always up to date

The law changes, but Nolo is on top of it! We offer several
ways to make sure you and your Nolo products are up to date:

 Nolo's Legal Updater
We'll send you an email whenever a new edition of this book
is published! Sign up at **www.nolo.com/legalupdater**.

 Updates @ Nolo.com
Check www.nolo.com/update to find recent changes
in the law that affect the current edition of your book.

 Nolo Customer Service
To make sure that this edition of the book is the most
recent one, call us at **800-728-3555** and ask one of
our friendly customer service representatives.
Or find out at **www.nolo.com**.

NOLO

please note

We believe accurate, plain-English legal information should help you solve many of your own legal problems. But this text is not a substitute for personalized advice from a knowledgeable lawyer. If you want the help of a trained professional—and we'll always point out situations in which we think that's a good idea—consult an attorney licensed to practice in your state.

NOLO

12th Edition

How to Form a
Nonprofit
Corporation
in California

By Attorney Anthony Mancuso

TWELFTH EDITION	JUNE 2007
Editor	DIANA FITZPATRICK
Book Production	MARGARET LIVINGSTON
CD-ROM Preparation	ELLEN BITTER
Proofreading	ROBERT WELLS
Index	THÉRÈSE SHERE
Printing	DELTA PRINTING SOLUTIONS, INC.

Mancuso, Anthony.

  How to form a nonprofit corporation in California / by Anthony Mancuso. -- 12th ed.

    p. cm.

  Includes index.

  ISBN-13: 978-1-4133-0649-1 (pbk.)

  ISBN-10: 1-4133-0649-7

    1. Nonprofit organizations--Law and legislation--California--Popular works. 2. Incorporation--California--Popular works. I. Title. II.Title: Nonprofit corporation in California.

KFC342.Z9M36 2007

346.794'064--dc22

2007002249

Quantity sales: For information on bulk purchases or corporate premium sales, please contact the Special Sales Department. For academic sales or textbook adoptions, ask for Academic Sales. Call 800-955-4775 or write to Nolo, 950 Parker Street, Berkeley, CA 94710.

Acknowledgments

The author extends a special thanks to Bethany Laurence and Diana Fitzpatrick, my editors, to Jake Warner, my publisher, and to all the hardworking people at Nolo.

About the Author

Anthony Mancuso is a corporations and limited liability company expert. He graduated from Hastings College of Law in San Francisco, studies advanced business taxation at Golden Gate University in San Francisco, and is an active member of the California State Bar. Mr. Mancuso writes books and programs software in the fields of corporate and LLC law. He has been a consultant for Silicon Valley EDA (Electronic Design Automation) companies working on C++ software project teams.

Mr. Mancuso is the author of Nolo's bestselling titles on forming and operating corporations (both profit and nonprofit) and limited liability companies. His titles include *Incorporate Your Business* (national and California editions), *How to Form a Nonprofit Corporation* (national and California editions), *Form Your Own Limited Liability Company*, and *LLC or Corporation?* He researched, wrote, and programmed *LLCMaker* and *Incorporator Pro* software programs, published by Nolo, which generate state-by-state articles and other forms for organizing corporations and LLCs in each of the states. His books and software have shown over a quarter of a million businesses and organizations how to form an LLC or corporation. He also is a licensed helicopter pilot and performs as a guitarist in various musical idioms, including jazz and blues.

Table of Contents

10 Final Steps in Organizing Your Nonprofit

11 After Your Corporation Is Organized

12 Lawyers, Legal Research, and Accountants

A Appendix A: How to Use the CD-ROM

Corporate Forms

Incorporation Checklist

Articles for a Public Benefit Corporation

Articles for a Religious Corporation

Special Article Provisions for an Unincorporated Association

Cover Letter for Filing Articles

Bylaws for Public Benefit Corporation

Membership Bylaw Provisions for Public Benefit Corporation

Bylaw Provisions for Religious Corporation

Membership Bylaw Provisions for Religious Corporation

Offer to Transfer Assets

Bill of Sale for Assets

Minutes of First Meeting of Board of Directors

Membership Certificate

IRS, FTB, and AG Forms and Publications

Name Availability Inquiry Letter

Name Reservation Request Form

California FTB 3500 Exemption Application (2006)

IRS Form 1023: Application for Recognition of Exemption (6/2006)

Instructions for IRS Form 1023 (6/2006)

Form SS-4: Application for Employer Identification Number (2/2006)

Instructions for Form SS-4 (2/2006)

Form 5768: Election/Revocation of Election by an Eligible Section 501(c)(3)
    Organization to Make Expenditures to Influence Legislation (12/2004)

Publication 557: Tax Exempt Status for Your Organization (3/2005)

Publication 4220, Applying for 501(c)(3) Tax-Exempt Status (9/2003)

Publication 4221, Compliance Guide 501(c)(3) Tax-Exempt Organizations (9/2003)

Publication 1828, Tax Guide for Churches and Religious Organizations (9/2006)

IRS Revenue Procedure 75-50

IRC Section 4958, Taxes on Excess Benefit Transactions

IRS Regulations Section 53.4958-0, Table of Contents

Your Legal Companion for Forming a Nonprofit Corporation in California

Forming a nonprofit corporation may sound like a daunting task that you should hand over to a lawyer as quickly as you can—after all, isn't there a lot of paperwork and filings, and complicated IRS nonprofit tax laws to learn? There is paperwork, and you will need to deal with the IRS, but the truth is, you can do it yourself. Forming a nonprofit corporation in California is actually a fairly straightforward process. And, with the help of our line-by-line instructions, you can also obtain tax exempt status from the IRS for your newly formed nonprofit corporation. Thousands of people have gone through the entire process of incorporating a nonprofit and obtaining 501(c)(3) tax exempt status with this book to guide them.

Along the way, there may be decisions you need to make where you should seek professional advice. We'll let you know when you need outside help. And even if you do decide to hire a lawyer to handle some of the work for you, the information in this book will help you be an informed client—and get the most for your money.

This book explains, in plain English, how to incorporate your nonprofit in California and obtain 501(c)(3) tax exempt status from the IRS. We show you how to:

- prepare and file nonprofit corporation articles and bylaws
- apply for and obtain 501(c)(3) tax exempt status from the IRS
- satisfy IRS conflict-of-interest and excess-benefit guidelines
- qualify as a 501(c)(3) public charity
- prepare minutes for your first board meeting
- take care of post-incorporation filings and tasks.

There are legal and tax technicalities that nonprofits must deal with in exchange for the substantial benefits they receive as nonprofits. We give you the information and tools you need both to form your tax exempt nonprofit and understand the practical and ongoing issues related to running a nonprofit.

We know that any legal process can be challenging. We hope this book, with its step-by-step approach to incorporation and obtaining tax exempt status from the IRS, will help you through the legal hoops and over the hurdles of incorporating your nonprofit in California and obtaining tax exempt status from the IRS. Congratulations on taking your first steps towards success in your new nonprofit endeavor!

Is Nonprofit Incorporation Right for You?

Deciding to form a nonprofit corporation will be a big step for you and the members of your group. It will involve more paperwork and government forms, on both the state and federal level, than anyone will like; and you'll have to conduct your business within the legal framework of various state and federal laws. Fortunately, there are big payoffs to all this work and attention, including the ability to attract donors and grant funds, obtain real and personal property tax exemptions and special nonprofit mailing rates, avoid corporate income taxes, and shield officers and directors from legal liability. Before starting down the path of nonprofit incorporation, however, you'll want to learn a little more about who can form a nonprofit and the consequences of doing so. In this chapter, we'll explain:

- the kinds of groups that can—and can't—form a nonprofit using this book
- the benefits you'll enjoy as a nonprofit—and some of the disadvantages to choosing this route
- how nonprofits can raise start-up funds and earn money, should they wish to do so
- the process you'll go through (following the instructions in this book) to incorporate and obtain your tax-exempt status, and
- for those considering incorporating in another state, considerations to bear in mind before doing so.

Is Your Group a Nonprofit That Can Use This Book?

A for-profit corporation can be formed for any lawful purpose. Nonprofit corporations, however, must be established under California law for one of three broad purposes: 1) for the benefit of the public (a public benefit corporation), 2) for religious purposes (a religious corporation), or 3) for the mutual benefit of the members of the nonprofit (a mutual benefit corporation). It's easy to form a nonprofit corporation in California: just prepare articles of incorporation that say you are formed for one of these three broad nonprofit purposes and then file your articles with the California Secretary of State. This creates your legal corporate entity. However, having a nonprofit corporation recognized by the California Secretary of State is only your first hurdle. The next important step is to obtain the necessary state and federal corporate income tax exemptions for your nonprofit corporation. To obtain these exemptions, your nonprofit must be formed for one or more specific purposes described in the income tax statutes.

This book has been written specifically for nonprofits that want to qualify for a federal income tax exemption under Section 501(c)(3) of the Internal Revenue Code. This means your nonprofit must be formed for religious, charitable, scientific, literary, and/or educational purposes. If you want to organize as a religious purpose group, we will show you how to form a California religious nonprofit corporation. If you want to organize as a nonprofit to engage in any of the other 501(c)(3) tax-exempt purposes, we will show you how to form a California public benefit corporation. This book is not for groups that want to form a mutual benefit corporation, because mutual benefit nonprofits usually obtain their tax exemption under a subsection of Section 501(c) other than 501(c)(3). It is also not for certain special types of nonprofits (including some public benefit corporations) that do not fall under Section 501(c)(3). See discussion below, "Special Types of California Public Benefit Corporations," and "Mutual Benefit Corporations."

When thinking about incorporating your nonprofit, consider which purpose you fall

Corporation Basics

You don't have to understand all there is to know about corporations in order to follow this book or form your nonprofit. But there are a few basic concepts you'll want to have under your belt as you go through the process. Here they are, with special emphasis on any differences between for-profit corporations and nonprofits.

- **A corporation is a separate legal entity.** A corporation is a legal entity that allows a group of people to pool energy, time, and money for profit or nonprofit activities. It acquires legal existence after its founders comply with their state's incorporation procedures and formalities. The law treats a corporation as a separate "person," distinct from the people who own, manage, or operate it. The corporation can enter into contracts, incur debts, and pay taxes. Corporations are either for-profit (business corporations) or nonprofits.

- **For-profit, or business, corporations versus nonprofits.** Business corporations can be formed for any legal purpose. They can issue shares of stock to investors in return for money or property, or services performed for the corporation. Shareholders receive a return on their investment if dividends are paid or if, upon dissolution of the corporation, any

corporate assets remain to be divided among the shareholders after payment of all creditors. Nonprofits, on the other hand, generally cannot issue shares of stock or pay dividends under state law (unless they are some type of hybrid such as consumer or producer co-ops). The federal tax code also prohibits 501(c)(3) tax-exempt nonprofit corporations from paying dividends or profits to their members or other individuals. When a 501(c)(3) tax-exempt nonprofit corporation dissolves, it must distribute its remaining assets to another tax-exempt nonprofit group.

- **In-state and out-of-state corporations.** Corporations formed in California are known in California as "domestic" corporations. Corporations formed in other states, even if physically present and engaging in activities in California, are called "foreign" corporations. For example, a corporation formed in California is a domestic corporation as far as California is concerned, but a foreign corporation when considered by other states. At the end of this chapter, we give you more information on doing business outside California and deciding whether to incorporate in another state.

under for Section 501(c)(3). Once you know you fall within one of the 501(c)(3) purposes, you can rest assured that this book can help you through the process. First we'll help you create your corporate entity in California by showing you how to prepare and file articles of incorporation for a public benefit or religious corporation. Then we'll show you how to obtain your state and federal nonprofit income tax exemptions for 501(c)(3) status.

Public Benefit Corporations

Under state law, public benefit corporations are corporations formed for a "public purpose" or "charitable purpose." Most groups forming public benefit corporations also want to qualify for Section 501(c)(3) status. These groups usually organize for one of the specified purposes under Section 501(c)(3)—charitable, scientific, literary, or educational. All of these 501(c)(3) purposes are considered "charitable" purposes under California law. For example, a school or educational facility would organize as a California public benefit corporation formed under state law for "charitable" purposes but its 501(c)(3) purposes would be "educational." The public purpose classification under state law is for groups that want to form civic league or social welfare public benefit corporations (see discussion below on civic league and social welfare groups). Don't worry—we show you how to fill in your articles so you put in the right purposes under California law and also satisfy the federal and state tax exemption requirements.

Religious Corporations

Just as the name indicates, religious corporations are formed primarily or exclusively for religious purposes. These groups can qualify as religious organizations under both state incorporation law and Section 501(c)(3). You need not set up a formal church to form a religious nonprofit corporation; these groups can have a general religious purpose. For example, a group organized to promote the study and practice of a particular religion could incorporate as a religious nonprofit corporation.

Special Types of California Public Benefit Corporations

This book covers the incorporation of California public benefit and religious nonprofits that want to obtain their tax exemption under Section 501(c)(3) of the Internal Revenue Code. There are several other types of California public benefit corporations that obtain tax exemption under *other* sections of the Internal Revenue Code or that must meet special state law requirements. Below, we list several of the most common types of these special California nonprofit corporations. If you plan to form one of these special nonprofits, you'll need to do your own research or get legal help to form your corporation—this book does not cover the incorporation of these special groups. See "Where to Go for Help for Non-501(c)(3) Nonprofits," below.

- **Civic leagues and social welfare groups.** Civic leagues and social welfare groups are formed as California public benefit corporations and seek their exemption from federal corporate income taxation under Section 501(c)(4) of the Internal Revenue Code. Because this book covers only nonprofits exempt under Section 501(c)(3) of the Internal Revenue Code, you won't be able

to use this book to incorporate these types of public benefit corporations. (See *Special Nonprofit Tax-Exempt Organizations*, in Appendix B, for a list of organizations that qualify for tax-exempt status under a subsection of 501(c) other than Subsection 3).

- **Medical or legal service corporations.** These are nonprofit corporations operated to assume or defray the cost of medical or legal services. These corporations may be organized as California public benefit corporations or mutual benefit corporations. Special provisions of the California Corporations Code apply (see California Corporations Code §§ 10810–10841).

- **Humane societies.** A humane society, formed to prevent cruelty to children or animals, can be formed as a California public benefit corporation. The Department of Justice must perform a criminal history check on all incorporators and issue a certificate before the secretary of state will accept the articles of incorporation for filing (California Corporations Code §§ 10400–10406).

It is unlikely that the California Secretary of State's office, where you'll file your articles of incorporation, will question whether your religious activities are genuine. This type of debate is more likely to occur (if it occurs at all) when you apply for your state or federal tax exemptions.

Mutual Benefit Corporations

This book is not intended for mutual benefit corporations. Unlike public benefit corporations and religious corporations, these groups usually qualify for tax-exempt status under a subsection of 501(c) other than 501(c)(3). Examples of mutual benefit corporations include trade associations, automobile clubs, and social groups, such as tennis clubs. Chambers of commerce, boards of trade, and mechanics' institutes, which are generally formed to promote trade and commerce, can organize as mutual benefit corporations or as regular, for-profit corporations. Cooperatives, comprising producers or consumers organized for their mutual benefit, can also qualify as mutual benefit nonprofits with special added restrictions applicable to them.

Because these groups do not qualify for tax-exempt status under Section 501(c)(3), they are not entitled to many of the benefits enjoyed by public benefit and religious corporations. For example, contributions to mutual benefit corporations are normally not tax deductible, and other benefits (such as special nonprofit mailing rates and real and personal property tax exemptions) are not available to mutual benefit corporations. Mutual benefit corporations also cannot distribute gains, profits, or dividends to those designated in their articles or bylaws as members, but may provide them with other benefits such as services and facilities. On the other hand, members of a mutual benefit corporation can own part of the corporation. When the corporation dissolves and all its debts and liabilities are paid, the remaining assets, gains, and profits can be distributed to its members.

Benefits of the Nonprofit Corporation

Now that you understand that this book is intended for nonprofits organized for religious, charitable, scientific, literary, and/or educational purposes that want to qualify for a tax exemption under Section 501(c)(3) of the Internal Revenue Code (and hopefully your nonprofit is among them), let's look at the benefits you'll enjoy as a 501(c)(3) tax-exempt nonprofit corporation. The relative importance of each of the following benefits will vary from group to group, but at least one of them should be very significant for your organization.

If you finish this section and conclude that nothing here is very important for your group, you'll want to consider whether it makes sense to incorporate at all. Many groups accomplish their nonprofit purposes just fine as unincorporated nonprofit associations, without formal organizational paperwork or written operational rules. If you can continue to accomplish your nonprofit purposes and goals informally, you may be happier staying small.

Tax Exemptions

Nonprofit corporations are eligible for state and federal exemptions from payment of corporate income taxes, as well as other tax exemptions and benefits. At federal corporate tax rates of 15% on the first $50,000 of taxable income, 25% on the next $25,000, and 34% and higher on income over $75,000, it goes without saying—at least if you expect to earn a substantial amount of money (from services, exhibits, or performances, for example)—that you'll want to apply for an exemption. The

California corporate income tax exemption is equally attractive, as are county real and personal property tax exemptions. Chapters 3, 4, and 5 cover tax exemptions in detail.

SEE AN EXPERT

Get the help of a competent tax adviser as soon as you decide to incorporate. Make sure you choose someone experienced in the special field of nonprofit bookkeeping. Ask the adviser to help you (especially your treasurer) set up a good record-keeping system. Have the tax helper periodically review the system to be sure that you have met accepted bookkeeping standards and have filed your tax forms on time.

Receiving Public and Private Donations

One of the primary reasons for becoming a 501(c)(3) nonprofit corporation is that it increases your ability to attract and receive public and private grant funds and donations.

- **Public sources.** Tax-exempt government foundations (like the National Endowment for the Arts or Humanities, the Corporation for Public Broadcasting, or the National Satellite Program Development Fund) as well as private foundations and charities (such as the Ford Foundation, the United Way, or the American Cancer Society) are usually required by their own operating rules and federal tax regulations to donate their funds only to 501(c)(3) tax-exempt organizations.

- **Private sources.** Individual private donors can claim personal federal income tax deductions for contributions made to 501(c)(3) tax-exempt groups. At death, a complete federal estate tax exemption is available for bequests made to 501(c)(3) groups.

Where to Go for Help for Non-501(c)(3) Nonprofits

If you want to form a nonprofit for any purpose other than one recognized under Section 501(c)(3) of the Internal Revenue Code, this book is not for you. For example, if you are a civic league or social welfare group that wants nonprofit status, you will want to organize as a public benefit corporation under Section 501(c)(4) of the Internal Revenue Code. Or, if your group is a California mutual benefit corporation, you will seek tax-exempt status under a subsection of 501(c) other than 501(c)(3). This book is not intended for these special types of nonprofits.

If you are a special nonprofit that is not covered by this book, you can find legal forms and tax exemption help online. For sample articles of incorporation for mutual benefit corporations and public benefit civic leagues and social welfare groups, go to the California Secretary of State Corporations Section website at www.ss.ca.gov/business/business.htm. If you are seeking tax exemption for a nonprofit under a subsection of 501(c) other than 501(c)(3), go to the IRS website at www.irs.gov and obtain IRS Package 1024. The IRS 1024 package contains forms and instructions to use to apply for a nonprofit tax exemption under Internal Revenue Code Sections 501(c)(2), (4), (5), (6), (7), (8), (9), (10), (12), (13), (15), (17), (19), and (25). The California Franchise Tax Board website at www.ftb.ca.gov has state tax exemption application forms to download and use to apply for your state corporate income tax exemption for these special non-501(c)(3) groups. IRS Publication 557 and IRS Form 1024 also contain information and instructions on forming some of these special purpose nonprofits.

In short, if you plan to ask people to give you significant amounts of money in furtherance of your nonprofit purpose, you need to demonstrate to your donors that you have 501(c)(3) tax-exempt status.

Protection From Personal Liability

Protecting the members of your group from personal liability is one of the main reasons for forming a corporation (either profit or nonprofit). Once you're incorporated, in most situations directors or trustees, officers, employees, and members of a corporation won't be personally liable for corporate debts or liabilities, including unpaid organizational debts and unsatisfied lawsuit judgments against the organization, as they normally would be if they conducted their affairs without incorporating. Creditors can go after only corporate assets to satisfy liabilities incurred by the corporation—not the personal assets (car, home, or bank accounts) of the people who manage, work for, or volunteer to help the nonprofit corporation.

EXAMPLE:

A member of the audience sued a nonprofit symphony orchestra when the patron fell during a concert, claiming that the symphony (which also owned the concert hall) provided an unsafe ramp. The patron won a judgment that exceeded the orchestra's insurance policy limits. The amount of the judgment in excess of insurance is a debt of the corporation, but not of its individual directors, members, managers, or officers. By contrast, had the orchestra been an unincorporated association of musicians, the principals of the unincorporated group could be held personally liable for the excess judgment amount.

In a few situations, however, people involved with a nonprofit corporation may be personally liable for the corporation's liabilities. Here are some major areas of potential personal liability:

- **Taxes.** State and federal governments can hold the corporate employee who is responsible for reporting and paying corporate taxes (usually the treasurer) personally liable for any unpaid taxes, penalties, and interest due for failure to pay taxes or file necessary returns. With proper planning, your nonprofit corporation should be tax exempt, but you may still have to file informational returns and annual reports with the secretary of state, as well as pay employee withholding and other payroll taxes and taxes on income unrelated to your nonprofit purposes. IRS penalties for delinquent tax payments and returns are substantial, so keep this exception to limited liability in mind—particularly if you will be the treasurer.

- **Dues.** Members of a nonprofit corporation are personally liable for any membership fees and dues they owe the corporation. In most cases, this is a minor obligation since dues are normally set at modest amounts.

- **Violations of statutory duties.** Corporate directors are legally required to act responsibly (not recklessly) when managing the corporation. They may be held personally financially liable if they fail to act responsibly. Personal liability of this sort is the exception, not the rule. Generally, as long as directors attend meetings and carry out corporate responsibilities conscientiously, they should have little to worry about—the corporate limited liability shield insulates directors from all but the most reckless and irresponsible decisions.

- **Intermingling funds or other business dealings.** A nonprofit corporation must act so that its separate existence is clear and respected. If it mixes up corporate funds with the personal funds of those in charge, fails to follow legal formalities (such as failing to operate according to bylaws, hold director meetings, or keep minutes of meetings), or risks financial liability without sufficient backup in cash or other assets, a court may disregard the corporate entity and hold the principals responsible for debts and other liabilities of the corporation. In legalese, this is known as "piercing the corporate veil." Piercing the veil is the exception, not the rule, and only happens when a court decides that it is necessary to prevent a gross injustice or fraud perpetuated by the founders or principals of a corporation.

- **Private foundation managers.** If the nonprofit corporation is classified as a private foundation, foundation managers can be held personally liable for federal excise taxes associated with certain prohibited transactions. They may also be held personally liable for penalties and interest charged for failing to file certain tax returns or pay required excise taxes. (As explained in Chapter 4, a private foundation is a 501(c)(3) corporation that does not qualify as a public charity—you'll see that most 501(c)(3) nonprofits qualify as public charities and are not subject to the private foundation requirements.)

- **Loans.** When a nonprofit corporation takes a loan to cover its operating costs or buys property subject to a mortgage, banks and commercial lending institutions sometimes insist on the personal guarantee of its directors or officers. If the directors or officers agree to personally guarantee the loan or mortgage, the protection that they would normally enjoy as a result of their organization's corporate status goes away. It is somewhat unusual for nonprofit directors or officers to sign a personal guarantee. Obviously, if they do, they will be liable to repay the loan if the corporation cannot do so.

Separate and Perpetual Legal Existence

A corporation is a legal entity that is separate from the people who work in it. Again, one benefit of this separate existence is that corporate liabilities are not the liabilities of the managers, officers, or members of the corporation (known as the corporate characteristic of limited liability). Another benefit is that this corporate legal person is, in a sense, immortal; the nonprofit corporation continues to exist as a legal entity despite changes in management or other corporate personnel caused by the resignation, removal, or death of the people associated with it. It may, of course, be dissolved or drastically affected by the loss of key people, but its inherent perpetual existence makes it more likely that the group's activities will continue, an attractive feature to the private or public donor who prefers funding activities that are organized to operate over the long term.

Employee Benefits

Another benefit of the nonprofit corporation is that its principals can also be employees and, therefore, eligible for employee fringe benefits not generally available to the workers in unincorporated organizations. These benefits include group term life insurance, reimbursement of medical expenses, and coverage by a qualified corporate employee pension or retirement income plan.

Formality and Structure

The formal corporate documents—the articles, bylaws, minutes of meetings, and board resolutions—that you'll prepare as a nonprofit will actually be quite useful to your organization. They'll outline the group's purposes, embody its operating rules, and provide structure and procedures for decision making and dispute resolution. This is important for any collective activity, but for nonprofit groups it is vital, especially if the board includes members of the community with diverse interests and viewpoints. Without the clear-cut delegation of authority and specific operating rules in the articles and bylaws, running the organization might be a divisive, if not futile, affair.

Miscellaneous Benefits

Additional advantages are available to nonprofits that engage in particular types of activities or operations. These benefits can be helpful, and in some cases are critical, to the success of a nonprofit organization. Here are examples of some of the benefits available to certain types of tax-exempt nonprofits.

- Your nonprofit may qualify for exemptions from county real and personal property taxes.
- 501(c)(3) organizations receive lower postal rates on third-class bulk mailings.
- Many publications offer cheaper classified advertising rates to nonprofit organizations.
- Nonprofits are the exclusive beneficiaries of free radio and television public service announcements (PSAs) provided by local media outlets.
- Many stores offer lower membership rates to nonprofit employees.
- Nonprofit employees are often eligible to participate in job training, student intern, work-study, and other federal, state, and local employment incentive programs (where salaries are paid substantially out of federal and state funds).
- 501(c)(3) performing arts groups are qualified to participate in the performance programs sponsored by federally supported colleges and universities.
- Certain 501(c)(3) educational organizations are eligible for a tax refund for gasoline expenses (for example, in running school buses).

EXAMPLE:

A senior citizens' botany club began as an informal organization. Initially, six members took a monthly nature walk to study and photograph regional flora. Everyone chipped in to buy gas for whoever drove to the hike's starting point. Recently, however, membership increased to 15 and the group decided to collect dues from members to pay the increased expenses—gas money, guidebooks, maps, and club T-shirts— associated with more frequent field trips. To avoid mixing club monies with personal funds, a treasurer was designated to open a bank account on behalf of the organization. Several people suggest that it is time to incorporate the club.

Does incorporation make sense at this time? Probably not. There is no new pressing need to adopt the corporate form or to obtain formal recognition as a tax-exempt nonprofit. Most banks will allow an unincorporated group without a federal Employer Identification Number or IRS tax exemption to open up a non-interest-bearing account. However, should the club decide to seek funding and contributions to spearhead a drive to save open space in the community, it might be a good idea to incorporate.

The Disadvantages of Going Nonprofit

If your group has come together for 501(c)(3) tax-exempt purposes, and if reading about the benefits of becoming a nonprofit above prompted a "Wow! We would really like to be able to do *that!*" then chances are you've decided to tackle the rules and forms necessary to establish your status as a legal nonprofit. Before jumping in, however, take a minute to read the following descriptions of some of the hurdles and work you'll encounter along the way, especially if you have been operating informally (and successfully) without financial or employee record keeping or controls. If any of the following appear insurmountable to you, think again about incorporating.

Official Paperwork

One disadvantage in forming any corporation is the red tape and paperwork. You'll begin by preparing initial incorporation documents (articles of incorporation, bylaws, and minutes of first meeting of the board of directors). Although this book will show you how to prepare your own incorporation forms and bylaws with a minimum of time and trouble, the process will still take you a few hours. You and your compatriots must be prepared for some old-fashioned hard work.

After you've set up your corporation, you'll need to file annual information returns with the state (the Franchise Tax Board and the attorney general) as well as the Internal Revenue Service. Also, you will need to regularly prepare minutes of ongoing corporate meetings, and, occasionally, forms for amending articles and bylaws. The annual tax reporting forms will require the implementation of an organized bookkeeping system plus the help of an experienced nonprofit tax adviser as explained below.

Fortunately, keeping minutes of these meetings is not all that difficult to do once someone volunteers for the task (typically the person you appoint as corporate secretary). Sample forms for amending nonprofit articles are available from the California Secretary of State Corporations Section website at www.ss.ca .gov/business/business.htm.

Annual nonprofit informational tax returns do present a challenge to a new group unfamiliar with state tax reporting forms and requirements. Other record-keeping and reporting chores, such as double-entry accounting procedures and payroll tax withholding and reporting, can be equally daunting. At least at the start, most nonprofits rely on the experience of a tax advisor, bookkeeper, or other legal or tax specialist on the board or in the community to help them set up their books and establish a system for preparing tax forms on time. See Chapter 12 for recommendations on finding legal and tax professionals for your nonprofit.

Incorporation Costs and Fees

For nonprofit incorporators unwilling to do the job themselves, a main disadvantage of incorporating a nonprofit organization is the cost of paying an attorney to prepare the incorporation forms and tax exemption applications. Putting some time and effort into understanding the material in this book can help you eliminate this disadvantage, leaving you with only the actual cost of incorporation. Including the typical $300 federal tax exemption application fee, total fees to incorporate are approximately $350 to $400. (Costs are $350 higher for nonprofits that anticipate gross receipts of more than $10,000. These groups pay a $750, rather than a $300, federal tax exemption application fee.)

Time and Energy Needed to Run the Nonprofit

When a group decides to incorporate, the legal decision is often part of a broader decision to increase not just the structure, but the overall scope, scale, and visibility of the nonprofit. With a larger, more accountable organization come a number of new tasks: setting up and balancing books and bank accounts, depositing and reporting payroll taxes, and meeting with an accountant to extract and report year-end figures for annual informational returns. Although these financial, payroll, and tax concerns are not exclusively corporate chores, you'll find that most unincorporated nonprofits keep a low employment, tax, and financial profile and get by with minimum attention to legal and tax formalities.

EXAMPLE:

A women's health collective operates as an unincorporated nonprofit organization. It keeps an office open a few days a week where people stop by to read and exchange information on community and women's health issues. The two founders donate their time and the office space and pay operating costs (such as phone, utilities, and photocopying) that aren't covered by contributions from visitors. The organization has never made a profit, there is no payroll, and tax returns have never been filed. There is a minimum of paperwork and record keeping.

The founders could decide to continue this way indefinitely. However, the founders want to expand the activities and revenues of the collective. They decide to form a 501(c)(3) nonprofit corporation in order to be eligible for tax-deductible contributions and grant funds from the city, and to qualify the group to employ student interns and work-study students. This will require them to prepare and file articles of incorporation and a federal corporate income tax exemption application. They must select an initial board of directors and prepare organizational bylaws and formal written minutes of the first board of directors' meeting.

After incorporation, the group holds regular board meetings documented with written minutes, sets up and uses a double-entry bookkeeping system, implements regular federal and state payroll and tax procedures and controls, files exempt organization tax returns each year, and expands its operations. A full-time staff person is assigned to handle the increased paperwork and bookkeeping chores brought about by the change in structure and increased operations of the organization.

This example highlights what should be one of the first things you consider before you decide to incorporate: Make sure that you and your coworkers can put in the extra time and effort that an incorporated nonprofit organization will require. If the extra work would overwhelm or overtax your current resources, we suggest you hold off on your incorporation until you get the extra help you need to accomplish this task smoothly (or at least more easily).

Restrictions on Paying Directors and Officers

As a matter of state corporation law and the tax exemption requirements, nonprofits are restricted in how they deal with their directors, officers, and members. None of the gains, profits, or dividends of the corporation can go to individuals associated with the corporation, including directors, officers, and those defined as members in the corporation's articles or bylaws. State self-dealing rules apply as well, regulating action by the board of directors if a director has a financial interest in a transaction. Finally, with respect to California public benefit corporations (if you form a 501(c)(3) tax-exempt nonprofit corporation for nonreligious purposes, you will form a California public benefit corporation), a majority of the board of directors cannot be paid (other than as a director), or related to other persons who are paid, by the corporation. This can represent a significant restriction because it eliminates the close-knit, family organizations many picture when they think of a small, grass-roots nonprofit corporation.

Restrictions Upon Dissolution

One of the requirements for the 501(c)(3) tax exemption is that upon dissolution of the corporation, any assets remaining after the corporation's debts and liabilities are paid must go to another tax-exempt nonprofit, not to members of the former corporation.

Restrictions on Your Political Activities

Section 501(c)(3) of the Internal Revenue Code establishes a number of restrictions and limitations that apply to nonprofits. Here, we discuss a limitation that may be very significant to some groups—the limitation on your political activities. Specifically, your organization may not participate in political campaigns for or against candidates for public office, and cannot substantially engage in legislative or grassroots political activities except as permitted under federal tax regulations.

EXAMPLE:

Society for a Saner World, Inc., has as one of its primary objectives lobbying hard to pass federal and local legislation that seeks

to lessen societal dependency on fossil fuels. Since a substantial portion of the group's efforts will consist of legislative lobbying, the group's 501(c)(3) tax exemption probably will be denied by the IRS. Instead, the group should seek a tax-exemption under IRC § 501(c)(4) as a social welfare group, which is not limited in the amount of lobbying the group can undertake. Of course, the benefits of 501(c)(4) tax exemption are fewer too—contributions to the group are not tax-deductible and grant funds will be more difficult to obtain—see *Special Nonprofit Tax-Exempt Organizations,* in Appendix B.

Oversight by the Attorney General

The California Attorney General has broad power to oversee the operations of California public benefit corporations, more so than it does with other California nonprofits. (Remember: If you form a nonreligious 501(c)(3) tax-exempt corporation, you will be forming a California public benefit corporation.) The state can even take the corporation to court to make sure it complies with the law.

By contrast, California religious purpose nonprofit corporations have wider flexibility in managing their internal affairs. If a religious corporation does not set up its own operating rules, provisions of the nonprofit law will apply to its operations by default. These are less stringent than those that would apply to a public benefit corporation under similar circumstances.

How Nonprofits Raise, Spend, and Make Money

Most nonprofits need to deal with money—indeed, being able to attract donations is a prime reason for choosing nonprofit status. Nonprofits can also make money. Nonprofit does not literally mean that a nonprofit corporation cannot make a profit. Under federal tax law and state law, as long as your nonprofit is organized and operating for a recognized nonprofit purpose, it can take in more money than it spends in conducting its activities. A nonprofit may use its tax-free profits for its operating expenses (including salaries for officers, directors, and employees) or for the benefit of its organization. It cannot, however, distribute any of the profits for the benefits of its officers, directors, or employees (as dividends, for example).

This section explains how nonprofits raise initial funds and how they make money on an ongoing basis.

Initial Fundraising

A California nonprofit corporation is not legally required to have a specified amount of money in the corporate bank account before commencing operations. This is fortunate, of course, because many beginning nonprofits start out on a shoestring of meager public and private support.

So, where will your seed money come from? As you know, nonprofit corporations cannot issue shares, nor can they provide investment incentives, such as a return on capital through the payment of dividends to investors, benefactors, or participants in the corporation (see "Corporation Basics" at the beginning of this chapter).

Nonprofits have their own means and methods of obtaining start-up funds. Obviously,

the most common method is to obtain revenue in the form of contributions, grants, and dues from the people, organizations, and governmental agencies that support the nonprofit's purpose and goals. Also, if you are incorporating an existing organization, its assets are usually transferred to the new corporation—these assets may include the cash reserves of an unincorporated group, which can help your corporation begin operations. You can also borrow start-up funds from a bank, although for newly formed corporations a bank will usually require that incorporators secure the loan with their personal assets—a pledge most nonprofit directors are understandably reluctant to make.

Often, of course, nonprofits receive initial and ongoing revenues from services or activities provided in the pursuit of their exempt purposes (ticket sales, payments for art lessons or dance courses, school tuition, or clinic charges).

For information on meeting California's special fundraising rules, see "State Solicitation Laws and Requirements" in Chapter 5.

Making Money From Related Activities

Many nonprofits make money while they further the goals of the organization. The nonprofit can use this tax-exempt revenue to pay for operating expenses (including reasonable salaries) and to further its nonprofit purposes. For example, an organization dedicated to the identification and preservation of shore birds might advertise a bird-watching and counting hike for which they charge a fee; the group could then use the proceeds to fund their bird rescue operations. What it cannot do with the money, however, is distribute it for the benefit of officers, directors, or employees of the corporation (as the payment of a patronage dividend, for example).

EXAMPLE:

Friends of the Library, Inc., is a 501(c)(3) nonprofit organized to encourage literary appreciation in the community and to raise money for the support and improvement of the public library. It makes a profit from its sold-out lecture series featuring famous authors and from its annual sale of donated books. Friends can use this tax-exempt profit for its own operating expenses, including salaries for officers and employees, or to benefit the library.

Making Money From Unrelated Activities (Unrelated Income)

Nonprofits can also make money in ways unrelated to their nonprofit purpose. Often this income is essential to the survival of the nonprofit group. This unrelated income, however, is usually taxed as unrelated business income under state and federal corporate income tax rules. While earning money this way is permissible, it's best not to let unrelated business activities reach the point where you start to look more like a for-profit business than a nonprofit one. This can happen if the unrelated income-generating activities are absorbing a substantial amount of staff time, requiring additional paid staff or volunteers, or producing more income than your exempt-purpose activities. If the unrelated revenue or activities of your tax-exempt nonprofit reach a substantial level, the IRS can decide to revoke the group's 501(c)(3) tax-exemption—a result your nonprofit will no doubt wish to avoid.

EXAMPLE:

Many thousands of books are donated to Friends of the Library for its annual book sale, one of its major fundraising events. Although the sale is always highly successful, thousands of books are left over.

Friends decides to sell the more valuable books by advertising in the rare and out-of-print books classified sections in various magazines. The response is overwhelming; soon, there are six employees cataloguing books. In addition, Friends begins a business purchasing books from other dealers and reselling them to the public. Such a situation could attract attention from the IRS and prompt it to reconsider Friends' 501(c)(3) tax-exempt status.

Making Money From Passive Sources

Although it's not typical for the average non-profit, a nonprofit corporation can make money from passive sources such as rents, royalties, interest, and investments. This income is nontaxable in some cases.

Your Path to Nonprofit Status

Nonprofit organizations first obtain nonprofit corporate status with the California Secretary of State—a simple formality accomplished by filing articles of incorporation. Then they go on to obtain a corporate income tax exemption with the California Franchise Tax Board and the Internal Revenue Service. In sum, your path to nonprofit status is a basic two-step process—first you incorporate with the California Secretary of State, then you apply for tax-exempt recognition from the California Franchise Tax Board and the Internal Revenue Service. Because the two tax exemption applications are similar, most groups prepare both tax applications at the same time. When you're done with this book, you'll have completed each of these steps.

State Law Requirements for Nonprofits

The California Secretary of State must officially recognize all California nonprofit corporations. To obtain state recognition, you'll file articles of incorporation with the secretary of state's office stating that your organization is entitled to receive nonprofit corporate status. This book covers the basic requirements for obtaining recognition by California's Secretary of State as a nonprofit corporation. The California Nonprofit Corporation Law (California Corporations Code §§ 5000-9927) governs the organization and operations of California nonprofit corporations.

We focus on public benefit corporations in this book (those formed for public or charitable purposes) because these corporations make up the majority of nonprofit corporations eligible for exemption under Section 501(c)(3) of the Internal Revenue Code. Requirements for religious corporations are noted only if they are different from the requirements for public benefit corporations.

Tax Exempt Status Under Federal and State Tax Law

Both state and federal tax laws apply to California nonprofit corporations. To obtain tax-exempt status, nonprofits must comply with initial and ongoing requirements under the California Revenue and Taxation Code and the federal Internal Revenue Code. In most ways, understanding and complying with state and federal tax rules is more important (and more challenging) than fulfilling the state corporate law requirements. This book focuses on nonprofit corporations seeking tax-exempt status under Section 510(c)(3) of the Internal Revenue Code, which are nonprofits organized for religious, charitable, educational, scientific, or literary purposes.

Incorporating in Another State—Don't Fall for It

Corporations formed in a particular state are known in that state as domestic corporations. When viewed from outside that state, these corporations are considered foreign. A foreign corporation that plans to engage in a regular or repeated pattern of activity in another state must qualify to do business there by obtaining a certificate of authority from the secretary of state. For example, a corporation formed in Nevada that intends to do regular business in California is a foreign corporation here, and must qualify the corporation with our secretary of state.

Incorporators who plan to operate in another state besides California have naturally considered whether it makes sense to incorporate in that other state. Maybe the incorporation fees or corporate taxes are lower than those in California or the nonprofit statutes are more flexible. Then, the reasoning goes, one could qualify the corporation in California as a foreign corporation. As tempting as this end run may appear, it's not usually worth it. This section explains why, and also advises you of out-of-state activities that you can engage in without worrying about qualifying in another state.

Qualifying as a Foreign Corporation in California Will Cost You More

The process of qualifying a foreign corporation to operate in California takes about as much time and expense as incorporating a domestic corporation. This means that you will pay more to incorporate out-of-state since you must pay the regular California qualification fees plus out-of-state incorporation fees.

Two Sets of Tax Exemptions

Your corporation will still be subject to taxation in each state in which it earns or derives income or funds. If the state of incorporation imposes a corporate income tax, then the nonprofit corporation will need to file for and obtain two state corporate tax exemptions—one for California, the state where the corporation will be active, and one for the state of incorporation. Similarly, double sales, property, and other state tax exemptions may often be necessary or appropriate.

Two Sets of State Laws

Your out-of-state corporation will still be subject to many of the laws that affect corporations in California. Many of California's corporate statutes that apply to domestic corporations also apply to foreign corporations.

Out-of-State Activities Below the Radar

For the above reasons, most readers who flirt with the idea of incorporating in a state other than California would be well advised to skip it. This doesn't mean, however, that you'll have to trim all of your activities to stay within California. Fortunately, there are many things nonprofits can do as a foreign corporation in another state without obtaining a certificate of authority from the secretary of that state. Here are some that are recognized in many (but not all) states:

- maintaining, defending, or settling any legal action or administrative proceeding, including securing or collecting debts, and enforcing property rights
- holding meetings of corporate directors or of the membership and distributing information to members
- maintaining bank accounts and making grants of funds
- making sales through independent contractors and engaging in interstate or foreign commerce
- conducting a so-called isolated transaction that is completed within 30 days and is not one of a series of similar transactions, and
- exercising powers as an executor, administrator, or trustee, so long as none of the activities required of the position amounts to transacting business.

When Out-of-State Incorporation Makes Sense

There may be a few of you for whom incorporation in another state makes sense. If you plan to set up a multistate nonprofit with corporate offices and activities in more than one state (a tristate environmental fund for example), you may want to consider incorporating in the state that offers the greatest legal, tax, and practical advantages. To help you decide where to incorporate, you can refer to *How to Form a Nonprofit Corporation*, by Anthony Mancuso (Nolo). This book contains the basic nonprofit corporation law for each state. For further information on state-by-state differences, check a local nonprofit resource center library (for nonprofit library resources online, type "nonprofit resource libraries" into your search engine—you'll find a host of online libraries at your disposal). An experienced nonprofit lawyer or consultant can also help you determine which state is the most convenient and least costly to use as the legal home for your new nonprofit corporation.

References to IRS Articles and Materials

Throughout the book, there are references to IRS articles and materials included on the CD-ROM that comes with this book. Some of this material includes articles and information made available by the IRS on its website as part of its Exempt Organizations Continuing Professional Education Technical Instruction Program, which regularly publishes articles for tax-exempt organizations. The IRS has the following statement on its website regarding this material: "These materials were designed specifically for training purposes only. Under no circumstances should the contents be used or cited as authority for setting or sustaining a technical position." In other words, use this material to learn about IRS tax issues, but don't expect to be able to rely on it if you end up in a dispute with the IRS. Nolo includes this material on the CD-ROM as a convenience to the reader and as an alternative to directing you to an IRS website link to this material. This material is taken directly from the IRS website at www.irs.gov/charities/article/0,,id=161088,00.html. If you are interested in one of the issues, you should check the IRS website for any updated articles or information on your topic.

Legal Rights and Duties of Incorporators, Directors, Officers, Employees, and Members

Even though a corporation is a legal person capable of making contracts, incurring liabilities, and engaging in other activities, it still needs real people to act on its behalf to carry out its activities. These people decide to incorporate, select those who will be responsible for running the organization, and actually manage and carry out the nonprofit's goals and activities.

This chapter explains the rights and responsibilities of those in your group who will organize and operate your nonprofit corporation. These incorporators, directors, officers, members, and employees have separate legal rights and responsibilities. Later, after your nonprofit is up and running, you may want to refer back to this chapter if you have questions regarding the powers and duties of these important people.

The Importance of Protecting Your Corporate Status

Before you start looking for people to help run your nonprofit, take a moment for a reality check: Many potential helpers will hesitate to become involved because they've read in the press about a few notorious, high-visibility lawsuits where nonprofit directors have been held personally liable for misconduct by executives of the nonprofit (for example, the executive of a large, public membership nonprofit misappropriates program funds to buy a yacht or high-priced apartment for personal use). On a more down-to-earth level, a potential treasurer for your nonprofit may hesitate to serve if he thinks he'll be personally responsible for the organization's tax reporting penalties or a potential director may be worried about being personally sued by a fired employee of the nonprofit. Fortunately, these types of personal liability are extremely rare. Most nonprofits should be able to assure potential director and officer candidates that the nonprofit will be run accountably and sensibly without undue risk of tax or legal liability for the directors.

One obvious way to reassure candidates is to purchase directors' and officers' liability insurance from an insurance broker who handles nonprofit corporate insurance (called D & O errors and omissions insurance). This type of insurance, however, is expensive and usually beyond the reach of newly formed small nonprofits. Also, D & O coverage often excludes the sorts of potential liabilities that your directors and officers may be worried about (personal injury and other types of legal tort actions, claims of illegality, or intentional misconduct and the like). If you decide to investigate the cost of D & O insurance, you will want to make sure to go over the areas of coverage and exclusion in the policy very carefully before you buy in.

California nonprofit law recognizes that nonprofits often can't afford D & O liability insurance with adequate claim coverage and it contains provisions that help limit *volunteer* directors' and officers' exposure to liability. Corporations must also indemnify (advance or pay back) a director for legal expenses incurred in a lawsuit under certain conditions. These special California statutes are discussed in more detail in "Directors," below, and they can provide added comfort to people considering serving as a California nonprofit corporation director or officer. Again, we believe the best and most practical way to reassure directors and officers to hitch their wagon to your nonprofit organization's star is to be able to show them you will operate your nonprofit fairly, responsibly, and safely without undue risk of lawsuits by employees or complaints by the public.

Incorporators and Their Role as Promoters

An incorporator is the person (or persons) who signs and delivers the articles of incorporation to the secretary of state for filing. In practice, the incorporator is often selected from among the people who serve as the initial directors of the corporation. Once the corporation is formed, the incorporator's legal role is finished.

During the organizational phase, it's not unusual for an incorporator to become a "promoter" of the corporation. An incorporator's promotional activities can quickly go beyond enthusiastic talk about the organization. Promotional activities may involve obtaining money, property, personnel, and whatever else it takes to get the nonprofit corporation started. Arranging for a loan or renting office space will require signatures and promises—to repay the loan and pay the rent. But will the newly formed corporation automatically become responsible? Future directors may hesitate to join a new organization that is saddled already by contracts negotiated by an eager (but perhaps unsavvy) promoter. The promoters themselves will naturally be nervous that they'll be personally responsible if the incorporation plans go awry. And what about the third parties—they may not be inclined to do business with promoters unless they are assured that there will be a responsible party at the other end. After explaining how a promoter must approach every transaction—with the corporation's best interests in mind—we'll show you how to address the concerns of the eventual directors, the promoters themselves, and the third parties with whom they do business.

A Promoter Must Act With the Corporation's Best Interests in Mind

When an incorporator acts as a promoter, she is considered by law to be its fiduciary. This legal jargon simply means she has a duty to act in the best interests of the corporation, and must make full disclosure of any personal interest and potential benefits she may derive from business transacted for the nonprofit.

EXAMPLE:

When the incorporator/promoter arranges to sell property she owns to the nonprofit corporation, she must disclose to the nonprofit's board of directors both her ownership interest in the property and any gain she stands to make on the sale.

Directors Must Ratify a Promoter's Actions

Most of the time, a nonprofit corporation won't be bound by an incorporator's preincorporation contract with a third party unless the board of directors ratifies the contract or the corporation accepts the benefits of the contract. For example, if a nonprofit board votes to ratify the lease signed by an incorporator before the date of incorporation, the corporation will be bound to honor the lease. Similarly, if the nonprofit moves into its new offices and conducts business there, their actions will constitute a ratification and the nonprofit will be bound.

Promoters Can Avoid Personal Liability

Fortunately, if promoters carefully draft documents—such as any loan papers and leases—they can avoid the risk of personal liability in the event that the corporation doesn't ratify the deal (or if the corporation never comes into being). Incorporators will not be personally liable for these contracts if they sign in the name of a proposed corporation, not in their individual name, clearly inform the third party that the corporation does not yet exist and may never come into existence, and tell the third party that even if it does come into existence, it may not ratify the contract.

Convincing Third Parties to Do Business With a Promoter

As you might imagine, a cautious third party may balk at doing business with an individual whose yet-to-be-formed nonprofit may repudiate the deal. One way to provide some assurance to a third party is for an incorporator to bind himself personally to the contract—in essence, become a guarantor for the loan, lease, or other contract. Understandably, few incorporators will be able or willing to put their personal finances on the line, unless they are absolutely sure that the corporation will in fact be formed and will ratify the deal. The other solution is to incorporate quickly—which you can do with the help of this book!

EXAMPLE:

An incorporator/promoter enters into an agreement to lease office space for its organization. Six months later, the organization obtains nonprofit corporate status. The newly formed nonprofit is not bound by the lease agreement unless its board of directors ratifies the agreement or the organization used the office space during the preincorporation period.

Directors

Directors meet collectively as the board of directors, and are responsible—legally, financially, and morally—for the management and operation of your nonprofit corporation. A nonprofit in California must have at least one director, although many nonprofits have three or more. Often, the people who formed the corporation (the incorporators) also become the corporation's first directors and they are also the ones who prepare and file the articles of incorporation. Although there are no residency requirements (you can have out-of-state directors) or age requirements, your directors should be over the age of 18 to avoid contractual problems.

Selecting Directors

Choosing directors is one of the most important decisions you will make when organizing your nonprofit. Here are some important things to consider that will help you make the best possible choice for your organization.

Commitment to Your Nonprofit's Purpose

Your directors are a crucial link between your organization and its supporters and benefactors. Make sure that the members of the community that you plan to serve will see your directors as credible and competent representatives of your group and its nonprofit goals. Their status and integrity will be crucial to encouraging and protecting public trust in your organization, and their connections will be vital to attracting recognition, clients, donations, and other support.

- Consider members of the communities you will serve who have a proven commitment to the goals of your organization. There may be more than one community you'll want to consider. For example, your draw may be local (city, county, or state), regional, or national. If you are an environmental group concerned with issues in the southern part of the state, you have both a geographic community (people in the area) and a community of interest (environmentalists generally). Your board should reflect a cross section of interested and competent people from both these communities.

- Look for people with contacts and real-world knowledge and experience in the specific area of your nonprofit's interest. If you are starting a new private school or health clinic, someone familiar with your state's educational or public health bureaucracy would be a big help.

- If your organization is set up to do good works that will benefit a particular group, don't overlook the value of including a member of that recipient group. You may learn important things about your mission and get valuable buy-in from the beneficiaries of your hard work.

Business Knowledge and Expertise

Directors' responsibilities include developing and overseeing organizational policies and goals, budgeting, fundraising, and disbursing a group's funds. The board of directors may hire an administrator or executive director to supervise staff and daily operations, or it may supervise them directly. Either way, your board of directors should be a practical-minded group with strong managerial, technical, and financial skills. In making your selection, try to find people with the following skills and experience:

- **Fundraising experience.** While many large nonprofits have a staff fundraiser, smaller groups often can benefit from the advice of an experienced board member.

- **Experience managing money.** A professional accountant or someone with expertise in

record keeping and budgeting can be a godsend. Many nonprofits get into difficulty because their record-keeping and reporting techniques aren't adequate to produce the information required by the federal and state governments. Many are simply inattentive to financial responsibilities, such as paying withholding taxes or accounting properly for public or private grant monies.

- **Useful practical skills.** Do you need the professional expertise of a doctor, lawyer, or architect; or operational assistance in areas such as public relations, marketing, or publishing? If so, make finding one of these professionals a high priority during your board search.

Public Officials Are a Good Choice

The IRS likes to see that you have a representative (and financially disinterested) governing body that reflects a range of public interests, not simply the personal interests of a small number of donors. While it's by no means required, the presence of a sympathetic public official on your board can enhance its credibility with both the IRS and the community.

Avoid Conflicts of Interest

When selecting board members, you may need to inquire about, or at least consider, a prospective member's agenda or motives for joining the board. Obviously, people who want to join for personal benefit rather than for the benefit of the organization or the public should not be asked to serve. This doesn't mean that everyone with a remote or potential conflict of interest should be automatically disqualified. It does mean that any slight or possible conflict of interest should be fully recognized and discussed. If the conflict is limited, the director may be able to serve constructively if he refrains from voting on certain issues.

The bylaws included in this book have conflict-of-interest provisions that contain rules and procedures for avoiding or approving transactions, including compensation arrangements, that benefit the nonprofit's directors, officers, employees, or contractors. See Article 9 of the bylaws and "Limitation on Profits and Benefits" in Chapter 3 for more information on this topic.

Develop a Realistic Job Description

Your board of directors should be prepared to put time and energy into the organization. Make sure every prospective director has a realistic and clear understanding of what the job entails. Before you contact prospective candidates, we suggest that you prepare a job description that specifies at least the following:

- the scope of the nonprofit's proposed activities and programs
- board member responsibilities and time commitments (expected frequency and length of board meetings, extra duties that may be assigned to directors), and
- the rewards of serving on your board (such as the satisfaction of working on behalf of a cause you care about or the experience of community service).

A clear and comprehensive job description will help with decision making and will also help avoid future misunderstandings with board members over what is expected of them.

Train Your New Directors

The organizers of a nonprofit corporation often need to give initial directors orientation and training about the nonprofit's operations and activities. This training should continue so that board members can handle ongoing operational issues as well. For example, if your nonprofit corporation is organized to provide health care services, board members may need to learn city, state, and federal program requirements that impact your operations, and should get regular updates on changes made to these rules and regulations.

> **TIP**
>
> **Choose the right number of directors.** You'll want enough to ensure a wide basis of support (particularly with respect to fundraising), but not so many as to impede efficiency in the board's operation. Boards with between nine and 15 directors often work well.

Paying Your Directors

Nonprofit directors usually serve without compensation. We believe this is generally wise. Having nonprofit directors serve without pay reinforces one of the important legal and ethical distinctions of the nonprofit corporation: Unlike its for-profit counterpart, its assets are used to promote its goals, not for the private enrichment of its incorporators, directors, agents, members, or employees.

If you compensate directors, do so at a reasonable rate, related to the actual performance of services and established in advance by a board resolution. (See Article 9 of the bylaws included in this book for specific procedures to follow when approving compensation arrangements.) Most nonprofits reimburse directors only for necessary expenses incurred in performing director duties, such as travel expenses—typically a gas or mileage allowance—to attend board meetings. Sometimes directors are paid a set fee for attending meetings.

The bylaws included with this book contain conflict-of-interest and compensation approval policies that help a nonprofit obtain its 501(c)(3) tax exemption. These policies require disinterested members of the board or a committee of the board (such as a compensation committee) to approve all compensation paid to directors, officers, and others who exert control over a nonprofit (substantial contributors, higher-paid employees, or contractors). Before approving the compensation, the board or committee must determine that the pay is comparable to the amounts paid to others who serve in similar roles for similar organizations. For more information on these bylaw provisions, see Chapter 7, the sample bylaws for a public benefit corporation, special instruction 12.

Public Benefit Corporations and the "51% Rule"

If you form a California public benefit corporation and choose to compensate your directors for performing nondirector services for your corporation, you'll need to understand the 51% rule, a state law provision applicable to public benefit corporations (California Corporations Code § 5227). This rule specifies that a majority of directors of a public benefit corporation cannot be interested persons. A director is interested if she receives payment from the corporation for services rendered in any capacity *other than* as a director, or is related to such a person (for example, a director also serves and is paid as an officer or consultant to the corporation). Under the statute, related means a brother, sister, ancestor, descendant, spouse, brother-in-law, sister-in-law, son-in-law, daughter-in-law, father-in-law, or mother-in-law of any such paid person. This means that a majority of the board, including relatives of board members, cannot be paid as officers, employees, or independent contractors of the corporation.

EXAMPLE:

A 501(c)(3) education nonprofit corporation, organized as a California public benefit corporation, has three directors on its board, each of whom is paid a modest amount for attending board meetings. All three directors can be paid for attending meetings without violating the 51% rule. One of the board members is also paid a salary as the organization's chief operating officer and another director is also paid as a legal consultant to the nonprofit. The nonprofit is in violation of the 51% rule because only one-third of the board is "disinterested," not the required 51% or greater. If the board member who is the legal consultant agrees to render legal advice and services for free, the nonprofit will be in compliance with the 51% rule because then two-thirds of the board would be disinterested (only one board member, the chief operating officer, would be interested).

The California Attorney General enforces the 51% disinterested director rule. How will the attorney general know if you're in violation of the rule? Every year, you'll file a Periodic Report form (Form RRF-1) with the attorney general's office, in which you'll be asked about your directors' interested or disinterested status. If you are a public benefit corporation and the attorney general learns that a majority of your board (including relatives of board members) is not disinterested, it will, at the very least, send your corporation a letter requiring compliance.

Larger nonprofit corporations and those that rely on grant funds (where even stricter conflict-of-interest rules often apply) will already be familiar with director compensation limitations and are less likely than their smaller counterparts to run into problems with the 51% rule. Smaller groups, however, tend to rely more heavily on the same group of people (and their family members) to act as directors and also as officers, employees, and independent contractors of their organization. These smaller public benefit corporations may need to look for extra, unrelated people to fill some of the directors' positions so that the more active directors (or their family members) can also be paid salaries as officers or employees.

The following examples highlight some of the problems that small nonprofits run into with the 51% disinterested directors rule.

EXAMPLE 1:

Your public benefit corporation has four directors: you, your sister Blanche, and two unrelated persons, Bob and Ray. Bob's brother-in-law, Alfredo, is one of the paid officers of the corporation. If you get paid for doing occasional work as an independent contractor, your corporation has violated the 51% rule. Why? Because you are an interested person (you are getting paid for services other than acting as a director) and your sister Blanche is an interested person (she is related to you). Even if you replace Blanche with an unrelated unpaid board member, your public benefit corporation board will still be in violation of the 51% rule because Bob is an interested person as well (his brother-in-law is a paid employee of the corporation). Remember, a majority of the board cannot be paid for nondirector work or related to anyone who is paid by the corporation.

EXAMPLE 2:

A two-person board consists of two unrelated, unpaid people who run a small, nonprofit public benefit corporation. From time to time, they consult the spouse of one of the directors, who is an accountant

and does not charge the corporation. After a big project, they decide to make a token payment to the accountant for all the tax work done on the project. Whoops! The director who is the accountant's spouse just became an interested person and because there are only two people on the board, the board is now in violation of the 51% rule.

Term of Office

You can set the term of office for your directors in your bylaws (if you don't, the law provides that directors of public benefit and religious corporations can serve only for one year). Should you decide to set the term, you'll need to abide by the rules for public benefit corporations and religious corporations.

Public Benefit Corporations

The maximum term for directors of a public benefit corporation depends on whether the corporation has members. (For a discussion of members, see "Membership Nonprofits," below). If the public benefit corporation has members, the maximum term is three years; without members, the maximum term is six years. A director whose term has expired, however, can be reelected immediately and can serve an unlimited number of additional consecutive terms.

Public benefit corporations can get around the three-year (or six-year) term limitation by including a special provision in their bylaws authorizing the designation, instead of election, of directors. The bylaws can provide that one or more persons, usually the more active directors, are authorized to designate the other directors for any prescribed term. Generally, public benefit corporations with members can use this procedure for only one-third of their authorized number of directors.

Religious Corporations

Religious corporations can set up their own rules for the term, election, selection, designation, removal, and resignation of directors. These rules can be specified in the corporation's articles or by-laws.

> **TIP**
>
> **We suggest a three-year term for directors.** You'll get the most out of what a director has to contribute and will ensure continuity in operations. In return, the director will get the satisfaction of long-term service and hopefully will see some goals fulfilled.

Staggered Elections for Board Members

In the interest of continuity, staggered elections of board members may be a good idea. For example, rather than replacing the entire board at each annual election, you may wish to reelect ⅓ of the board members each year to serve a three-year term. To start this staggered system out with a 15-member board—five of the initial directors would serve for one year, five for two years, and the remaining five for the full three-year term. At each annual reelection, ⅓ of the board would be elected to serve three-year terms.

Quorum Rules

For the board of directors to take action at a meeting, a specified number of directors of the corporation—called a quorum—must be present. Unless otherwise provided in the bylaws, a majority of the number of directors in office represents a quorum. Most small nonprofits restate this majority quorum rule in their bylaws.

If you want a lower quorum requirement, you can provide for it in your bylaws, subject to certain restrictions. A public benefit corporation must have a quorum of at least two directors, or one-fifth of the total number of directors, whichever is larger. A public benefit corporation with only one director, however, may of course have a one-person quorum. Religious corporations can choose any quorum requirement they wish.

EXAMPLE:

A public benefit corporation with five directors must have at least a two-director quorum. A 15-director public benefit corporation must have at least a three-person quorum.

Voting Rules

Once a quorum is present at a meeting, a specified number of votes is needed to pass a board resolution. Unless otherwise stated in the articles or bylaws, a resolution must be passed by a majority vote of the directors present at a meeting where there is a quorum. In some cases, the votes of interested directors cannot be counted. This is discussed more in "How to Avoid Self-Dealing," below.

EXAMPLE:

The bylaws of a corporation with ten board members specify that a quorum consists of a majority of the board and that action by the board can be taken by a majority of the directors present. This means that a quorum of at least six people (a majority of the ten-person board) must be present to hold a board meeting and, at the very least, four votes (a majority of the six members present at a meeting) are required to pass a resolution. If eight of the ten directors attend the meeting, action must be approved by at least five votes—a majority of those present at the meeting.

If a quorum is present initially at a meeting and one or more board members leaves, action can sometimes still be taken even if you lose your quorum. As long you can still obtain the number of votes that represents a majority of the required quorum stated in the bylaws, the board can take action even though a quorum is no longer present at the meeting (this is known as the initial quorum rule). Going back to the example above, in a ten-director board, the required quorum for board action is six directors (a majority of the ten) and at least four votes (a majority of those present) are needed to take board action. Under the initial-quorum rule, two directors can leave the meeting and the four remaining votes will still be sufficient to pass a resolution. Why? Because a quorum was initially present and four board members, representing a majority of the required quorum of six, can vote to pass a resolution.

TIP

Get a quorum by teleconferencing.
Your board of directors doesn't necessarily have to meet in person to take action. Directors can take action (following their regular voting rules) using a conference telephone call.

Executive Committees

The board of directors can delegate some or even a significant part of the board's duties to an executive committee of two or more directors. This arrangement is often used when some directors are more involved in running and managing the nonprofit's affairs and business than others. Even the passive directors,

however, should still keep an eye on what their more active colleagues are up to and actively participate in regular meetings of the full board. To encourage passive directors to stay involved, courts have held the full board responsible for the actions of the executive committee.

Fortunately, keeping the full board abreast of executive committee actions isn't very difficult. The full board should receive regular, timely minutes of executive committee meetings and should review and, if necessary, reconsider important executive committee decisions at each regularly scheduled meeting of the full board. The full board should retain the power to override decisions of the executive committee.

There are certain actions that can't be delegated to an executive committee. Specifically, an executive committee cannot be given authority to:

- approve action that requires approval by the membership
- fill vacancies on the board or other committees
- fix directors' compensation
- alter bylaws
- appoint committees, or
- use corporate funds to support a nominee to the board after more people have been nominated than can be elected.

Don't confuse this special executive committee of directors with other corporate committees. The board typically appoints several specialized committees to keep track of and report on corporate operations and programs. These committees act as working groups that are more manageable in size and help make better use of the board's time and its members' talents. They may include finance, personnel, buildings and grounds, new projects, fundraising, or other committees.

These committees, often consisting of a mix of directors, officers, and paid staff, do not normally have the power to take legal action on behalf of the corporation; their purpose is to report and make recommendations to the full board or the executive committee.

EXAMPLE:

The board of directors appoints a finance committee charged with overseeing the organization's fundraising, budgeting, expenditures, and bookkeeping. The corporation's treasurer chairs the committee. Periodically, this committee makes financial recommendations to the full board. The board could also appoint a personnel committee to establish hiring and employment policies and to interview candidates for important positions. A plans and programs committee might be selected to put together the overall action plan for accomplishing the goals of the organization. Any action taken based on a committee's report or recommendation would be subject to approval by the board.

Directors Must Act Carefully

Corporate directors and officers have a legal duty to act responsibly and in the best interests of the corporation—this is called their statutory "duty of care." The statutes defining this phrase use general, imprecise legal terms that are not very helpful in understanding what exactly it means. As a result, the meaning of the term has developed over time as judges and juries, faced with lawsuits, decide whether a director's acts did (or did not) live up to the duty of care. Fortunately, most of it boils down to common sense, as the following discussions show.

Personal Liability for Directors' Acts

In general, you shouldn't be overly concerned about the prospect of personal liability for your directors. Broadly speaking, courts are reluctant to hold nonprofit directors personally liable, except in the clearest cases of dereliction of duty or misuse of corporate funds or property. In the rare cases when liability is found, the penalties are usually not onerous or punitive—typically, the court orders directors to repay the losses their actions caused.

Ordinary negligence or poor judgment is usually not enough to show a director breached his duty of care. Instead, there generally must be some type of fraudulent or grossly negligent behavior. *Volunteer* directors and executive officers of nonprofits enjoy extra protection from personal liability. These personal immunity laws are discussed in detail in "Special Protections for Volunteer Directors and Officers," below.

EXAMPLE:

A committee of the nonprofit advises the board of an unsafe condition on the corporation's property. The committee recommends certain remedial actions to get rid of the problem. If the board fails to implement any remedial measures or otherwise take steps to deal with the problem, a court could hold the directors personally liable for any ensuing damage or injuries.

Although the risk of being held personally liable is small, there are some things a director can and should do to minimize the risk of personal liability. Most importantly, all directors, whether active participants or casual community observers, should attend board meetings and stay informed of, and participate in, all major board decisions. If the board makes a woefully wrongheaded or ill-advised decision that leads to monetary damages, the best defense for any board member is a "No" vote recorded in the corporate minutes.

Also, all boards should try to get an experienced financial manager on their board or use the services of a prudent accountant who demands regular audited financial statements of the group's books. Legalities aside, what is most likely to put nonprofit directors at risk of personal liability is bad financial management, such as failing to pay taxes, not keeping proper records of how much money is collected and how it is disbursed, and commingling funds, either directors' personal funds with corporate funds or mixing restricted with nonrestricted funds.

Reliance on Regular Business Reports: A Safe Haven

To help directors accomplish their managerial duties, directors can rely on information from reliable, competent sources within the corporation (officers, committees, and supervisory staff), or on outside professional sources (lawyers, accountants, and investment advisors). If this information later turns out to be faulty or incorrect, the directors will not be held personally liable for any decision made in reliance on the information, unless the directors had good reason to question and look beyond the information presented to the board and failed to do so.

For example, if a nonprofit's treasurer tells the board that the organization has sufficient cash to meet ongoing payroll tax requirements, and the report seems reasonable (perhaps because the nonprofit has a budget surplus), the IRS will probably find that the individual board members were entitled to rely on the treasurer's report, even if there is not enough money to pay the taxes. However, if the board knows or

should have known that the nonprofit is having a difficult time paying its bills despite reports to the contrary by the treasurer, and the board does not direct the treasurer to make sure to set money aside to pay payroll taxes, the IRS may try to hold board members personally liable for unpaid taxes.

Investment Decisions Involving Corporate Assets

Directors of a public benefit corporation must use more caution when making investment decisions than when they decide routine business matters. That's because when they make investment decisions involving corporate funds, directors have an added duty of care under California nonprofit law to avoid speculation and protect those funds—a stricter standard of care than the normal standard discussed above. According to this stricter standard of care, directors must "avoid speculation, looking instead to the permanent disposition of the funds, considering the probable income, as well as the probable safety of the corporation's capital." (California Corporations Code § 5240(b)(1).)

This stricter investment standard does not apply to religious corporations. Directors of religious corporations are held to the lighter duty of care for the investments of nonprofit funds.

EXAMPLE:

The treasurer of a performing arts group tells the group's directors that the group has a hefty surplus of funds because of its recent road tour. The board decides to invest this money in a stable asset mutual fund rather than one of several high-risk equity funds that reported double-digit declines in the last several quarters. If challenged by the attorney general or a complaining member, the directors should be able to show that they've met the statutory investment standard—they attempted to preserve the capital of the corporation by investing in a stable fund with a predictable positive return track record rather than a riskier fund that was more likely to lose money.

Directors Must Be Loyal

A director has a duty of loyalty to the corporation. This means that the director must give the corporation a "right of first refusal" on business opportunities he becomes aware of in his capacity as director. If the corporation fails to take advantage of the opportunity after full disclosure, or if the corporation clearly would not be interested in the opportunity, the director can take advantage of the opportunity himself.

EXAMPLE:

Bob is a volunteer director on the board of Help Hospices, a nonprofit hospice and shelter organization. He agrees to shop around for a low-rent location in a reasonably safe neighborhood for the next nonprofit hospice site. He learns of three low-rent locations, one of which would also be ideal as a low-cost rental studio for his son who wants to move out of his parents' house as soon as possible. Bob reports all three locations to the board, and tells them that he plans to apply for a lease in his son's name on one of the rental units only if the board decides that it is not interested in leasing the space for nonprofit purposes. This type of specific disclosure is exactly what is required for Bob to meet his duty of loyalty to the nonprofit. Bob can apply for the lease for his son if the board gives him the go-ahead after deciding the nonprofit is not interested in leasing the space for itself.

How to Avoid Self-Dealing

Directors must guard against unauthorized self-dealing—that is, involving the corporation in any transaction in which the director has a material, or significant, financial interest without proper approval. Any transaction that has a material financial impact on a director can trigger the self-dealing rules. Once the self-dealing rules are triggered, the transaction must be properly approved before it can be consummated (see the California Corporations Code § 5233 for public benefit corporations; § 9243 for religious corporations).

The self-dealing rules and proper approval requirements can arise in many different types of transactions, including the purchase or sale of corporate property, the investment of corporate funds, or the payment of corporate fees or compensation.

EXAMPLE:

A board votes to authorize the corporation to lease or buy property owned by a director, or to purchase services or goods from another corporation in which a director owns a substantial amount of stock. Either of these could be considered a prohibited self-dealing transaction if not properly disclosed and approved, because a director has a material financial interest in each transaction and neither falls within one of the specific statutory exceptions.

A corporation must follow one of several distinct procedures to approve a transaction involving the corporation and one or more directors with a material financial interest in the transaction. Some of these procedures are similar to the duty of disclosure rules discussed above for directors who want to take advantage of an opportunity that could benefit the corporation. Self-dealing transactions, however, are ones where the corporation has decided to pursue the opportunity and the transaction will benefit the director.

If proper self-dealing procedures are not followed, the corporation, any of its directors or officers, or the California Attorney General can, on the attorney general's motion or upon complaint to the attorney general by a nonprofit insider or member of the public, sue the directors for the return of assets or repayment of money obtained through the self-dealing transaction.

See Article 9 of the bylaws included in this book for specific procedures to follow when approving transactions that benefit directors, officers, employees, or contractors associated with the nonprofit.

Get Attorney General Approval

The safest and most effective way to handle a situation where there is potential for self-dealing is to obtain the attorney general's approval of the transaction. You can do this before or after the deal is consummated (before is better).

If you don't want to seek the attorney general's approval, you can simply notify the attorney general of the transaction (and get approval of the transaction from the board as explained in the next section). This is not as good a safeguard for your deal as getting attorney general approval, but it does limit the time in which a lawsuit can be filed to two years from the date of the written notice. Without attorney general approval or notice, the attorney general has up to ten years after the transaction is consummated to file a lawsuit, and anyone else has up to three years.

California religious nonprofits have extra leeway in self-dealing situations. See the *Attorney General's Guide for Charities* (contained on the CD-ROM) that contains a statement regarding the attorney general's overall hands-off policy with respect to the oversight of religious corporations.

RESOURCE

Go over the *Attorney General's Guide for Charities*. It has information on seeking attorney general approval and sending a notice of transaction to the attorney general, and provides detailed information on how to comply with other nonprofit reporting and filing requirements. You can browse or download the *Attorney General's Guide for Charities* (plus occasional separate supplements), at the California Attorney General's website at http://ag.ca.gov/charities/publications.php. The *Guide* also contains excellent summaries of the legal responsibilities and liabilities of nonprofit directors under California law, as well as practical information on fundraising, fiscal management, and other important nonprofit issues. We recommend all California nonprofits obtain a copy of this valuable sourcebook.

CD-ROM

The *Attorney General's Guide for Charities* (2005) is included on the CD-ROM.

Obtain Approval From Disinterested Board Members

If you don't have the time to get the attorney general's approval for a self-dealing transaction, the transaction can be approved by a disinterested board, or committee of the board, upon a showing of certain facts. This approach is a lot less safe than getting attorney general approval, but it may be appropriate if you are absolutely certain a self-dealing transaction is completely fair to your nonprofit, even though a director is incidentally benefited by the transaction. For the board approval to be valid, it must occur before the transaction is entered into and the director who has a financial interest in the transaction cannot vote, although he can be counted for purposes of determining whether a quorum is present. In addition, the board must:

- have full knowledge of the economic benefit to the interested director
- determine that the transaction is fair and benefits the corporation, and
- determine that it is the best business deal that the corporation can make.

A properly authorized committee of the board can make these findings, as long as the board ratifies the committee's findings as soon as possible.

For religious corporations, the board or committee must simply determine that the transaction is fair or in furtherance of the religious purposes of the corporation.

Exceptions to Self-Dealing Rules

Exceptions to the self-dealing rules allow corporations to make certain decisions without having to follow the strict procedures that might otherwise apply. Here are some actions that might financially benefit a director but can be approved by normal board action:

- a board resolution fixing the compensation of a director or officer of the corporation
- a transaction that is part of the public, charitable, or religious program of the corporation, as long as it is approved without unjustified favoritism and benefits directors or their families only because they are in the class of persons intended to be benefited by the particular corporate program, and
- a transaction involving less than 1% of the corporation's previous year's gross receipts or $100,000, whichever is less, provided the interested director has no knowledge of the transaction.

Loans and Guarantees

Any loan or guarantee to a director of a public benefit corporation must be approved by the attorney general. Excluded from this requirement is a director's repayment obligation to a corporation for premiums paid on a life insurance policy, provided the obligation is secured by the proceeds of the policy and its cash surrender value. Loans made to an officer for the purchase of a principal residence are also not subject to this requirement, as long as the loan is necessary, in the board's opinion, to secure the services or continued services of the officer and is secured by real property in California.

Loans and guarantees to directors of religious corporations do not require the approval of the attorney general. Instead, they must be made under the general duty of care guidelines discussed above in "Directors Must Act Carefully."

SEE AN EXPERT

Consult a lawyer before approving any loans or providing any guarantees to directors. Because a nonprofit's activities cannot in any way benefit individuals involved in its operations, it's easy to see why a loan to a director from tax-exempt funds might appear questionable, even if it falls outside the attorney general's approval rules. If you plan to make a loan or guarantee to a director, check with a lawyer to make sure you comply with the applicable attorney general approval rules, and make sure the loans and guarantees are fair and in furtherance of the nonprofit's goals and activities.

Special Protections for Volunteer Directors and Officers

Special laws protect volunteer directors from personal liability for actions taken in connection with their duties as directors. These laws were passed to provide incentive and protection to people willing to serve on boards and work on behalf of nonprofit organizations. The protections offered by these laws have not proved to be of major significance. They can be helpful, however, particularly for small nonprofits during the early years when they often can't afford director and officer liability insurance yet need to attract outside people to help with their organizations.

Of course you should do everything possible to minimize potential risks involving your group's activities at the outset. For example, make sure that employees perform their work in a safe manner and that anyone required to perform a skilled task is properly trained and licensed. In addition, the corporation should obtain insurance coverage whenever possible for any specific known risks: motor vehicle insurance to cover drivers of corporate vehicles, and general commercial liability insurance to cover the group's premises. This will help reduce the risk of any personal liability for directors. And make sure your nonprofit meets all payroll and corporate tax return requirements imposed by the state and the IRS. Failure to withhold and pay payroll taxes or file timely corporate information returns can lead to hefty penalties and fines against the organization and the individuals responsible for the nonprofit's tax filings.

Public Benefit Corporations

California's nonprofit law protects a volunteer director or executive officer (such as the president, vice president, secretary, or treasurer) of a public benefit corporation from personal liability for negligent acts or omissions committed in the performance of his duties (California Corporations Code § 5239). This protection applies only to certain third-party lawsuits for monetary damages, such as a

personal injury claim against a director by a participant in a fundraising event. To get this protection, the following conditions must be met:

- the act or omission must be within the scope of the director's or executive officer's duties
- the act or omission must be performed in good faith
- the act or omission must not be reckless, wanton, intentional, or grossly negligent, and
- damages caused by the act or omission must be covered by a liability insurance policy (either in the form of a general liability policy, a directors' and officers' (D & O) liability policy, or a policy issued personally to the director or executive officer), *or*, if there is no such policy, good faith efforts must have been made to obtain liability insurance.

It is important to remember that these laws protect only *volunteer* directors and executive officers of public benefit corporations. You can be reimbursed for expenses such as gas mileage or receive a per diem payment and still be considered a volunteer. You cannot, however, receive a salary, fee, or other consideration for services to the corporation. The law isn't intended to cover day-to-day ministerial actions of corporate employees.

If the nonprofit does not have the insurance as mentioned in the final point above, the organization must be able to show that it made good faith efforts to obtain it. Fortunately, the law gives some meaning to the term, good faith efforts. Here are the rules:

- If you are a 501(c)(3) public benefit nonprofit and your annual budget is less than $25,000, you can show this good faith effort if your corporate records prove that you made at least one inquiry each year for $500,000 in general liability coverage, and that the quotes received equaled or exceeded 5% of your annual budget for the prior year.

- Larger nonprofits should get one or more quotes for coverage per year and keep a record of the dates of their contacts with insurance brokers, agents, and companies, the types and amounts of coverage sought, and quotes or responses received from each contact. Documentation of this sort should also be kept if a larger nonprofit gets less insurance than it originally sought.

- Volunteer directors and executive officers must also make reasonable efforts on their own to obtain insurance and these efforts should be carefully documented.

EXAMPLE:

The Better Books Network has an annual budget of $20,000. The Treasurer contacts a nonprofit insurance broker and gets a quote for $500,000 worth of general liability coverage at a cost of more than $1,000 (more than 5% of the nonprofit's previous annual budget). Under the statute, they qualify as having made a reasonable effort to obtain insurance. They don't have to take the policy; they just have to be able to show that they asked for and obtained this quote (by making a note in the corporate records and, if possible, attaching a faxed or written copy of the quote obtained from their insurance broker). They must obtain similar quotes for all years in which they hope to take advantage of this statutory escape hatch.

A volunteer director or officer may still be personally liable to the corporation for negligence in actions brought by other directors in the name of the corporation or by the attorney general. And the corporation itself remains liable for damages to third parties, even if its directors and officers fall under the protection of these rules. Also, if a plaintiff sues for something other than monetary damages (such as a court order for restitution), these rules do not apply.

There is a separate provision of California's nonprofit law (California Corporations Code § 5047.5) that protects volunteer directors and officers of public benefit corporations in a manner similar to the protections offered by Section 5239. To qualify under this section, the public benefit corporation must be tax-exempt under Section 501(c)(3) of the Internal Revenue Code, have an annual budget of less than $50,000, and take out a general liability insurance policy of at least $500,000. Larger 501(c)(3) tax-exempt corporations must be insured for at least $1 million. This section specifically requires that the nonprofit obtain a general liability policy, whereas Section 5239 requires only that you be able to show the nonprofit made attempts to obtain insurance.

Religious Corporations

Section 9247 of the California Corporations Code protects volunteer directors and officers of California nonprofit religious corporations in a manner similar to Section 5239, discussed above. Section 5047.5, discussed above, also applies to religious nonprofits that are tax-exempt under Section 501(c)(3) of the Internal Revenue Code.

Indemnification for Lawsuits

Generally, a California corporation must indemnify (reimburse) a director for legal expenses incurred in a lawsuit related to the performance of his duties as director, if the director wins the lawsuit. If the director loses the lawsuit, he can still be reimbursed for legal expenses if the board, membership, or the court approves the payment and finds that the director was acting in good faith and in a manner he believed to be in the best interests of the corporation.

Indemnification is more difficult to obtain if the lawsuit involves self-dealing or if the indemnification is for judgments, fines, or settlements in actions brought by the corporation itself or by the California Attorney General.

Insurance

A nonprofit corporation can purchase insurance to cover a director's legal expenses, judgments, fines, and settlements incurred in connection with a lawsuit or other proceeding brought against the director for either a breach of duty to the corporation, or simply because of her status as a director of the corporation. Of course, D & O liability insurance, as noted above in "Ways to Reassure Potential Officers and Directors," can be costly and beyond the reach of many small nonprofits. Insurance cannot, as a matter of California law, be purchased to cover any liability that arises from breaking the self-dealing rules discussed above.

Officers

A California nonprofit corporation must have at least three officers: a president (or chairperson of the board), secretary, and treasurer (as the chief financial officer). Typically, officers are selected from the board of directors. One person may fill one or more of the officer positions, except that the person who holds the office of secretary or treasurer cannot also be the president. There are no residency or age requirements for officers.

Duties and Responsibilities

The powers, duties, and responsibilities of officers are specified in the corporation's articles or bylaws, or by resolution of the board of directors. Generally, officers are in charge of supervising and implementing the day-to-day business of the corporation. This authority does not usually include the authority to enter into major business transactions, such as the mortgage or sale of corporate property. These kinds of major transactions are left to the board of directors. If the board wants the officers to have the power to make one or more major business decisions, special authority should be delegated by board resolution.

Officers have a duty to act honestly and in the best interests of the corporation. Officers are considered agents of the corporation and can subject the corporation to liability for their negligent or intentional acts if their acts cause damage and are performed in the scope of their employment.

Officers May Bind the Corporation

Generally, the actions and transactions of an officer are legally binding on the corporation. A third party is entitled to rely on the apparent authority of an officer and can require the corporation to honor a deal, regardless of whether the officer was actually empowered by the board to enter into the transaction. To avoid confusion, if you delegate a special task to an officer outside the realm of the officer's normal duties, it's best to have your board pass a resolution granting the officer special authority to enter into the transaction on behalf of the corporation.

And, of course, any action taken by an officer on behalf of a corporation will be binding if the corporation accepts the benefits of the transaction or if the board ratifies the action, regardless of whether or not the officer had the legal authority to act on the corporation's behalf.

Compensation of Officers

Officers can receive reasonable compensation for services they perform for a nonprofit corporation. It is appropriate to pay officers who have day-to-day operational authority, and not to pay the officers who limit themselves to presiding over the board of directors or making overall nonprofit policy decisions. In smaller nonprofits, it is more common for officers and directors to also assume staff positions and be paid for performing these operational tasks. Remember, though, that under the 51% disinterested directors rule, only 49% of the directors of a public benefit corporation can receive compensation as officers or for another nondirectorial position of the same corporation.

EXAMPLE:

In a larger nonprofit organization, a paid executive director or medical director (these are staff positions, not board of director posts) might oversee routine operations of a medical clinic, and the paid principal or administrator (also staff positions) will do the same for a private school. However, in a smaller nonprofit, the corporate president or other officer may assume these salaried tasks.

The bylaws included with this book contain conflict-of-interest and compensation approval policies that help a nonprofit obtain its 501(c)(3) tax exemption. These policies require disinterested members of the board or a committee of the board (such as a compensation committee) to approve all compensation paid to directors, officers, and others who exert control over a nonprofit (substantial contributors, higher-paid employees, or contractors). Before approving the compensation, the board or committee must determine that the pay is comparable to the amounts paid to others who serve in similar roles for similar organizations. For more information on these bylaw provisions, see, in Chapter 7, "Bylaws for a Public Benefit Corporation," special instruction 12 in "Instructions for Completing Your Bylaws."

The California Nonprofit Integrity Act of 2004 contains special California rules for the approval of executive compensation. Under the law, the board or a committee of the board of all "charitable" nonprofits (generally, public benefit nonprofits except schools and hospitals) must review and approve as "just and reasonable" any compensation paid to the nonprofit's president (or chief executive officer) and treasurer (or chief financial officer). Compensation includes salary, benefits, and any other amounts paid. You must obtain board or committee approval initially upon hiring the officer, when the term of employment is renewed or extended, and whenever the officer's compensation is modified. However, separate approval of the CEO and CFO's compensation is not required if compensation is modified for substantially all employees.

If you already have a nonprofit CEO or CFO who is an at-will employee with no employment contract, your board should review and approve the officer's compensation. If you are organizing your nonprofit and are appointing your initial officers, you should add your finding as to the reasonableness of CEO, CFO, and other officer compensation in the Compensation of Officers resolution in your Minutes of First Meeting of the Board of Directors, prepared as explained in "Prepare Minutes of Your First Board of Directors' Meeting" in Chapter 10.

Here are some Internet resources you can use to learn more about the rules under the California Nonprofit Integrity Act of 2004:

- Go to the California Attorney General's website at http://ag.ca.gov/charities/publications.php, select the links to the "Guide to the Nonprofit Integrity Act of 2004."

- To read the sections of California law amended or added by the Act, go to www.leginfo.ca.gov/calaw.html, select and read Government Code Sections 12581, 12582, 12583, 12584, 12585, 12586, 12599, 12599.1, 12599.3, 12599.6, and 12599.7, and Business and Professions Code Section 17510.5.

Loans, Guarantees, and Immunity Laws

Loans and guarantees to officers are governed by the same rules that apply to loans and guarantees to directors (see "Loans and Guarantees," above). The special personal immunity laws for volunteer directors of nonprofits also apply to volunteer executive officers of nonprofit corporations. These laws are discussed in detail above in "Loans and Guarantees." The executive officers who fall under the protection of the personal immunity laws are the president, vice president, secretary, treasurer, and anyone who assists in establishing the policy of the corporation, at least with respect to their policy-making decisions. A corporation can also insure or indemnify its officers against personal liability for their actions on behalf of the corporation.

Employees

Employees of nonprofit corporations work for and under the supervision of the corporation and are paid a salary in return for their services.

Paid directors and officers are considered employees for purposes of individual income tax withholding, Social Security, state unemployment, and other payroll taxes the employer must pay. Employees have the usual duties to report and pay their taxes, and the usual personal liability for failing to do so.

Employee Immunity

Employees are generally not personally liable for any financial loss their acts or omissions may cause to the corporation or to outsiders, as long as they are acting within the course and scope of their employment. If the harm is done to outsiders, it is the corporation, not the employees, that must assume the burden of paying for the loss.

CAUTION

Employees may be personally liable for taxes. An important exception to the rule of employee nonliability concerns the employee whose duty it is to report or pay federal or state corporate or employment taxes. The responsible employee (or officer or director) can be held personally liable for failure to report or pay such taxes. The IRS may take a broad view as to who is "responsible" for such duties—see "Federal and State Corporate Employment Taxes" in Chapter 11.

Employee Compensation

Salaries paid to officers or regular employees should be reasonable and given in return for services actually performed. A reasonable salary is one roughly equal to that received by employees rendering similar services elsewhere. If salaries are unreasonably high, they are apt to be treated as a simple distribution of net corporate earnings and could jeopardize the nonprofit's tax-exempt status. Nonprofits should avoid paying discretionary bonuses at the end of a good year—this may look like a payment from the earnings and profits of the corporation, a no-no for nonprofits. In reality, since the pay scale for nonprofit personnel is usually lower than that of their for-profit counterparts, most of this cautionary advice shouldn't be needed.

Employee Benefits

Among the major advantages associated with being an employee of a corporation are the employment benefits it can provide, such as corporate pension plans, corporate medical expense reimbursement plans, and corporate group accident, health, life, and disability insurance. Generally, amounts the corporation pays to provide these benefits (such as the payment of insurance premiums by the corporation) are not included in the employee's individual gross income and therefore are not taxed to the employee. Also, the benefits themselves (such as insurance proceeds) are often not taxed when the employee receives them. These corporate employee benefits can sometimes be an important collateral reason for forming a nonprofit corporation. They are often more favorable than those allowed noncorporate employees.

The nonprofit itself enjoys a tax break when offering benefits in certain situations. Benefits are deductible by a nonprofit corporation if taxes are owed by the corporation in connection with an activity that uses the services of these employees. For example, if a nonprofit generates $20,000 in gross revenue unrelated to its exempt purposes, but pays wages of $10,000 plus benefits of $5,000 to generate this income, its net unrelated business income is reduced to $5,000.

Nonprofits may establish some of the employee benefits plans available to employees of business corporations. The rules are complicated, however. For information on setting up qualified employee plans and other benefits, consult your tax adviser or a benefit plan specialist.

Membership Nonprofits

California nonprofit law assigns a very specific meaning to the terms member and membership nonprofit. At the time you incorporate, you must decide whether to establish a formal membership structure for your nonprofit. If you choose to have a membership structure, your members will be the ones who approve or disapprove major corporate decisions. In a nonmembership structure, the board of directors makes the major corporate decisions. Most smaller groups choose not to form a membership corporation because it is simpler to operate without members.

Nonmembership Corporations

First, then, let's review how the majority of nonprofits run—without a formal membership. In a nonmembership corporation, only the directors participate in the legal affairs of the corporation. This structure avoids the extra time, work, and expense involved in having major corporate decisions subject to formal member approval.

California nonprofit law gives members the right to approve various corporate decisions. However, if the nonprofit's articles and bylaws do not provide for members, the law specifically says that directors act in the place of members whenever membership approval of an action is required. So if you read the California nonprofit law and see references to approval by members, this means approval by directors in a nonmembership nonprofit. In addition, in a nonmembership corporation, any membership action can be approved by regular board approval (normally majority vote) even if there is a greater membership vote requirement for the action specified in the nonprofit law.

There may be many interested people associated with a nonmembership organization—

folks who pay annual dues or fees to support the organization or to receive attendance privileges, mailings, or discounts to events—but they're not members as the term is legally defined. These people are often called supporters, patrons, contributors, advisors, or even members, but they don't participate in the legal affairs of the nonprofit because they have not been specifically granted legal membership rights by the corporation.

EXAMPLE:

Susan, a patron of the Art Museum, has a museum membership that entitles her to free admissions, participation in educational programs and events, use of a special facility, or attendance at exhibition previews. The membership does not give Susan any say in the museum's operation and management, which she would have if she were a legal, formal member.

If you already know that your nonprofit will not have members, you may skip the rest of this section. If you're not sure about whether to have members, this section should guide you in your decision. And should you decide to form a membership nonprofit, you'll need to refer back to this discussion as you go about the normal steps of setting up and running your nonprofit.

Who Is a Member Under Law?

Under California nonprofit law, a member is someone who is given the right in the corporation's articles or bylaws to vote for the election of directors, the sale of substantially all of the assets of the corporation, a merger of the corporation, or its dissolution (California Corporations Code § 5056). A member also means any person who is designated a member in the corporation's articles or bylaws and has the right to vote on amendments to the corporation's articles or bylaws. Sometimes a nonprofit will refer informally to its members or charge admission fees, dues, or assessments to enroll and maintain an informal nonprofit membership. These people, even if referred to informally as members, are not members under law unless you set up a membership structure in your articles and bylaws and give them specific voting rights.

Members Elect and Remove Directors

Members elect the directors in a membership corporation. The election must take place at a regular membership meeting or, subject to some exceptions, can be by written ballot. Regular meetings of members should coincide with the time for reelection of directors. There are specific rules that govern director nomination and election procedures.

Special meetings of members for the purpose of removing directors can be called by 5% or more of the members. If the corporation has fewer than 50 members, removal of directors must be approved by a majority of all members. Normal voting requirements apply to the removal of directors if the corporation has 50 or more members.

Members Amend Bylaws and Articles

The voting members may, on their own, adopt, amend, or repeal provisions of the bylaws. This can be done by unanimous written consent, by written ballots received from at least a quorum of members, or by a majority of a quorum vote at a meeting. Because a quorum for a membership meeting can be greater or less than a majority of the total membership voting power (see quorum rules below), a relatively small percentage of membership votes may be sufficient to change the bylaws.

EXAMPLE:

If a nonprofit corporation has 20 voting members, each with one vote, and the bylaws require that less than a majority (eight) be present at a meeting to represent a quorum, then five members can change the bylaws at a meeting.

We think it is wise for the bylaws to contain higher quorum and voting requirements when it comes to changing the bylaws—amending the bylaws is a major decision and should be decided by a substantial number of members of the corporation.

Once formal members have been admitted, a bylaw or bylaw amendment fixing or changing the authorized number of directors can only be passed by the members and not by the board. With few exceptions, members must also approve a board resolution to amend the articles of incorporation, following normal membership voting rules.

Members Approve Mergers and Consolidations

The principal terms of an agreement to merge or consolidate the nonprofit corporation with another corporation usually must be approved by the members.

Members Approve the Sale of Corporate Assets

Members of a nonprofit corporation must approve a board resolution to sell substantially all of the corporation's assets, unless the sale is made for the purpose of securing the payment or performance of any corporate contract, note, bond, or obligation, or is in the regular course of business (this latter exception won't normally apply—few nonprofit corporations are organized for the purpose of selling corporate assets).

Classes of Membership

If you decide to set up a membership structure in your bylaws, you can establish different classes of membership, such as voting and nonvoting membership classes. For example, a large botanical society might have one class of voting members who elect the board of directors, and an informal nonvoting membership consisting of persons who receive the society's magazine and newsletters.

If you have different memberships, the rights, privileges, restrictions, and obligations associated with each class of membership must be stated in the articles of incorporation or bylaws. In addition, the corporation must maintain a membership book containing the name, address, and the class of membership, if applicable, of each member.

Membership Quorum and Voting Rules

Unless the articles or bylaws state otherwise, each member is entitled to one vote on any matter submitted for approval to the members. Again, it's possible to have several classes of membership with different voting rights attached to each membership. A quorum for a membership corporation is a majority of all members, unless the bylaws provide for a different number (which can be greater or less than a majority). If you provide for a membership quorum of less than one-third of all members, then special notice of members' meetings will be required if less than one-third of the members actually attend the meeting.

Larger membership nonprofits rarely call and hold meetings with the expectation that members will attend and vote at the meeting in person. Rather, membership proxies (written votes) are usually solicited by mail well in advance of the meeting. The corporate secretary tallies and reports these votes at the membership meeting. The main business of the membership—the reelection of the board—is usually accomplished through this proxy-by-mail procedure in large membership nonprofits.

Membership Action to Dissolve the Nonprofit

A majority of all of a membership corporation's members (not just a majority of members present at a meeting at which a quorum is present) can elect to voluntarily dissolve the corporation for any reason. The board of directors with normal membership approval (the votes of a majority of a quorum) can also elect to voluntarily dissolve the corporation. In a few special cases, the board can, on its own, elect to dissolve the corporation without obtaining membership approval.

Lower membership vote requirements are imposed for an involuntary dissolution. An involuntary dissolution, discussed in more detail in Chapter 11, is a dissolution for a specific reason, usually indicating a failure on the part of the corporation to effectively carry out its corporate purposes. For an involuntary dissolution, one-third of the votes of all the members of the corporation is required. The votes of members who have participated in any of the acts which form the basis for requesting involuntary dissolution cannot be counted.

Expelling Members

A member cannot be expelled unless it is done "in good faith and in a fair and reasonable manner." There is a specific procedure that public benefit corporations can use to be sure that their procedure for expulsion of a member is fair and reasonable. We've included this procedure in the bylaw provisions for public benefit membership corporations contained in this book. The law doesn't address what constitutes a good faith reason for expulsion—it only deals with the procedure for expulsion. There have been a number of court cases that have ruled on the fairness of specific reasons for expelling members, but there's no general rule. If a question involving the expulsion of members arises, see a lawyer.

A member can resign from the corporation at any time. The rights of a member cease upon his expulsion, death, termination from membership, or upon dissolution of the corporation.

Complying With Securities Laws

Memberships in a nonprofit corporation are considered securities and, as such, are regulated by laws governing the offer and sale of securities. Generally, the offer to sell or the sale of securities requires the approval of the California Commissioner of Corporations, often involving the preparation and filing of complicated and costly documents. Obtaining this approval is called qualifying the sale of securities and, as you might guess, most small corporations wish to avoid having to obtain this approval.

Fortunately, nonprofit corporations exempt under Section 501(c)(3) of the Internal Revenue Code (and the parallel state tax exemption section of the California Revenue & Taxation Code § 23701(d)) will, in most cases, be eligible for an automatic exemption from qualifying the issuance of their memberships. To qualify for this automatic exemption:

- the issuer must be organized exclusively for educational, benevolent, fraternal, religious, charitable, social, or reformatory purposes, and not for profit

- no part of the net earnings of the issuer can inure to the benefit of any member or other individual, and

- the promoters of the nonprofit corporation must not expect, intend to, or actually make a profit directly or indirectly from any business or activity associated with the organization or operation of the nonprofit organization, or from remuneration received from such nonprofit corporation.

These requirements are basically the same as the requirements for obtaining 501(c)(3) status, so you shouldn't have any trouble meeting them. In fact, these requirements are a little looser than the Section 501(c)(3) requirements because they include additional purposes. Except for memberships issued by a group organized and operated for social purposes, memberships that meet the first two requirements above are also exempt from registration with the Securities and Exchange Commission under Section 3(a)(4) of the federal Securities Act. ●

Requirements for Section 501(c)(3) Tax Exemption

Corporations, like individuals, are normally subject to federal and state income taxation. One reason to establish a nonprofit corporation is to obtain an exemption from corporate income taxes. Exemption is not automatic—a corporation must apply and show that it is in compliance with nonprofit exemption requirements to receive it. This chapter focuses on the basic federal tax exemption available to nonprofits under Section 501(c)(3) of the Internal Revenue Code and what is required to obtain tax-exempt status under this provision. In later chapters, we discuss the state exemption (which is very similar to the federal exemption) and also take you line by line through the federal tax exemption application.

You'll notice in going through the material in this chapter that many IRS tax exemption requirements are broad and seemingly applicable to a wide range of activities, both commercial and noncommercial. In fact, many commercial organizations are engaged in activities that could qualify for 501(c)(3) tax-exempt status. For example, there are for-profit scientific organizations that perform research that could qualify as 501(c)(3) scientific research. Similarly, many commercial publishing houses publish educational materials that could qualify the organization for 501(c)(3) status.

So why do only some organizations obtain tax-exempt status? Because a corporation must choose to apply for tax-exempt status from the IRS. Many organizations that might be eligible for 501(c)(3) status prefer to operate as commercial enterprises because they do not want to be subject to the moneymaking, profit distribution, and other restrictions applicable to nonprofits. (See Chapter 1 for a discussion of these restrictions). By defining and organizing your activities as eligible for 501(c)(3) status and then seeking tax-exempt status from the IRS, you distinguish your organization from similar commercial endeavors.

Section 501(c)(3) Organizational Test

Under Section 501(c)(3) of the Internal Revenue Code, groups organized and operated exclusively for charitable, religious, scientific, literary, and educational purposes can obtain an exemption from the payment of federal income taxes. The articles of incorporation of a 501(c)(3) corporation must limit the group's corporate purposes to one or more of the allowable 501(c)(3) purposes and must not empower it to engage (other than as an insubstantial part of its activities) in activities that don't further one or more of these tax-exempt purposes. This formal requirement is known as the 501(c)(3) organizational test.

A group can engage in more than one 501(c)(3) tax-exempt activity. For example, a group's activities can be characterized as charitable and educational, such as a school for blind or physically handicapped children.

A nonprofit cannot, however, engage simultaneously in a 501(c)(3) exempt purpose activity and in an activity that is exempt under a different subsection of Section 501(c). Thus, a group cannot be formed for educational *and* social or recreational purposes because social and recreational groups are exempt under Section 501(c)(7) of the Internal Revenue Code (see "Is Your Group a Nonprofit That Can Use This Book?" in Chapter 1 for a discussion of non-501(c)(3) tax-exempt groups). As a practical matter, this problem rarely occurs, because the non-501(c)(3) subsections are custom-tailored to specific types of organizations, such as war veterans' organizations and cemetery companies.

Valid Purposes Under Section 501(c)(3)

Now let's take a closer look at the most common 501(c)(3) purposes—charitable, religious, scientific, literary, and educational— and the requirements for each of these purposes. In addition to the valid purpose requirements discussed in this section, there are other general requirements that all 501(c)(3) groups must comply with to obtain 510(c)(3) status. These other requirements are discussed below in "Other Requirements for 501(c)(3) Groups."

Humane Societies and Sports Organizations

There are other, less commonly used exemptions available under Section 501(c)(3) that we do not cover in this book. For example, groups organized to prevent cruelty to children or animals or to foster national or international amateur sports competitions can claim a tax exemption under Section 501(c)(3). However, these groups must meet narrowly defined 501(c)(3) requirements, and, for humane societies, special state requirements. See IRS Publication 557 for specifics on each of these special 501(c)(3) groups and contact the state attorney general's office for special incorporation requirements for humane societies.

Charitable Purposes

The charitable purpose exemption is the broadest, most all-encompassing exemption under Section 501(c)(3). Not surprisingly, it is also the most commonly used exemption.

Benefit to the Public

The word charitable as used in Section 501(c)(3) is broadly defined to mean "providing services beneficial to the public interest." In fact, other 501(c)(3) purpose groups— educational, religious, and scientific groups— are often also considered charitable in nature because their activities usually benefit the public. Even groups not directly engaged in a religious, educational, or scientific activity, but whose activities indirectly benefit or promote a 501(c)(3) purpose can qualify as a 501(c)(3) charitable-purpose group.

Groups that seek to promote the welfare of specific groups of people in the community (handicapped or elderly persons or members of a particular ethnic group) or groups that seek to advance other exempt activities (environmental or educational) will generally be considered organized for charitable purposes because these activities benefit the public at large and are charitable in nature.

Groups that advance religion, even if they do not have a strictly religious purpose or function, are often considered charitable purpose organizations under Section 501(c)(3). The IRS reasons that the advancement of religion is itself a charitable purpose. Examples of some of these charitable purpose groups include:

- **Monthly Newspaper.** A group that published and distributed a monthly newspaper with church news of interdenominational interest was held to accomplish a charitable purpose because it contributed to the advancement of religion.

- **Coffee House.** A nonprofit organization formed by local churches to operate a supervised facility known as a coffee house was found to have a valid 501(c)(3) charitable purpose because it advanced religion and education by bringing together college age people with church leaders, educators, and leaders from the business community for discussions and counseling on religion, current events, social, and vocational problems.

- **Genealogical Research.** An organization formed to compile genealogical research data on its family members to perform religious observances in accordance with the precepts of their faith was held to advance religion and be a charitable organization under 501(c)(3).

- **Missionary Assistance.** A missionary group established to provide temporary low-cost housing and related services for missionary families on furlough in the United States from their assignments abroad was held to be a charitable purpose organization under Section 501(c)(3).

Other examples of activities and purposes that have met the IRS organizational test for charitable purpose (and possibly another 501(c)(3) purpose as well) include:

- relief of the poor, distressed, or under-privileged

- advancement of education or science

- erection or maintenance of public buildings, monuments, or works

- lessening the burdens of government

- lessening neighborhood tensions

- elimination of prejudice and discrimination

- promotion and development of the arts

- defense of human and civil rights secured by law

- providing facilities and services to senior citizens

- maintaining a charitable hospital

- providing a community fund to support family relief and service agencies in the community

- providing loans for charitable or educational purposes, and

- maintaining a public interest law firm.

Class or Group of Beneficiaries

A charitable organization must be set up to benefit an indefinite class of people, not particular persons. The number of beneficiaries can be relatively small as long as the benefited class is open and the beneficiaries of the group are not specifically identified.

EXAMPLE 1:

A charitable nonprofit corporation cannot be established under Section 501(c)(3) to benefit Jeffrey Smith, an impoverished individual. But Jeffrey Smith can be selected as a beneficiary of a 501(c)(3) charitable group whose purpose is to benefit needy individuals in a particular community (as long as he is a member of that community).

EXAMPLE 2:

A foundation that awards scholarships solely to undergraduate members of a designated fraternity was found to be a valid charitable organization under 501(c)(3), even though the number of members in the benefited group is small.

The following groups, all charitable in nature and benefiting a defined but indefinite group of people, were found to be valid charitable purpose organizations under Section 501(c)(3):

- an organization formed to build new housing and renovate existing housing for sale to low-income families on long-term, low-payment plans

- a day care center for children of needy, working parents

- a group created to market the cooking and needlework of needy women

- a self-help housing program for low-income families

- homes for the aged where the organization satisfies the special needs of an aged person for housing, health care, and financial security. (The requirements for housing and health care will be satisfied if the organization is committed to housing residents who become unable to pay and if services are provided at the lowest possible cost.)

- an organization that takes care of patients' nonmedical needs (reading, writing letters, and so on) in a privately owned hospital

- an organization that provides emergency and rescue services for stranded, injured, or lost persons

- a drug crisis center and a telephone hotline for persons with drug problems, and

- a legal aid society offering free legal services to indigent persons.

Health care nonprofits, whether hospitals or less formal, noninstitutional health care facilities or programs, can qualify as charitable 501(c)(3) organizations. However, the IRS is particularly concerned about conflicts of interest and business dealings between doctors who do work for the nonprofit and also rent space or have other commercial dealings with the nonprofit. The IRS recommends that the health care nonprofit form a community board and have conflict-of-interest provisions in their bylaws.

Services Need Not Be Free

Section 501(c)(3) charitable organizations are not required to offer services or products free or at cost. Nevertheless, doing so, or at least providing services at a substantial discount from the going commercial rate, can help convince the IRS of your group's bona fide charitable intentions. Charging full retail prices for services or products does not usually demonstrate a benefit to the public. Other restrictions applicable to a nonprofit's ability to make money are discussed below in "Other Requirements for 501(c)(3) Groups."

Religious Purposes

For Section 501(c)(3) purposes, a religious purpose group can be either a loosely defined religious organization that practices or promotes religious beliefs in some way or a formal institutional church. Groups formed to advance religion often qualify as charitable purpose organizations under Section 501(c)(3).

Qualifying as a Religious Organization

Traditionally, the IRS and the courts have been reluctant to question the validity or sincerity of religious beliefs or practices held by a group trying to establish itself as a religious purpose organization. As long as the organization's beliefs appear to be "truly and sincerely held" and their related practices and rituals are not illegal or against public policy, the IRS generally does not challenge the validity of the religious tenets or practices. However, the IRS will question the nature and extent of religious activities (as opposed to religious beliefs) if they do not appear to foster religious worship or advance a religious purpose, or if they appear commercial in nature.

EXAMPLE:

A group that holds weekly meetings and publishes material celebrating the divine presence in all natural phenomena should qualify as a religious purpose group. However, an organization that sells a large volume of literature to the general public, some of which has little or no connection to the religious beliefs held by the organization, could be regarded by the IRS as a regular trade or business, not as a tax-exempt religious organization.

A religious group need not profess belief in a supreme being to qualify as a religious organization under Section 501(c)(3).

Religious corporations also have the widest flexibility in managing their internal affairs. (See the *Attorney General's Guide for Charities* (2005) (contained on the CD-ROM) that contains a statement regarding the attorney general's overall hands-off policy with respect to oversight of religious corporations.)

Qualifying as a Church

You can also qualify under the 501(c)(3) religious purpose category as a church, but doing so is more difficult than simply qualifying as a 501(c)(3) religious organization. One of the advantages of qualifying as a church is that a church automatically qualifies for 501(c)(3) *public charity status*—a status that all 501(c)(3) groups want to obtain, as we explain later in Chapter 4.

CD-ROM

The IRS has a guide to assist churches and clergy in complying with the religious purpose requirement of the Internal Revenue Code. The publication is intended to be a user-friendly compilation, set forth in question-and-answer format. A copy of this guide, IRS Publication 1828, *Tax Guide for Churches and Religious Organizations*, is included on the CD-ROM. Most church and religious-purpose groups will find the information in this publication extremely helpful when preparing their federal exemption application (see Chapter 9).

Under IRS rulings, a religious organization should have the following characteristics to

qualify as a church (not all are necessary but the more the better):

- a recognized creed or form of worship
- a definite and distinct ecclesiastical government
- a formal code of doctrine and discipline
- a distinct religious history
- a membership not associated with any other church or denomination
- a complete organization of ordained ministers
- a literature of its own
- established places of worship
- regular congregations, and
- regular religious services.

Courts have used similar criteria to determine whether or not a religious organization qualifies as a church. In one case, the court looked for the presence of the following "church" factors:

- services held on a regular basis
- ordained ministers or other representatives
- a record of the performance of marriage, other ceremonies, and sacraments
- a place of worship
- some support required from members
- formal operations, and
- satisfaction of all other requirements of federal tax law for religious organizations.

All religious purpose groups that claim church status must complete a special IRS schedule with specific questions on some of the church characteristics listed above. We discuss this tax application and the special IRS schedule for churches in Chapter 9.

Traditional churches, synagogues, associations, or conventions of churches (and religious orders or organizations that are an integral part of a church and engaged in carrying out its functions) can qualify as 501(c)(3) churches without difficulty. Less traditional and less formal religious organizations may have a harder time. These groups often have to answer additional questions to convince the IRS that they qualify as tax-exempt churches.

Some churches stand a greater chance of being audited by the IRS than others. Not surprisingly, the IRS is more likely to examine and question groups that promise members substantial tax benefits for organizing their households as tax-deductible church organizations.

Scientific Purposes

Groups that engage in scientific research carried on in the public interest are also eligible for tax-exempt status under 501(c)(3). Under IRS regulations, research incidental to commercial or industrial operations (such as the normal inspection or testing of materials or products, or the design or construction of equipment and buildings) does not qualify as a scientific purpose under Section 501(c)(3). In an IRS case involving a pharmaceutical company, the company's clinical testing of drugs was held not to be "scientific" under Section 501(c)(3) because the clinical testing in question was incidental to the pharmaceutical company's commercial operations.

Generally, research is considered in the public interest if the results (including any patents, copyrights, processes, or formulas) are made available to the public; that is, the scientific research must be published for others to study and use. Research is also considered in the public interest if it is performed for the United States or a state, county, or city government, or if it is conducted to accomplish one of the following purposes:

- to aid in the scientific education of college or university students

- to discover a cure for a disease, or

- to aid a community or region by attracting new industry, or by encouraging the development or retention of an existing industry.

EXAMPLE:

An organization was formed by a group of physicians specializing in heart defects to research the causes and treatment of cardiac and cardiovascular conditions and diseases. The physicians practiced medicine in a private practice facility that was separate and apart from the organization's research facility, which was used exclusively for the research program. Although some patients from the physicians' private practice were accepted for the research program, they were selected on the same criteria as other patients. The IRS found that the physician's research group met the scientific purpose organizational test for Section 501(c)(3) purposes.

If you are applying for a scientific exemption under Section 501(c)(3), your federal exemption application (covered in Chapter 9) should show that your organization is conducting public interest research and you should provide the following information:

- an explanation of the nature of the research

- a description of past and present research projects

- how and by whom research projects are determined and selected, and

- who will retain ownership or control of any patents, copyrights, processes, or formulas resulting from the research.

CD-ROM
For a list of the specific information the IRS requires from scientific groups, see IRS Publication 557, page 14.

Literary Purposes

This is a seldom-used Section 501(c)(3) category because most literary purpose nonprofits are classified as educational by the IRS. Nevertheless, valid 501(c)(3) literary purposes include traditional literary efforts, such as publishing, distribution, and book sales. These activities must be directed toward promoting the public interest as opposed to engaging in a commercial literary enterprise or serving the interests of particular individuals (such as the proprietors of a publishing house). Generally, this means that literary material must be available to the general public and must pertain to the betterment of the community.

A combination of factors helps distinguish public interest publishing from private publishing. If you publish materials that are clearly educational and make them available to the public at cost, or at least below standard commercial rates, then you might qualify as a 501(c)(3) literary purpose organization. However, if your material seems aimed primarily at a commercial market and is sold at standard rates through regular commercial channels, chances are that your literary organization will be viewed by the IRS as a regular business enterprise ineligible for a 501(c)(3) tax exemption. For example, publishing textbooks at standard rates will probably not qualify as a tax-exempt literary purpose under Section 501(c)(3) because the activity is more private than public in nature. On the other hand, publishing material to promote highway safety or the education of handicapped children is likely to qualify as a bona fide 501(c)(3) literary purpose.

EXAMPLE:

A publishing house that only published books related to esoteric Eastern philosophical thought applied for 501(c)(3) literary exemption. Their books were sold commercially but at modest prices. The IRS granted the tax exemption after requesting and reviewing the manuscript for the nonprofit's first publication. The IRS found that the material was sufficiently specialized to render it noncommercial in nature.

Educational Purposes

The type of educational activities that qualify as educational purpose under 501(c)(3) are broad, encompassing instruction both for self-development and for the benefit of the community. The IRS allows advocacy of a particular intellectual position or viewpoint if there is a "sufficiently full and fair exposition of pertinent facts to permit an individual or the public to form an independent opinion or conclusion. However, mere presentation of unsupported opinion is not (considered) educational."

If a group takes political positions, it may not qualify for an exemption (see discussion on political activities in "Other Requirements for 501(c)(3) Groups," below). An educational group that publishes a newsletter with a balanced analysis of issues, or at least with some room devoted to debate or presentation of opposing opinions, should qualify as a 501(c)(3) educational purpose group. If its newsletter is simply devoted to espousing one side of an issue, platform, or agenda, the educational purpose tax exemption may not be granted.

Examples of activities that qualify as educational purpose include:

- publishing public interest educational materials

- conducting public discussion groups, forums, panels, lectures, and workshops

- offering a correspondence course or a course that uses other media such as television or radio

- operating a museum, zoo, planetarium, symphony orchestra, or performance group

- serving an educational institution, such as a college bookstore, alumni association, or athletic organization, or

- publishing educational newsletters, pamphlets, books, or other material.

CD-ROM

See the CD-ROM file *Education, Propaganda, and the Methodology Test* for guidelines used by the IRS and courts to determine if a nonprofit qualifies as an educational purpose organization under Section 501(c)(3).

Formal School Not Necessary

To qualify as a 501(c)(3) educational organization, a group does not need to provide instruction in traditional school subjects or organize as a formal school facility with a regular faculty, established curriculum, and a regularly enrolled student body.

CAUTION

You may need formal school attributes for other reasons. Groups setting up nontraditional schools aren't required to have a regular faculty, full-time students, or even a fixed curriculum to qualify for a 501(c)(3) educational purpose tax exemption. As a practical matter, however, they may need some or all of these things to qualify for state or federal support, participate in federal student loan programs, and obtain accreditation.

Child Care Centers

Providing child care outside the home qualifies as a 501(c)(3) educational purpose under special provisions contained in Internal Revenue Code Section 501(k) if:

- the care enables parent(s) to be employed, and

- the child care services are available to the general public.

A child care facility that gives enrollment preference to children of employees of a specific employer, however, will not be considered a 501(c)(3) educational purpose organization.

Private School Nondiscrimination Requirements

If you set up a 501(c)(3) private school, you must include a nondiscrimination statement in your bylaws and publicize this statement to the community served by the school. This statement must make it clear that the school does not discriminate against students or applicants on the basis of race, color, or national or ethnic origin.

Here is a sample statement taken from IRS Revenue Procedure 75-50:

NOTICE OF NONDISCRIMINATORY POLICY AS TO STUDENTS
The [name of school] admits students of any race, color, national and ethnic origin to all the rights, privileges, programs, and activities generally accorded or made available to students at the school. It does not discriminate on the basis of race, color, national and ethnic origin in administration of its educational policies, admissions policies, scholarship, and loan programs, and athletic and other school-administered programs.

RESOURCE

Additional information on the history and status of 501(c)(3) private school nondiscrimination requirements is on the IRS website (www.irs.gov), in a tax topic update titled *Private School Update*. For further information on IRS private school antidiscrimination rules and procedures, see IRS Revenue Procedure 75-50 and IRS Publication 557, *Private Schools* (included on the CD-ROM).

CD-ROM

The CD-ROM at the back of this book contains the following related IRS material:

- *Tax-Exempt Status for Your Organization*
- *Private School Update*
- *IRS Revenue Procedure 75-50*.

Other Requirements for 501(c)(3) Groups

In addition to being organized primarily for one or more allowable tax-exempt purposes, a nonprofit must not engage in other activities that conflict or substantially interfere with its valid 501(c)(3) purposes. This section discusses some of the requirements that keep a 501(c)(3) from straying too far from its exempt-purpose activities.

Unrelated Business Activities

To obtain 501(c)(3) status, a corporation cannot substantially engage in activities unrelated to the group's tax-exempt purposes. Or, put differently, your nonprofit corporation can conduct activities not directly related to its exempt purpose as long as these activities don't represent a substantial portion of your total activities. Some unrelated activity is allowed because as a practical matter, most nonprofits need to do some unrelated business to survive.

For example, a nonprofit dance group might rent unused portions of its studio space to an outside group for storage. Another nonprofit might invest surplus funds to augment its income.

Most groups need not be overly concerned with this limitation unless activities unrelated to exempt purposes start to involve a significant amount of the group's energy or time, or if these activities produce "substantial" income. If the activities are themselves nonprofit, they should be included in the organization's exempt purposes and classified as related activities. The IRS keeps an eye out for tax-exempt groups that regularly engage in profit-making businesses with little or no connection to their exempt purposes (a church running a trucking company). Business activities necessary to further the group's exempt purposes, such as hiring and paying employees and paying rent for space used for the group's exempt purpose, are considered related activities.

Most new nonprofits work full time simply tending to their exempt purposes and do not explore unrelated moneymaking activities until later, if at all. However, if you plan to engage in unrelated business from the start, be careful. It's hard to pin down exactly when these activities become substantial enough to jeopardize the corporation's tax-exempt status. Also, income derived from unrelated business activities is subject to federal and state corporate income tax, even if it is not substantial enough to affect the group's 501(c)(3) tax-exempt status.

CD-ROM

For more information on the federal unrelated business income tax that applies to nonprofit 501(c)(3) groups, see the CD-ROM file *UBIT: Current Developments*.

Limitation on Profits and Benefits

A 501(c)(3) nonprofit corporation cannot be organized or operated to benefit individuals associated with the corporation (directors, officers, or members) or other persons or entities related to, or controlled by, these individuals (such as another corporation controlled by a director). In tax language, this limitation is known as the prohibition on private inurement and means that 501(c)(3) groups can't pay profits to, or otherwise benefit, private interests.

Two specific 501(c)(3) requirements implement this prohibition on self-inurement:

- no part of the net earnings of the corporation can be distributed to individuals associated with the corporation, and

- upon dissolution, the assets of a 501(c)(3) group must be irrevocably dedicated to another tax-exempt group (another 501(c)(3) or a federal, state, or local government for a public purpose).

These requirements are basically the same as the state law requirements that apply to California public benefit and religious corporations. Note that the IRS and state law allow a nonprofit to pay reasonable salaries to directors, officers, employees, or agents for services rendered in furtherance of the corporation's tax-exempt purposes.

Excess Benefit Rules

In recent years, the IRS has adopted strict rules and regulations regarding the payment of money, benefits, or property to nonprofit directors, officers, sponsors, donors, and others associated with the nonprofit. The main purpose for these rules, called the excess benefit rules, is to make sure nonprofit organizations do not pay out lavish benefits or skim off program funds to line the pockets or serve the private interests of individuals associated with the nonprofit. The excess benefit rules are also called the IRS intermediate sanctions, a government-speak euphemism that is meant to have an appropriately harsh ring. These rules are contained in Section 4958 of the Internal Revenue Code and Section 53.4958 of the IRS Regulations.

The excess benefit rules apply to individuals associated with 501(c)(3) nonprofit public charities. (As explained more fully in Chapter 4, in all likelihood you will be forming a public charity nonprofit.) The individuals subject to the rules include nonprofit directors, officers, and trustees as well as major sponsors, donors, or anyone else in a position to exercise substantial influence over the affairs of the nonprofit. The rules also apply to family members and entities owned by any of the individuals subject to the rules.

Under the rules, an excessive benefit transaction is any transaction where the nonprofit gives cash, property, or anything of value to a recipient that exceeds the value of the services performed by the recipient (or the value of any other cash, property, or thing of value given to the nonprofit by the recipient). If a nonprofit pays $100 to an officer who has contributed $75 worth of services, the excess benefit is $25. Of course, the IRS is looking for much bigger numbers, sometimes in the realm of thousands, or hundreds of thousands of dollars worth of extra benefits paid from the nonprofit coffers to directors, officers, consultants, sponsors, and donors.

The remedy, as you might guess, is a tax that must be paid by both the recipient of the excess benefit as well as the nonprofit managers (the directors and executive officers) who approved the excess benefit transaction. The recipient of the excess benefit can be assessed a 25% tax on the excess benefit, and the manager or managers who approved it can be assessed a 10% tax, with a limit on a manager's liability capped at $20,000 per transaction. A director must object to the transaction to be excluded from those considered to have approved it—silence or abstention at a board meeting that results in the excess benefit payment is not a defense. The recipient must repay or return the excess benefit to the nonprofit or the recipient will be charged an additional 200% tax. The message is clear— if you receive an undeserved benefit from your nonprofit, expect a substantial financial slap on the wrist, plus a whopping big penalty if you don't return the benefit to the nonprofit.

The IRS regulations add detail about the scope and operation of the excess benefit rules. For example, disqualified persons is broadly defined to include all sorts of people paid by or associated with the nonprofit organization. Excess salaries, contract payments, benefits, privileges, goods, services, or anything else of value paid or provided to almost anyone associated with your nonprofit can potentially trigger the excess benefit tax rules.

The regulations also contain a safe-harbor provision for deals or decisions that provide an economic benefit to a director, officer, contractor, or other key nonprofit person. To qualify for the protection of the safe harbor rule, a number of conditions must be met, including:

- disinterested members of the board or committee must approve the transaction in advance
- the decision must be based on comparability data reviewed and relied on by the board that shows the property is transferred at fair market value or compensation is paid at a rate similar to that paid by other organizations for comparable services, and

- the decision must be documented in the corporate records at the time the transaction is approved.

Falling within the safe harbor provision creates a presumption that your deal or decision was fair. The IRS can rebut this presumption if it obtains evidence to the contrary.

If you are interested in reading more information about these rules, you can use the CD-ROM files listed below.

CD-ROM

The CD-ROM at the back of this book contains the following files with information on the excess benefit rules and regulations:

- IRC Section 4958, *Taxes on Excess Benefit Transactions.*
- IRS Regulations Section 53.4958-0, *Table of Contents.* This file contains the IRS regulations promulgated under Section 4958.
- *Intermediate Sanctions (IRC 4958) Update.*

The last thing you want to have happen is to subject board members, officers, contractors, sponsors, donors, and others who deal with your nonprofit to the prospect of having to pay back money or the value of benefits previously paid out or provided by your nonprofit plus very hefty taxes, interest, and penalties.

Conflict of Interest Provisions

Article 9 of the bylaws included in this book contains rules and procedures for approving or avoiding conflict-of-interest transactions, including compensation arrangements. This bylaw provision contains the conflicts-of-interest language recommended by the IRS (included in the sample conflict-of-interest policy in Appendix A of the instructions to IRS Form 1023). It also has language for the approval of compensation arrangements that attempts to comply with the safe harbor provisions of the excess benefit rules (See Article 9, Section 5). You will need to become familiar with Article 9 of your bylaws and refer to those provisions whenever your board, or a committee of your board, decides to set or increase salaries, enter into contracts, or approve deals with individuals or other organizations.

If you have any question about whether a transaction, contract, compensation decision, or other economic decision is reasonable or whether it may be outside the safe harbor provisions of the excess benefit rules, ask a nonprofit lawyer for help.

Limitation on Political Activities

A 501(c)(3) corporation is prohibited from participating in any political campaigns for or against any candidate for public office. Participation in or contributions to political campaigns can result in the revocation of 501(c)(3) tax-exempt status and the assessment of special excise taxes against the organization and its managers. (See Internal Revenue Code §§ 4955, 6852, and 7409.)

Voter Education Activities

Section 501(c)(3) groups can conduct certain voter education activities if they are done in a nonpartisan manner (see IRS Revenue Ruling 78-248). If you want to engage in this type of political activity, we recommend you consult an attorney. Your organization can request an IRS letter ruling on its voter education activities by writing to the address listed in IRS Publication 557, Chapter 3, "Political Activity."

CD-ROM

For information on restrictions on political candidate campaign activity by 501(c)(3) organizations, see *Election Year Issues* in the CD-ROM. It also contains information about other laws

and restrictions applicable to political campaign nonprofits—non-501(c)(3) groups organized primarily to support or oppose political candidates under Internal Revenue Code § 527.

Influencing Legislation

Section 501(c)(3) organizations are prohibited from acting to influence legislation, "except to an insubstantial degree." In the past, courts have found that spending more than 5% of an organization's budget, time, or effort on political activity was substantial. More recently, courts have tended to look at the individual facts of each case. Generally, if a nonprofit corporation contacts, or urges the public to contact, members of a legislative body, or if it advocates the adoption or rejection of legislation, the IRS considers it to be acting to influence legislation.

Lobbying to influence legislation also includes:

- any attempt to affect the opinions of the general public or a segment of the public, and

- communication with any member or employee of a legislative body, or with any government official or employee who might participate in the formulation of legislation.

However, lobbying to influence legislation does not include:

- making available the results of nonpartisan analysis, study, or research

- providing technical advice or assistance to a government body, or to its committee or other subdivision, in response to a written request from it, where such advice would otherwise constitute the influencing of legislation

- appearing before, or communicating with, any legislative body with respect to a possible decision that might affect the organization's existence, powers, tax-exempt status, or the deductibility of contributions to it, or

- communicating with a government official or employee, other than for the purpose of influencing legislation.

Also excluded from the definition of lobbying efforts are communications between an organization and its members about legislation (or proposed legislation) of direct interest to the organization and the members, unless these communications directly encourage members to influence legislation.

EXAMPLE:

A Housing Information Exchange keeps its members informed of proposed legislation affecting low-income renters. This should not be considered legislative lobbying activity unless members are urged to contact their political representatives in support of, or in opposition to, the proposed legislation.

In determining whether a group's legislative activities are substantial in scope, the IRS looks at the amount of time, money, or effort the group spends on legislative lobbying. If they are substantial in relation to other activities, 501(c)(3) tax status might be revoked and, again, special excise taxes can be levied against the organization and its managers. See IRC § 4912.

Political Expenditures Test

Under the political expenditures test in IRC § 501(h), limitations are imposed on two types of political activities: lobbying expenditures and grassroots expenditures. Lobbying expenditures are those made for the purpose of influencing legislation, while grassroots expenditures are those made to influence public opinion.

For examples of these two types of activities, see IRS Publication 557, the "Lobbying Expenditures" section. The monetary limits are different for each of the categories and the formulas for computing them are somewhat complicated.

If your 501(c)(3) nonprofit elects the political expenditures test, you must file IRS Form 5768, *Election–Revocation of Election by an Eligible Section 501(c)(3) Organization to Make Expenditures to Influence Legislation*, within the tax year in which you wish the election to be effective. This election is also available under similar rules at the state level. A copy of this form is included on the CD-ROM provided with this book.

The Alternative Political Expenditures Test

Since it is impossible to know ahead of time how the IRS will assess the substantiality of a group's legislative activity, the IRC allows 501(c)(3) public charities (most 501(c)(3) groups will qualify as public charities—see Chapter 4) to elect an alternative expenditures test to measure permissible legislative activity. Under this test, a group may spend up to 20% of the first $500,000 of its annual expenditures on lobbying, 15% of the next $500,000, 10% of the next $500,000, and 5% of its expenditures beyond that, up to a total limit of $1 million each year.

> **CAUTION**
>
> **Some groups can't use the political expenditures test.** This expenditures test and its provisions for lobbying and grassroots expenditures are not available to churches, an integrated auxiliary of a church, a member of an affiliated group of organizations that includes a church, or to private foundations.

If your nonprofit corporation plans to do considerable lobbying activity, mostly by unpaid volunteers, then electing the expenditures test might be a good idea. Why? Because the minimal outlay of money to engage in these activities will probably keep you under the applicable expenditure limits. If you didn't make this election, your 501(c)(3) tax exemption might be placed in jeopardy if the IRS considers your political activities to be a substantial part of your overall purposes and program.

If you plan to engage in more than a minimum amount of political lobbying or legislative efforts, you need to decide whether it is to your advantage to elect the expenditures test based on the facts of your situation. If you find that these alternative political expenditures rules are still too restrictive, you might consider forming a social welfare organization or civic league under Section 501(c)(4) of the Internal Revenue Code—this exemption requires a different federal exemption application, IRS Form 1024, and does not carry with it all the attractive benefits of 501(c)(3) status (access to grant funds, tax deductible contributions, etc.). See "Is Your Group a Nonprofit That Can Use This Book?" in Chapter 1, and IRS Publication 557 for further information on 501(c)(4) organizations.

> **CAUTION**
>
> **Additional limitations.** Federally funded groups may be subject to even more stringent political expenditure tests than those discussed here (for example, political activity and expenditure restrictions imposed by the federal Office of Management and Budget).

> **CD-ROM**
>
> For a thorough discussion of the rules that apply to lobbying activities by 501(c)(3) organizations and detailed information on the Section 501(h) political expenditures test election, see *Lobbying Issues* on the CD-ROM.

Political Action Organizations

The IRS can also challenge a 501(c)(3) group's political activities by finding that it is an action organization: one so involved in political activities that it is not organized exclusively for a 501(c)(3) tax-exempt purpose. Under these circumstances the IRS can revoke the organization's tax-exempt status. Intervention in political campaigns or substantial attempts to influence legislation, as discussed above, are grounds for applying this sanction. In addition, if a group has the following two characteristics, it will be classified as an action organization and lose its 501(c)(3) status:

1. Its main or primary objective or objectives—not incidental or secondary objectives—may be attained only by legislation or defeat of proposed legislation, and

2. It advocates or campaigns for the attainment of such objectives rather than engaging in nonpartisan analysis, study, or research and making the results available to the public.

In determining whether a group has these characteristics, the IRS looks at the surrounding facts and circumstances, including the group's articles and activities, and its organizational and operational structure.

The point here is to be careful not to state your exempt purposes in such a way that they seem only attainable by political action. Even if you indicate that your activities will not be substantially involved with legislative or lobbying efforts, the IRS may decide otherwise and invoke this special classification to deny or rescind 501(c)(3) status.

If the IRS classifies a group as an action organization, the group can still qualify as a social welfare group under 501(c)(4).

EXAMPLE:

A group that has a primary purpose of "reforming the judicial system in the United States" will likely sound like a political action organization to the IRS, because this sounds like a political goal that must be accomplished mostly by political means. However, if the group rephrases its primary purpose as "educating the public on the efficacy of mediation, arbitration, and other alternative nonjudicial dispute resolution mechanisms," it stands a better chance of having the IRS approve its application, even if it lists some political activity as incidental to its primary educational purpose.

CAUTION

Check the Federal Election Commission website (FEC). Politically active groups should go to the FEC website at www.fec.gov to read about the ever-changing federal election campaign laws and how they may impact their nonprofit's political activities.

Information for Specific Questions About Your Group's Activities

Even after reading through this chapter, you might still have some questions about whether your specific nonprofit activities meet the IRS definition of educational, charitable, or religious purposes under Section 501(c)(3) of the Internal Revenue Code. Or, after you take a closer look at Chapter 4, you might wonder whether your nonprofit can qualify for special public charity treatment as a school or church.

Answers to these types of questions used to be left to the expertise of highly paid lawyers and tax professionals—this is no longer true. It is remarkably easy to find out more about how the IRS might look at your nonprofit organization when it reviews your tax exemption application. The IRS website disseminates most of the material necessary to answer many technical questions as long as you are persistent enough to search the site thoroughly and uncover the material. Specifically, IRS publications and regulations, as well as the technical manuals the IRS examiners use when reviewing tax exemption applications, are available online.

This chapter refers to special IRS training materials from the IRS website and includes this material on the CD-ROM that accompanies this book. We describe how each of these articles helps explain and illustrate a specific issue related to obtaining and maintaining a 501(c)(3) tax exemption. There is a lot more helpful material on the IRS website, and we encourage you to browse it to learn as much as you'd like about nonprofit organization tax issues.

Here is one way to search the IRS site for nonprofit tax exemption answers:

Go to the main page of the IRS website at www.irs.gov and click the Charities and Non-profits link. This page contains special nonprofit tax topics, resources, and links to additional information. If you don't find what you're looking for, in the search box type in a word or phrase which succinctly describes your question.

You can also try to find your topic by clicking on the Site Map link that appears at the top of most of the site's Web pages. You should see a list of links for Charities and Non-profits, which you can use to navigate through the site to find the material you're looking for.

Another more advanced approach is to click the Site Map link at the top of the Web page, then click the Internal Revenue Manual listed under the Tax Professionals heading. This link takes you to a table that lists different sections of the internal IRS procedures manual used by IRS examiners and field agents. It contains a wealth of technical material about IRS procedures, rulings, and policies. Part 7 is the main area of interest for nonprofit groups applying for their 501(c)(3) tax exemption. Select this link, then scroll down the heading list until you see the heading, "7.25 Exempt Organizations Determinations Manual." Click on the link under this heading to "7.25.3, Religious, Charitable, Educational, Etc., Organizations." This chapter contains examples of groups that have and have not qualified under each of the 501(c)(3) tax-exempt purposes.

If you want to learn even more, you can examine any IRS rulings and cases that you uncover in your website search. Rulings are compiled in *IRS Cumulative Bulletins*, the most recent of which are available for browsing on the IRS website. Click the Site Map link at the top of any IRS site Web page, then select Resources for Tax Professionals, and scroll down and select the Internal Revenue Bulletins link. Then select the volume for the year when the ruling was issued and scroll through the beginning table of contents to find the page where the ruling begins (the first two numbers of a ruling indicate its year—for example, Ruling 2004-51 was issued in 2004, so you would look at the *Bulletin* for 2004 to find the text of the ruling). Most years have more than one *Bulletin* volume, and some rulings are placed in the next year's volume. It takes persistence to track down rulings, but they can be enormously helpful in understanding why the IRS accepted or rejected a nonprofit organization's application for a 501(c)(3) tax exemption. Another (easier) way to track down rulings is to go to TaxLinks.com. Click on the appropriate year in the heading (for example, 1980), then scroll through the numbered rulings for that year and select the appropriate ruling number (for example, 80-106 to find Revenue Ruling 80-106). For more information on doing your own research, see Chapter 12.

RESOURCE

For an in-depth discussion and analysis of the requirements that apply to each type of 501(c)(3) nonprofit, supplemented annually with the latest IRS and court rulings in each area, see *The Law of Tax-Exempt Organizations*, by Bruce R. Hopkins, (John Wiley & Sons, New York, N.Y.).

Public Charities and Private Foundations

In this chapter, we explain why it is not enough to simply obtain your 501(c)(3) tax-exempt status—you also need to be recognized as a 501(c)(3) public charity. Getting this extra recognition is essential to make your life as a nonprofit easier to manage. Even though the last thing you may be interested in at this point is delving into more tax technicalities, it will help you enormously to have a general understanding of the distinction between public charity and private foundation tax status before you do your federal tax exemption application. You will understand the importance of some of the most technical questions on the application and you'll know how to answer questions to show you qualify for public charity tax status.

We help you get through this information by explaining the different public charity classifications and requirements in plain English. You don't need to master this material. In fact, many nonprofits let the IRS decide which public charity category works for them. For now, simply read through the information to get a general understanding of the concepts. You can come back to this chapter when you do your federal tax exemption application and reread the sections that apply to you.

Throughout this chapter, we refer to the Internal Revenue Code sections that apply to the different public charity classifications. You don't need to pay attention to these section references. They will be useful later as a reference when you prepare your federal tax exemption application.

The Importance of Public Charity Status

The IRS classifies all 501(c)(3) tax-exempt nonprofit corporations as either private foundations or public charities. Initially, most 501(c)(3) corporations are presumed to be private foundations. It's extremely important to understand that your group, too, will initially be viewed as a private foundation. The problem with this classification is that private foundations are subject to strict operating rules and regulations that don't apply to groups classified as public charities. You'll want to get yourselves out from under this presumption because, like most 501(c)(3) groups, you would probably find it impossible to operate under the rules and restrictions imposed on private foundations. To overcome this presumption, you must show on your federal 501(c)(3) tax exemption application that you qualify as a public charity.

A few special groups are not presumed to be private foundations and do not have to apply for public charity status—the same groups that are not required to file a 501(c)(3) tax exemption application. We think it's foolhardy in most cases not to apply for, and obtain, official notification from the IRS that you are a public charity. (For a discussion of this issue, see "Do You Need to File Form 1023?" in Chapter 9.)

How to Qualify for Public Charity Status

As explained above, almost all 501(c)(3) nonprofits want to overcome the private foundation presumption and establish themselves as a public charity. There are three basic ways to do this:

- **Form one of the types of nonprofits that automatically qualify.** Particular types of nonprofit organizations, such as churches, schools, or hospitals, automatically qualify for public charity status because of the nature of their activities.

EXAMPLE:

A church that maintains a facility for religious worship would most easily obtain *automatic* public charity status. A church qualifies for recognition as a public charity because of the nature of its activities rather than its sources of support.

- **Derive most of your support from the public.** If your group receives support primarily from individual contributions, government, or other public sources, you can qualify for public charity status as a publicly supported organization.

EXAMPLE:

An organization formed to operate a center for rehabilitation, counseling, or similar services, that plans to carry on a broad-based solicitation program and depend primarily on government grants, corporate contributions, and individual donations, would most likely seek public charity status as a *publicly supported organization.*

- **Receive most of your revenue from activities related to your tax-exempt purposes.** If your group receives most of its revenue from activities related to its tax-exempt purposes, you can qualify under a special public charity support test that applies to many smaller nonprofits.

EXAMPLE:

An arts group deriving most of its income from exempt-purpose activities (lessons, performances, and renting studio facilities to other arts groups) would probably choose the *support* test. This public charity test, unlike those that apply to publicly supported organizations, allows groups to count income

derived from the performance of their exempt purposes as qualified support.

CD-ROM

For additional information on the rules that apply to each of the three public charity tests, see the file *Public Charity or Private Foundation Status Issues under IRC §§ 509(a)(1)-(4), 4942(j)(3), and 507,* on the CD-ROM. For information on the public charity requirements associated with each type of automatically recognized public charity (churches, schools, hospitals, and others), see the section titled, *Type A. Organizations That Engage in Inherently Public Activity (IRC 509(a)(1) and IRC 170(b)(1)(A)(i)-(v)).* For information on the public charity test we call the public support test, see the section titled, " Publicly Supported Organizations Described in IRC §§ 509(a)(1) and 170(b)(1)(A)(vi)." For information on the public charity test we call the exempt-activities support test, see the section titled, "Publicly Supported Organizations Described in IRC § 509(a)(2)."

You Can Let the IRS Decide Your Public Charity Classification

It's sometimes hard to figure out whether your organization will meet the public support test or the exempt activities test discussed below. To make this decision, an organization must second-guess future sources of support and tackle quite a few tax technicalities. Fortunately, if you have doubts, the IRS will help. Simply check a box on the federal tax exemption application and the IRS will decide this question for you based upon the financial and program information you submit with your application.

For the specifics on making this election, see the Chapter 9 instructions to Part X, Line 5(i), of the federal tax exemption application.

Automatic Public Charity Status

The IRS automatically recognizes certain 501(c)(3) groups as public charities because they perform particular services or engage in certain charitable activities. The following groups automatically qualify:

Churches

Religious purpose groups that qualify as churches for 501(c)(3) tax exemption purposes also automatically qualify as a public charity. (IRC §§ 509(a)(1) and 170(b)(1)(A)(i).) Qualifying as a church under Section 501(c)(3) is more difficult than qualifying as a 501(c)(3) religious purpose organization. To qualify as a church, the organization must have the institutional and formal characteristics of a church. (See "Religious Purposes" in Chapter 3.) If your religious-purpose 501(c)(3) group does not qualify as a church, it can still qualify for public charity status under one of the other public charity tests described below.

Schools

Certain educational institutions that have the institutional attributes of a school automatically qualify as public charities. (IRC §§ 509(a)(1) and 170(b)(1)(A)(ii).) Generally, these are educational organizations whose primary function is to present formal instruction. These schools usually have a regular faculty and curriculum, a regularly enrolled body of students, and a place where their educational activities are carried on.

This school category for automatic public charity recognition is geared toward primary or secondary preparatory or high schools, and colleges and universities with regularly enrolled student bodies. The farther an educational group strays from the institutional criteria mentioned above, the harder it will be to qualify as a public charity. This doesn't mean that less structured educational institutions can't automatically qualify for public charity status as schools, it just may be more difficult. Nontraditional groups have a better chance of obtaining automatic public charity status if they have some conventional institutional attributes, such as regional accreditation and a state-approved curriculum. If your educational-purpose 501(c)(3) group does not fall within this school category for automatic recognition, it can still qualify for public charity status under the public support test or exempt activities support test, described below.

Hospitals and Medical Research Organizations

Nonprofit health care groups that operate charitable hospitals or facilities and whose main function is to provide hospital or medical care, medical education, or medical research automatically qualify as public charities. (IRC §§ 509(a)(1) and 170(b)(1)(A)(iii).) These charitable hospitals generally have the following characteristics:

- doctors selected from the community at large who are part of the courtesy staff
- a community-oriented board of directors
- emergency room facilities available on a community-access basis
- admission of at least some patients without charge (on a charitable basis)
- nondiscrimination with respect to all admissions (particularly Medicare or Medicaid patients), and
- a medical training and research program that benefits the community.

Other 501(c)(3) health care organizations, such as rehabilitation groups, outpatient clinics, community mental health programs, or drug treatment centers, can qualify as hospitals if their principal purpose is to provide hospital or medical care. A health organization that uses consultation services of certified medical personnel such as doctors and nurses will have an easier time meeting the hospital criteria. The IRS does not, however, recognize convalescent homes, homes for children or the aged, or institutions that provide vocational training for the handicapped as fitting within this public charity category.

Medical education and research organizations do not qualify under these IRC sections unless they actively provide on-site medical or hospital care to patients as an integral part of their functions. Medical research groups must also be directly and continuously active in medical research with a hospital, and this research must be the organization's principal purpose.

TIP

Hospitals and other tax-exempt health care organizations may want to adopt a community board and a conflict-of-interest policy in their bylaws. We explain how hospitals and medical care groups can modify the conflict-of-interest provisions in the bylaws included in this book to add provisions recommended by the IRS. (See Chapter 9, Part VIII, Line 20, "Filling in Schedule C.")

Public Safety Organizations

Groups organized and operated exclusively for public safety testing automatically qualify for public charity status. Generally, these organizations test consumer products to determine their fitness for use by the general public. (IRC § 509(a)(4).)

Government Organizations

Certain government organizations operated for the benefit of a college or university automatically qualify as public charities. (IRC §§ 509(a)(1) and 170(b)(1)(A)(iv).) You won't

be forming a government corporation, but we mention it because this type of organization is included in the list of public charities on the federal tax exemption application form.

Supporting Organizations

Organizations operated solely for the benefit of, or in connection with, one or more of the above organizations, or publicly supported groups or groups that meet the exempt activities support test (described below in "Public Support Test" and "Exempt Activities Support Test"), are also automatically classified as public charities (except those that benefit a public safety organization). (IRC § 509(a)(3).)

CD-ROM

For further information on organizations listed above, see IRS Publication 557, *Tax Exempt Status for Your Organization,* "Section 509(a)(1) Organizations." For supporting organizations, see Publication 557, "Section 509(a)(3) Organizations." Also, note that recent federal rules have been enacted as part of the Pension Protection Act of 2006 that impose additional requirements on supporting organizations and private foundations that fund them. Ask your tax adviser for more information.

Public Support Test

To be classified as a publicly supported public charity, a group must regularly solicit funds from the general community. It must normally receive money from government agencies and/or from a number of different private contributors or agencies. (IRC §§ 509(a)(1) and 170(b)(1)(A)(vi).) The term "normally" has a special meaning in this context that is explained below. We call this public charity test the public support test because the main requirement is that the organization must receive a substantial portion of its funds from broad-based public support sources.

In general, museums, libraries, and community centers that promote the arts should qualify under this public charity test if they rely on broad-based support from individual members of the community or from various public and private sources. Organizations that expect to rely primarily on a few private sources or occasional large grants to fund their operations will probably not meet the requirements of this section. This support test is difficult for small, grassroots groups to meet because income from the performance of tax-exempt purposes does not count as qualifying public support income—a source of support commonly relied upon by these groups.

To determine whether your group qualifies as a publicly supported public charity, you will need to do some basic math and understand some technical rules. Try not to get overwhelmed or discouraged by this technical material. For now, you can simply read through the information to get a sense of the basic criteria for this test and whether or not you might qualify. You can revisit anything that might seem applicable to you later when you fill in your federal tax exemption application.

More importantly, you may decide to let the IRS figure out which public support test works for you. In most cases, unless you know your nonprofit easily fits within the automatic public charity classification, the best and easiest approach is to let the IRS decide whether the public support test (covered in this section) or the exempt activities support test (discussed below) works for your nonprofit. After all, the technical staff on the IRS Exempt Organizations Determinations staff knows this material inside out. Why not use their expertise and let them apply the public charity support tests to your group's past and projected sources

of public support which you will disclose in your federal tax exemption application.

CD-ROM

For more detailed information on qualifying as a public charity using the public support test, see IRS Publication 557 (included on the CD-ROM), *Tax Exempt Status for Your Organization,* "Publicly Supported Organizations." Also check the IRS website at www.irs.gov under the "Public Charities and Non-Profits" section.

How Much Public Support Do You Need?

The IRS will usually consider an organization qualified under the public support test if it meets one of the following tests:

- The group normally receives at least ⅓ of its total support from governmental units, from contributions made directly or indirectly by the general public, or from a combination of the two (including contributions from other publicly supported organizations), or

- The organization receives at least $1/10$ of its support from these sources *and* meets an additional "attraction of public support" requirement (we discuss the attraction of public support test below).

We call this ⅓ or $1/10$ figure "public support." To keep your percentage high enough, you'll want the IRS to classify as much of your income as possible as public support (the numerator amount), and keep your total support figure (the denominator amount) as low as possible. This will make your final percentage of public support as high as possible. Of course, the IRS has many rules, and exceptions to the rules, to define public support and total support. We provide a guide to the basic technical terms used below.

Some basic math must be used to estimate your organization's percentage of support. As we explain later, only certain types of support can be included in the numerator of the fraction—the support funds classified as qualified public support. The denominator of the fraction includes the organization's total support, which includes most sources of support received by the nonprofit. You will want as much support as possible to show up in the numerator as qualified public support. If some support received by the nonprofit does not qualify as public support, then it is better to have the support also excluded from the total support. This will keep the excluded support from reducing your public support percentage since both the numerator and denominator will be left intact.

What Is Public Support?

Qualified public support (support included in the numerator of the fraction) includes funds from private and public agencies as well as contributions from corporate and individual donors. However, the IRS limits how much qualified support your group can receive from one individual or corporation. Also, some membership fees can be included as qualified support. We discuss these special rules in more detail below.

What Does "Normally" Mean?

An organization must "normally" receive either $1/3$ or $1/10$ of its total support from public support sources. This means that one tax year won't make or break your chances of meeting the test—the IRS bases its decision on four years' cumulative receipts. Your organization will meet either the $1/3$ or $1/10$ support test for both its current and the following tax year if, during the four tax years before its current tax year, its cumulative public support equals $1/3$ or $1/10$ of its cumulative total support.

Advance and Definitive Rulings

There are two ways to request public charity status if you are seeking it: either under the public support test or under the exempt activities support test.

If your organization has been operating for one tax year consisting of at least eight months at the time you complete your federal exemption application, you can ask for a definitive ruling on your public charity status. The IRS will use the past support received by the group to determine if it qualifies as a publicly supported organization.

Existing groups can, and new groups must, request an advance ruling on their public charity status. If your expected sources of support seem likely to qualify you under either the public support test or the exempt activities support test, the IRS will grant you one of these tentative rulings. Later, at the end of an advance ruling period consisting of the corporation's first five tax years, the IRS will give a definitive ruling. If the group's public support during the advance ruling period satisfies the support requirements of the appropriate public charity test, the organization will qualify as a public charity.

In granting advance rulings under the public support test, the IRS always looks to see if your organization will meet the attraction of public support factors (discussed below) whether you plan to meet the $1/3$ or $1/10$ public support test.

For further information on definitive and advance public charity ruling requests, see Chapter 9.

EXAMPLE:

Open Range, Inc., is a nonprofit organization for medical research on the healthful effects of organic cattle ranching. ORI's cumulative total support was $60,000 for 1996 through 2000, and its cumulative public support was $25,000. The organization will, therefore, be considered a publicly supported public charity for 2000 and the following tax year. This remains true even if, for one or more of the previous four years, public support did not equal ⅓ of the total support—it's the cumulative total that counts.

What Is a "Government Unit"?

Money received from a government unit is considered public support. Government units include federal or state governmental agencies, county, and city agencies, and so on. The most common example of governmental support is a federal or state grant.

The 2% Limit Rule

Direct or indirect contributions from the general public are considered public support. Indirect contributions include grants from private trusts or agencies also funded by contributions from the general public, such as grants from Community Chest or the United Fund.

However, there is a major restriction applicable to these contributions. The total contributions from one individual, trust, or corporation made during the preceding four tax years can be counted only to the extent that they do not exceed 2% of the corporation's total support for those four years. Contributions from government units, publicly supported organizations, and unusual grants are not subject to this 2% limit. These exceptions are discussed below.

EXAMPLE:

If your total support over the previous four-year period was $60,000, then only $1,200 (2% of $60,000) contributed by any one person, private agency, or other source can count as public support.

Note that the total amount of any one contribution, even if it exceeds this 2%, four-year limitation, is included in the corporation's total support. Paradoxically, therefore, large contributions from an individual or private agency can have a disastrous effect on your status as a publicly supported charity. You get to include such contributions as public support only to the extent of 2% of the previous four years' total income, but the total income figure is increased by the full amount of the contribution. This makes it more difficult for you to meet the ⅓ or $1/10$ public support requirement.

EXAMPLE:

On Your Toes, a ballet troupe, received the following contributions from 2004 through 2007:

2004	$10,000	from individual X
2005	20,000	from individual Y
2006	60,000	from Z Community Chest
2007	10,000	as an additional contribution from individual X
	$100,000	Total Support

All support for the four-year period is from contributions, direct or indirect, from the general public. However, in view of the 2% limit, On Your Toes will have trouble maintaining its publicly supported public charity status. While all contributions count toward total support, only $2,000 (2% x $100,000) from any one contributor counts as public support.

Therefore, the troupe's public support for this period is only $6,000 ($2,000 from each contributor, X, Y, and Z), which falls $4,000 short of the minimum $1/10$ public support requirement.

Now, suppose On Your Toes received $2,000 each from 50 contributors over the four-year period. It still has $100,000 total support, but because no one contributor gave more than 2% of the four years' total support, it can count the entire $100,000 as public support.

TIP

Increase your chances of qualifying as a publicly supported public charity. One way to do this is to solicit smaller contributions through a broad-based fundraising program and don't rely constantly on the same major sources. This way, you'll beat the 2% limit and have a better chance of qualifying contributions as public support.

Exceptions to the 2% Limit Rule

There are two major exceptions to the 2% limit.

Money From Government Units or Publicly Supported Organizations

Contributions received from a government unit or other publicly supported organization are not subject to the 2% limit, except those specifically earmarked for your organization by the original donor.

EXAMPLE:

Ebeneezer Sax gives $1 million to National Public Music, a national government foundation that promotes musical arts. NPM then gives your organization the million dollars as a grant. If Sax made the contribution to NPM on the condition that the foundation

give it to your organization, it is considered earmarked for you and the 2% limit applies. If not, the limit doesn't apply—and you can count the whole donation as public support.

Except for earmarked contributions or grants, you can rely on large contributions or grants from specific government agencies or other publicly supported organizations every year, since all such contributions will be counted as public support.

Money From Unusual Grants

Another major exception to the 2% limit is for unusual grants from the private or public sector. A grant is unusual if it:

- is attracted by the publicly supported nature of your organization
- is unusual—this means you don't regularly rely on the particular grant and it is an unexpectedly large amount, and
- would, because of its large size, adversely affect the publicly supported status of your organization (as we've seen, because of the 2% limit, large grants can cause trouble).

If a grant qualifies as an unusual grant, you can exclude the grant funds from both your public support and total support figures for the year in which they are given.

EXAMPLE:

The National Museum of Computer Memorabilia, Inc., is a nonprofit corporation that operates a museum of computers and artificial intelligence memorabilia. The years 2000 through 2002 are difficult ones and the museum raises very little money. But in 2008 the organization receives an unexpected windfall grant. A look at the receipts for 2005 to 2008 helps illustrate the importance of the unusual grant exception. All amounts are individual contributions from the general public unless indicated otherwise:

2005	$1,000	from A
	1,000	from B
2006	1,000	from C
2007	1,000	from D
	1,000	from E
2008	100,000	from Z, a private grant agency
	$105,000	Total Receipts

Assume that the 2008 grant qualifies as an unusual grant. The total support computation for the four-year period would be:

2005	$1,000	from A
	1,000	from B
2006	1,000	from C
2007	1,000	from D
	1,000	from E
2008	0	the $100,000 grant drops out from total support
	$5,000	Total Support

Because the total support is $5,000, the museum can only count a maximum of 2% times $5,000, or $100, received from any one individual during this period as public support. Therefore, the public support computation for this period looks like this:

2005	$100	from A
	100	from B
2006	100	from C
2007	100	from D
	100	from E
2008	0	the $100,000 contribution also drops out from the public support computation
	$500	Total Public Support

The museum meets the 10% support test because total public support of $500 equals 10% of the total support of $5,000 received over the four-year period. If the organization also meets the attraction of public support requirement (which must be met by groups whose public support is less than $\frac{1}{3}$ of total support), it will qualify as a publicly supported public charity for 2008 and 2009.

If the $100,000 contribution did not qualify as an unusual grant, the nonprofit would not meet the 10% public support test. Total support would equal total receipts of $105,000; a maximum of 2% times $105,000, or $2,100, from each individual and the grant agency would be classified as public support. Public support received over the four-year period would consist of $1,000 from individuals A, B, C, D, and E, and the maximum allowable sum of $2,100 from the grant agency, for a total public support figure of $7,100. The percentage of public support for the four-year period would equal $7,100 divided by $105,000, or less than 7%, and the group would not qualify as a publicly supported public charity in 2008. Again, you can see how a large grant can hurt you if it does not qualify as an unusual grant.

Membership Fees as Public Support

Membership fees are considered public support as long as the member does not receive something valuable in return, such as admissions, merchandise, or the use of facilities or services. If a member does receive direct benefits in exchange for fees, the fees are not considered public support. These fees are, however, always included in the total support computation.

What's Not Public Support?

We've already mentioned some sources of support that are excluded because of special circumstances (they exceed the 2% limit or are paid by members in return for something of value). There are additional types of support that are never included as public support. The following types of income are not considered public support and, in some cases, are also not included in the total support figure (in which case they would drop entirely from the percentage of ⅓ or $^{1}/_{10}$ support calculation).

Unrelated Activities and Investment

Net income from activities unrelated to exempt purposes as well as gross investment income, which includes rents, dividends, royalties, and returns on investments, are not considered public support. Both these types of income are added to the total support figure (they stay in the denominator of your ⅓ or $^{1}/_{10}$ support calculation).

Sales of Assets or Performing Tax-Exempt Activity

The following types of income are not considered as public support or part of total support (as with unusual grants, they drop out of both computations):

- **Gains from selling a capital asset.** Generally, capital assets are property owned by the corporation for use in its activities. Note that capital assets do not include any business inventory or resale merchandise, business accounts or notes receivable, or real property used in a trade or business. Gains from selling these noncapital asset items are characterized as gross investment income and are not considered public support, but are added to the total support figure.

- **Receipts from performing tax-exempt purposes.** Examples include money received from admissions to performances of a tax-exempt symphony, fees for classes given by a dance studio and tuition, or other charges paid for attending seminars, lectures, or classes given by an exempt educational organization.

Since we're dealing with tax laws, you'd probably expect at least one complicating exception. Here it is. If your organization relies primarily on gross receipts from activities related to its exempt purposes (such as an educational nonprofit that receives most of its support from class tuition), this exempt-purpose income will *not* be considered public support. Instead it will be computed in total support (so it will decrease your percentage of support calculation by making the fraction smaller). If your group falls in this category, it will probably not be able to qualify as a publicly supported public charity and should attempt to qualify under the public charity exempt activities support test discussed below.

Attraction of Public Support Test

Groups that can't meet the ⅓ public support requirements can qualify for public charity status if they receive at least $^{1}/_{10}$ of their total support from qualified public income sources and meet the additional attraction of public support requirement. Only groups trying to qualify for public charity status using the $^{1}/_{10}$ (as opposed to ⅓) public support requirements must satisfy this attraction of public support test. The IRS considers a number of factors in determining whether a group meets the test. Only Factor 1, below, must be met; none of the other factors are required.

The IRS looks favorably on organizations that meet one or more of the attraction of public support factors listed below. Meeting as many of these factors as possible will not only help you obtain public charity status, it also shows that you satisfy the basic 501(c)(3) tax-exempt status requirements—namely, that your nonprofit is organized and operated in the public interest and has broad-based community support and participation. Finally, if you request an advance ruling to see if your organization meets the public support test, the IRS will decide whether you meet the attraction of public support requirement, regardless of whether you expect to meet the ⅓ or the ¹/₁₀ public support percentage (see "Advance and Definitive Rulings," above).

Factor 1. Continuous Solicitation of Funds Program

Your group must continually attract new public or governmental support. You will meet this requirement if you maintain a continuous program for soliciting money from the general public, community, or membership—or if you solicit support from governmental agencies, churches, schools, or hospitals that also qualify as public charities (see "Automatic Public Charity Status," above). Although this factor concerns broad-based support, the IRS allows new groups to limit initial campaigns to seeking seed money from a select number of the most promising agencies or people.

Factor 2. Percentage of Financial Support

At least 10% of your group's total support must come from the public. However, the greater the percentage of public support, the better. Remember that if your public support amounts to ⅓ or more, you do not have to meet the attraction of public support factors listed in this subsection.

Factor 3. Support From a Representative Number of People

If your group gets most of its money from government agencies or from a broad cross section of people as opposed to one particular individual or a group with a special interest in your activities, it will more likely meet the attraction of public support requirement.

Factor 4. Representative Governing Body

A nonprofit corporation whose governing body represents broad public interests, rather than the personal interest of a limited number of donors, is considered favorably by the IRS. The IRS is more likely to treat an organization's governing body as representative if it includes:

- public officials
- people selected by public officials
- people recognized as experts in the organization's area of operations
- community leaders or others representing a cross section of community views and interests (such as members of the clergy, teachers, and civic leaders), or
- for membership organizations, people elected under the corporate articles or bylaws by a broad-based membership.

Factor 5. Availability of Public Facilities or Services

If an organization continuously provides facilities or services to the general public, the IRS will consider this favorably. These facilities and services might include a museum open to the public, an orchestra that gives public performances, a group that distributes educational literature to the public, or an old-age home that provides nursing or other services to low-income members of the community.

Factor 6. Additional Factors

Corporations are also more likely to meet the attraction of public support requirement if:

- members of the public with special knowledge or expertise (such as public officials, or civic or community leaders) participate in or sponsor programs

- the organization maintains a program to do charitable work in the community (such as job development or low-income housing rehabilitation), or

- the organization gets a significant portion of its funds from another public charity or a governmental agency to which it is, in some way, held accountable as a condition of the grant, contract, or contribution.

Factor 7. Additional Factors for Membership Groups Only

A membership organization is more likely to meet the attraction of public support requirement if:

- the solicitation for dues-paying members attempts to enroll a substantial number of people in the community or area, or in a particular profession or field of special interest

- membership dues are affordable to a broad cross section of the interested public, or

- the organization's activities are likely to appeal to people with some broad common interest or purpose—such as musical activities in the case of an orchestra or different forms of dance in the case of a dance studio.

Exempt Activities Support Test

Don't worry if your Section 501(c)(3) group does not qualify as a public charity either automatically or through the ⅓ or ¹⁄₁₀ public support test described above. There is another way to qualify as a public charity. The exempt activities support test is likely to meet your needs if your 501(c)(3) group intends to derive income from performing exempt-purpose activities and services (IRC § 509(a)(2)).

Although IRS publications sometimes include groups that meet the support test described in this section as publicly supported organizations, we do not. For us, publicly supported organizations are those that qualify under the public support test described above. We use the term exempt activities support test to describe this test.

For more detailed information on this public charity category, see IRS Publication 557, *Tax Exempt Status for Your Organization*, "509(a)(2) Organizations."

> **TIP**
>
> **Let the IRS do the work for you.** You can let the IRS do the hard part of deciding how each of the special rules described below applies to your group's anticipated sources of financial support. We show you how to check a box on the federal exemption application to do this. For now, just read through this material and you can come back to a particular section if you need to later when you fill in your IRS tax exemption application.

What Type of Support Qualifies and How Much Do You Need?

To qualify under the exempt activities public charity support test, a 501(c)(3) nonprofit organization must meet two requirements:

1. The organization must normally receive more than ⅓ of its total support in each tax year as qualified public support. Qualified public support is support from any of the following sources:

    - gifts, grants, contributions, or membership fees, and

    - gross receipts from admissions, selling merchandise, performing services, or providing facilities in an activity related to the exempt purposes of the nonprofit organization.

2. The organization also must normally not receive more than ⅓ of its annual support from unrelated trades or businesses or gross investment income. Gross investment income includes rent from unrelated sources, interest, dividends, and royalties—sources of support far removed from the activities of most small nonprofit organizations. However, it does not include any taxes you pay on income from unrelated businesses or activities—these amounts are deducted before the ⅓ figure is calculated.

Again, the most important aspect of this test, and the one that makes it appropriate for many 501(c)(3) groups, is that it allows the ⅓ qualified public support amount to include the group's receipts from performing its exempt purposes. Hence, this public charity classification is appropriate for many self-sustaining nonprofits that raise income from their tax-exempt activities, such as performing arts groups, schools, and other educational-purpose organizations, and nonprofit service organizations. School tuition, admissions to concerts or plays, or payments for classes at a pottery studio count as qualified public support under this public charity test.

Support Must Be From Permitted Sources

Qualified public support under this test must come from permitted sources including:

- individuals
- government agencies, and
- other 501(c)(3) public charities—generally, those that qualify as public charities under one of the tests described in "Automatic Public Charity Status" or "Public Support Test," above.

Permitted sources do not include disqualified persons (defined under IRC Section 4946)—people who would be considered disqualified if the organization were classified as a private foundation. These include substantial contributors, the organization's founders, and certain related persons.

Membership Fees and Dues Get Special Treatment

Dues paid to provide support for or to participate in the nonprofit organization, or in return for services or facilities provided only to members, are considered valid membership dues and can be counted in full as qualified public support. On the other hand, fees or dues paid in return for a discount on products or services provided to the public, or in return for some other monetary benefit, are not valid membership fees. However, these payments can still be counted as qualified public support if the fee entitles the member to special rates for exempt-purpose activities—in which case the payments would qualify as receipts related to the group's exempt purposes, but the payments may be subject to the 1% or $5,000 limitation discussed in the next section below.

EXAMPLE:

People pay $50 to become members of All Thumbs, a nonprofit group dedicated to rebuilding interest in the unitar, a near-extinct one-stringed guitar-like musical instrument. All Thumbs' members are allowed $50 worth of reduced rate passes to all unitar concerts nationwide. Although these fees can't be counted as valid member-ship fees because they are paid in return for an equivalent monetary benefit (a $50 discount at unitar concerts), they still count as receipts related to the performance of the group's exempt purposes (putting on these concerts is an exempt purpose and activity of the group). Therefore, the fees can be counted by the organization as qualified public support (we assume the fees paid by each individual do not exceed the 1% or $5,000 limitation that applies to exempt-purpose receipts as discussed in the next section below).

Are You Selling Services or Information That the Federal Government Offers for Free?

If your nonprofit plans to sell services or information, check to see if the same service or information is readily available free (or for a nominal fee) from the federal government. If so, you may need to tell potential clients and customers of this alternate source. This rule applies to all tax-exempt nonprofits (including any 501(c)(3) organization, whether classified as a public charity or private foundation). (IRC § 6711.) Failure to comply with this disclosure requirement can result in a substantial fine. For further information on these disclosure requirements, see IRS Publication 557.

The 1% or $5,000 Limit for Exempt-Purpose Income

There is one major limitation on the amount of income from exempt-purpose activities that can be included in the ⅓ qualified public support figure. In any tax year, receipts from individuals or government units from the performance of exempt-purpose services that exceed $5,000 or 1% of the organization's total support for the year, whichever is greater, must be excluded from the organization's qualified public support figure. This limitation applies only to exempt-purpose receipts and not to gifts, grants, contributions, or membership fees received by the organization.

EXAMPLE:

Van-Go is a visual arts group that makes art available to people around the nation by toting it around in specially marked vans. In 2007, Van-Go derives $30,000 total support from the sale of paintings. The funds are receipts related to the performance of the group's exempt purposes. Any amount over $5,000 paid by any one individual cannot be included in computing its qualified public support for the year, although the full amount is included in total support. Of course, if Van-Go's total support for any year is more than $500,000, then the limitation on individual contributions will be 1% of the year's total support, since this figure exceeds $5,000.

Some Gifts Are Gross Receipts

When someone gives money or property without getting anything of value in return, we think of it as a gift or contribution. But when people give a nonprofit money or property in return for admissions, merchandise, services performed, or facilities furnished to the contributor, these aren't gifts. They are considered gross receipts from exempt-purpose activities and are subject to the $5,000 or 1% limitation.

EXAMPLE:

At its annual fundraising drive, the California Cormorant Preservation League rewards $100 contributors with a book containing color prints of cormorants. The book normally retails for $25. Only $75 of each contribution is considered a gift; the remaining $25 payments are classified as gross receipts from the performance of the group's exempt purposes and are subject to the $5,000 or 1% limitation.

Some Grants Are Gross Receipts

It is sometimes hard to distinguish money received as a grant from exempt-purpose gross receipts. The IRS rule is that when the granting agency gets some economic or physical benefit in return for its grant, such as a service, facility, or product, the grant is classified as gross receipts related to the exempt activities of the nonprofit organization. This means that the funds will be subject to the 1% or $5,000 limitation that applies to exempt-purpose receipts. Money contributed to benefit the public will be treated as bona fide grants by the IRS, not as exempt-purpose receipts. This type of bona fide grant is not subject to the 1% or $5,000 limitation.

EXAMPLE 1:

A pharmaceutical company, Amalgamated Mortar & Pestle, provides a research grant to a nonprofit scientific and medical research organization, Safer Sciences, Inc. The company specifies that the nonprofit must use the grant to develop a more reliable childproof cap for prescription drug containers (the results of the nonprofit research will be shared with the commercial company). The money is treated as receipts received by Safer Sciences in carrying out its exempt purposes and is subject to the $5,000 or 1% limitation.

EXAMPLE 2:

Safer Sciences gets a grant from the federal Centers for Disease Control and Prevention to build a better petri dish for epidemiological research. Since the money is used to benefit the public, the full amount will be included in the nonprofit organization's qualified public support figure.

Unusual Grants Drop Out of the Computation

To be included as qualified support (in the numerator of the support fraction), the support must be from permitted sources. Disqualified persons include founders, directors, or executive officers of the nonprofit. A large grant from one of these sources could undermine the ability of the nonprofit to qualify under this public charity test.

To avoid this result for nonprofits that would otherwise qualify under the exempt activities support test, unusual grants are ignored—that is, they drop out of both the numerator and denominator of the support calculation. (There is a similar exclusion for unusual grants under the public support test discussed above.) A grant will be classified as unusual if the source of the grant is not regularly relied on or actively sought out by the nonprofit as part of its support outreach program and if certain other conditions are met. If you want to learn more about these unusual grant requirements for groups that qualify as a public charity under the exempt-activities support test, see IRS Publication 557 (included on the CD-ROM).

Rents Related to Exempt Purposes Are Not Gross Investment Income

Rents received from people or groups whose activities in the rented premises are related to the group's exempt purpose are generally not considered gross investment income. This is a good thing. Why? Remember: Under this public charity test, the organization must normally not receive more than 1/3 of its total support from unrelated trades or businesses or from gross investment income.

EXAMPLE:

Good Crafts, Inc., a studio that provides facilities for public education in historic crafts, rents a portion of its premises to an instructor who teaches stained glass classes. This rent would probably not fall into the gross investment income category. However, if the tenant's activities in the leased premises were not related to the nonprofit's purposes, then the rent would be included as gross investment income and, if all the unrelated and investment income of the nonprofit exceeded ⅓ of its total support, the nonprofit could lose its public charity status under the exempt activities support test.

Keep this exception in mind if your group owns or rents premises with extra space. It may be important to rent (or sublease, if you are renting, too) to another person or group whose activities are directly related to your exempt purposes. (If you're renting, be sure the terms of your lease allow you to sublease; most of the time, you'll need your landlord's permission.)

SEE AN EXPERT

When to consult a tax expert. If you plan to supplement your support with income from activities unrelated to your exempt purposes (as more and more nonprofits must), check with your tax adviser. You'll want to make sure this additional income will not exceed 1/3 of your total support and jeopardize your ability to qualify under this public charity category.

There's That Word "Normally" Again

To qualify as a public charity under the support test, groups must "normally" meet the ⅓ qualified support requirements set forth in "Public Support Test," above. As with publicly supported organizations, this means that the IRS looks at the total amount of support over the previous four-year period to decide if the organization qualifies as a public charity for the current and the following tax year. (See "What Does 'Normally' Mean?" above.)

TIP

You can quality under a definitive or advance ruling. Like the publicly supported public charities discussed earlier, the groups discussed here can qualify for public charity status under a definitive or advance ruling. For further information on advance and definitive rulings, see "Advance and Definitive Rulings," in "Public Support Test," above, and Chapter 9.

Private Foundations

Initially, the IRS will classify your 501(c)(3) corporation as a private foundation. As we mentioned at the beginning of this chapter, almost all nonprofits will want to overcome this presumption and establish themselves as a public charity instead. Because you are probably interested in public charity status, you can skip this section or read through it quickly if you want learn about private foundations and the operating limitations and restrictions applicable to them. If you want to form a private foundation, you can use this book as an introduction to the subject, but you will probably also need the help of a nonprofit lawyer or tax specialist with experience setting up private foundations. The rules that apply to private foundations are very complicated and the penalties for not obeying the rules are stiff.

Background

Broadly speaking, the reason that private foundations are subject to strict operating limitations and special taxes, while public charities are not, is to counter tax abuse schemes by wealthy individuals and families. Before the existence of private foundation restrictions, a person with a lot of money could set up his own 501(c)(3) tax-exempt organization (such as The William Smith Foundation) with a high-sounding purpose (to wipe out the potato bug in Northern Louisiana). The potato bugs, though, were never in any danger, because the real purpose of the foundation was to hire all of William Smith's relatives and friends down to the third generation. Instead of leaving the money in a will and paying heavy estate taxes, William Smith neatly transferred money to the next generation tax free by use of a tax-exempt foundation that just happened to hire all of his relatives.

To prevent schemes such as this, Congress enacted the private foundation operating restrictions, special excise taxes, and other private foundation disincentives discussed in the next section.

Operating Restrictions

Private foundations must comply with operating restrictions and detailed rules, including:

- restrictions on self-dealing between private foundations and their substantial contributors and other disqualified persons

- requirements that the foundation annually distribute its net income for charitable purposes

- limitations on holdings in private businesses

- provisions that investments must not jeopardize the carrying out of the group's 501(c)(3) tax-exempt purposes, and

- provisions to assure that expenditures further the group's exempt purposes.

Violations of these provisions result in substantial excise taxes and penalties against the private foundation and, in some cases, against

its managers, major contributors, and certain related persons. Keeping track of and meeting these restrictions is unworkable for the average 501(c)(3) group, which is the main reason why you'll want to avoid being classified by the IRS as a private foundation.

Note: The Pension Protection Act of 2006 increased the excise taxes that apply to private foundations and made other technical changes. If you are interested in more information, ask your nonprofit tax advisor.

Limitation on Deductibility of Contributions

Generally, a donor can take personal income tax deductions for individual contributions to private foundations of up to only 30% of the donor's adjusted gross income. Donations to public charities, on the other hand, are generally deductible up to 50% of the donor's adjusted gross income.

Of course, the overwhelming number of individual contributors do not contribute an amount even close to the 30% limit, so this limitation is not very important. The real question of importance to contributors is whether you are a qualified 501(c)(3) organization so that charitable contributions to your group are tax deductible.

RESOURCE

IRS Publication 526, *Charitable Contributions*, discusses the rules limiting deductions to private foundations (called 30% limit organizations) and public charities (50% limit organizations), including special rules that apply to donations of real estate, securities, and certain types of tangible personal property. 501(c)(3) organizations (both public charities and private foundations) and other qualified groups eligible to receive tax-deductible charitable contributions are listed in IRS Publication 78, *Cumulative List of Organizations*.

Special Types of Private Foundations

The IRS recognizes two special types of private foundations that have some of the advantages of public charities: private operating, and private nonoperating foundations. We mention them briefly below because they are included in IRS nonprofit tax publications and forms. Few readers will be interested in forming either of these special organizations.

Private Operating Foundations

To qualify as a private operating foundation, the organization generally must distribute most of its income to tax-exempt activities and must meet one of three special tests (an assets, support, or endowment test). This special type of 501(c)(3) private foundation enjoys a few benefits not granted to regular private foundations, including the following:

- **More generous deductions for donors.** As with public charities, individual donors can deduct up to 50% of adjusted gross income for contributions to the organization.

- **Extended time to distribute funds.** The organization can receive grants from a private foundation without having to distribute the funds received within one year (and these funds can be treated as qualifying distributions by the donating private foundation).

- **No excise tax.** The private foundation excise tax on net investment income does not apply.

All other private foundation restrictions and excise taxes apply to private operating foundations.

CD-ROM

For additional information on the rules that apply to private operating foundations, see *Public Charity or Private Foundation Status Issues under IRC §§ 509(a)(1)-(4), 4942(j)(3), and 507,* on the CD-ROM included at the back of this book. See the section titled, "IRC 4942(j)(3)—Private Operating Foundations."

Private Nonoperating Foundations

This special type of private foundation is one that either:

- distributes all the contributions it receives to public charities and private operating foundations (discussed just above) each year, or

- pools its contributions into a common trust fund and distributes the income and funds to public charities.

Individual contributors to private nonoperating foundations can deduct 50% of their donations. However, the organization is subject to all excise taxes and operating restrictions applicable to regular private foundations.

Other Tax Benefits and Requirements

In this chapter we discuss additional federal tax issues that affect nonprofits, such as the deductibility of contributions made to 501(c)(3) nonprofits and what happens if a 501(c)(3) makes money from activities not related to its tax-exempt purposes. We also cover nonprofit tax benefits and tax and nontax requirements that apply to 501(c)(3) nonprofits under California law.

Federal and State Tax Deductions for Contributions

A donor (corporate or individual) can claim a personal federal income tax deduction for contributions made to a 501(c)(3) tax-exempt organization. These contributions are called charitable contributions. Generally, California follows the federal tax deductibility rules for charitable contributions made to nonprofit corporations.

Corporations can make deductible charitable contributions of up to 10% of their annual taxable income. Individuals can deduct up to 50% of adjusted gross income in any year for contributions made to 501(c)(3) public charities and to some types of 501(c)(3) private foundations, as explained in Chapter 4. Donations to most types of private foundations are limited to 30% of an individual's adjusted gross income in each year.

What Can Be Deducted

A donor can deduct the following types of contributions:

- **Cash.**
- **Property.** Generally, donors can deduct the fair market (resale) value of donated property. Technical rules apply to gifts of appreciated property (property that has increased in value) that may require donors

to decrease the deduction they take for donating appreciated property—see IRS Publication 526, *Charitable Contributions*, "Giving Property That Has Increased In Value."

- **Unreimbursed car expenses.** These include the cost of gas and oil incurred by the donor while performing services for the nonprofit organization, and
- **Unreimbursed travel expenses.** These include expenses incurred by the donor while away from home and performing services for the nonprofit organization, such as the cost of transportation, meals, and lodging.

What Cannot Be Deducted

Certain types of gifts cannot be deducted as charitable contributions. Nondeductible gifts include:

- **The value of volunteer services.** For example, if you normally are paid $40 per hour for bookkeeping work, and you volunteer ten hours of your time to a nonprofit to help them prepare their annual financial statements, you cannot claim a charitable deduction for the value of your time donated to the nonprofit (you can't claim a charitable deduction of $400).
- **The right to use property.** If you rent out office space for $1,000 per month and allow a nonprofit to use $1/10$ of the total space for a small office, you cannot claim a charitable deduction of $100 per month for letting the nonprofit use the space for free.
- **Contributions to political parties.** These contributions, however, can be taken as a tax credit, subject to dollar and percentage limitations.
- **Direct contributions to needy individuals.**
- **Tuition.** Even amounts designated as donations, which must be paid in addition to

tuition as a condition of enrollment, are not deductible.

- **Dues paid to labor unions.**
- **The cost of raffle, bingo, or lottery tickets, or other games of chance.**
- **Child care costs paid while performing services for a nonprofit organization.**

Donations That Can Be Partially Deducted

Contributions that a nonprofit receives in return for a service, product, or other benefit (such as membership fees paid in return for special membership incentives or promotional products, or donations charged for attending a performance) are only partially deductible. Donors may deduct for these only to the extent that the value of the contribution exceeds the fair market value of the service, product, or benefit received by the donor.

EXAMPLE:

If a member of a 501(c)(3) organization pays a $30 membership fee and receives a record album that sells for $30, nothing is deductible. But if a $20 product is given in return for the $30 payment, $10 of the fee paid is a bona fide donation and may be deducted by the member as a charitable contribution.

501(c)(3) nonprofit groups should always clearly state the dollar amount that is deductible when receiving contributions, donations, or membership fees in return for providing a service, product, discount, or other benefit to the donor.

Reporting Requirements

Individuals can claim deductions for charitable contributions by itemizing the gifts on IRS

Schedule A and filing this form with their annual 1040 income tax return. IRS rules require donors to obtain receipts for all charitable contributions claimed on their tax returns. Receipts must describe the contribution and show the value of any goods or services received from the nonprofit by the donor as part of the transaction. See IRS publications mentioned below for more information on how to prepare donor receipts for your organization.

RESOURCE

The IRS requirements for deducting and reporting charitable contributions change from year to year. For current information, see IRS Publication 526, *Charitable Contributions*. For information on valuing gifts, see IRS Publication 561, *Determining the Value of Donated Property*.

Federal Estate and Gift Tax Exemptions

Gifts made as part of an individual's estate plan (through a will or trust document) can be an important source of contributions for 501(c)(3) nonprofits. When the individual dies, the 501(c)(3) organization receives the money and the money is excluded from the taxable estate of the individual.

The tax savings for the donor can be enormous, since taxable estates can be taxed at a rate as high as 45%. This tax is scheduled to be repealed in its entirety in 2010 (see Caution below). Only estates that are quite large are subject to tax, however, because all estates receive an automatic tax credit that is quite significant. By 2009, the amount of the automatic tax credit for estates will be $3.5 million. Nevertheless, more and more people are realizing that their estate may be big enough to get hit with an estate tax. This is particularly true of people who own real estate in large urban centers where real estate values have kept going up. Many people are motivated, therefore, to engage in estate planning, including making charitable gifts to nonprofit organizations.

> **CAUTION**
>
> **The repeal of the estate tax "sunsets" at the end of 2010.** This double negative means that the estate tax repeal is temporary, unless Congress renews it or takes some other action on it. So, unless Congress votes to make the repeal permanent, the estate tax will be reinstated in 2011. Keep in touch with your tax advisor and check the IRS website at www.irs.gov for the latest changes.

Traditionally, colleges and universities and larger environmental and health organizations have actively solicited estate charitable giving by providing information to members and donors about estate planning and the benefits of charitable bequests. Increasingly, smaller nonprofits are starting to understand the game and are pursuing similar strategies in their fundraising efforts. If you understand how charitable giving affects the donor's taxes, you'll be better able to persuade potential donors to give to your cause.

An individual does not pay taxes on gifts made during his lifetime. However, gifts to an individual (who isn't the giver's spouse) or to a nonqualified organization will reduce the donor's unified estate and gift tax credit to the extent the gifts exceed $12,000 in one calendar year. For example, a $13,000 gift to a struggling writer, who will use the money to support himself while he writes the great American novel, will not be taxed to you. But the excess of $1,000 will be counted as part of your estate tax credit. On the other hand, gifts made to a 501(c)(3) nonprofit (even if they exceed $12,000) do not reduce this federal and estate gift tax credit. Tax-wise, you might be better off giving the money to a literary nonprofit that, in turn, gives grants to promising writers (unfortunately, you could not earmark the money for a particular writer, as explained in "Charitable Purposes" in Chapter 3.

> **RESOURCE**
>
> **For further information on federal and state estate and gift taxes and individual estate planning techniques,** see *Plan Your Estate*, by Denis Clifford and Cora Jordan (Nolo).

Federal Unrelated Business Income Tax

All tax-exempt nonprofit corporations, whether private foundations or public charities, may have to pay tax on income derived from activities unrelated to their exempt purposes. The first $1,000 of unrelated business income is not taxed. After that, the normal federal corporate tax rate applies: 15% on the first $50,000 of taxable corporate income; 25% on the next $25,000, and 34% on taxable income over $75,000 (with a 5% surtax on taxable income between $100,000 and $335,000). Higher corporate tax rates (35% and an interim 38% surtax) apply to corporate taxable incomes over $10 million dollars.

> **CAUTION**
>
> **Be careful with unrelated income.** As explained in "Unrelated Business Activities" in Chapter 3, if unrelated income is substantial, it may jeopardize the organization's 501(c)(3) tax exemption.

CHAPTER 5 | OTHER TAX BENEFITS AND REQUIREMENTS | 89

CD-ROM

For past history and current developments in the federal treatment of an exempt organization's unrelated business income tax, see *Current Developments*, on the CD-ROM included at the back of this book.

Activities That Are Taxed

Unrelated business income comes from activities that are not directly related to a group's exempt purposes. An unrelated trade or business is one that is regularly carried on and not substantially related to a nonprofit group's exempt purposes. It is irrelevant that the organization uses the profits to conduct its exempt-purpose activities.

EXAMPLE 1:

Enviro-Home Institute is a 501(c)(3) nonprofit organized to educate the public about environmentally sound home design and home construction techniques. Enviro-Home develops a model home kit that applies its ideas of appropriate environmental construction and is very successful in selling the kit. The IRS considers this unrelated business income because it is not directly related to the educational purposes of the organization.

EXAMPLE 2:

A halfway house that offers room, board, therapy, and counseling to recently released prison inmates also operates a furniture shop to provide full-time employment for its residents. This is not an unrelated trade or business because the shop directly benefits the residents (even though it also produces income).

Activities That Are Not Taxed

A number of activities are specifically excluded from the definition of unrelated trades or businesses. These include activities in which nearly all work is done by volunteers, and those that:

- are carried on by 501(c)(3) tax-exempt organizations primarily for the benefit of members, students, patients, officers, or employees (such as a hospital gift shop for patients or employees)
- involve the sale of mostly donated merchandise, such as thrift shops
- consist of the exchange or rental of lists of donors or members
- involve the distribution of low-cost items, such as stamps or mailing labels worth less than $5, in the course of soliciting funds, and
- involve sponsoring trade shows by 501(c)(3) groups—this exclusion extends to the exempt organization's suppliers, who may educate trade show attendees on new developments or products related to the organization's exempt activities.

Some of these exceptions have been hotly contested by commercial business interests at congressional hearings. The primary objection is that nonprofits receive an unfair advantage by being allowed to engage, tax free, in activities that compete with their for-profit counterparts. Expect more hearings and future developments in this volatile area of nonprofit tax law.

Also excluded from this tax is income not derived from services (termed gross investment income in the Internal Revenue Code). Remember, this tax applies to unrelated activities, not necessarily to unrelated income. Examples of nontaxable income include:

- dividends, interest, and royalties
- rent from land, buildings, furniture, and equipment (some forms of rent are taxed if the rental property was purchased or improved subject to a mortgage, or if the rental income is based on the profits earned by the tenant), and
- gains or losses from the sale or exchange of property.

See Section 512(b) of the Internal Revenue Code for the complete list of these untaxed sources of income and the exceptions that exist for certain items.

SEE AN EXPERT

It is often difficult to predict whether the IRS will tax an activity or income as unrelated business. Furthermore, IRS regulations and rulings and U.S. Tax Court decisions contain a number of rules classifying specific activities as unrelated businesses that are subject to tax. In short, you should do more research or consult a tax specialist if you plan to engage in activities or derive income from sources not directly related to your exempt purposes. Please note, this isn't the same thing as saying you shouldn't engage in an unrelated activity—many nonprofits must engage in commercial businesses unrelated to their exempt purposes to survive. But to avoid jeopardizing your 501(c)(3) tax-exempt status and to understand the tax effects of engaging in unrelated business, you simply need good tax advice.

California Unrelated Business Income Tax

California, like the federal government, taxes the unrelated business income of a tax-exempt nonprofit corporation. The state's definition of an unrelated trade or business is similar to that used by the IRS. Basically, any trade or business not substantially related to the organization's exempt purposes is considered an unrelated trade or business.

The tax rate for unrelated income is the standard California corporate franchise tax rate. (Franchise tax is the name of the tax in California that applies to the taxable income of most corporations.) This rate is currently set at 8.84%, and it applies to the net amount of unrelated business income (gross unrelated business income minus deductions for expenses directly connected with carrying on the unrelated business activity). Tax-exempt organizations are allowed a $1,000 deduction before computing their California taxable unrelated business income.

EXAMPLE:

A Section 501(c)(3) traveler's aid society earns $7,000 a year selling baked goods to passers-by. Cost of the ingredients and all expenses related to this profit-making activity total $3,000. The society pays state unrelated business taxes on the $3,000 net amount ($7,000 − $1,000 deduction − $3,000 cost of goods sold).

The state does not tax certain activities as unrelated trade or business. The state exceptions are similar to the IRS exceptions and include any trade or business:

- where most of the work is performed by volunteers
- that exists mostly for the convenience of the members, students, patients, officers, or employees, or
- that sells merchandise, most of which was given to the organization as gifts or contributions.

Like the federal law, California also generally excludes specific kinds of passive income, such as rent and interest income, from unrelated business income tax.

California Nonprofit Tax Exemption

California corporations are subject to an annual corporate franchise tax of 8.84% on the net income of the corporation. A minimum franchise tax of $800 must be paid annually, starting in the corporation's second tax year. (California Revenue and Taxation Code § 23701(d).) California nonprofit corporations can apply for an exemption from this corporate franchise tax.

Section 23701(d) of the California tax law exempts the same groups that are exempt under Section 501(c)(3) of the Internal Revenue Code. This means that religious, charitable, scientific, literary, and educational organizations—the most common types of nonprofit corporations and the ones this book is primarily concerned with—can apply for a state exemption from corporate franchise taxes. The California 23701(d) nonprofit corporation tax exemption parallels the federal 501(c)(3) tax exemption. Chapter 8 provides step-by-step instructions on how to fill out and file your state corporate tax exemption application.

California tax law, like the federal 501(c)(3) scheme, imposes restrictions on the political activity of 23701(d) tax-exempt groups. California rules are very similar to the federal rules in that California recognizes both the substantial activities test and the alternative political expenditures test. These tests limit the amount of political lobbying and expenditures that can be undertaken by tax-exempt nonprofits. (See "Other Requirements for 501(c)(3) Groups" in Chapter 3.)

California does not make a separate determination as to whether your tax-exempt nonprofit corporation is a private foundation or public charity. The state simply follows the determination made by the IRS. If your organization is classified by the IRS as a 501(c)(3) public charity, it will be considered a public charity in California.

California Attorney General Reporting Requirements

All charitable corporations and trustees holding property for charitable purposes must register with the California Attorney General's Office, Registry of Charitable Trusts. After registering with the attorney general, you will file annual financial disclosure returns showing how you operate your nonprofit and how your charitable funds are used. Most public benefit corporations (not just those formed for a specific charitable purpose) are considered charitable corporations for the purpose of these registration and annual reporting requirements. Religious corporations are not subject to these reporting requirements. The registration and annual reporting requirements are meant to ensure that the corporate funds are not misused in any way.

After you incorporate a California nonprofit public benefit corporation, you will receive a letter from the attorney general's office. The letter will include a pamphlet with information on the registration requirements, other statutes affecting charitable organizations, and a registration form and instructions. Don't be confused by the legal jargon in these documents— basically, the registration and annual reporting requirements apply to all 501(c)(3) nonprofit groups, except for religious corporations and certain schools and hospitals.

The attorney general registration and reporting requirements are a formality for most Section 501(c)(3) groups. However, if your public benefit corporation solicits funds for specific charitable purposes (such as to provide a free meal program), and the attorney general receives numerous complaints from the public claiming that your organization misrepresents itself when asking for donations or misapplies donated funds to nonprogram purposes, the attorney general will probably look over your annual reports closely. If the complaints sound credible and your reports look incomplete or inaccurate, you will probably receive an inquiry letter from the attorney general asking for more information. If the attorney general is not satisfied with your response, it can take your nonprofit to court and sue both the nonprofit corporation and its principals for the payback of funds fraudulently solicited from the public or misapplied to non-program purposes. For further information on submitting these required forms, see "File an Initial Report With the Attorney General" in Chapter 10.

California Welfare Exemption

Many California tax-exempt nonprofit corporations own or lease real property (or portions of property). Real property includes land, buildings, and fixtures attached to a building. For example, your group may own its building; or perhaps you are a tenant in someone else's structure. Your group may also own (or lease) movable property, known as personal property, such as equipment or vehicles.

For-profit businesses pay property taxes on the land and buildings they own and personal taxes on their business equipment and inventory. However, when a qualified 501(c)(3) uses real or personal property *exclusively* to carry out its exempt purposes, it gets a wonderful tax break—no taxes! This rule is known as the welfare exemption, contained in Section 214 of the California Revenue

and Taxation Code. To apply for the welfare exemption, call your local county tax assessor and ask for a welfare exemption application and materials.

The welfare exemption can provide tremendous savings for your organization. For example, if you own property and pay relatively high taxes, your property tax bills will go down to zero after you incorporate and obtain a welfare exemption. Or, if you lease property from a nonprofit group that has itself qualified for the welfare exemption, the property tax attributed to your portion of the premises will be dropped from the property tax rolls once you obtain a welfare exemption.

TIP

If you're a tenant, remember the welfare exemption when negotiating your lease. Your landlord (assuming the landlord is a nonprofit that also qualifies for the exemption) will enjoy a tax break when you qualify for the welfare exemption. Ask the landlord to pass some of his tax savings on to you, in the form of decreased rent, as soon as you qualify. (See "Leasing and the Welfare Exemption," below, for more information.)

RESOURCE

The material in this section is based on the *Assessor's Handbook* published by the California State Board of Equalization. A copy of the Welfare, Church and Religious Exemptions section of the *Handbook* is included on the CD-ROM. If you want to see if there's an updated version, go to the California State Board of Equalization website at www.boe.ca.gov. Select the Property Tax link from the link list and click Assessor's Handbook. You can view and print the *Handbook* by section from the website.

Section 214 Exemption Requirements

Many nonprofit corporations qualify for the California welfare exemption. The general requirements for the exemption under Section 214 of the California Revenue and Taxation Code are:

- The property must be used exclusively for religious, hospital, scientific, or charitable purposes and be owned and operated by community chests, funds, foundations, or corporations organized and operated for religious, hospital, scientific, or charitable purposes.

- The owner must be a nonprofit corporation or other organization exempt from taxes under Section 501(c)(3) of the Internal Revenue Code or under Section 23701(d) of the California Revenue and Taxation Code.

- No part of the net earnings of the owner can inure to the benefit of any private shareholder or individual (see "No Benefit to Individuals," below, for more information on this point).

- The property must be used for the actual operation of the exempt purposes of the group, and it must not exceed the amount of property reasonably necessary to accomplish the group's exempt purposes.

- The property cannot be used or operated by the owner or by any other person so as to benefit any officer, trustee, director, shareholder, member, employee, contributor, bondholder of the owner or operator, or any other person, through the distribution of profits, payments of excessive charges or compensation, or the more advantageous pursuit of their business or profession.

- The property cannot be used by the owner or members for fraternal or lodge purposes or for social club purposes, except where such use is clearly incidental to a primary religious, hospital, scientific, or charitable purpose.

- The property must be irrevocably dedicated to religious, charitable, scientific, or hospital purposes and upon the liquidation, dissolution, or abandonment by the owner, will not inure to the benefit of any private person except a fund, foundation, or corporation organized and operated for religious, scientific, or charitable purposes. Irrevocable dedication is explained below in "Irrevocable Dedication of Property."

Most 501(c)(3) nonprofit corporations meet the welfare exemption requirements because they are the same as, or similar to, those which must be met to obtain federal and state income tax exemptions. Although certain types of property owned and operated for religious purposes are covered by the welfare exemption, religious-purpose groups generally seek property exemptions under the more flexible church and religious exemptions discussed below.

No Benefit to Individuals

The State Board of Equalization will deny the exemption if the use of the property benefits an individual. In making this determination, the Board takes into account:

- whether a capital investment made by the owner or operator for expansion of a physical plant is justified by the contemplated return on the investment and is required to serve the interests of the community

- whether the property for which the exemption is claimed is used for the actual operation of an exempt activity (under

Section 214, the welfare exemption provision) and does not exceed the amount of property necessary to accomplish the exempt purpose

- whether the services and expenses of the owner or operator are excessive, based upon like services and salaries in comparable public institutions, and

- whether the operations of the owner or operator, either directly or indirectly, materially enhance the private gain of any individual or individuals.

Irrevocable Dedication of Property

To qualify for the welfare exemption, property must be dedicated to religious, charitable, scientific, or hospital purposes irrevocably, which means the dedication can't be rescinded. Since an irrevocable dedication clause of all of the nonprofit corporation's property is required by Section 501(c)(3) of the Internal Revenue Code and by Section 23701(d) of the California Revenue and Taxation Code to obtain the federal and state income tax exemptions, you can satisfy all three of these requirements with one irrevocable dedication clause in the articles of incorporation. You can make a specific dedication to a particular group or (as is more common) the dedication can be to a designated class of organizations, such as those that are tax-exempt under federal and state law and satisfy the requirements of Section 214. The articles included on the CD-ROM in this book contain an irrevocable dedication clause that meets these three requirements.

Dedication Clause for Educational and Scientific Purposes

If property is dedicated to scientific or educational purposes, these purposes must fall within the specific meaning of scientific and educational for the welfare exemption.

(We explain the requirements for scientific and educational purpose below and provide legal language that satisfies these requirements in "Prepare Articles of Incorporation" in Chapter 6.)

Special Statutory Categories

Under California law, certain nonprofit uses of property are specifically mentioned as eligible for the welfare exemption. In some cases, all of the welfare exemption requirements must be met; sometimes, specific requirements are waived. Here are a few examples:

Homeless Shelters

Property owned by a qualifying organization that is used wholly or partially to provide temporary shelter for homeless people qualifies for the welfare exemption. The exemption on the property is granted in proportion to the space used for this purpose.

Educational TV and FM Stations

Property used exclusively by a noncommercial educational FM broadcast station or an educational TV station that is owned and operated by a religious, hospital, scientific, or charitable fund, foundation, or corporation is within the meaning of the welfare exemption. In addition, one or both of the following requirements must be satisfied:

- **TV.** The educational TV station must receive at least 25% of its operating expense revenues from contributions from the general public or dues from its members.

- **FM radio.** The station must be a noncommercial educational FM broadcast station licensed and operated under Federal Communications Commission rules (Section 73.501 and following of Title 47 of the Code of Federal Regulations).

Preservation of the Environment or Animals

Property used for the preservation of native plants or animals, preserved or protected for its geographical formations of scientific or educational interest, or open space land used solely for recreation and for the enjoyment of scientific beauty (nature trails, tidal pool exploration, and the like) can qualify as exempt from taxation. The property must be open to the general public, subject to reasonable restrictions concerning the uses of the land, and be owned and operated by a scientific or charitable fund, foundation, or corporation that meets the other requirements of Section 214.

Property Leased to the Government

Property that is leased to, and exclusively used by, a government entity for its interest and benefit is exempt if all the other requirements of Section 214 are met, except for the irrevocable dedication requirement. The dedication will be deemed to exist if the lease provides that the owner's entire interest in the property will pass completely to the government entity upon the liquidation, dissolution, or abandonment of the owner, or when the last rental payment is made under the lease, whichever occurs first, and if certain other formal requirements are met.

Property Under Construction or Demolition

Facilities under construction, together with the land where the facilities are located, fall under the welfare exemption, as long as the property and facilities will be used exclusively for religious, hospital, or charitable purposes. The same is true for property that is being demolished with the intent of replacing it with facilities to be used exclusively for religious, hospital, or charitable purposes.

Volunteer Fire Departments, Zoos, and Public Gardens

Property used by volunteer fire departments will fall within the welfare exemption, as long as it also meets certain other requirements. Property used exclusively for the operation of a zoo or for horticultural displays by a zoological society can also qualify for the welfare exemption.

Educational Purposes That Entitle Nonprofits to Use the Welfare Exemption

Educational purposes and activities that benefit the community as a whole (not just a select membership of the nonprofit organization) qualify as charitable purposes under the welfare exemption. Below are examples of the types of educational purposes and activities that meet the requirements of the welfare exemption.

Elementary and High Schools

Real and personal property used by elementary and high schools owned and operated by religious, hospital, or charitable funds, foundations, or corporations fall within the welfare exemption if all of the other requirements of Section 214 are met and the school is an institution of learning with one of the following characteristics:

- attendance at the school exempts a student from attendance at a public full-time elementary or secondary day school under Section 12154 of the Education Code; or

- a majority of its students have been excused from attending a full-time elementary or secondary day school under Section 12152 or 12156 of the Education Code.

Basically, this special provision exempts the property of an educational purpose group that sets up a private, institutionalized elementary or high school with state-approved curriculum and other state-approved institutionalized attributes (such as regular attendance and certified faculty). If you set up a private college in conjunction with a private elementary or high school, you can also seek to obtain the welfare exemption under this provision. If, however, your educational purpose is to set up a private college by itself, you will usually have to meet the requirements of the separate California college exemption to be exempt from personal and real property taxes (see "Other California Tax Exemptions," below).

Special rules extend the welfare exemption to certain property owned by colleges and certain property used for housing facilities for elderly or handicapped persons. Check with the tax assessor's office for further information on these special rules.

Other Educational-Purpose Groups

Many general purpose educational groups qualify for the welfare exemption. For example, groups that give instruction in dance, music, or other art forms, or groups that publish instructional literature can qualify for the welfare exemption. The courts and the assessor's office have set up a number of general guidelines for determining whether a general educational-purpose group is eligible for the welfare exemption. These include:

- The organization can't be a formal college, secondary, or elementary school (see the definition of elementary and secondary schools in "Elementary and High Schools," above).

- The organization can't receive support from public (governmental) agencies.

- The educational program should be available to the community at large and provide a social benefit to the general public—not just a select number of people. In other

words, the educational program must have some charitable attributes that instruct or benefit those who attend as well as the general public. The fact that admission fees are charged for attendance at performances, or that tuition is charged for instruction, does not negate the charitable nature of the educational activities.

EXAMPLE 1:

In a leading case, the court ruled that a theater group whose primary activities consisted of charging admissions to theatrical performances open to the general public was charitable in nature and its educational purpose was one within the meaning of the welfare exemption. In reaching this conclusion, the court took note of the fact that the only real estate owned by the group was a playhouse used for the production of popular plays and musical comedies. The real estate was not used to benefit any officer, trustee, director, shareholder, member, employee, contributor, or bondholder of the corporation. All productions were of amateur standing. Membership in the theater group was unrestricted and was obtained by anyone who purchased a season ticket. In addition, the theater obtained revenue from the sale of tickets to the general public for single performances and from gifts.

The court considered these facts favorably, as well as the fact that the theater group was dedicated to providing educational benefits both to those who took part in the productions and to members of the general public (members of the audience). These benefits were found to be beneficial to the community, and therefore charitable, so the group's educational purposes were found to be within the meaning of the welfare exemption. The group was granted the welfare exemption and the real and personal property owned by the group was held exempt. (*Stockton Civic Theatre*, 66 Cal.2d 13 (1967).)

EXAMPLE 2:

In another important case, an educational-purpose group was denied the welfare exemption. This case involved an educational-purpose mortuary school that was an accredited junior college offering a one-year course in mortuary science leading toward an AA degree. The court found that because the school was a quasi-diploma mill, it did not qualify for the college exemption; and because it was of collegiate grade, it did not meet the welfare exemption's statutory requirements. The court went on to say that the organization was ineligible in any event, because its educational program (mortuary science) did not benefit the community at large or an ascertainable and indefinite portion of the community. All benefits went to a specific segment of the community (the funeral service industry) by providing it with competently trained personnel. (*California College of Mortuary Science*, 23 Cal.App.3d 702 (1972).)

Whether the tax assessor's office will consider your educational activities charitable in nature will depend on the particular activities of your group. If you show the assessor's office that your educational-purpose activities (seminars, lectures, publications, courses, and performances) benefit the community at large (which most do), you should qualify for the welfare exemption.

Scientific Purposes That Entitle Nonprofits to Use the Welfare Exemption

Scientific purposes are narrowly defined for purposes of the welfare exemption. Under Section 214, scientific purposes are limited to medical research whose objects are the encouragement or conduct of scientific investigation, research, and discovery for the benefit of the community at large, unless the research is carried on by an institution chartered by the U.S. government.

Religious Purposes That Entitle Nonprofits to Use the Welfare Exemption

Property owned by religious purpose groups and used for religious purposes is eligible for the welfare exemption. The courts have interpreted the terms religious and religion broadly under the welfare exemption. For example, property owned and operated for religious worship (such as a church building) and property used for general religious purposes (such as church schools, retreats, summer camps, reading rooms, and licensed church nursery schools) qualifies for the welfare exemption. Although the welfare exemption applies to this broad range of religious purposes, most religious groups use California's separate religious welfare exemption because it is easier to qualify for and use.

The religious exemption is a separate exemption under Section 207 of the California Revenue and Taxation Code. This exemption provides a streamlined and coordinated procedure that many nonprofit religious groups can now use to obtain their real and personal property tax exemptions. In the past, religious groups applied for both the church exemption (discussed below) and the welfare exemption.

The church exemption was used for religious worship property, such as a church building; and the welfare exemption was used for other religious uses not involving religious worship.

The religious exemption exempts property owned and used by a nonprofit religious organization for religious purposes (not just religious worship) and involves a simplified application and renewal procedure. This consolidated exemption specifically lists church property used for preschool, nursery school, kindergarten, elementary, and secondary school purposes as exempt religious purposes. Like the welfare exemption, the religious exemption does not exempt college-level institutions. As a result, under this exemption a church need file only a single form to obtain an exemption on property owned by the church and used for religious worship as well as property used for school purposes.

All religious corporations, whether or not they own and operate church schools, should call their local county tax assessor's office (exemption division) and determine if they are eligible to use the religious exemption and its simplified application and reporting requirements.

The religious exemption does not apply to particular uses such as hospitals, educational FM radio or television stations, and certain housing owned by churches. In these cases, use the welfare exemption.

California law also provides certain religious groups with another property tax exemption: the church exemption. Although religious-purpose groups usually use the religious exemption explained above, we briefly discuss this third exemption in case you don't qualify for the other exemptions and need to use this one instead.

The church exemption applies to personal and real property used exclusively by a church. This includes property owned or leased from another nonprofit or profit-making group. This is a broader exemption than the welfare exemption or religious exemption, because under this special religious exemption, it is strictly the use, and not the ownership of the property, that is determinative. As with the term religious, property used for church purposes has been liberally interpreted by the courts. Broadly speaking, the courts define property that qualifies for this separate exemption as "any property or facility that is reasonably necessary for the fulfillment of a generally recognized function of a complete, modern church" (see *Cedars of Lebanon Hospital v. County of Los Angeles*, 35 Cal.2d 729 (1950)). Consequently, church property includes not only property used directly for religious worship, but also property used for activities related to the function of churches, such as administrative and business meetings of the church governing body, religious instructional sessions, practice sessions of the choir, and most activities of auxiliary organizations accountable to the local church authority. For further information on the church exemption, call the local tax assessor's office or the main headquarters of the California State Board of Equalization in Sacramento.

Leasing and the Welfare Exemption

We have looked at some types of ownership, operation, and uses of property that will be considered religious, hospital, scientific, or charitable under the welfare exemption. The above discussion, for the most part, assumes that the group seeking the exemption both uses and owns the property. But what about leasing? How does a tax-exempt group that leases property benefit from the welfare exemption? What problems are encountered when the tax-exempt group is the landlord?

Even groups that do not qualify for the welfare exemption can obtain a property tax exemption on leased premises rented to government or charitable organizations and used for public libraries, museums, public schools, colleges, or educational purposes by nonprofit colleges or universities. (See Revenue & Taxation Code §§ 251 and 442.)

Your Nonprofit Is the Renter

Let's first consider the situation in which your group, qualified as tax-exempt under the welfare exemption, leases property from another person or group.

Your group will be exempt from paying any personal property taxes on property located on the premises, regardless of the status (exempt or nonexempt) of your landlord. Although you don't own and operate the real property as required by Section 214, your group does own and operate the *personal* property located on the premises. You will therefore be exempt from paying any personal property taxes that are levied on equipment, furniture, and other movable items located on the premises.

If your group is renting from another group that itself qualifies for and obtains the welfare exemption, then the exemption will apply to both the personal and real property taxes associated with the leased property. If you lease from a tax-exempt qualified lessor, you and the landlord should agree clearly in writing that the rent you pay will be lessened by an amount equal to the real property tax exemption for the leased premises for each year in which your group qualifies for the welfare exemption. This is a way of making sure that the benefits of the welfare exemption that apply to the leased premises will be passed on to you.

The only other way to obtain an exemption from payment of both personal and real property taxes on leased premises is for your group to fall within another exemption, other than the welfare exemption (see "Other California Tax Exemptions," below). Again, if this is true, the lease agreement should clearly state that a reduction or elimination of real property taxes on the owner's tax bill should be passed on to you for each year in which you qualify for the particular exemption.

Your Nonprofit Is the Landlord

Now let's look at the situation where your group qualifies for the welfare exemption and you lease property or portions of property to another organization. For example, if your group owns a building that is too large for your needs, it makes sense to lease out some of the extra space.

- If you lease the property to an organization that meets the welfare exemption requirements, the leased premises will continue to be exempt from real property taxes.

- If you lease to a group that meets the requirements of some other real property exemption provided under other provisions of California law, the leased premises will continue to be exempt from real property taxes.

- If you lease the property to a group that cannot meet any of the above three tests, you won't lose your entire exemption. However, your welfare exemption will apply only to the buildings or portions of buildings that you occupy or use. Your group will receive a real property tax bill for any portion of the facilities rented out to nonexempt tenants and, as the owner of the property, you'll have to pay these taxes. Of course, in this case, the owner organization will want to make sure that the lease agreement passes these taxes on to the nonexempt tenants in the form of rent.

Other California Tax Exemptions

Section 501(c)(3) nonprofits and other groups that do not qualify for the welfare exemption may be eligible for other tax exemptions under different provisions of California law. We've already touched on the separate college, religious, and church exemptions above. The following is a partial list of special property tax exemptions that can benefit nonprofit groups.

This is only a partial list and is subject to change—for current information on property tax exemptions that might apply to your nonprofit group, call your local county tax assessor's office or the main headquarters of the California State Board of Equalization in Sacramento.

Other Property Tax Exemptions		
Type of Owner or Property	Personal Property Exemption	Real Property Exemption
Cemeteries	X	X
Churches	X	X
Colleges	X	X
Exhibitions	X	X
Free museums	X	X
Religious organizations	X	X
Veterans' organizations	X	X
Works of art	X	

State Solicitation Laws and Requirements

Fundraising is a way of life for most nonprofit organizations because these organizations depend on contributions solicited from the general public, and public and private grants, for their operating funds. Most states, including California, regulate how a 501(c)(3) public charity can solicit contributions from the general public. State regulation of charitable solicitations is meant to serve two main purposes:

- to curb fundraising abuses by monitoring the people involved and their activities, and
- to give the public access to information on how much an organization spends to raise whatever ultimately goes into funding its charitable, educational, religious, or other nonprofit purpose.

The rules that apply to fundraising are beyond the scope of this book, but we recommend that you make learning about state charitable solicitation rules one of your top priorities after you incorporate. The U.S. Supreme Court has put the brakes on attempts by states to regulate what a nonprofit must disclose directly to potential contributors. However, California, like many other states, has enacted laws regulating disclosures by commercial fundraisers paid by a nonprofit. California also regulates the activities of consultants hired by nonprofits to help them raise funds. Both fundraisers and consultants are required to make periodic reports to the California Attorney General. California also imposes annual reporting requirements for any charity soliciting contributions or sales that collects more than 50% of its annual income and more than $1,000,000 in contributions from California donors during the calendar year, if the charity spent more than 25% of its annual income on nonprogram expenses. (See Business & Professions Code §§ 17510.9 and 17510.95 for the complete text.)

The best way to learn about the rules is to go to the California Attorney General's website at caag.state.ca.us/charities/publications/99char.pdf and view or download the latest California Attorney General's Office *Guide to Charitable*

Solicitation. It contains a thorough discussion of the various state operational and reporting requirements that apply to charitable solicitations by fundraisers in California. (The *Guide*, is also included on the CD-ROM.)

The California Nonprofit Integrity Act of 2004 imposes additional restrictions on the fundraising activities of charitable nonprofits. It primarily applies to nonprofit public benefit corporations (except schools and hospitals) and the commercial fundraisers (and lawyers) that they pay. Here is a partial summary of the Act:

- Commercial fundraisers hired by a charitable nonprofit must notify the attorney general before starting to work on a solicitation campaign, and they must have a written contract with the charitable organization. A charitable organization can cancel a contract with a fundraiser if the commercial fundraiser is not registered with the attorney general's Registry of Charitable Trusts.

- Fundraising contracts must contain other disclosures and provisions, including the charitable purpose of the solicitation campaign and the fees or percentages that will be paid to the fundraiser. The contract must require that all contributions the fundraiser receives either be deposited in a bank account controlled by the charitable organization or delivered in person to the charitable organization within five days. The charitable organization must have the right to cancel the contract without liability for ten days after the date it is signed. The organization must also have the right to cancel the contract for any reason at any time on 30 days notice to the fundraiser.

- The Act imposes numerous other obligations and restrictions on charitable organizations and their commercial fundraisers. These rules were designed to ensure that donations solicited from the public are used

for the stated purposes of each fundraising campaign and to protect the public from misrepresentations and fraudulent fundraising practices. For example, the new rules say that a charity may accept contributions only for a charitable purpose that is expressed in the solicitation for contributions and that conforms to the charitable purpose expressed in the articles of incorporation or other governing instrument of the charitable organization, and the nonprofit must apply any contributions only in a manner consistent with that purpose. To help ensure accountability under the Act, fundraisers are required to keep records of fundraising drives for at least ten years.

Here are some Internet resources you can use to learn more about the rules under the California Nonprofit Integrity Act of 2004:

- Go to the California Attorney General's website at http://ag.ca.gov/charities/ publications.php, select the links to the Nonprofit Integrity Act of 2004.

- To read the sections of California law amended or added by the Act, go to www. leginfo.ca.gov/calaw.html, select and read Government Code Sections 12581, 12582, 12583, 12584, 12585, 12586, 12599, 12599.1, 12599.3, 12599.6, and 12599.7, and Business and Professions Code Section 17510.5.

Regulation of charitable solicitation is an active and changing area of law. At the federal level, Congress has proposed putting multistate nonprofit fundraising activities under Federal Trade Commission (FTC) regulation, and thereby under federal court jurisdiction, while single-state fundraising would remain under state and local jurisdiction. You should do you best to keep your nonprofit network antennae tuned to developments in this area.

Choose a Name and File Your Articles of Incorporation

This chapter shows you how to form your California nonprofit corporation. To do this, you must first choose a name for your corporation; then you prepare and file articles of incorporation with the California Secretary of State. You'll see that it is a relatively simple and straightforward process and mostly involves filling in blanks on standard forms using information you already have at your fingertips. Take your time and relax; you'll be surprised at how easy it all is.

TIP

Forming your corporation will be the first step you take to obtain nonprofit status. Your corporation must be in existence when you apply for your state and federal tax exemptions. We recommend, however, that before you file your articles, you read through and prepare some of the other documents required later in the process, such as your bylaws and tax exemption applications. That way you'll know what is required to complete the process before you form your corporation. (See "Don't Rush to File," below).

All the forms you need to prepare and file your articles are on the CD-ROM or appendix included with this book. These forms include the name availability and name reservation forms, articles of incorporation for a public benefit or religious corporation, and a cover letter for filing your articles of incorporation. Instructions for using the CD-ROM are in Appendix A.

The secretary of state's business portal website also has forms, such as the name availability and name reservation form, that you can complete online, print, and mail in. (See www.ss.ca.gov/business/business.htm.) This website also has sample corporate documents, such as articles of incorporation and certificates of amendment to articles of incorporation. These sample corporate documents are intended for use as a guide only—they can't be completed online or copied and mailed in.

CAUTION

Check fees and addresses before you prepare or file your incorporation forms. Fees, procedures, and addresses often change. Current filing fees and the address for each secretary of state branch office are listed on the California Secretary of State's business portal website at www.ss.ca.gov/business/business.htm.

As you begin the process of forming your corporation, we suggest that you use the tear-out Incorporation Checklist in Appendix B (or, access the checklist file on the CD-ROM) to chart your way through the incorporation steps in Chapters 6 through 10. Look through the steps on the chart and check the box labeled "My Group" for each step that applies to you. When you complete each step, go back and mark the "Done" box. This will help you keep track of where you are and can greatly simplify the incorporation process for you.

Choose a Corporate Name

The first step in forming your corporation is to choose a name that you like and one that also meets the requirements of state law. The California Secretary of State will approve your corporate name when you file your articles of incorporation. As explained more below, you can check name availability and reserve a corporate name before you file your articles.

Keeping or Changing Your Name

If you are incorporating an existing organization, you may want to use your current name as your corporate name, particularly if it has become associated with your group, its activities, fundraising efforts, products, or services. Many new corporations do this by simply adding "Inc." to their old name (for example, The World Betterment Fund decides to incorporate as The World Betterment Fund, Inc.). Using your old name is not required, however. If you have been thinking about a new name for your organization, this is your chance to change it.

As a practical matter, your corporate name is one of your most important assets. It represents the goodwill of your organization. We don't use the term goodwill here in any legal, accounting, or tax sense; rather, your name is significant because people in the community, grant agencies, other nonprofits, and those with whom you do business will identify your nonprofit primarily by its name. For this reason, as well as to avoid having to print new stationery, change promotional literature, or create new logos, you should pick a name you'll be happy with for a long time.

There are certain legal requirements for corporate names in California. If you don't meet these requirements, the secretary of state will reject your corporate name (and will also reject your articles of incorporation).

Your Name Must Be Unique

Your proposed corporate name must not be the same as, or confusingly similar to, a corporate name already on file with the secretary of state. The list of corporate names maintained by the secretary of state includes:

- existing California corporations
- out-of-state corporations qualified to do business in California
- names registered with the secretary of state by out-of-state corporations, and
- names reserved for use by other corporations.

In deciding whether a corporate name is too similar to one already on file, the secretary of state's office will usually look only at similarities between the corporate names themselves, not at similarities in the types and locations of the corporations using the names. If you attempt to form a corporation with a name that is similar in sound or wording to the name of another corporation on the corporate name list, the secretary of state's office may reject your name and return your articles of incorporation to you. For example, suppose your proposed name is "Open Spaces." If another corporation is on file with the secretary of state with the name "Open Spaces International, Inc.," your name will probably be rejected as too similar.

The secretary of state does not compare proposed corporate names against the names of other types of legal entities on file with its office. For example, it does not check proposed corporate names against the names of limited liability companies (LLCs), limited partnerships, or registered limited liability partnerships (RLLPs). However, you should do your best to avoid names used by all other types of organizations and businesses, not just corporations. If your name is likely to mislead the public or create confusion because it is too similar to the name of an existing business, then you can be stopped from using that name, regardless of the types of business entities involved. For information on trademark and trade name law, see "Perform Your Own Name Search," below. For information on how to compare your proposed corporate name to corporate and LLC names already on file with the secretary of state, see "Check Existing Corporate Names Online," below.

You Can't Use Certain Terms

A California nonprofit corporation cannot use the words "bank," "trust," or "trustee" in its name. These financial institutions are regulated by special California laws and there are special regulations that govern their formation.

No Need to Use "Inc."

Unlike many other states, California does not require a corporate designator in corporate names, such as "Corporation," "Incorporated," "Limited," or an abbreviation of one of these words ("Corp.," "Inc.," or "Ltd."). For example, The Actors' Workshop and The Actors' Workshop, Inc., are both valid corporate names in California. Most incorporators, however, want to use one of these corporate designators precisely because they want others to know that their organization is incorporated.

Using Two Names and Changing Your Name

If you want to adopt a formal corporate name in your articles that's different than the one you have used (or plan to use) to identify your nonprofit organization, you can do so. You'll need to file a fictitious business name statement (also known as a "dba statement") with the local county clerk.

You can also change your corporate name after you've filed your articles. After making sure that the new name is available for use (as explained further below), you can amend your articles and file the amendment with the secretary of state.

> **CAUTION**
>
> **Having your name approved by the secretary of state when you file your articles of incorporation does not guarantee that you will have the absolute legal right to use it.** As explained in more detail in "Perform Your Own Name Search," below, another organization or business may already be using the name as its business name or may be using it as a trademark or service mark. If someone else is using the name, they may be able to prevent you from using it, depending on their location, type of business, and other circumstances. We show you how to do some checking on your own to be relatively sure that no one else has a prior claim to your proposed corporate name based on trademark or service mark.

Practical Suggestions for Selecting a Name

Now that we've looked at the basic legal requirements related to your choice of a corporate name, here are some practical suggestions to help you do it.

Use Common Nonprofit Terms in Your Name

There are a number of words that broadly suggest 501(c)(3) nonprofit purposes or activities. Choosing one of these names can simplify the task of finding the right name for your organization and will alert others to the nonprofit nature of your corporate activities. "Common Nonprofit Names," below, shows a few examples.

Names to Avoid

When selecting a corporate name, we suggest you avoid, or use with caution, the types of words described and listed below. Of course, there are exceptions. If one of these words relates to your particular nonprofit purposes or activities, it may make sense to use the word in your name.

Avoid words that, taken together, signify a profit-making business or venture, such as Booksellers Corporation, Jeff Baxter & Company, Commercial Products Inc., or Entrepreneurial Services Corp.

Avoid words that describe or are related to special types of nonprofit organizations (those that are tax exempt under provisions of the IRC other than Section 501(c)(3)), such as Business League, Chamber of Commerce, Civic League, Hobby, Recreational or Social Club, Labor, Agricultural or Horticultural Organization, Political Action Organization, Real Estate Board, and Trade Group.

 CROSS REFERENCE

For a listing of these special tax-exempt nonprofit groups and a brief description of each group, see "Special Nonprofit Tax-Exempt Organizations," in Appendix B.

EXAMPLE:

The name Westbrook Social Club, Inc., would clearly identify a social club, tax exempt under IRC § 501(c)(7)—for this reason, you shouldn't use this type of name for your 501(c)(3) nonprofit. However, The Social Consciousness Society might be an appropriate name for a 501(c)(3) educational-purpose organization. Also, although The Trade Betterment League of Pottersville would identify a 501(c)(6) business league and The Millbrae Civic Betterment League a 501(c)(4) civic league, The Philanthropic League of Castlemont might be a suitable name for a 501(c)(3) charitable giving group.

Common Nonprofit Names

Academy	House
Aid	Human
American	Humane
Appreciation	Institute
Assistance	International
Association	Learning
Benefit	Literary
Betterment	Mission
Care	Music
Center	Orchestra
Charitable	Organization
Coalition	Philanthropic
Community	Philharmonic
Congress	Program
Conservation	Project
Consortium	Protection
Council	Public
Cultural	Refuge
Education	Relief
Educational	Religious
Environmental	Research
Exchange	Resource
Fellowship	Scholarship
Foundation	Scientific
Friends	Service
Fund	Shelter
Health	Social
Help	Society
Heritage	Study
Home	Troupe
Hope	Voluntary
Hospice	Welfare
Hospital	

Avoid words or abbreviations associated with nationally known nonprofit causes, organizations, programs, or trademarks. You can bet that the well-known group has taken steps to protect its name as a trademark or service mark. Steer clear of the names in "These Names Are Already Taken," below.

These Names Are Already Taken

Here is a small sampling of some well-known —and off-limits—nonprofit names and abbreviations:

AAA

American Red Cross

American Ballet Theatre or ABT

American Conservatory Theatre or ACT

Audubon

Blue Cross

Blue Shield

Environmental Defense Fund

National Geographic

National Public Radio or NPR

Sierra Club

Public Broadcasting System or PBS

Avoid words with special symbols or punctuation that might confuse the secretary of state's computer name-search software, such as: @ # $ % ^ & * () + ? and > or <.

Pick a Descriptive Name

It's often a good idea to pick a name that clearly reflects your purposes or activities (for example, Downtown Ballet Theater, Inc.; Good Health Society, Ltd.; Endangered Fish Protection League, Inc.). Doing this allows potential members, donors, beneficiaries, and others to easily locate and identify you. More fanciful names (The Wave Project, Inc., Serendipity Unlimited Inc.) are usually less advisable because it might take a while for people to figure out what they stand for, although occasionally their uniqueness can provide better identification over the long term.

EXAMPLE:

Although the name Northern California Feline Shelter, Inc., will alert people at the start to the charitable purposes of the nonprofit group, Cats' Cradle, Inc., may stay with people longer once they are familiar with the activities of the organization.

Limit Your Name Geographically or Regionally

If you use general or descriptive terms in your name, you may need to further qualify it by geographic or regional descriptions to avoid conflicts or public confusion.

EXAMPLE 1:

Your proposed name is The Philharmonic Society, Inc. Your secretary of state rejects this name as too close to a number of philharmonic orchestras on file. You refile using the proposed name, The Philharmonic Society of East Creek, and your name is accepted.

EXAMPLE 2:

Suppose you are incorporating the AIDS Support Group, Inc. Even if this name does not conflict with the name of another corporation on file in your state, it is still a good idea to limit or qualify the name to avoid confusion by the public with other groups in other parts of the country that share the same purposes or goals. You could do this by changing the name to the AIDS Support Group of Middleville.

Choose a New Name Instead of Trying to Distinguish Yourself

Instead of trying to distinguish your proposed name from another established group by using a regional or other identifier, it's usually better to choose a new and different name if the public is still likely to confuse your group with the other group.

EXAMPLE:

Your proposed nonprofit name is The Park School, Inc. If another corporation (specializing in a nationwide network of apprentice training colleges) is already listed with the name Park Training Schools, your secretary of state may reject your name as too similar.

You may be able to limit your name and make it acceptable (The Park Street School of Westmont, Inc.) but this may not be a good idea for two reasons: First, members of the public who have heard of the Park Training Schools might think that your school is simply a Westmont affiliate of the national training program. Second, you might still be infringing the trademark rights of the national group (they may have registered their name as a state or federal trademark).

Use a Corporate Designator in Your Name

Even though not legally required in California, you might want to include a corporate designator in your name to let others know that your organization is a corporation. Here are some examples: Hopi Archaeological Society, Inc., The Children's Museum Corporation, Mercy Hospital, Incorporated, and The Hadley School Corp.

Take Your Time

Finding an appropriate and available name for your corporation will take time and patience. It's usually best not to act on your first impulse—try a few names before making your final choice. Ask others both inside and outside the organization for feedback. And remember: Your proposed name might not be available for your use—have one or more alternate names in reserve in case your first choice isn't available.

Check Name Availability

The secretary of state will reject your articles of incorporation if the name you've chosen for your corporation is not available. Any name already being used by another corporation on file with the secretary of state's office is considered unavailable. To avoid having your articles rejected, it's often wise to check if the name you want is available before you try to file your articles.

Check Your Proposed Name by Mail

You can request a corporate name check by sending a Name Availability Inquiry Letter to the secretary of state's office in Sacramento. You can check up to three corporate names per request and there is no filing fee. The secretary will respond to your written request within one to two weeks.

The Name Availability Inquiry Letter is available online at the secretary of state's business portal website at www.ss.ca.gov/business/corp/corp_naav2.htm. You can fill out the form online, print it, and mail it to the secretary of state. A blank tear-out copy of the Inquiry Letter is also included in Appendix B and on the CD-ROM in PDF format included at the back of this book.

CAUTION

Checking the availability of a name doesn't reserve the name or give you any rights to the name. Even if the secretary of state indicates by return mail that a corporate name is available, it may not be available when you file your articles. To avoid this problem and to save time, you can check and reserve a name for a small fee as explained in the next section.

Check Existing Corporate Names Online

You can check the names of existing corporations registered with the secretary of state online at the secretary of state's business portal website at www.ss.ca.gov/business/business. htm. Click the California Business Search link, then enter your proposed name in the corporate records search box. You will see the existing corporate names on file that contain the word or words you typed in the search box. We also recommend you check your corporate name against any registered LLC (limited liability company) names by entering your proposed name in the LLC search box as well. Even though the secretary of state may let you use a corporate name that conflicts with an LLC name, we advise against doing this. To avoid legal disputes, it's best to stay clear of any business name (whether a corporate, LLC, or unincorporated business name) that is the same as or similar to your proposed corporate name. The fact that an LLC name has a different ending than your corporate name (for example, "Racafrax, LLC" and you want to use "Racafrax" as your corporate name) does not mean you will be allowed to use your proposed name. If the names are substantially similar, a court may stop you from using your proposed name, even if you use it for a corporation and the competing business name is used by an LLC.

If your proposed corporate name is not the same as or similar to an existing name listed online, you may decide it's safe to go ahead and file your articles without formally checking name availability or reserving your name with the secretary of state. If you discover a match to your proposed name, and the corporation is still active (the name search tells you whether the corporation is active or not), you need to look for another name. If you discover a similar corporate name, the secretary of state may find that it is too similar to your proposed name to let you use it. The only way to tell whether the secretary of state will allow you to use a name that is similar to an existing corporate name is to do a formal name availability check or try to reserve the name. If the secretary of state reports that the name is not available or won't reserve it for your use, you know the name was too similar to the existing corporation's name.

What to Do When There's a Name Conflict

If using your proposed name is crucial to you and the secretary of state's office tells you that it is too similar to an existing corporate name already on file, there are a few things you can do.

Appeal the Decision

You can ask the secretary of state's legal counsel to review the staff's determination regarding your name's acceptability. This will involve filing a written request, and you may decide to seek the help of a lawyer. Here's why: The legal question of whether or not a name is so close to another name so as to cause confusion to the public is a difficult one, and involves looking at a number of criteria contained in court decisions. Factors such as the nature of each trade name user's business (the term "trade name" simply means a name used in conjunction with the operation of a trade or business), the geographical proximity of the two businesses, and other factors work together in ways that are difficult to predict. We cover trade name issues in more detail below but, for now, we simply note that if you do get into this sort of debate, you will probably want to see a lawyer who is versed in the complexities of trade name or trademark law or do some additional reading on your own.

Get Permission

An obvious resolution would be to obtain the written consent of the other corporation. Some-times, profit corporations that have registered a name similar to the proposed name of a non-profit corporation will be willing to allow the nonprofit corporation to use the similar name. We think this is too much trouble. Besides, most businesses jealously guard their name, and it is unlikely any business or organization will let you ride on the coattails of their existing name. If you are told your proposed corporate name is too similar to another name, we recom-mend you move on and choose another name that is available for your use.

Pick Another Name

You may decide that it's simpler (and less trouble all the way around) to pick another name for your nonprofit corporation. We usually recommend this approach.

> **CAUTION**
>
> **A name check gives you only a prelimi-nary indication whether your proposed corporate name is available.** Don't order your stationery, business cards, or office signs until the secretary of state has formally accepted your name by approving your Name Reservation Request or filing your articles of incorporation.

Reserve Your Corporate Name

For a small fee, you can reserve an available corporate name with the secretary of state. It makes sense to reserve a name if you will not be filing your articles immediately—available corporate names are hard to find, and reserving a name allows you to hold on to the name while you complete your initial paperwork for incorporation.

To reserve a name, you can prepare and file a Name Reservation Request Form with the secretary of state. When filling in the form, you can list up to three names in order of preference. The first available name will be reserved for your use. If a name is accepted, only the person who filled in the Name Reservation form can file articles with the reserved name or a similar name during the 60-day reservation period.

The Name Reservation Request Form is avail-able online at the secretary of state's business portal website at www.ss.ca.gov/business/corp/pdf/naavreservform.pdf. You can fill out the form online, print it, and mail it to the secretary of state. There is a $10 filing fee. A blank, tear-out copy of the form is also included in Appendix B and on the CD-ROM.

You can also reserve a corporate name in person at any of the secretary of state's regional offices. The addresses and telephone numbers of these offices are listed at the beginning of Appendix B. The fee for reserving a name in person is $20. The clerk will ask for two $10 checks. If your proposed name is not available, the clerk will keep $10 and return one $10 check to you.

If your proposed name is accepted, the secretary of state will send you a certificate of reservation that is valid for 60 days from the date it is issued. If you cannot file your articles within that time, you can rereserve the name by preparing a new reservation letter. The secretary of state must receive the second reservation letter at least one day after the first certificate expires. You are not allowed two consecutive reservations of corporate name—therefore the requests must be separated by at least one day.

> **CAUTION**
>
> **Reservation fees are subject to change.** To be sure the fee amounts are correct, call the secretary of state at 916-657-5448, or check current fee information at the secretary of state's website at www.ss.ca.gov/business/corp/corp_formsfees.htm.

> **CAUTION**
>
> **The person whose name is on the reservation form must sign the articles of incorporation.** Make sure that the person submitting the reservation form (whose name is inserted in the top box of the form) will be available to sign articles of incorporation on behalf of your organization. The corporate name is reserved for this person's use only.

Perform Your Own Name Search

Approval by the secretary of state's office of your corporate name doesn't necessarily mean that you have the legal right to use this name. Acceptance of your corporate name by the secretary of state's office simply means that your name does not conflict with that of another corporation already on file with the secretary of state. The secretary of state does not, however, check the state trademark/service mark registration lists maintained in the secretary of state's office, nor does it check your corporate name against the names of noncorporate

entities on file with the office—such as LLCs, limited partnerships, and registered limited liability partnerships (RLLPs). Thus, another organization (corporate or noncorporate, profit, or nonprofit) may already have the right to use this same name (or one similar to it) as a federal or state trademark or service mark used to identify their goods or services. Also, another organization (corporate or noncorporate) may already be presumed to have the legal right to use the name in a particular county if they are using it as trade name (as the name of their business or organization) and have filed a fictitious business name statement with their county clerk.

The secretary of state will send you a letter after you file your articles, repeating everything we've just said. The secretary puts it a bit more legalistically, warning you that filing articles of incorporation does not, in itself, authorize the use a corporate name if that use would violate another person's right to use the name, including rights in a trade name, rights under state or federal trademark laws, or state fictitious business name laws, and rights that arise under principles of common law (the law expressed in court decisions). You're probably wondering—If someone is using my proposed name already, does that mean that I can't use the name either? And how can I discover whether someone is using the name in the first place? The sections below will give you some guidance.

Who Should Perform This Search?

In many circumstances, you will know that your name is unique and unlikely to infringe on another organization's name. This would probably be the case, for example, if you called your group the Sumner County Crisis Hotline, or the Southern California Medieval Music Society. By qualifying your name this way, you know that you are the only nonprofit in your area using the name. However, in some circumstances you may be less sure of your right to use a name. For example, the names Legal Rights for All or The Society to Cure Lyme Disease may be in use by a group in any part of the country. Read on.

Who Gets to Use a Name?

The basic rule is that the ultimate right to use a particular name will usually be decided based on who was first in time to actually use the name in connection with a particular trade, business, activity, service, or product. In deciding who has the right to a name, the similarity of the types of businesses or organizations and their geographical proximity are usually taken into account.

Finding Users of Your Name

Below we list self-help name checking procedures you may want to use to be more certain that your proposed corporate name is unique. Do these name search procedures before you file your articles. Obviously, you can't be 100% certain—you can't possibly check all names in use by all other groups. However, you can check obvious sources likely to expose names similar to the one you wish to use. Here are some places to start.

Fictitious Business Name Files

Check the county clerk in the county or counties where you plan to operate to see if your name has already been registered by another person, organization, or business as a fictitious business name. Most county clerks will require you to come in and check the fictitious business files yourself—it takes just a few minutes to do this.

State Trademarks and Service Marks

Call the California Secretary of State's trademark and service mark registration section (the phone number is 916-653-4984) and ask if your proposed corporate name is the same as or similar to trademarks and service marks registered with the state. They will check up to two names against their list of registered marks over the phone at no charge. The trademark and service mark section's Web page is located at www.ss.ca.gov/business/ts/ts.htm. At the time of this edition, marks could not be searched online.

Check Directories

Check major metropolitan phone book listings, nonprofit directories, business and trade directories, and so on to see if another company or group is using a name similar to your proposed corporate name. Large public libraries keep phone directories for many major cities throughout the country, as well as trade and nonprofit directories. A local nonprofit resource center or business branch of a public library may have a special collection of nonprofit research materials—check these first for listings of local and national nonprofits. One commonly consulted national directory of nonprofit names is the *Encyclopedia of Associations* published by Gale Research Company.

Consult the Federal Trademark Register

If your name is the type that might be used to market a service or product or to identify a business activity of your nonprofit corporation, you should check federal trademarks and service marks. You can check the *Federal Trademark Register* for free at www.uspto.gov. You can also go to a large public library or special business and government library in your area that carries the *Federal Trademark Register*, which lists trademark and service mark names broken into categories of goods and services.

Use Other Internet Databases

Most of the business name listings mentioned above, including Yellow Page listings and business directory databases and the federal and state trademark registers, are available as part of several commercial computer databases. For example, the federal and state registers can be accessed through the TRADEMARKSCAN databases using SAEGIS, Dialog, or Westlaw online services. (Use your browser's search engine to find links to these services.) Subscription databases charge fees for your research time (unlike the www.uspto.gov site which is free).

Further Searching

Of course, if you wish to go further in your name search, you can pay a private records search company to check various databases and name listings. Alternatively, or in conjunction with your own efforts or search procedures, you can pay a trademark lawyer to oversee or undertake these searches for you (or to render a legal opinion if your search turns up a similar name). Most organizers of smaller nonprofits, particularly those who believe that a specialized or locally based name is not likely to conflict with anyone else's name, will not feel the need to do this and will be content to undertake the more modest self-help search procedures mentioned above.

The Consequences of Using Another's Name

To avoid problems, we suggest using the name selection techniques discussed above, and performing the kind of commonsense checking described earlier. Disputes involving trade names, trademarks, and service marks tend to arise in the private, commercial sector. It is unlikely that your nonprofit will wish to market products and services as aggressively as a regular commercial concern and thereby run afoul of another business's trademark or service mark (you'd also be jeopardizing your tax-exempt status by engaging in a substantial amount of commercial activity). Nonetheless, as a matter of common sense, and to avoid legal disputes later on, you should do your best to avoid names already in use by other profit and nonprofit organizations, or in use as trademarks or service marks.

If You Use Another Company's Trade Name or Trademark

Legal remedies for violation of trade name or trademark rights vary under federal and state laws and court decisions. Most of the time, the business with the prior claim to the name can sue to enjoin (stop) you from using your name or can force you to change it. The court may also award the prior owner money damages for loss of sales or goodwill caused by your use of the name. If you violate a trademark or service mark registered with the U.S. Patent and Trademark Office, the court may award treble damages (three times the actual money damages suffered as a result of the infringement), any profits you make from using the name, and court costs; and may order that the goods with the offending labels or marks to be confiscated and destroyed.

Here's an example of how this works. A company called Foul Weather Gearheads has been in business for ten years selling foul weather gear such as rain slicks and hip boots via catalogues and the Internet. For the first seven to eight years, Foul Weather averaged gross annual sales of approximately $2 million. Another company, calling itself Rainy Day Gearheads, starts selling competing products and Foul Weather's gross revenues slip by about 25% over the next two years. If Foul Weather can prove that the Rainy Day Gearheads trademark likely caused customer confusion which resulted in Foul Weather's decrease in sales, Foul Weather can recover its lost profits. Or, if prior to the infringement, Foul Weather had registered its name on the Principal Trademark Register maintained by the U.S. Patent and Trademark Office, it could choose to go after Rainy Day's profits (instead of recovering its own losses), attorneys' fees, and treble damages.

For further information see *Patent, Copyright & Trademark—An Intellectual Property Law Desk Reference*, by Stephen Elias and Rich Stim (Nolo).

Protect Your Name

Once you have filed your articles of incorporation, you may want to take some additional steps to protect your name against later users. For example, if your name is also used to identify your products or services, you may wish to register it with the California Secretary of State and the United States Patent and Trademark Office as a trademark or service mark. You may also want to register in other states if you plan to conduct operations there.

Federal registration costs $200. You can register your name if:

- you have actually used the name in interstate commerce (that is, in two or more states) in connection with the marketing of goods or services, or

- you intend to use the name in interstate commerce in connection with the marketing of goods or services.

If you specify the second ground in your trademark application, you must file an affidavit (sworn statement) within six months stating that the name has been placed in actual use—and pay an additional $100. This six-month period may be extended for additional six-month periods (at a fee of $100 for each extension), up to a total extension of two and one-half years. To obtain these extensions, you have to convince the Patent and Trademark Office that you have good cause for delaying your use of the name. Because trademark application procedures are relatively simple and inexpensive, you may wish to tackle this task yourself—your local county law library should have practice guides available to help you handle state and federal trademark and service mark filing formalities.

Applying for a Federal Trademark

To apply for a federal trademark, go to the website of the Patent and Trademark Office (PTO) at www.uspto.gov and download a trademark application. Fill out the form following the instructions. A month or so after mailing the form, you should hear from the PTO. If there are any problems, you will receive a written list of questions together with the telephone number of a trademark examiner. The examiner should be able to address any questions and issues you can't handle yourself and should help you finalize your application without undue difficulty or delay.

Prepare Articles of Incorporation

The next step in organizing your corporation is to prepare articles of incorporation. This is your primary incorporation document—your corporation becomes a legal entity on the date you file your articles with the secretary of state. You must complete this step before you send in your state and federal tax exemption applications, because both the state and the IRS require you to submit a filed copy of your articles with your tax exemption application.

TIP

Prepare your bylaws and look over the tax application early in the process. Even though you have to file your articles before you send in your state and federal tax exemption applications, we recommend that you prepare bylaws and review or complete some of the work on the tax applications before you file your articles. That way, you'll know what else is required to obtain nonprofit status and you won't be surprised late in the process (after you've already incorporated) about a condition or other requirement you can't or don't want to meet. See the discussion in "Don't Rush to File," below.

There are two types of articles included on the CD-ROM: one for California public benefit corporations and one for California religious corporations. If you are incorporating an existing nonprofit organization that was organized and operated as an unincorporated association (with formal articles of association, a charter or association bylaws), you will need to add some special provisions to the standard articles shown below. Most preexisting nonprofit organizations are not unincorporated associations and will not need to concern themselves with these provisions.

Rules for Preparing and Printing Your Documents

When preparing and printing articles of incorporation for any type of corporation (public benefit or religious), printouts should be legible with sufficient contrast for photocopying. If you are printing on a dot matrix printer and have the capability, you should set it for "Correspondence," "Near-Letter-Quality," or a similar high-resolution mode. Using paper with a good weight and fiber content also improves legibility. For example, use 20 lb. 25% cotton paper (available in most stationery stores) instead of regular bond paper if your printer can accept it.

> **CAUTION**
>
> **Most nonprofits will find our articles sufficient, and won't need to alter them.** If you want to modify the articles, do so only after making sure your changes conform to the California Nonprofit Corporation Law. (See Chapter 12 for suggestions on doing your own research or finding a lawyer to help you make modifications.)

Preparing Articles for a Public Benefit Corporation

To prepare articles for a public benefit corporation, open and fill in the Articles of Incorporation for California Public Benefit Corporations included on the CD-ROM, following the sample form and special instructions below.

Here are some general instructions to help you prepare your articles:

- The parenthetical blanks, "(_____)," in the sample form indicate information that you must complete on the CD-ROM.
- Corresponding blanks in the computer form are marked with a series of underlined characters.
- Replace the blanks in the computer form (each series of underlined characters) with the information indicated in the sample form below.
- Each circled number in the sample form (for example, ❶) refers to a special instruction that provides specific information to help you complete an item.

Articles of Incorporation
of
_____Name of Corporation_____ ❶

a California Public Benefit Corporation

ONE: The name of this corporation is ___(name of corporation)___.❶

TWO: This corporation is a nonprofit public benefit corporation and is not organized for the private gain of any person. It is organized under the Nonprofit Public Benefit Corporation Law for charitable ❷ purposes. The specific purposes for which this corporation is organized are ___(include statement of specific purposes in one or two short sentences here)___
_____.❸

THREE: The name and address in the State of California of this corporation's initial agent for service of process is ___(indicate name and address of the corporation's agent for service of process)___.❹

FOUR: (a) This corporation is organized and operated exclusively for ___(indicate your 501(c)(3) tax-exempt purpose or purposes; e.g., "charitable," "educational," "scientific," "literary")___ ❺ purposes within the meaning of Section 501(c)(3) of the Internal Revenue Code.

(b) Notwithstanding any other provision of these articles, the corporation shall not carry on any other activities not permitted to be carried on (1) by a corporation exempt from federal income tax under Section 501(c)(3) of the Internal Revenue Code or (2) by a corporation contributions to which are deductible under Section 170(c)(2) of the Internal Revenue Code.

(c) No substantial part of the activities of this corporation shall consist of carrying on propaganda, or otherwise attempting to influence legislation, and the corporation shall not participate or intervene in any political campaign (including the publishing or distribution of statements) on behalf of, or in opposition to, any candidate for public office.

FIVE: The names and addresses of the persons appointed to act as the initial Directors of this corporation are:

Name   Address
(show name and business or residence address of initial director(s) on lines below) ❻

_____   _____
_____   _____
_____   _____
_____   _____
_____   _____

SIX: The property of this corporation is irrevocably dedicated to __**(allowable dedication purpose or purposes—see instruction)**__ ❼ and no part of the net income or assets of the organization shall ever inure to the benefit of any director, officer, or member thereof or to the benefit of any private person.

On the dissolution or winding up of the corporation, its assets remaining after payment of, or provision for payment of, all debts and liabilities of this corporation, shall be distributed to a nonprofit fund, foundation, or corporation which is organized and operated exclusively for __**(allowable dedication purpose or purposes—see instruction)**__ ❼ and which has established its tax-exempt status under Section 501(c)(3) of the Internal Revenue Code.

Date: _____

__**(signatures of director(s) listed in Article FIVE)**__ ❽
(typed name) _____ , Director

_____ , Director

_____ , Director

_____ , Director

_____ , Director

We, the above-mentioned initial directors of this corporation, hereby declare that we are the persons who executed the foregoing articles of incorporation, which instrument is our act and deed.

__**(signatures of director(s) listed in Article FIVE)**__ ❽
(typed name) _____ , Director

_____ , Director

_____ , Director

_____ , Director

_____ , Director

Special Instructions for Public Benefit Corporations

The following numbered instructions correspond to circled numbers on the sample articles.

❶ Type the name of your corporation in the heading and in Article One. If you have reserved a corporate name, make sure the name shown here is exactly the same as the name shown on your Certificate of Reservation.

❷ Article Two states that your corporation is organized under the Nonprofit Public Benefit Corporation Law for charitable purposes. This statement is simply meant to satisfy the requirements of the California Corporations Code, not the 501(c)(3) tax-exempt purposes. Remember: public benefit corporations must be organized under state law for a charitable or public purpose, and the accepted practice for nonreligious 501(c)(3) public benefit groups—the type of group you are incorporating—is to indicate a charitable (as opposed to public) purpose in this sentence.

❸ Type a short statement of your group's specific purposes in the blanks at the end of Article Two. It's important to be brief—to satisfy state law requirements, all you need is one or two short sentences. You will provide much more detail on your nonprofit purposes and activities in your tax exemption applications. See "Examples of Specific Purpose Statements," below, for some ideas on what to write. Your statement will begin by completing the last sentence of Article Two: "The specific purposes for which this corporation is organized are…." Keep the following in mind when completing this short statement of purposes:

- Your statement should make clear that you fall within one or more of the nonreligious 501(c)(3) tax exemption categories (charitable, educational, scientific, or literary). Make sure you use the key words associated with one or more of these categories (for example, "charitable" or "educational"). If necessary, describe the kinds of activities you pursue in any one or more of these categories with language the IRS can clearly identify with one of the tax-exempt purposes.

- Remember, although you may qualify as tax-exempt under one or more categories of Section 501(c)(3) (for example, a charitable and educational organization), you cannot *also* fall within another tax-exempt section of the Internal Revenue Code (for example, you can't be both a charitable group under 501(c)(3) *and* a social welfare group under Section 501(c)(4)). Be careful to avoid using key words associated with these other tax-exempt sections—such as social, fraternal, or recreational.

EXAMPLE:

An educational and social welfare organization would not be eligible for a 501(c)(3) tax exemption because social welfare groups are exempt under the provisions of a different Internal Revenue Code section.

❹ Type the name and residence or business address of the corporation's initial agent for service of process—this is the person to whom legal documents in any future lawsuit against the corporation must be sent. Normally, you'll use the name of one of the initial directors (see special instruction ❻) and give the address of the corporation. You cannot use a post office box number in this address.

❺ Indicate your 501(c)(3) tax-exempt purpose or purposes in this blank: type the word "charitable," "educational," "scientific," "literary," or a combination of these words ("charitable and educational").

Examples of Specific Purpose Statements

The purposes and activities of each nonprofit group differ, which means there's no simple, custom-tailored clause that works for everyone. The following examples are illustrations that will not necessarily apply to your group. Look at the examples to get a feel for the kind of information you should provide in your statement. Then, refer back to the 501(c)(3) tax-exempt purpose categories discussed in Chapter 3. Write a few sentences describing your specific purposes, then reduce these sentences to one or two short sentences that summarize your tax-exempt purposes.

Educational: Publishing and Lectures. This sample clause is for a group that wants to publish books and give public lectures:

> The specific purposes for which this corporation is organized are to develop an institution to teach and disseminate educational material to the public, including, but not limited to, material relating to _[the areas of instruction are mentioned here]_, through publications, lectures, or otherwise.

> The group's purpose is clearly stated as educational in nature. There is, however, no need to mention any institutional attributes such as a full-time faculty, standard curriculum, or regularly enrolled student body.

Educational: Dance Group. This sample clause is for a group that wants to set up studios where it can teach dance and hold dance performances.

> The specific and primary purposes for which this corporation is organized are to educate the general public in dance and other art forms. The means of providing such education includes, but is not limited to, maintaining facilities for instruction and public performances of dance and other art forms.

The term education is clearly stated and the general public is specified as the recipient of these tax-exempt services. The group's statement is broad enough to allow it to expand to other art forms in the future and still be within its purpose clause. That way, any future revenue from other types of educational activities (music or art, for example), would still be considered related to the group's stated purpose and, therefore, tax-exempt.

Charitable and Educational: Housing Improvement. This sample clause is for a group that plans to get grants and tax exemptions to improve housing conditions for low- and moderate-income people by organizing a housing information and research exchange.

> The specific purposes for which this corporation is organized are to provide education and charitable assistance to the general public by organizing a housing information and research exchange.

> The purpose statement simply restates the group's mission (to organize a housing information and research exchange), and characterizes the purpose as charitable and educational and for the general public.

Charitable: Medical Clinic. This sample clause is for a community health care clinic for low-income people.

> The specific purposes for which this corporation is organized are to establish and maintain a comprehensive system of family-oriented health care aimed primarily at the medically underserved areas of _[city and county]_.

❻ Indicate the names and addresses of the initial directors of the corporation. You can organize a public benefit corporation with just one director, but will probably want to provide for more. You can give the business address (usually the address of the corporation) or the residence address of each initial director. Remember, public benefit corporations must have at least two unpaid directors for each paid director, and the two unpaid directors must be unrelated to the one paid director (see "Directors" in Chapter 2).

❼ Article Six contains a clause that irrevocably dedicates the property of the corporation to specific tax-exempt purposes. This dedication clause satisfies federal and state tax-exemption requirements and allows qualifying nonprofit groups to obtain personal and real property tax exemptions under California's welfare exemption.

There are two blanks to be completed in Article Six. In each blank, state the same purposes—ones that meet both the requirements of 501(c)(3) of the Internal Revenue Code and the California welfare exemption. Because the allowable purposes of these sections are different, you must choose purposes that are allowed by both sections —namely, charitable, religious, educational, or scientific.

Most public benefit corporations choose charitable, educational, or scientific purpose, or some combination of these, and not religious purpose. You can choose purposes that are different from the tax-exempt purposes of your group, or you can indicate purposes that are the same as your 501(c)(3) tax-exempt purposes (see special instruction ❺, above). Many groups choose "charitable purposes." To do this, you simply fill in both blanks with those exact words: "charitable purposes." If you choose educational or scientific, you must also specifically include that it meets the requirements of Section 214 of the California Revenue and Taxation Code.

After you have decided which purposes you want, fill in both blanks with one of the following phrases (both blanks should say the same thing):

- charitable purposes
- educational purposes meeting the requirements of Section 214 of the California Revenue and Taxation Code, or
- scientific purposes meeting the requirements of Section 214 of the California Revenue and Taxation Code.

The word "purposes" is not included in the computer form. Be sure to include this word in each response.

❽ There are two sets of signature lines at the end of the articles—each director (each person named in Article Five as an initial director) signs this form twice—once in each set of signature lines. First, type each director's name under the signature lines in both sections. Then, after printing the form, date the articles and have each director sign both signature lines above his or her name. Remember to print this form on letter-sized paper, using one side of a page only.

Preparing Articles for a Religious Corporation

To prepare articles for your religious corporation, fill in the Articles of Incorporation for California Religious Corporations included on the CD-ROM, following the sample form and special instructions below. This form contains fewer blanks than the public benefit form because the term "religious purposes" has already been inserted where appropriate.

Here are some general instructions to help you prepare your articles:

- The parenthetical blanks that look like this "(_____)" in the sample form indicate information that you must complete on the CD-ROM.
- Corresponding blanks in the computer form are marked with a series of underlined characters.
- Replace the blanks in the computer form (each series of underlined characters) with the information indicated in the sample form below.

Each circled number in the sample form (for instance, ❶) refers to an instruction that will help you complete an item.

Special Instructions for Religious Corporations

The following numbered instructions correspond to a circled number on the sample articles:

❶ Type the name of your corporation in the heading and in Article One. If you have reserved a corporate name, make sure the name shown here is exactly the same as the name shown on your Certificate of Reservation.

❷ Read special instruction ❸ for the Articles of Public Benefit Corporation, above, to get a general idea of what this specific purpose statement is meant to accomplish and how it should be written. Complete the sentence at the end of Article Two using one or two short sentences.

For example, a religious corporation that plans to establish a formal church might simply state its specific purposes this way: "The specific purposes for which this corporation is organized are to establish and maintain a church for religious worship." A less formal religious purpose nonprofit might describe its religious purposes as follows: "The specific purposes for which this corporation is organized are to disseminate information on and establish a community for the practice of the faith of [name of belief system]."

❸ Type the name and residence or business address of the corporation's initial agent for service of process—this is the person to whom legal documents in any future lawsuit against the corporation must be sent. Normally, you'll list the name of one of the initial directors (see special instruction ❹) along with the address of the corporation. You cannot use a post office box number in this address.

❹ Type the names and addresses of the initial directors of the corporation. You can organize a religious corporation with just one director. However, most religious groups will name three or more directors. You can give the business address—usually the address of the corporation—or the residence address of each initial director.

❺ Note that there are two sets of signature lines at the end of the articles—each director (each person named in Article Five as an initial director) signs this form twice—once in each set of signature lines. First, type each director's name under the signature lines in both sections. Then, after printing the form, date the articles and have each director sign both signature lines above his or her name. Remember to print this form on letter-sized paper, using one side of a page only.

Articles of Incorporation
of
<u>   **Name of Corporation**   </u> ❶

a California Religious Corporation

ONE: The name of this corporation is <u>   (name of corporation) </u>. ❶

TWO: This corporation is a religious corporation and is not organized for the private gain of any person. It is organized under the Nonprofit Religious Corporation Law exclusively for religious purposes. The specific purposes for which this corporation is organized are <u> **(include statement of specific purposes in one or two short sentences here)** </u> <u> </u>.❷

THREE: The name and address in the State of California of this corporation's initial agent for service of process is <u> **(indicate name and address of the corporation's agent for service of process)** </u>. ❸

FOUR: (a) This corporation is organized and operated exclusively for religious purposes within the meaning of Section 501(c)(3) of the Internal Revenue Code.

(b) Notwithstanding any other provision of these articles, the corporation shall not carry on any other activities not permitted to be carried on (1) by a corporation exempt from federal income tax under Section 501(c)(3) of the Internal Revenue Code or (2) by a corporation contributions to which are deductible under Section 170(c)(2) of the Internal Revenue Code.

(c) No substantial part of the activities of this corporation shall consist of carrying on propaganda, or otherwise attempting to influence legislation, and the corporation shall not participate or intervene in any political campaign (including the publishing or distribution of statements) on behalf of, or in opposition to, any candidate for public office.

FIVE: The names and addresses of the persons appointed to act as the initial directors of this corporation are:

Name   Address

(show name and business or residence address of initial director(s) on lines below) ❹

_____   _____

_____   _____

_____   _____

_____   _____

_____   _____

SIX: The property of this corporation is irrevocably dedicated to religious purposes and no part of the net income or assets of the organization shall ever inure to the benefit of any director, officer, or member thereof or to the benefit of any private person.

On the dissolution or winding up of the corporation, its assets remaining after payment of, or provision for payment of, all debts and liabilities of this corporation, shall be distributed to a nonprofit fund, foundation, or corporation which is organized and operated exclusively for religious purposes and which has established its tax-exempt status under Section 501(c)(3) of the Internal Revenue Code.

Date: _____

(signatures of director(s) listed in Article FIVE) ❺

(typed name) _____ , Director

_____ , Director

_____ , Director

_____ , Director

_____ , Director

We, the above-mentioned initial directors of this corporation, hereby declare that we are the persons who executed the foregoing articles of incorporation, which instrument is our act and deed.

(signatures of director(s) listed in Article FIVE) ❺

(typed name) _____ , Director

_____ , Director

_____ , Director

_____ , Director

_____ , Director

Preparing Articles for an Unincorporated Association

This section is for unincorporated associations that want to incorporate. An unincorporated association is a group of people who operate a collective organization according to a formal set of rules (such as articles of association, a charter, or bylaws) and under the supervision of a governing board (usually directors, officers, or similar officials). A typical example is an unincorporated church organized and operated under a formal church charter and governed by a board of directors or elders. Most existing nonprofit organizations are not organized as unincorporated associations and do not need to read this section.

If you are incorporating a formal unincorporated association of the type described above, start by preparing articles for a public benefit or religious corporation as explained above. Then, you need to make a few changes to the standard form as described below.

TIP

You can type your articles manually or you can save yourself some time and work by copying and pasting files from the CD-ROM into your articles file. To use the CD-ROM, open the file on the disk titled Special Article Provisions for an Unincorporated Association. Fill in the article provisions in the same manner described above for the other articles on the CD-ROM.

To modify your articles, you'll need to add two provisions. First, add a new Article Seven to your articles immediately after Article Six and before the first date line and first set of signature lines, as follows:

SEVEN: The name of the existing unincorporated association, now being incorporated by the filing of these Articles of Incorporation, is __**(type name of unincorporated association here)**__.

Next, add the following declaration at the end of your articles (after the second set of signature lines):

DECLARATION

__**(Name of association board member or officer)**__ and __**(name of association board member or officer)**__ declare under penalty of perjury that they are the __**(titles of association board members or officer)**__ of __**(name of unincorporated association)**__, the unincorporated association referred to in the Articles of Incorporation to which this declaration is attached, and that said association has duly authorized its incorporation by means of said Articles of Incorporation.

Date: __**(date of signing)**__

__**(signature of association board member or officer)**__
(typed name)

__**(signature of association board member or officer)**__
(typed name)

Any two officers (for example, a president, vice president, secretary, or treasurer) or any two members of the governing board of the unincorporated association (such as directors or trustees) can prepare and sign the above declaration. State their names and positions in the blanks provided and, after printing the form, have the two association officers or two association governing members sign in the blanks below the declaration.

After making these changes, the last portion of your modified articles should read as follows:

SEVEN: The name of the existing unincorporated association, now being incorporated by the filing of these articles of incorporation, is _____.

Date: _____

____**(signatures of director(s) listed in Article FIVE)**____

(typed name) _____, Director

_____, Director

_____, Director

_____, Director

_____, Director

We, the above-mentioned initial directors of this corporation, hereby declare that we are the persons who executed the foregoing articles of incorporation, which instrument is our act and deed.

____**(signatures of director(s) listed in Article FIVE)**____

(typed name) _____, Director

_____, Director

_____, Director

_____, Director

_____, Director

DECLARATION

_____ and _____ declare under penalty of perjury that they are the _____ of _____, the unincorporated association referred to in the articles of incorporation to which this declaration is attached, and that said association has duly authorized its incorporation by means of said articles of incorporation.

Date: _____

_____

_____

After printing your articles, date and sign the form. Your initial directors date and sign in the first and second set of signature lines. The two officers or board members of the association date and sign after the declaration at the very end of the articles.

Remember the secretary of state document requirements for all articles of incorporation described in "Rules for Preparing and Printing Your Documents" at the beginning of this section.

Special Rules When Incorporating an Unincorporated Association

The incorporation of the association must be approved by the association in accordance with its rules and procedures (usually at least a majority vote of association members is required). A failure to obtain proper association approval of its incorporation could result in legal action being taken against the new corporation by the previous members of the unincorporated association.

Once an unincorporated association becomes a corporation, the property of the association becomes the property of the corporation. Also, if association members had any voting rights similar to those that entitle members of a corporation to be formal members (for example, the right to vote for directors or dissolution), then these association members become formal members of the corporation (you must organize as a membership corporation). See Chapter 2 for a discussion of the rules and consequences of formal membership in a corporation.

All rights of creditors of the association and all liens on the property of the association remain intact after the incorporation. This means that creditors can still look to property transferred to the new corporation to satisfy creditor claims. If legal action is pending against the association at the time of its incorporation, any judgment in the legal action will bind the corporation, and creditors can satisfy their judgments by going after the assets of the corporation that were transferred to it from the unincorporated association.

File Your Articles

When you file your articles of incorporation with the California Secretary of State, your corporation becomes a legal entity. Filing your articles is also the first step along the way to obtaining 501(c)(3) tax-exempt status, since you must include a certified copy of your articles of incorporation with your state and federal tax exemption applications. Thus, your corporation must already be in existence when you apply for tax-exempt status from the state and the IRS.

Don't Rush to File

Even though filing your articles is the first step in the process, we recommend that you prepare bylaws and at least start your state tax exemption application before you file your articles with the secretary of state. Taking these additional steps gives you the opportunity to think through your decision to incorporate more thoroughly. When you prepare bylaws, you must decide on basic organizational matters, such as the composition of your board of directors and whether you want to set up a membership or nonmembership structure for your nonprofit. Having to think through some of these issues may lead you to rethink your decision to incorporate.

When preparing your state exemption application, you might realize that your organization will have difficulty qualifying for the tax exemption. There may be questions on the application that you didn't anticipate or requirements that you realize you can't meet. You might decide that it's best to postpone your decision to form a nonprofit corporation until you get tax or legal advice. Or, if preparing the state tax exemption application (which is very similar in scope and complexity to the federal tax application) is just too much trouble, you might decide to put off your nonprofit plans for now. You might decide to form your tax-exempt nonprofit corporation later when you have more enthusiasm for the task (or at least a little more help).

If you change your mind at this point (before filing your articles), you won't incur any additional cost and there won't be additional work involved. On the other hand, if you rush to file your articles right away and then decide you really don't want to form a nonprofit corporation, it's too late. Your nonprofit legal entity will already be formed and you will either have to dissolve your corporation immediately (see "Dissolving a Nonprofit Corporation" in Chapter 11), or you will have to prepare and file regular state and federal corporate income tax returns each year and pay income taxes on any revenue remaining after the payment of deductible expenses.

CAUTION

There's always some uncertainty and risk. The California Secretary of State will not accept articles for a nonprofit and hold them for filing while you obtain your state tax exemption—it used to do this, but decided to drop this wait-and-see procedure. Before you apply for your state and federal tax exemptions, your nonprofit corporation must be formed. The problem is: There is no guarantee that you will ultimately obtain both your federal and state income tax exemptions. Without these exemptions, your nonprofit corporation will not obtain the benefits you undoubtedly wanted when you started this whole process (federal and state tax exemptions, eligibility for grant funds, tax-deductible contributions). But there is no way around it. Filing articles to form a nonprofit corporation is always a bit of a gamble. All you can do is reduce the risk by reading this book carefully and going through Chapters 8 and 9 ahead of time to get a sense of what the state and IRS expect from you to qualify for a nonprofit tax exemption. By reading our examples and sample responses in these chapters, you can learn how to best characterize and describe your organization's goals and programs to qualify for your tax exemptions and to make your nonprofit corporation a viable, tax-exempt entity.

Make Copies

You will need copies of your original articles of incorporation for the filing package you submit to the California Secretary of State. If you are forming a public benefit corporation, make four copies of your original articles of incorporation (three for your filing package and one for your records). In all other cases, you need three copies of your articles (two for the filing package and one for your records).

You need these copies for the following purposes: You'll place one file copy in your corporate records book. You will send two copies to the California Secretary of State. These two copies will be certified at no charge by the secretary of state and returned to you. Each certified copy has a facing page containing the seal of the state of California and an official certification statement. When you get the certified copies back, you will mail one certified copy with your state tax exemption to the Franchise Tax Board. The other certified copy you will mail to the IRS with your federal tax exemption application. Before you mail out these copies, make one photocopy of a certified copy to place in your corporate records book.

If you're forming a public benefit corporation, you'll send one additional copy of your articles to the California Secretary of State, who will forward it to the Attorney General, Registry of Charitable Trusts (see "File an Initial Report With the Attorney General" in Chapter 10).

Prepare Your Cover Letter

Prepare the cover letter to the California Secretary of State included on the CD-ROM, *Cover Letter for Filing Articles*. This cover letter requests the secretary to file the original articles and certify the two copies of the articles. Prepare the cover letter following the sample form and special instructions below.

- The parenthetical blanks, that is, "(_____)," in the sample form below indicate information which you must complete on the computer form on the CD-ROM.

- Corresponding blanks in the computer form are marked with a series of underlined characters.

- Replace the blanks in the computer form (each series of underlined characters) with the information indicated in the sample form below.

Each circled number in the sample form (such as, ❶) refers to a special instruction, which provides specific information to help you complete an item.

❶ One of the initial directors named in your articles should prepare and sign this letter as the incorporator of your organization. If you have reserved a corporate name, the person who reserved the corporate name should prepare and sign this cover letter.

❷ Public benefit corporations must submit at least three copies; religious corporations at least two copies. There is no extra charge above the standard filing fee for these copies. You can submit extra copies for certification by the secretary of state if you wish. The fee for comparing and certifying each additional copy is $8 per copy. Make sure to change the amount of your check to the secretary of state and the language of the cover letter if you submit extra copies for certification.

❸ In this blank, indicate whether you are filing articles for a public benefit or a religious corporation.

❹ The fee for filing articles of incorporation for a nonprofit corporation is currently $30. Staple a check made payable to the California Secretary of State for this amount to your cover letter.

> **CAUTION**
>
> **Check that your fee amounts are current.** The fee for filing your articles (as well as other fees, such as the charge for comparing and certifying extra copies of the articles) changes from time to time. Call the secretary of state at 916-657-5448 to confirm the fee amounts given in this book before filing your papers. Alternatively, find the latest fee information on the California Secretary of State's website at www.ss.ca.gov/business/business.htm.

❺ If you have reserved the corporate name shown in your articles and are filing your articles within 60 days of the effective date of your Certificate of Reservation, type this optional paragraph at the bottom of your cover letter, supplying the number and date of your Certificate of Reservation.

❻ Type your incorporator's name under the signature line and print two copies of the cover letter. The incorporator should sign at the bottom of the letter. Make sure to place a copy of the printed cover letter in your corporate records book.

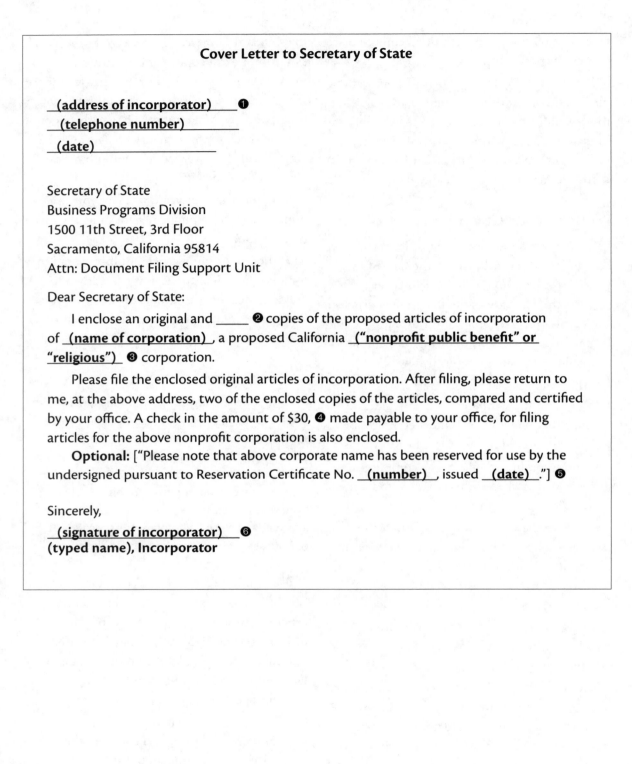

Cover Letter to Secretary of State

__(address of incorporator)__ ❶
__(telephone number)__
__(date)__

Secretary of State
Business Programs Division
1500 11th Street, 3rd Floor
Sacramento, California 95814
Attn: Document Filing Support Unit

Dear Secretary of State:

I enclose an original and _____ ❷ copies of the proposed articles of incorporation of __(name of corporation)__ , a proposed California __("nonprofit public benefit" or "religious")__ ❸ corporation.

Please file the enclosed original articles of incorporation. After filing, please return to me, at the above address, two of the enclosed copies of the articles, compared and certified by your office. A check in the amount of $30, ❹ made payable to your office, for filing articles for the above nonprofit corporation is also enclosed.

Optional: ["Please note that above corporate name has been reserved for use by the undersigned pursuant to Reservation Certificate No. __(number)__ , issued __(date)__ ."] ❺

Sincerely,
__(signature of incorporator)__ ❻
(typed name), Incorporator

File Your Documents With the Secretary of State

After making your copies and completing the cover letter to the secretary of state, mail the following documents to the Business Programs Division of the secretary of state's Sacramento office at the address indicated in the cover letter:

- one original and three copies (for public benefit corporations) or one original and two copies (for religious corporations) of your articles of incorporation

- a cover letter with a check made payable to the Secretary of State, and

- a stamped, self-addressed envelope.

If You're in a Hurry, File in Person

Articles can be filed in person for $15 extra at any branch office of the secretary of state. (Always check the California Secretary of State's website for changes to filing fees.) When you file in person at a secretary of state office other than the Sacramento office, you must submit an extra copy of your articles, which will be forwarded to the main Sacramento office. You can also do an expedited filing to get a response in four hours (for $500) or 24 hours (for $350). Expedited filing requests must be made in person at the Sacramento office. For more information, check the secretary of state's website at www.ss.ca.gov/business/precexp.htm.

Your next step is to wait. The secretary of state will make sure your corporate name is available for use and that your articles conform to law. If there are no problems, the secretary of state will file your articles and return the certified copies to you. Expect to wait two to four weeks or

longer before receiving the filed copies (unless you've ponied up the extra bucks for expedited filing by mail). California is notoriously slow with its filings.

When you receive your certified copies of your articles from the secretary of state, you will need to make copies for the following purposes:

- one copy to be filed with the post office to obtain a nonprofit mailing permit (see "Apply for a Mailing Permit" in Chapter 10)

- two copies to be filed with the local tax assessor's office if you wish to obtain an exemption from payment of local personal and real property taxes (see "Apply for Your Property Tax Exemption" in Chapter 10)

- additional copies to be filed in connection with any licenses or permits you wish to obtain (see "Licenses and Permits" in Chapter 11), and

- if you are incorporating an unincorporated association, one copy to be filed with the county recorder of each county in which the unincorporated association owns property (see "File Your Articles With the County Recorder" in Chapter 10).

If there are any problems, the secretary of state will usually return your articles, indicating the items that need correction. Often the problem is technical, not substantive, and easy to fix. If the problem is more complicated (such as an improper or insufficient corporate purpose clause), you may be able to solve the problem by rereading our examples and suggestions for completing the articles. If you get stuck, you will need to do a little research or obtain further help from a nonprofit lawyer with experience in drafting and filing nonprofit articles (see Chapter 12).

Sign Documents on Behalf of the Corporation

Congratulations! Once your articles are filed, your organization is a legally recognized nonprofit corporation. But before you rush out to pursue your nonprofit objectives, remember that your corporation is the one that is now doing business, not you as an individual. This means that signatures on any document, such as an agreement with a vendor, application for a grant, lease, or other financial or legal form, must clearly show that you're acting on behalf of the corporation (and not for yourself). Your signature should be a block of information (plus a signature), which looks like this:

> Parents for a Better Society, Inc. (the name of your nonprofit)
> By: ___(your signature)___
> Sarah Hovey, Director (your corporate title, such as director, president, secretary, and so on).

If you fail to sign documents on behalf of the corporation and in your capacity as a corporate director, officer, or employee, you are leaving yourself open to possible personal liability for corporate obligations. From now on, it is extremely important for you to maintain the distinction between the corporation that you've organized and yourself. As we've said, the corporation is a separate legal person and you want to make sure that other organizations, businesses, the IRS, and the courts respect this distinction.

Remember that until you obtain your state and federal tax exemptions, your corporation is liable for the payment of state and federal income taxes. Furthermore, until you obtain your federal 501(c)(3) tax exemption and public charity status, your corporation will be unable to receive most public and private grant funds, or assure donors that contributions made to the corporation are tax deductible. You must follow through with the procedures contained in the succeeding chapters—doing so is vital to the success of your new corporation.

CHAPTER

7

Bylaws

Your next step is to prepare your bylaws. This document is, for all practical purposes, your corporation's internal affairs manual. It sets forth the rules and procedures for holding meetings, electing directors and officers, and taking care of other essential corporate formalities. Specifically, the bylaws:

- Contain information central to the organization and operation of your corporation (for example, dates of meetings, quorum requirements).

- Restate the most significant legal and tax provisions applicable to tax-exempt nonprofit corporations. This is useful for your own reference and necessary to assure the IRS and the state that you are eligible for these tax exemptions.

- Provide a practical, yet formal, set of rules for the orderly operation of your corporation: to resolve disputes, provide certainty regarding procedures, and manage corporate operations.

Preparing bylaws for a nonprofit corporation is not difficult. It simply involves filling in several blanks in the appropriate bylaws for your group. There are four sets of bylaws on the CD-ROM; you'll open the one that corresponds to your group's purpose and follow along with us as we show you how to complete the forms. Before you begin work on your bylaws, you'll need to decide whether your nonprofit will have members. We guide you through that issue below.

The bylaw sets you will choose from are:

- Basic Bylaws for a Public Benefit Nonprofit Corporation

- Membership Bylaw Provisions for a Public Benefit Corporation

- Basic Bylaws for a Religious Corporation

- Membership Bylaw Provisions for a Religious Corporation.

Customizing Your Bylaws

The bylaws in this book contain standard, workable provisions for running a corporation. Any changes to these standard provisions that only affect administrative matters can be made without researching the law. For example, matters related to the payment of salaries, duties of officers, and composition of advisory or standing committees are usually left to the discretion of the nonprofit corporation. However, if you want to change basic legal provisions in your bylaws (such as notice or call of meeting rules, or voting or quorum provisions), you should check the Nonprofit Corporation Law prior to making these changes or let an experienced nonprofit lawyer help you.

CAUTION

Don't think of your bylaws as meaningless fine print. On the contrary, bylaws are crucial to the functioning of your organization. Be sure to read them carefully, making sure you understand the purpose and effect of the different provisions included.

Choose a Membership or Nonmembership Structure

Your first step in preparing bylaws is to decide whether you want your nonprofit corporation to be a membership or nonmembership corporation. There are significant differences between the two structures and significant legal consequences that will result from your decision. See "Membership Nonprofits" in Chapter 2 for a discussion of the two different types of structures and the legal consequences of setting up a membership versus a nonmembership structure.

Most groups want a nonmembership corporation because it is simpler to establish and operate. Nonmembership corporations are run by a board of directors, as opposed to membership corporations, where members have the right to vote on major corporate decisions (the election of directors, dissolution of the corporation, sale of substantially all of the corporation's assets, or changes to the articles or bylaws of the corporation). And you don't lose any significant advantages by not having members—most people who might want to support your group aren't interested in having the technical legal rights given to members.

Some groups, however, will decide that the nature of their activities requires a membership structure. This is a reasonable decision in circumstances where membership participation in the affairs of the nonprofit corporation is essential or desirable (for example, to increase member involvement in the nonprofit's mission and program).

Bylaws for a Public Benefit Corporation

All public benefit corporations start by preparing the public benefit corporation bylaws contained in the CD-ROM. These bylaws are for any type of 501(c)(3) public benefit corporation: membership or nonmembership; and charitable, educational, scientific, or literary (for 501(c)(3) purposes). Groups with a formal membership structure need to add special provisions to these basic public benefit corporation bylaws. California religious corporations will use a different form to prepare their bylaws.

Don't Be Confused by References to Members in Bylaw Provisions

The basic public benefit corporation bylaws contain references to "the members, if any," of the corporation, and make certain provisions applicable to the corporation only if the corporation has members. These provisions have no effect on nonmembership corporations. As a practical matter, nonmembership corporations will simply approve by normal board approval, matters that reference approval by the membership of a membership corporation. Leaving in the references to members simply allows membership corporations to use the same basic provisions as nonmembership corporations. It also allows nonmembership corporations to more easily amend their bylaws later if they ever decide to adopt a membership structure.

General Instructions

To prepare bylaws for a public benefit corporation, fill in the Bylaws for a Public Benefit Corporation included on the CD-ROM. Follow the sample form and special instructions below.

Here are some general instructions to help you prepare your bylaws:

- The parenthetical blanks, "(_____)," in the sample form indicate information that you must complete on the CD-ROM.
- Corresponding blanks in the computer form are marked with a series of underlined characters.
- Replace the blanks in the computer form (each series of underlined characters) with the information indicated in the sample form below.

- Each circled number in the sample form (e.g., ❶) refers to a special instruction that provides specific information to help you complete an item.
- A vertical series of dots in the sample form below indicates a gap where we have skipped over language in the computer form.

Sample Bylaws

The sample bylaws below are an abbreviated version of the complete form contained on the CD-ROM. In the text below, we provide sample language and instructions for the few sections that contain blanks.

Instructions for Completing Your Bylaws

Open Bylaws for a Public Benefit Corporation on the CD-ROM and follow these instructions. The numbers on the instructions correspond to the relevant place on the bylaw form.

❶ Type the name of your corporation in the heading of the bylaws.

❷ Type the name of the county where the corporation's principal office is located. The principal office is the legal address of the corporation. If your nonprofit is ever sued, most of the time the lawsuit will have to be filed in the county where your principal office is located.

❸ Don't fill in the blanks in this section at this time. Use these blanks later to change the principal office of the corporation to another location, within the same county, by showing the new address and date of the address change.

❹ This section allows you to state in more detail the primary objectives and purposes of your nonprofit corporation. (Remember, your statement of specific purposes in your articles of incorporation is brief.) Here you can go into as much detail as you want, describing the specific purposes and activities of your corporation. You can be concise, but we suggest you provide some detail about your organization. You should state your major objectives and describe the activities that you plan to engage in. Doing this will give insiders a sense of certainty regarding the specific goals you intend to achieve and the means by which you plan to achieve them. A more detailed statement here will also give the state franchise board and the IRS additional information, which they will use to determine if the specific activities you plan to engage in entitle you to the necessary tax exemptions.

In all cases, refer back to "Prepare Articles of Incorporation" in Chapter 6, and reread the sections on nonprofit purposes (which you studied when preparing a statement of purposes for your articles of incorporation). These considerations apply here too, except that you don't need (and probably don't want) to be as brief this time.

Below you'll see an example of an expanded list of objectives and purposes that an educational dance group could use. This is the same group we used when illustrating how to prepare a short statement of specific purposes (see "Prepare Articles of Incorporation" in Chapter 6). If you compare this more detailed statement with the educational dance group example given in "Examples of Specific Purpose Statements" in Chapter 6, we think you'll get the idea of what this bylaw provision is meant to accomplish and how to prepare it.

Bylaws
of
_____Name of Corporation_____ ❶

a California Public Benefit Corporation

ARTICLE 1
OFFICES

SECTION 1. PRINCIPAL OFFICE

The principal office of the corporation for the transaction of its business is located in
___**(name of county)**___ County, California. ❷

SECTION 2. CHANGE OF ADDRESS

The county of the corporation's principal office can be changed only by amendment of
these bylaws and not otherwise. The board of directors may, however, change the principal
office from one location to another within the named county by noting the changed
address and effective date below, and such changes of address shall not be deemed an
amendment of these bylaws:

(Fill lines in below later, if and when address changes) ❸

_____   Dated: _____

_____   Dated: _____

_____   Dated: _____

SECTION 3. OTHER OFFICES

The corporation may also have offices at such other places, within or without the State of
California, where it is qualified to do business, as its business may require, and as the board
of directors may, from time to time, designate.

ARTICLE 2
PURPOSES

SECTION 1. OBJECTIVES AND PURPOSES

The primary objectives and purposes of this corporation shall be: ❹

___**(provide specific statement of your group's nonprofit purposes and activities)**___

_____

_____

_____

_____

_____

ARTICLE 3
DIRECTORS

SECTION 1. NUMBER

The corporation shall have __(number of directors)__ ❺ directors and collectively they shall be known as the board of directors. The number may be changed by amendment of this bylaw, or by repeal of this bylaw and adoption of a new bylaw, as provided in these bylaws.

.
.
.

SECTION 5. COMPENSATION

Directors shall serve without compensation except that they shall be allowed and paid __("their actual and necessary expenses incurred in attending directors' meetings" or state other provisions allowing reasonable compensation for attending meetings)__ . ❻ In addition, they shall be allowed reasonable advancement or reimbursement of expenses incurred in the performance of their regular duties as specified in Section 3 of this Article. Directors may not be compensated for rendering services to the corporation in any capacity other than director unless such other compensation is reasonable and is allowable under the provisions of Section 6 of this Article. Any payments to directors shall be approved in advance in accordance with this corporation's conflict of interest policy as set forth in Article 9 of these bylaws.

.
.
.

SECTION 8. REGULAR AND ANNUAL MEETINGS

Regular meetings of directors shall be held on __(date)__ ❼ at __(time)__ M, ❼ unless such day falls on a legal holiday, in which event the regular meeting shall be held at the same hour and place on the next business day.

If this corporation makes no provision for members, then, at the annual meeting of directors held on __(date)__, ❼ directors shall be elected by the board of directors in accordance with this section. Cumulative voting by directors for the election of directors shall not be permitted. The candidates receiving the highest number of votes up to the number of directors to be elected shall be elected. Each director shall cast one vote, with voting being by ballot only.

.
.
.

SECTION 13. QUORUM FOR MEETINGS

A quorum shall consist of __(state number or percentage, e.g., "a majority of the board of")__ ❽ directors.

SECTION 15. CONDUCT OF MEETINGS

Meetings of the board of directors shall be presided over by the chairperson of the board, or, if no such person has been so designated or in his or her absence, the president of the corporation or, in his or her absence, by the vice president of the corporation or, in the absence of each of these persons, by a chairperson chosen by a majority of the directors present at the meeting. The secretary of the corporation shall act as secretary of all meetings of the board, provided that, in his or her absence, the presiding officer shall appoint another person to act as secretary of the meeting.

Meetings shall be governed by __("Robert's Rules of Order" or state other rules or procedures for conduct of directors' meeting)__ , ❾ as such rules may be revised from time to time, insofar as such rules are not inconsistent with or in conflict with these bylaws, with the articles of incorporation of this corporation, or with provisions of law.

.
.
.

ARTICLE 5
COMMITTEES

SECTION 1. EXECUTIVE COMMITTEE

The board of directors may, by a majority vote of directors, designate two (2) or more of its members (who may also be serving as officers of this corporation) to constitute an executive committee and delegate to such committee any of the powers and authority of the board in the management of the business and affairs of the corporation, except with respect to:

(a) The approval of any action which, under law or the provisions of these bylaws, requires the approval of the members or of a majority of all of the members.

(b) The filling of vacancies on the board or on any committee which has the authority of the board.

(c) The fixing of compensation of the directors for serving on the board or on any committee.

(d) The amendment or repeal of bylaws or the adoption of new bylaws.

(e) The amendment or repeal of any resolution of the board which by its express terms is not so amendable or repealable.

(f) The appointment of committees of the board or the members thereof.

(g) The expenditure of corporate funds to support a nominee for director after there are more people nominated for director than can be elected.

(h) The approval of any transaction to which this corporation is a party and in which one or more of the directors has a material financial interest, except as expressly provided in Section 5233(d)(3) of the California Nonprofit Public Benefit Corporation Law.

By a majority vote of its members then in office, the board may at any time revoke or modify any or all of the authority so delegated, increase or decrease but not below two (2) the number of its members, and fill vacancies therein from the members of the board. The committee shall keep regular minutes of its proceedings, cause them to be filed with the corporate records, and report the same to the board from time to time as the board may require. ❿

.
.
.

ARTICLE 8
FISCAL YEAR

SECTION 1. FISCAL YEAR OF THE CORPORATION

The fiscal year of the corporation shall begin on the ___**(day and month, e.g., "first day of January")**___ ⓫ and end on the ___**(day and month, e.g., "last day of December")**___ ⓫ in each year.

.
.
.

ARTICLE 9 ⓬
CONFLICT OF INTEREST AND COMPENSATION APPROVAL POLICIES

SECTION 1. PURPOSE OF CONFLICT OF INTEREST POLICY

.
.
.

ARTICLE 13 ⓭
MEMBERS

SECTION 1. DETERMINATION OF MEMBERS ⓮

If this corporation makes no provision for members, then, pursuant to Section 5310(b) of the Nonprofit Public Benefit Corporation Law of the State of California, any action which would otherwise, under law or the provisions of the articles of incorporation or bylaws of this corporation, require approval by a majority of all members or approval by the members, shall only require the approval of the board of directors.

WRITTEN CONSENT OF DIRECTORS ADOPTING BYLAWS ⓯

We, the undersigned, are all of the persons named as the initial directors in the articles of incorporation of ___**(name of corporation)**___, ⓯ a California nonprofit corporation, and, pursuant to the authority granted to the directors by these bylaws to take action by unanimous written consent without a meeting, consent to, and hereby do, adopt the foregoing bylaws, consisting of ___**(number of pages)**___ ⓯ pages, as the bylaws of this corporation.

Dated: ___**(date)**___ _____**(signature of director)**_____ ⓯

_____**(typed name)**_____, Director

_____**(typed name)**_____, Director

_____**(typed name)**_____, Director

_____**(typed name)**_____, Director

_____**(typed name)**_____, Director

CERTIFICATE

This is to certify that the foregoing is a true and correct copy of the bylaws of the corporation named in the title thereto and that such bylaws were duly adopted by the board of directors of said corporation on the date set forth below.

(Fill in Certificate date and signature of secretary later, after first board meeting) ❶❻

Dated: ___(date)___ ___(signature of secretary)___

(typed name)   , Secretary

Response for an Educational Group

ARTICLE 2
PURPOSES
SECTION 1. OBJECTIVES AND PURPOSES

The primary objectives and purposes of this corporation shall be:

(a) to provide instruction in dance forms such as jazz, ballet, tap, and modern dance;

(b) to provide instruction in body movement and relaxation art forms, such as tumbling, tai-chi, and yoga;

(c) to give public performances in dance forms and creative dramatics;

(d) to sponsor special events involving the public performance of any or all of the above art forms as well as other performing arts by the corporation's performing troupe as well as by other community performing arts groups; and

(e) to directly engage in and to provide facilities for others to engage in the promotion of the arts, generally.

❺ Indicate the total number of persons authorized to serve on your board. This number will usually be the same as the number of people you've already indicated as the first directors of the corporation in Article Five of the articles of incorporation. However, you may at this time state a greater number to allow for additional directors to be elected at a future meeting of the board. Don't forget to abide by the "51% Rule," which means that a majority of the board must not be paid by the corporation or related to another person who is paid by the corporation. See "Directors" in Chapter 2 for more information on public benefit corporations and the 51% rule.

A few groups might want to change this section to provide for a range of numbers of directors, with the exact number to be later fixed by resolution of the board of directors. For example, you might want to retype this section to provide as shown in the sample below.

Variation on Numbers of Directors

SECTION 1. NUMBER

The corporation shall have not fewer than two (2) nor more than five (5) directors, with the exact number to be fixed within these limits by approval of the board of directors or the members, if any, in the manner provided in these bylaws.

❻ Indicate in this blank any specific payments that will be allowed to board members for attending meetings of the board (note that reasonable advancement and reimbursement of expenses for performing other director duties are allowed by this section). You can enter a specific per-meeting amount (or you can use the sample language shown in the blank on the sample form above to authorize payment of "actual and necessary" expenses incurred by directors in attending board meetings). If, as is often the case, you do not wish to pay directors for attending meetings, simply type "no payments authorized" in this blank. Paying a director (a small amount) solely for attending board meetings does not make a director an "interested person" for purposes of the 51% rule (Corp. Code § 5227).

Payments to Directors

Directors shall serve without compensation except that they shall be allowed and paid **$50 for attending each meeting of the board of directors.**

Directors shall serve without compensation except that they shall be allowed and paid **no payment authorized.**

❼ In the blanks in the first paragraph, indicate the date and time when regular meetings of the board will be held. Many nonprofits hold regular board meetings, while others simply schedule regular meetings once each year and call special meetings during the year when required. In any case, make sure to indicate in the blanks that you will hold a regular board meeting at least annually.

Responses

Regular meetings of directors shall be held on **the first Friday of each month** at **9 o'clock AM**…

Regular meetings of directors shall be held on **the second Monday of December** at **1 o'clock PM**…

Regular meetings of directors shall be held on **July 1st and February 20th** at **9 o'clock AM**…

In the second paragraph of this section, fill in the blank to indicate which one of your regular board meetings will be specified as the annual regular meeting of the board to elect (or reelect) directors of your corporation. In a nonmembership corporation, the directors vote for their own reelection or replacements, with each director casting one written vote. Of course, if a corporation has provided for only one regular meeting each year in the first paragraph of this section, then the date of this regular meeting will be repeated in this blank as the date of the annual meeting of directors.

Responses for Annual Meeting Date

If this corporation makes no provision for members, then, at the annual meeting of directors held on **January 1st**, directors shall be elected…

If this corporation makes no provision for members, then, at the annual meeting of directors held on **the first Friday of July**, directors shall be elected…

The provisions in the second paragraph of this section apply only to nonmembership corporations. Membership corporations can leave this line blank, since they will add provisions to their bylaws specifying that the members, not the directors, elect directors of the corporation.

❽ A quorum (a minimum number of directors) must be present at a director's meeting in order to conduct business. Indicate the number of directors who will constitute a quorum. Although the usual practice is to provide for a majority, you can choose a larger or smaller number. However, you cannot choose a quorum of less than one-fifth of the authorized number of directors (the number given in special instruction ❺, above), or two, whichever is larger. Of course, one-director corporations can and will provide for a quorum of one director. For example, a seven-director corporation can't provide for a quorum of fewer than two directors, while a 15-director corporation must have at least a three-director quorum.

Whatever number or percentage you decide on, you should realize that this section of the bylaws concerns a quorum, not a vote requirement. A meeting can be held only if at least a quorum of directors is present, but a vote on any matter before the board must, generally, be passed by the vote of a majority of those present at the meeting.

EXAMPLE:

If a public benefit corporation with seven directors provides for a minimum quorum of two, and just two directors hold a meeting, action can be taken by the unanimous vote of these two directors. However, if all seven directors attend the meeting, action must be approved by at least four directors (a majority of those present at the meeting).

Many public benefit corporations will want a less-than-majority quorum rule. The reason is because these corporations must have a majority of "disinterested" directors on their board. Sometimes, corporations have difficulty getting nonsalaried directors to attend board meetings on a regular basis. A lower quorum requirement can help ensure that enough directors for a quorum will be present at meetings.

❾ In this blank, indicate the rules of order that will be used at directors' meetings. Most nonprofits specify Robert's Rules of Order here, but you may choose any set of procedures for proposing, approving, and tabling motions. With a small board, you can leave this line blank if you see no need to specify formal procedures for introducing and discussing items of business at your board meetings.

❿ This section follows a state law provision that allows the board of a public benefit corporation to set up an executive committee of the board consisting of board members only. The law allows the executive committee to have much of the management power of the full board (as specified in this section of the bylaws). Although at least two board members must serve on this committee, in practice, most nonprofit corporations establish an executive board committee of from three to five board members. Of course, you don't have to set up an executive committee of the board, and you can set up other types of committees with or without board members (see Section 2 of this Article in the CD-ROM bylaws).

⓫ The fiscal year of the corporation is the period for which the corporation keeps its books (its accounting period), and will determine the corporation's tax year for purposes of filing certain tax returns and reports. Indicate the beginning and ending dates of the corporation's fiscal year in this space. You can choose the calendar year from January 1 to December 31, which most nonprofits do. Or, you can use what the IRS considers a true fiscal year, consisting of a 12-month period ending on the last day of any month other than December (for example, from July 1 to June 30).

⓬ Article 9 of the bylaws included in this book contains rules and procedures for approving or avoiding conflict of interest transactions, including compensation arrangements, between your nonprofit and its directors, officers, employees, contractors, and others.

This bylaw provision contains the conflicts-of-interest language recommended by the IRS (included in the sample conflict-of-interest policy in Appendix A of the instructions to IRS Form 1023). It also contains language for the approval of compensation arrangements that attempts to comply with the safe harbor provisions of the excess benefit rules (see the discussion on the excess benefit rules in "Limitation on Profits and Benefits" in Chapter 3). You will need to become familiar with this provision, and make sure you are comfortable with its procedures for the approval and review of financial transactions with, and salary and other compensation paid to, your directors, officers, and others who are in a position to influence your nonprofit. If you decide to make changes to this provision, do so only after reading, in Chapter 9, "Prepare Your Tax Exemption Application," instructions to Part V, where we refer to this bylaw provision when providing sample responses to question on the application. If you make any changes, you will need to create your own responses to some of the questions on the 501(c)(3) application.

❸ The last portion of the basic bylaws (Article 13, Written Consent of Directors, and the Certificate section) is for nonmembership groups only. Membership public benefit corporations do not need to fill in and use this last portion of the basic bylaws—we show you how to add membership provisions to complete your bylaws below.

❹ Section 1 of Article 13 makes it clear that the directors of nonmembership corporations can take the place of members in taking any action that, under law, otherwise requires membership approval. In other words, the directors can act in place of the members in nonmembership corporations.

❺ Fill in the Written Consent of Directors paragraph, showing the name of the corpora-

tion and the number of pages in your final bylaws. Type your directors' names (the directors named in your articles) below the signature lines. After printing and dating the form, have each director sign the form.

❻ Don't fill in the blanks following the Certificate at bottom of the bylaws at this time. Your corporate secretary will complete these blanks after the first meeting of your board.

Bylaw Provisions for Schools and Federally Funded Groups

Some groups may need to add language or make other modifications to the bylaws on the CD-ROM. Here are three examples, schools, federally funded groups, and larger public benefit groups (with annual gross revenues of $2 million or more).

Schools

If your nonprofit activities will consist of operating a formal school, you will need to add an article to the sample bylaws consisting of a "nondiscriminatory policy statement." For information on the applicability of this statement to your group and how to prepare it, see the discussion on Part III in "Prepare Your Tax Exemption Application" in Chapter 9.

Participants in Federal Programs

If your nonprofit corporation plans to receive federal or other public grants or money, some funding agencies may require that you include provisions in your bylaws stating that no board member, officer, or other person exercising supervisory power in the corporation, or any of their close relatives, can benefit from the receipt of grant funds. Generally, provisions of this sort are meant to prohibit board members, officers (president, vice president, secretary, treasurer), and their families from being paid from, or directly benefited by, grant monies given to the organization.

TIP

If you plan to receive grant funds from government or other public sources, ask the funding agency for the exact language of any special provisions that you should include in your bylaws. In many cases, you won't want to provide for payment of directors or officers and should delete or modify Article 3, Sections 5 and 6; Article 4, Section 10; and Article 11, Section 1, of the bylaws on the CD-ROM.

Nonprofits With Revenues of $2 Million or More

Public benefit nonprofits with annual gross revenues of $2 million or more may wish to add provisions to their bylaws to reflect certain requirements under the California Nonprofit Integrity Act of 2004 that apply to them. These rules generally do not apply to schools or hospitals, and the $2 million threshold doesn't include grants received from government agencies if the nonprofit must provide an accounting of how it uses the governmental grant funds. However, if your nonprofit falls within the scope of these rules, you may want to include provisions in your bylaws that cover these requirements.

Here is a brief summary of the "larger non-profit" rules under the Act:

- The nonprofit must prepare audited annual financial statements which it must submit to the attorney general and make available for public inspection.

- The nonprofit board must appoint an audit committee that 1) helps hire and set the compensation of the auditors (CPAs) that prepare the organization's financial statements, 2) reviews the organization's audited statements, and 3) reports to the board its finding as to whether the nonprofit's financial affairs and financial statements are in order.

- The audit committee cannot include staff members, the president or chief executive officer, the treasurer, or the chief financial officer of the nonprofit. If an organization has a finance committee, members of that committee may serve on the audit committee, but cannot make up 50% or more of the audit committee.

To learn more about the California Nonprofit Integrity Act of 2004:

- Go to the California Attorney General's website at http://ag.ca.gov/charities/publications.php, select the link to the "Summary of New Law: Guide to the Nonprofit Integrity Act of 2004."

- To read the sections of California law amended or added by the Act, go to www.leginfo.ca.gov/calaw.html, select and read Government Code Sections 12581, 12582, 12583, 12584, 12585, 12586, 12599, 12599.1, 12599.3, 12599.6, and 12599.7, and Business and Professions Code Section 17510.5.

Membership Bylaw Provisions for a Public Benefit Corporation

This section applies only to membership corporations and shows how to add special membership provisions to the basic public benefit corporation bylaws. If you have decided to form a nonmembership public benefit corporation, this section does not apply to you and you should skip ahead to Chapter 8.

General Instructions

To add membership provisions to your public benefit corporation bylaws, fill in the blanks in the membership provisions file included on the CD-ROM, following the sample form and instructions below. Once completed, copy these membership provisions to your basic bylaws as explained in special instruction ❶ below.

- The parenthetical blanks, "(_____)," in the sample form below indicate information you must complete on the computer form on the CD-ROM.

- Corresponding blanks in the computer form are marked with a series of underlined characters.

- Replace the blanks in the computer form (each series of underlined characters) with the information indicated in the blanks in the sample form below.

- Each circled number in the sample form (for instance, ❶) refers to a special instruction that provides specific information to help you complete an item. The special instructions immediately follow the sample form.

- A vertical series of dots in the sample form indicates a gap where we have skipped over language in the computer form.

Sample Membership Provisions

Below is an example of membership provisions that a nonprofit with members might use. Don't be alarmed by the short size of the sample—it's an abbreviated version of the complete form, with sample language and instructions only for the sections on the form that contain blanks.

Special Instructions

❶ After completing these membership provisions, copy the full text of this file to your basic bylaws—this material replaces Article 13, the Written Consent, and the Certificate sections and signature lines at the end of your basic bylaws that you prepared above.

❷ Use this blank to indicate any special qualifications required for members (for example, over the age of 18 or currently enrolled students in a school's curriculum). Be careful here. The IRS likes 501(c)(3) tax-exempt corporations to have an open-admissions policy for members, and for membership in the corporation to be open to the general public. As a result, most public benefit corporations don't specify any qualifications for membership (see the suggested wording in the blank on the sample form).

❸ Most public benefit corporations do not require formal application for membership in the corporation. However, some will indicate that members must pay an admission fee and/ or annual dues prior to acceptance as a member in the corporation (see the suggested wording in the blank on the sample form).

❹ Indicate the manner of determining, or the amount of, admission fees and/or annual dues for members in the appropriate blanks (see the suggested wording in the blanks on the sample form).

❺ Indicate the date and time of the annual meeting of members. The members elect directors at this annual meeting. You may wish to coordinate this date with your annual directors' meeting (you might make it slightly before the annual directors' meeting).

❻ Type the date and time of any regular meetings of members. Many nonprofits will leave this line blank and decide to provide only for the annual meeting of members in their bylaws (in the previous paragraph). Those with a more active membership will indicate monthly or semiannual regular meetings of members here.

❼ You can set the quorum requirement for members' meetings at any number, whether greater or less than a majority. However, as indicated in the last paragraph of this section, if

Membership Provisions
of
__(name of corporation)__
a California Public Benefit Corporation

ARTICLE 13 ❶
MEMBERS

SECTION 1. DETERMINATION AND RIGHTS OF MEMBERS

The corporation shall have only one class of members. No member shall hold more than one membership in the corporation. Except as expressly provided in or authorized by the articles of incorporation or bylaws of this corporation, all memberships shall have the same rights, privileges, restrictions, and conditions.

SECTION 2. QUALIFICATIONS OF MEMBERS

The qualifications for membership in this corporation are as follows: __(specify qualifications or, if none, type "Any person is qualified to become a member of this corporation")__ . ❷

SECTION 3. ADMISSION OF MEMBERS

Applicants shall be admitted to membership __(state procedure, e.g., "on making application therefor in writing" and indicate if payment will be required, e.g., " and upon payment of the application fee and/or first annual dues, as specified in the following sections of this bylaw")__ . ❸

SECTION 4. FEES, DUES, AND ASSESSMENTS

(a) The following fee shall be charged for making application for membership in the corporation: __(state specific admission fee or leave to discretion of board, e.g., "in such amount as may be specified from time to time by resolution of the board of directors charged for, and payable with, the application for membership," or, if no fee, type "None")__ . ❹

(b) The annual dues payable to the corporation by members shall be __(state amount of annual dues, leave to discretion of board, e.g., "in such amount as may be determined from time to time by resolution of the board of directors," or type "None")__ . ❺

(c) Memberships shall be nonassessable.

.

.

.

ARTICLE 14
MEETINGS OF MEMBERS

SECTION 1. PLACE OF MEETINGS

Meetings of members shall be held at the principal office of the corporation or at such other place or places within or without the State of California as may be designated from time to time by resolution of the board of directors.

SECTION 2. ANNUAL AND OTHER REGULAR MEETINGS

The members shall meet annually on **(date, e.g., " the first Monday of July, September 30th")** ❺ in each year, at ____(time)____ M, ❺ for the purpose of electing directors and transacting other business as may come before the meeting. Cumulative voting for the election of directors shall not be permitted. The candidates receiving the highest number of votes up to the number of directors to be elected shall be elected. Each voting member shall cast one vote, with voting being by ballot only. The annual meeting of members for the purpose of electing directors shall be deemed a regular meeting and any reference in these bylaws to regular meetings of members refers to this annual meeting.

Other regular meetings of the members shall be held on __(date)__ ,❻ at __(time)__ M.❻ If the day fixed for the annual meeting or other regular meetings falls on a legal holiday, such meeting shall be held at the same hour and place on the next business day.

.

.

.

SECTION 5. QUORUM FOR MEETINGS

A quorum shall consist of __(state percentage, which may be more or less than a majority)__ ❼ of the voting members of the corporation.

The members present at a duly called and held meeting at which a quorum is initially present may continue to do business notwithstanding the loss of a quorum at the meeting due to a withdrawal of members from the meeting provided that any action taken after the loss of a quorum must be approved by at least a majority of the members required to constitute a quorum.

In the absence of a quorum, any meeting of the members may be adjourned from time to time by the vote of a majority of the votes represented in person or by proxy at the meeting, but no other business shall be transacted at such meeting.

When a meeting is adjourned for lack of a sufficient number of members at the meeting or otherwise, it shall not be necessary to give any notice of the time and place of the adjourned meeting or of the business to be transacted at such meeting other than by announcement at the meeting at which the adjournment is taken of the time and place of the adjourned meeting. However, if after the adjournment a new record date is fixed for notice or voting, a notice of the adjourned meeting shall be given to each member who, on the record date for notice of the meeting, is entitled to vote at the meeting. A meeting shall not be adjourned for more than forty-five (45) days.

Notwithstanding any other provision of this Article, if this corporation authorizes members to conduct a meeting with a quorum of less than one-third (1/3) of the voting power, then, if less than one-third (1/3) of the voting power actually attends a regular meeting, in person or by proxy, then no action may be taken on a matter unless the general nature of the matter was stated in the notice of the regular meeting.

.

.

.

SECTION 8. PROXY VOTING

Members entitled to vote ___(type "shall" or "shall not")___ ❽ be permitted to vote or act by proxy. If membership voting by proxy is not allowed by the preceding sentence, no provision in this or other sections of these bylaws referring to proxy voting shall be construed to permit any member to vote or act by proxy.

If membership voting by proxy is allowed, members entitled to vote shall have the right to vote either in person or by a written proxy executed by such person or by his or her duly authorized agent and filed with the Secretary of the corporation, provided, however, that no proxy shall be valid after eleven (11) months from the date of its execution unless otherwise provided in the proxy. In any case, however, the maximum term of any proxy shall be three (3) years from the date of its execution. No proxy shall be irrevocable and may be revoked following the procedures given in Section 5613 of the California Nonprofit Public Benefit Corporation Law.

If membership voting by proxy is allowed, all proxies shall state the general nature of the matter to be voted on and, in the case of a proxy given to vote for the election of directors, shall list those persons who were nominees at the time the notice of the vote for election of directors was given to the members. In any election of directors, any proxy which is marked by a member "withhold" or otherwise marked in a manner indicating that the authority to vote for the election of directors is withheld shall not be voted either for or against the election of a director.

If membership voting by proxy is allowed, proxies shall afford an opportunity for the member to specify a choice between approval and disapproval for each matter or group of related matters intended, at the time the proxy is distributed, to be acted upon at the meeting for which the proxy is solicited. The proxy shall also provide that when the person solicited specifies a choice with respect to any such matter, the vote shall be cast in accordance therewith.

SECTION 9. CONDUCT OF MEETINGS

Meetings of members shall be presided over by the chair of the board, or, if there is no chairperson, by the president of the corporation or, in his or her absence, by the vice president of the corporation or, in the absence of all of these persons, by a chair chosen by a majority of the voting members, present in person or by proxy. The secretary of the corporation shall act as secretary of all meetings of members, provided that, in his or her absence, the presiding officer shall appoint another person to act as secretary of the meeting.

Meetings shall be governed by __**(type "Robert's Rules of Order" or indicate other rules or procedures)**__ , ❾ as such rules may be revised from time to time, insofar as such rules are not inconsistent with or in conflict with these bylaws, with the articles of incorporation of this corporation, or with any provision of law.

.

.

.

WRITTEN CONSENT OF DIRECTORS ADOPTING BYLAWS

We, the undersigned, are all of the persons named as the initial directors in the articles of incorporation of __**(name of corporation)**__ , ❿ a California nonprofit corporation, and, pursuant to the authority granted to the directors by these bylaws to take action by unanimous written consent without a meeting, consent to, and hereby do, adopt the foregoing bylaws, consisting of __**(number of pages)**__ ❿ pages, as the bylaws of this corporation.

Date: _____

__**(signatures of director(s) listed in Article FIVE)**__ ❿
(typed name)   , Director

_____
                                                         , Director

_____
                                                         , Director

_____
                                                         , Director

_____
                                                         , Director

.

.

.

CERTIFICATE

This is to certify that the foregoing is a true and correct copy of the bylaws of the corporation named in the title thereto and that such bylaws were duly adopted by the board of directors of said corporation on the date set forth below.

(Fill in Certificate date and signature of secretary later, after first board meeting) ⓫

Dated: __**(date)**__   __**(signature of secretary)**__

                    (typed name)   , Secretary

your public benefit corporation sets a quorum at less than one-third of the voting power and less than one-third of the members actually attend a meeting, then no action may be taken at the meeting unless the notice of the meeting stated the general nature of the proposals to be acted upon. Fixing a quorum at less than one-third of the voting power, therefore, can make matters more complicated. The normal rule is that any action may be taken at a regular members' meeting, whether or not it was stated in the notice of the meeting (see Subsection (c) of this article in the computer form). In any case, it's a good idea to have at least a one-third quorum to help make members' meetings more representative of the entire membership.

❽ Indicate whether the corporation will allow proxy voting by members. (A proxy is simply a written authorization by a member allowing another person to vote for the member.) Many small membership corporations decide that proxy voting will not be permitted, which avoids problems and complications that can arise in times of controversy or difficult decisions, such as proxy wars or solicitations of proxies by outside or competing interests.

If you decide to allow proxies, the restrictions relating to proxies contained in the next sections of this article will apply.

❾ Indicate, if you wish, the sets of rules that will govern for proposing and taking action at your membership meetings. Robert's Rules of Order is the standard, of course, but you may specify another set of procedures or "none" if you wish to run your membership meetings loosely and informally.

❿ Fill in the Written Consent of Directors paragraph, showing the name of the corporation and the number of pages in your final bylaws. Type your directors' names (the directors named in your articles) below the signature lines. After printing and dating the form, have each director sign the form.

⓫ Do not fill in the blanks following the Certificate at the bottom of the bylaws at this time. Your corporate secretary will complete these blanks after the first meeting of your board.

You're almost done! Replace the corresponding sections of your basic bylaws (Article 13 through the end of the bylaws) with these completed membership provisions. Now turn to Chapter 8 for the next step in your journey toward nonprofit status.

Bylaws for a Religious Corporation

To form a religious corporation, you need special religious corporation bylaws or some other similar document that sets forth the ground rules for your corporation. The reason we mention a "similar document" is that the law governing religious corporations (Section 9150 of the Nonprofit Religious Corporation Law) defines the bylaws of religious corporations as "the code or code of rules used, adopted, or recognized for the regulation or management of the affairs of the corporation irrespective of the name or names by which such rules are designated." In essence, the state recognizes that religions are often governed by canons or other ecclesiastical documents instead of bylaws.

Special Rules for Religious Corporations

The law that applies to religious corporations is considerably more flexible and liberal than the law that applies to other nonprofit corporations. This is particularly true with respect to the form and content of a religious corporation's bylaws, which set forth the general operating rules for a corporation. The state is reluctant to get overly involved in this aspect of a religious corporation's affairs because of the constitutional protections afforded religions, the inappropriateness of state intrusion into most religious disputes, and the wide diversity of religious activities. (See the *Attorney General's Guide for Charities* (on the CD-ROM) that contains a statement regarding the attorney general's overall "hands-off" policy with respect to oversight of religious corporations.)

State Law Will Apply by Default

While the Nonprofit Religious Corporation Law provides certain fundamental rules regarding the operation of religious corporations, many of these rules apply only if the corporation's own canons or bylaws do not provide otherwise. In general, in areas most likely to involve doctrinal matters and First Amendment rights, such as membership meetings and member voting, religious corporations are given the most flexibility for establishing their own rules. See "Religious Purposes" in Chapter 3 for more on the flexibility afforded religious corporations in general.

Directors' Terms and Meetings

Religious corporations can set their own rules regarding the terms of office, election, selection, designation, removal, and resignation of directors. Subject to a few exceptions, religious corporations can also set their own rules about calling, noticing, and holding meetings of members or obtaining the approval of members. As mentioned above, if any of these subjects are not dealt with specifically in a religious corporation's bylaws, then the rules set forth in the Nonprofit Religious Corporation Law will apply.

You may remember from your reading of Chapter 2 that public benefit corporations are subject to the 51% rule, which requires at least 51% of the board to be "disinterested" (not paid for performing services other than as directors or related to any paid persons). Unlike public benefit corporations, all of the directors of a religious corporation can, if they wish, also serve as salaried officers, employees, or independent contractors of the corporation. (See Chapter 2 for a discussion of public benefit corporations and the 51% rule.)

Directors' Duty of Care

The general standard of conduct ("duty of care") for directors of religious corporations is similar to the standard that applies to public benefit corporation directors. Directors must act responsibly and in the best interests of the corporation. (See Chapter 2 for discussion about duty of care.) The duty of care for religious corporation directors is more lenient, however, because religious corporation directors can take into account the religious purposes of the corporation and its religious tenets, canons, laws, policies, and authority when making decisions.

In a public benefit corporation, directors can rely on business and financial reports prepared or presented by officers, employees, and experts, such as lawyers and accountants, when making business and financial decisions. Directors in religious corporations can also rely on information provided by religious authorities, ministers, priests, rabbis, or other people whose positions or duties in the religious organization the directors believe justify their reliance and confidence in them. This more lenient duty of care for religious corporations also applies to decisions relating to compensation for directors, loans to directors, guarantees of obligations of directors, and management of corporate investments. By contrast, for public benefit corporations, loans or guarantees to directors usually must be approved by the attorney general and there are stricter standards for managing corporate investments. See Chapter 2 for more on directors' duty of care.

The rules regarding the approval of self-dealing transactions for religious corporations (a transaction in which a director has a material financial interest, and that hasn't been properly approved by the board or a committee) are generally the same as those that apply to public benefit corporations, except for loans and guaranties to directors as mentioned above. However, directors of religious corporations can take into account the religious purposes of the corporation when considering approval of a self-dealing transaction.

Membership Inspection Rights

In public benefit corporations, members have the right to inspect the corporation's membership list, financial books, and records of members' and board meetings. For religious nonprofits, these membership inspection rights may be limited or totally eliminated by the corporation's bylaws. This is an area where the state felt it was inappropriate—or perhaps, unconstitutional—to require broad inspection rights or financial disclosure of corporate affairs to members. In the absence of any limitation on inspection rights, members of religious corporations have basically the same right to inspect as members of a public benefit corporation.

Attorney General Supervision

The Nonprofit Religious Corporation Law mandates a hands-off policy by the attorney general toward religious corporations, except to the extent the attorney general is empowered to act in the enforcement of the criminal laws. A few exceptions are also provided for the attorney general to step in based on the authority of the Religious Corporation Law. (See the *Attorney General's Guide for Charities* on the CD-ROM that contains a statement regarding the attorney general's overall hands-off policy with respect to oversight of religious corporations.)

The California Attorney General's traditional role of enforcing the charitable trust theory has, since 1980, been severely curtailed. A charitable trust, under Section 9142 of the Religious Corporation Law, is deemed to exist only under certain narrowly defined conditions. Moreover, the attorney general's office is, for the most part, prohibited from enforcing the terms of any implied or express trust (except with respect to certain property received by the corporation for a specific purpose from the general public, again subject to further restrictions, see Section 9230).

General Instructions

The bylaws for a religious corporation on the CD-ROM are basic, nonmembership religious corporation bylaws with standard provisions from the Nonprofit Religious Corporation Law. Nonmembership religious corporations can use these bylaws "as is." Religious corporations with a formal membership structure should start by preparing the basic religious corporation bylaws, then add the membership provisions as explained below.

To prepare bylaws for a religious corporation (member or nonmember), fill in the bylaws for a religious corporation included on the CD-ROM following the sample form and special instructions below.

Here are some general instructions to help you prepare your bylaws:

• The parenthetical blanks, "(_____)," in the sample form below indicate information that you must complete on the computer form on the CD-ROM.

- Corresponding blanks in the computer form are marked with a series of underlined characters.

- Replace the blanks in the computer form (each series of underlined characters) with the information indicated in the blanks in the sample form below.

- Each circled number in the sample form (for example, ❶) refers to a special instruction that provides specific information to help you complete an item. The special instructions follow the sample form.

- A vertical series of dots in the sample form below indicates a gap where we have skipped over language in the computer form.

Sample Bylaws

The sample bylaws below are an abbreviated version of the complete form contained on the CD-ROM. In the sample bylaws, we provide sample language and instructions for the few sections that contain blanks.

Many of you will want to take advantage of the flexibility allowed under the Nonprofit Religious Corporation Law and add customized provisions to these basic bylaws, tailoring them to your organizations' specific operating procedures. If you do this, make sure your changes conform to law. Review the legal provisions of the Nonprofit Religious Corporation Law (Sections 9110 through 9690 of the Nonprofit Corporation Law). You can read these provisions online at www.leginfo.ca.gov/calaw. html. Check the Corporations Code box, then click the Search button at the bottom of the page. Scroll down the heading list to Part 4, Nonprofit Religious Corporations. Click any of the Part 4 (9000 series) headings to read any provision of the Nonprofit Religious Corporation Law. You can also examine the law at a local county law library. You can also

ask a lawyer to make sure your variations are allowable (it shouldn't take the lawyer more than one or two hours to check the bylaws against the statutes).

Special Instructions

Here are the instructions to fill in the blanks in the standard religious corporation bylaws:

❶ Type the name of your corporation in the heading of the bylaws.

❷ Type the name of the county where the corporation's principal office is located. The principal office is the legal address of the corporation and, if your nonprofit is sued, will usually be the county where the lawsuit must be brought.

❸ Don't fill in the blanks in this section at this time. You may want to use these blanks later to change the principal office of the corporation to another location, within the same county, by showing the new address and date of the address change.

❹ This section allows you to state in more detail the primary objectives and purposes of your religious corporation (remember, your statement of specific purposes in your articles of incorporation should have been brief). Here you can go into as much detail as you want, describing the religious purposes and activities of your corporation. You can be brief here if you want, but a more detailed statement will give the state franchise board and the IRS additional information they'll use to determine if the specific activities you plan to engage in entitle you to the necessary tax exemptions. (See "Prepare Articles of Incorporation" in Chapter 6 for examples of sample responses by nonreligious groups.)

❺ Indicate the total number of persons authorized to serve on your board. Most of the time, this number will be the same as the number of people you've already indicated as

Bylaws

of

_____ (Name of Corporation) _____ ❶

a California Religious Corporation

ARTICLE 1
OFFICES

SECTION 1. PRINCIPAL OFFICE

The principal office of the corporation for the transaction of its business is located in **__(name of county)__** County, California.❷

SECTION 2. CHANGE OF ADDRESS

The county of the corporation's principal office can be changed only by amendment of these bylaws and not otherwise. The board of directors may, however, change the principal office from one location to another within the named county by noting the changed address and effective date below, and such changes of address shall not be deemed an amendment of these bylaws:

(Fill lines in below later, if and when address changes) ❸

_____   Dated: _____

_____   Dated: _____

_____   Dated: _____

SECTION 3. OTHER OFFICES

The corporation may also have offices at such other places, within or without the State of California, where it is qualified to do business, as its business may require and as the board of directors may, from time to time, designate.

ARTICLE 2
PURPOSES

SECTION 1. OBJECTIVES AND PURPOSES

The primary objectives and purposes of this corporation shall be: ❹

__(provide specific statement of your group's nonprofit purposes and activities)__

_____

_____

_____

ARTICLE 3
DIRECTORS

SECTION 1. NUMBER

The corporation shall have __**(number of directors)**__ ❺ directors and collectively they shall be known as the board of directors. The number may be changed by amendment of this bylaw, or by repeal of this bylaw and adoption of a new bylaw, as provided in these bylaws.

.

.

SECTION 5. COMPENSATION

Directors shall serve without compensation except that they shall be allowed and paid __**("their actual and necessary expenses incurred in attending directors' meetings" or state other provisions allowing reasonable compensation for attending meetings)**__. ❻ In addition, they shall be allowed reasonable advancement or reimbursement of expenses incurred in the performance of their regular duties as specified in Section 3 of this Article. Any payments to directors shall be approved in advance in accordance with this corporation's conflict of interest policy set forth in Article 9 of these bylaws.

.

.

SECTION 7. REGULAR AND ANNUAL MEETINGS

Regular meetings of directors shall be held on __**(date)**__ ❼ at __**(time)**__ M,❼ unless such day falls on a legal holiday, in which event the regular meeting shall be held at the same hour and place on the next business day.

If this corporation makes no provision for members, then, at the annual meeting of directors held on __**(date)**__, ❼ directors shall be elected by the board of directors in accordance with this section. Cumulative voting by directors for the election of directors shall not be permitted. The candidates receiving the highest number of votes up to the number of directors to be elected shall be elected. Each director shall cast one vote, with voting being by ballot only.

.

.

SECTION 12. QUORUM FOR MEETINGS

A quorum shall consist of __**(state number or percentage, e.g., "a majority of the Board of")**__ ❽ directors.

.

.

SECTION 14. CONDUCT OF MEETINGS

Meetings of the board of directors shall be presided over by the chairperson of the board, or, if no such person has been so designated or in his or her absence, the president of the corporation or, in his or her absence, by the vice president of the corporation or, in the absence of each of these persons, by a chairperson chosen by a majority of the directors present at the meeting. The secretary of the corporation shall act as secretary of all meetings of the board, provided that, in his or her absence, the presiding officer shall appoint another person to act as secretary of the meeting.

Meetings shall be governed by **("Robert's Rules of Order" or state other rules or procedures for conduct of directors' meeting)** , ❾ as such rules may be revised from time to time, insofar as such rules are not inconsistent with or in conflict with these bylaws, with the articles of incorporation of this corporation, or with provisions of law.

.

.

.

ARTICLE 5
COMMITTEES

SECTION 1. EXECUTIVE COMMITTEE

The board of directors may, by a majority vote of directors, designate two (2) or more of its members (who may also be serving as officers of this corporation) to constitute an executive committee and delegate to such committee any of the powers and authority of the board in the management of the business and affairs of the corporation, except with respect to:

(a) The approval of any action which, under law or the provisions of these bylaws, requires the approval of the members or of a majority of all of the members.

(b) The filling of vacancies on the board or on any committee which has the authority of the board.

(c) The fixing of compensation of the directors for serving on the board or on any committee.

(d) The amendment or repeal of bylaws or the adoption of new bylaws.

(e) The amendment or repeal of any resolution of the board which by its express terms is not so amendable or repealable.

(f) The appointment of committees of the board or the members thereof.

By a majority vote of its members then in office, the board may at any time revoke or modify any or all of the authority so delegated, increase or decrease but not below two (2) the number of its members, and fill vacancies therein from the members of the board. The committee shall keep regular minutes of its proceedings, cause them to be filed with the corporate records, and report the same to the board from time to time as the board may require. ❿

.

.

.

ARTICLE 8
FISCAL YEAR

SECTION 1. FISCAL YEAR OF THE CORPORATION

The fiscal year of the corporation shall begin on the __(day and month, e.g., "first day of January")__ ⓫ and end on the __(day and month, e.g., "last day of December")__ ⓫ in each year.

.

.

.

ARTICLE 9 ⓬
CONFLICT OF INTEREST AND COMPENSATION APPROVAL POLICIES

SECTION 1. PURPOSE OF CONFLICT OF INTEREST POLICY

.

.

.

ARTICLE 13 ⓭
MEMBERS

SECTION 1. DETERMINATION OF MEMBERS ⓮

If this corporation makes no provision for members, then, pursuant to Section 9310(b) of the Nonprofit Religious Corporation Law of the State of California, any action which would otherwise, under law or the provisions of the articles of incorporation or bylaws of this corporation, require approval by a majority of all members or approval by the members, shall only require the approval of the board of directors.

WRITTEN CONSENT OF DIRECTORS ADOPTING BYLAWS

We, the undersigned, are all of the persons named as the initial directors in the articles of incorporation of __(name of corporation)__, ⓖ a California nonprofit corporation, and, pursuant to the authority granted to the directors by these bylaws to take action by unanimous written consent without a meeting, consent to, and hereby do, adopt the foregoing bylaws, consisting of __(number of pages)__ ⓖ pages, as the bylaws of this corporation.

Date: _____

__(signatures of director(s) listed in Article FIVE)__ ⓖ
(typed name) , Director

_____, Director

_____, Director

_____, Director

_____, Director

.

.

.

CERTIFICATE

This is to certify that the foregoing is a true and correct copy of the bylaws of the corporation named in the title thereto and that such bylaws were duly adopted by the board of directors of said corporation on the date set forth below.

(Fill in Certificate date and signature of secretary later, after first board meeting) ⓰

Dated: __(date)__　　　　__(signature of secretary)__
(typed name) , Secretary

the first directors of the corporation in Article Five of the articles of incorporation. However, you may state a greater number to allow for additional directors who will be elected at a future meeting of the board.

For information on providing for a variable number of directors, see Bylaws for a Public Benefit Nonprofit Corporation, above, special instruction ❺.

❻ Use this blank if you wish to pay your directors a per-meeting fee or other compensation arrangement (such as a yearly payment) for attending board meetings. If, as is often the case, you do not wish to pay directors for attending meetings, simply type "no payments authorized" in this blank. The last sentence allows the corporation to advance or reimburse directors for actual expenses they incur in attending meetings (gas, tolls, and the like) and for performing any other director duties for the corporation.

❼ In the blanks in the first paragraph, fill in the date when the board will hold its regular meetings. Many nonprofits hold regular board meetings, while others simply schedule regular meetings once each year (and call special meetings during the year when required). In any case, make sure to indicate that you will hold a regular board meeting at least annually.

Responses for Board Meeting Dates

Regular meetings of directors shall be held on **the first Friday of each month** at **9 o'clock AM**…

Regular meetings of directors shall be held on **the second Monday of December** at **1 o'clock PM**…

Regular meetings of directors shall be held on **July 1st and February 20th** at **9 o'clock AM**…

In the second paragraph of this section, fill in the blank to indicate which of your regular board meetings will be the annual regular meeting of the board, when you'll elect (or re-elect) directors of your corporation. Note that in a nonmembership corporation, the directors vote for their own reelection or replacements, with each director casting one written vote. Of course, if a corporation has provided for only one regular meeting each year in the first paragraph of this section, then the date of this regular meeting will be repeated in this blank as the date of the annual meeting of directors.

Responses for Annual Meeting Dates

If this corporation makes no provision for members, then, at the annual meeting of directors held on **January 1st**, directors shall be elected…

If this corporation makes no provision for members, then, at the annual meeting of directors held on **the first Friday of July**, directors shall be elected…

The provisions in the second paragraph of this section affect only nonmembership corporations. Membership corporations can leave this line blank. Membership religious corporations will add membership provisions to their bylaws indicating the procedure for the election of directors by the members, as explained below.

❽ Indicate the number of directors who must be present at a directors' meeting to constitute a quorum so that business can be conducted. Although the usual practice is to provide for a majority, a nonprofit religious corporation can provide for a larger or smaller number.

Whatever number or percentage you decide on, understand that this section of the bylaws concerns a quorum, not a vote requirement. A meeting can be held only if at least a quorum of directors is present, but a vote on any matter before the board must be passed by the vote of a majority of those present at the meeting. (There are some exceptions to the majority-of-those-present rules—see Section 13 of Article 3 of the religious corporation bylaws.)

EXAMPLE:

If a religious corporation with five directors provides for a majority quorum, then a quorum of at least three directors must be present to hold a meeting of directors. If three directors actually attend, then action can be taken at the meeting by the vote of two of the directors present (the majority vote of those present at the meeting).

❾ In this blank, indicate the rules of order that directors will use at their meetings. Although many nonprofits specify Robert's Rules of Order here, religious groups may wish to refer to rules established by their organization for the conduct of business at directors' meetings. Alternatively, you may wish to leave this item blank if you see no need to specify formal procedures for introducing and discussing items of business at your board meetings.

❿ The Nonprofit Religious Corporation Law allows you to form an executive committee of the board, which must have at least two board members and can have much of the management power of the full board. This section of the bylaws provides for an executive committee of board members only. Although at least two board members must serve on this committee, in practice most nonprofit corporations establish an executive committee of from three to five board members. Of course, you can set up other types of committees with or without board members (see Section 2 of this article in the CD-ROM bylaws).

⓫ Indicate the beginning and ending dates of the fiscal year of the corporation. The fiscal year of the corporation is the period for which the corporation keeps its books (its accounting period) and will determine the corporation's tax year for purposes of filing certain tax returns and reports. It may be the calendar year, from January 1 to December 31 (this is the usual case for nonprofits); or it may be what the IRS considers a true fiscal year, consisting of a 12-month period ending on the last day of any month other than December (for example, from July 1 to June 30).

⓬ Article 9 of the bylaws included in this book contains rules and procedures for approving or avoiding conflict-of-interest transactions, including compensation arrangements, between your nonprofit and its directors, officers, employees, contractors, and others. This bylaw provision contains the conflicts-of-interest language recommended by the IRS (included in the sample conflict-of-interest policy in Appendix A of the instructions to IRS Form 1023). It also contains language for the approval of compensation arrangements that attempts to comply with the safe harbor provisions of the excess benefit rules (see the discussion on the excess benefit rules in "Limitation on Profits and Benefits" in Chapter 3). You will need to become familiar with this provision, and make sure you are comfortable with its procedures for the approval and review of financial transactions with, and salary and other compensation paid to, your directors, officers, and others who are in a position to influence your nonprofit. If you decide to make changes to this provision, do so only after reading, in Chapter 9, "Prepare Tax Exemption Application," instructions to Part V, where we refer to this bylaw provision when providing sample responses to questions on the application. If you make any changes, you will need to create your own responses to some of the questions on the 501(c)(3) application.

⑬ Last portion of Basic Religious Corporation Bylaws: The last portion of the basic bylaws (consisting of Article 13, Written Consent of Directors, and Certificate sections) is intended only for nonmembership groups. Membership religious corporations do not need to fill in and use this last portion of the basic bylaws—we show you how to add membership provisions to complete your bylaws below.

⑭ Section 1 of Article 13 makes it clear that the directors of nonmembership corporations can take the place of members in taking any action which, under law, otherwise requires membership approval (in other words, the directors can act in place of the members in nonmembership corporations).

⑮ Fill in the Written Consent of Directors paragraph, showing the name of the corporation and the number of pages in your final bylaws. Type your directors' names (the directors named in your articles) below the signature lines. After printing and dating the form, have each director sign the form.

⑯ Do not fill in the blanks following the Certificate at bottom of the bylaws at this time. Your corporate secretary will complete these blanks after the first meeting of your board.

Membership Bylaw Provisions for a Religious Corporation

This section applies only to religious membership corporations. If you have decided to form a nonmembership religious corporation, this section does not apply to you and you can skip ahead to Chapter 8.

Before we show you how to fill in your bylaws, let's deal with one possible area of confusion. Your religious corporation will probably want to refer to its supporters as "members"—of the congregation or church, for example. This gives your participants a feeling of participation, which will be important for you. Calling supporters members is perfectly okay, and you can do so without thereby establishing a formal membership corporation in the eyes of the IRS. In fact, most religious groups will not want a formal membership structure because of the active role legal members assume in the affairs of a membership corporation. As long as you don't, in your bylaws, give your members the legal status of formal members, you will not have established a formal membership corporation. See "Membership Nonprofits" in Chapter 2 for a complete discussion of member and nonmembership corporations.

General Instructions

Here are general instructions for filling in membership provisions for bylaws of a religious nonprofit corporation (included on the CD-ROM):

- The parenthetical blanks, "(_____)," in the sample form below indicate information that you must complete on the computer form on the CD-ROM.

- Corresponding blanks in the computer form are marked with a series of underlined characters.

- Replace the blanks in the computer form (each series of underlined characters) with the information indicated in the blanks in the sample form below.

- Each circled number in the sample form (for instance, **❶**) refers to a special instruction that provides specific information to help you complete an item.

- A vertical series of dots in the sample form below indicates a gap where we have skipped over language in the computer form.

- To add membership provisions to your basic religious corporation bylaws, fill in the blanks in the membership provisions file included on the CD-ROM, following the sample form and instructions below. Once completed, copy these membership provisions to your basic bylaws as explained in special instruction ❶ below.

Customizing Your Membership Bylaw Provisions

The Nonprofit Religious Corporation Law gives religious groups considerable flexibility to fashion many of their bylaw provisions. Accordingly, we've borrowed several membership provisions from the public benefit corporation bylaws discussed earlier. We think they make sense for most small membership religious organizations.

You may want to take advantage of the flexibility allowed religious corporations and customize these provisions. If you make modifications, make sure that they comply with the Nonprofit Religious Corporation Law (or have an attorney check your work). Most of the statutory religious corporation membership provisions are contained in Sections 9310 through 9420 of the Corporations Code. (See "Sample Bylaws," above, for instructions on how to find the Religious Corporation Law online).

Sample Membership Provisions

The sample bylaws below are an abbreviated version of the complete form contained on the CD-ROM. We've provided sample language and instructions for the few sections that contain blanks.

Special Instructions

Here are the instructions for filling in the blanks in the religious corporation membership provisions:

❶ After completing these membership provisions, copy the full text of this file to your basic religious bylaws—this material replaces Article 13, the Written Consent and Certificate sections, and signature lines at the end of your basic bylaws.

❷ Use this blank to indicate any special qualifications required for members. Please realize, however, that the IRS likes 501(c)(3) tax-exempt corporations to have membership in the corporation open to the general public. Consequently, most religious corporations will not specify any qualifications for membership (see the suggested wording in the blank on the sample form).

❸ Most religious corporations do not require members to formally apply for membership in the corporation. However, a few may wish to require members to pay an admission fee and/or annual dues prior to acceptance as a member in the corporation (see the suggested wording in the blank on the sample form).

❹ If you're going to require admission fees and/or annual dues for members, enter the amount or explain how you'll determine what the amount will be (see the suggested wording in the blanks on the sample form). If you won't charge application or admission fees (most groups won't), type "None" in both blanks.

Membership Provisions

of

_____**(name of corporation)**_____

a California Religious Corporation

.

.

.

ARTICLE 13 ❶

MEMBERS

SECTION 1. DETERMINATION AND RIGHTS OF MEMBERS

The corporation shall have only one class of members. No member shall hold more than one membership in the corporation. Except as expressly provided in or authorized by the articles of incorporation or bylaws of this corporation, all memberships shall have the same rights, privileges, restrictions, and conditions.

SECTION 2. QUALIFICATIONS OF MEMBERS

The qualifications for membership in this corporation are as follows __**(specify qualifications or, if none, type "Any person is qualified to become a member of this corporation")**__ . ❷

SECTION 3. ADMISSION OF MEMBERS

Applicants shall be admitted to membership __**(state procedure, e.g., "on making application therefor in writing" and indicate if payment will be required, e.g., "and upon payment of the application fee and/or first annual dues, as specified in the following sections of this bylaw")**__ . ❸

SECTION 4. FEES, DUES, AND ASSESSMENTS

(a) The following fee shall be charged for making application for membership in the corporation: __**(state specific admission fee or leave to discretion of board, e.g., "in such amount as may be specified from time to time by resolution of the board of directors charged for, and payable with, the application for membership," or, if no fee, type "None")**__ .

(b) The annual dues payable to the corporation by members shall be __**(state amount of annual dues, leave to discretion of board, e.g., "in such amount as may be determined from time to time by resolution of the board of directors," or type "None")**__ . ❹

(c) Memberships shall be nonassessable.

SECTION 9. TERMINATION OF MEMBERSHIP ❺

(a) Grounds for Termination. The membership of a member shall terminate upon the occurrence of any of the following events:

(1) Upon his or her notice of such termination delivered to the president or secretary of the corporation personally or by mail, such membership to terminate upon the date of delivery of the notice or date of deposit in the mail.

(2) Upon a determination by the board of directors that the member has engaged in conduct materially and seriously prejudicial to the interests or purposes of the corporation.

(3) If this corporation has provided for the payment of dues by members, upon a failure to renew his or her membership by paying dues on or before their due date, such termination to be effective thirty (30) days after a written notification of delinquency is given personally or mailed to such member by the secretary of the corporation. A member may avoid such termination by paying the amount of delinquent dues within a thirty- (30) day period following the member's receipt of the written notification of delinquency.

(b) Procedure for Expulsion. Following the determination that a member should be expelled under subparagraph (a)(2) of this section, the following procedure shall be implemented:

(1) A notice shall be sent by first-class or registered mail to the last address of the member as shown on the corporation's records, setting forth the expulsion and the reasons therefor. Such notice shall be sent at least fifteen (15) days before the proposed effective date of the expulsion.

(2) The member being expelled shall be given an opportunity to be heard, either orally or in writing, at a hearing to be held not less than five (5) days before the effective date of the proposed expulsion. The hearing will be held by the board of directors in accordance with the quorum and voting rules set forth in these bylaws applicable to the meetings of the Board. The notice to the member of his or her proposed expulsion shall state the date, time, and place of the hearing on his or her proposed expulsion.

(3) Following the hearing, the board of directors shall decide whether or not the member should, in fact, be expelled, suspended, or sanctioned in some other way. The decision of the board shall be final.

(4) If this corporation has provided for the payment of dues by members, any person expelled from the corporation shall receive a refund of dues already paid. The refund shall be prorated to return only the unaccrued balance remaining for the period of the dues payment.

SECTION 10. RIGHTS ON TERMINATION OF MEMBERSHIP

All rights of a member in the corporation shall cease on termination of membership as herein provided.

ARTICLE 14
MEETINGS OF MEMBERS ❻

SECTION 1. PLACE OF MEETINGS

Meetings of members shall be held at the principal office of the corporation or at such other place or places within or without the State of California as may be designated from time to time by resolution of the board of directors.

SECTION 2. ANNUAL AND OTHER REGULAR MEETINGS

The members shall meet annually on __(date, e.g., " the first Monday of July,__ __September 30th)"__ ❼ in each year, at __(time)__ M, ❼ for the purpose of electing directors and transacting other business as may come before the meeting. Cumulative voting for the election of directors shall not be permitted. The candidates receiving the highest number of votes up to the number of directors to be elected shall be elected. Each voting member shall cast one vote, with voting being by ballot only. The annual meeting of members for the purpose of electing directors shall be deemed a regular meeting and any reference in these bylaws to regular meetings of members refers to this annual meeting.

Other regular meetings of the members shall be held on __(date)__, ❽ at __(time)__ M. ❽

If the day fixed for the annual meeting or other regular meetings falls on a legal holiday, such meeting shall be held at the same hour and place on the next business day.

.
.
.

SECTION 8. PROXY VOTING

Members entitled to vote __("shall" or "shall not")__ ❾ be permitted to vote or act by proxy. If membership voting by proxy is not allowed by the preceding sentence, no provision in this or other sections of these bylaws referring to proxy voting shall be construed to permit any member to vote or act by proxy.

If membership voting by proxy is allowed, members entitled to vote shall have the right to vote either in person or by a written proxy executed by such person or by his or her duly authorized agent and filed with the secretary of the corporation, provided, however, that no proxy shall be valid after eleven (11) months from the date of its execution unless otherwise provided in the proxy. In any case, however, the maximum term of any proxy shall be three (3) years from the date of its execution. No proxy shall be irrevocable and may be revoked following the procedures given in Section 9417 of the California Nonprofit Religious Corporation Law.

If membership voting by proxy is allowed, all proxies shall state the general nature of the matter to be voted on and, in the case of a proxy given to vote for the election of directors, shall list those persons who were nominees at the time the notice of the vote for election of directors was given to the members. In any election of directors, any proxy which is marked by a member "withhold" or otherwise marked in a manner indicating that the authority to vote for the election of directors is withheld shall not be voted either for or against the election of a director.

If membership voting by proxy is allowed, proxies shall afford an opportunity for the member to specify a choice between approval and disapproval for each matter or group of related matters intended, at the time the proxy is distributed, to be acted upon at the meeting for which the proxy is solicited. The proxy shall also provide that when the person solicited specifies a choice with respect to any such matter, the vote shall be cast in accordance therewith.

SECTION 9. CONDUCT OF MEETINGS

Meetings of members shall be presided over by the chairperson of the board, or, if there is no chairperson, by the president of the corporation or, in his or her absence, by the vice president of the corporation or, in the absence of all of these persons, by a chairperson chosen by a majority of the voting members, present in person or by proxy. The secretary of the corporation shall act as secretary of all meetings of members, provided that, in his or her absence, the presiding officer shall appoint another person to act as secretary of the meeting.

Meetings shall be governed by __**("Robert's Rules of Order" or indicate other rules or procedures)**__ , ❿ as such rules may be revised from time to time, insofar as such rules are not inconsistent with or in conflict with these bylaws, with the articles of incorporation of this corporation, or with any provision of law.

.

.

.

WRITTEN CONSENT OF DIRECTORS ADOPTING BYLAWS

We, the undersigned, are all of the persons named as the initial directors in the articles of incorporation of __**(name of corporation)**__ , ⓫ a California nonprofit corporation, and, pursuant to the authority granted to the directors by these bylaws to take action by unanimous written consent without a meeting, consent to, and hereby do, adopt the foregoing bylaws, consisting of __**(number of pages)**__ ⓫ pages, as the bylaws of this corporation.

Date: _____

__**(signatures of director(s) listed in Article FIVE)**__ ⓫

(typed name)   , Director

_____

, Director

_____

, Director

_____

, Director

_____

, Director

.

.

.

CERTIFICATE

This is to certify that the foregoing is a true and correct copy of the bylaws of the corporation named in the title thereto and that such bylaws were duly adopted by the board of directors of said corporation on the date set forth below.

(Fill in Certificate date and signature of secretary later, after first board meeting) ⓬

Dated: __(date)__   __(signature of secretary)_____

                                                  (typed name)   , Secretary

---

❺ A membership corporation will need a process for removing members. The membership termination provisions in Section 9 of this Article are taken from the public benefit corporation law. They give due process to members, allowing them notice and an opportunity to be heard before the board decides whether they will be expelled. Although we think these provisions reflect a sensible set of rules, religious corporations are free to fashion their own procedures (Calif. Corp. Code § 9340(d)). If you wish to do so, replace the language of Section 9 with your own termination of membership rules.

❻ Under Section 9410(a) of the Corporations Code, religious corporations can specify any reasonable method of calling, noticing, and holding regular or special meetings of members (though there are some limitations, as mentioned below). Therefore, you may wish to replace the default procedures for calling, noticing, and holding meetings contained in the various sections of this Article with your own rules. For example, you might want to allow directors to call special meetings of members upon two days' telephone notice.

There are notice rules that apply when members approve certain types of actions by less than unanimous consent. These rules cannot be waived. These rules are listed in Section 4(f) of Article 14 of the religious corporation membership provisions in the CD-ROM file. We won't list all the special cases here. If you wish to change the notice rules and wish to check these special cases, see Section 9410(b) of the Corporations Code. If you have a lawyer review your changes, ask him or her to make sure your changes conform to this section of the Corporations Code.

❼ Indicate the date and time of the annual meeting of members. The members elect directors at this annual meeting. You may wish to coordinate this date with your annual directors' meeting (for example, slightly before the annual directors' meeting).

❽ Type the date and time of any regular meetings of members. Many nonprofits will leave this line blank and decide to provide for only the annual meeting of members in their bylaws (you did this in the previous paragraph). Those with a more active membership will indicate monthly or semiannual regular meetings of members here.

❾ Indicate whether the corporation will allow proxy voting by members. (A proxy is simply a written authorization by a member allowing another person to vote for the member.) Many small membership corporations decide against proxy voting, to avoid problems and complications that can arise in times of controversy or difficult decisions (such as proxy wars or solicitations of proxies by outside or competing interests).

If you decide to allow proxies, the restrictions relating to proxies contained in the next sections of this Article will apply.

❿ Indicate, if you wish, the sets of rules that will govern the proposing and taking of action at your membership meetings. Robert's Rules of Order is the standard, but you may specify another set of procedures.

⓫ Fill in the Written Consent of Directors paragraph, showing the name of the corporation and the number of pages in your final bylaws. Type your directors' names (the directors named in your articles) below the signature lines. After printing and dating the form, have each director sign the form.

⓬ Don't fill in the blanks following the Certificate at bottom of the bylaws at this time. Your corporate secretary will complete these blanks after your board's first meeting.

Replace the corresponding sections of your basic bylaws (Article 13 through the end of the bylaws) with these completed membership provisions. ●

Prepare Your State Tax Exemption

After filing your articles of incorporation and preparing bylaws, your next step is to prepare your state tax exemption application. There are a number of details here that require your attention, but if you approach this task with fresh energy and a little determination, you will easily complete this step.

If you think your nonprofit corporation meets the requirements for tax-exempt status under Section 501(c)(3), it should also meet the requirements for exemption from corporate income taxes under Section 23701(d) of the California Revenue and Taxation Code. To get the complete picture, glance at Chapter 9, which covers the federal form. You may conclude, as many incorporators do, that because the forms request similar information, you may as well prepare both tax applications at the same time.

When comparing the forms, you'll notice that information about your group's programs and finances is called for in both applications, though each form asks for the information in a slightly different format. Attachments and exhibits you prepare for the state form are also usually required for the federal form. The federal form differs from the state form in that it requires additional information, some of which is more technical than the state information because certain federal tax requirements (such as the federal public charity classification) do not apply under state tax law.

Before preparing the state tax exemption application, read the instructions for the application and review the material on obtaining 501(c)(3) tax-exempt status covered in Chapter 3.

The State Tax Exemption Application: Form FTB 3500

You will file the state tax exemption application form (Form FTB 3500) with the California Franchise Tax Board. This form is provided as part of the FTB 3500 booklet, which also contains official state instructions to the form. We have included a tear-out version of the form (2006) in Appendix B and the form with instructions on the CD-ROM.

Ways to Complete the Exemption Application

There are three ways to complete the state tax exemption application:

- Use the tear-out form in the book and fill it in by hand or typewriter.

- Open the FTB 3500 Exemption Application form on the CD-ROM. This booklet contains the state FTB 3500 form, plus official instructions to the form. Print one copy of the FTB 3500 form and fill in the blanks by hand or typewriter. The FTB 3500 file is provided in PDF format. To view and print this file, you must have Adobe Reader installed on your computer. This free program is provided on the CD-ROM, and also is available from the Adobe website at www.adobe.com.

- Go to the Franchise Tax Board's website and access the form online. To do this, go to www.ftb.ca.gov and click on the Forms tab at the top of the page. Under Forms and Publications, start with the most recent year and see if the FTB 3500 is listed for that year. If it doesn't show up, go back to the prior years until you find the most current version. You can also email the Franchise Tax Board to request a copy of the form by email. The file from the Franchise Tax Board is provided in PDF format.

⊘ **CAUTION**

Check that the 3500 form you are using is the most current. Before filling in the FTB 3500 form included with this book, check to see that it's current. Go to the Franchise Tax Board's website (www.ftb.ca.gov) and get the current year or the most recent year for which the form is available (as explained above). Compare the revision date on the first page of the latest online FTB 3500 booklet with the revision date for the form in this book (2006). If you prepare an FTB 3500 form that is newer than the one we provide with this book, the instructions below should still work to guide you through most of the form since changes to the form usually consist of reorganization and format changes. If a newer form contains questions not covered in this chapter, call the Franchise Tax Board (at 916-845-4171) and ask a tax-exempt organization specialist for help with the new material.

Attachments and Exhibits

As you go through the form, you'll see that you must include documents such as articles, bylaws, and financial statements with your completed Form FTB 3500. You'll also need to provide narrative answers to questions. You will use attachment pages for these purposes, as we explain in more detail below. You can use a separate attachment page for each question or you can have your attachment pages run together—that is, the attachment pages can contain answers to many questions. How you format and use the attachment pages is up to you—just be sure that the FTB can connect each response on your attachment pages with a particular question on the FTB 3500 form.

We have some suggestions to help you prepare attachment pages. Use 8 ½" x 11" paper, number the pages in the heading or footer on each page, and type or print the information needed. At the top of each attachment page, indicate that the material is an attachment to your exemption application and give the name of the corporation. Use the format in the sample below (you'll see that we provide you with plenty of sample language you can use in your responses on the attachment pages).

Attachment Page

ATTACHMENT TO FTB EXEMPTION APPLICATION OF

Blue Valley Education Foundation

Page 1:

Item: 6(b) "Any person is qualified to become a member of this corporation. The corporation shall have only one class of members and all memberships have the same rights, privileges, restrictions, and conditions. The number of members of the general public who will be admitted to the corporation is undetermined."

Item 7(a): Endorsed Articles of Incorporation attached, Exhibit A

Item 7(b): Copy of proposed Bylaws attached, Exhibit B

As you can see from some of the sample attachment responses above, you will need to attach legal documents as well as financial statements to your exemption application. Label the documents as exhibits and letter them in alphabetical order. You can write the exhibit number at the top of the document, or you can staple a separate blank page or note to the front of the document and write the exhibit reference on that page or note (for example "Exhibit A"). We recommend you do a separate exhibit reference page or note for your certified articles because the articles are supposed to be an exact copy of the articles you filed with the secretary of state. Make sure each document has a heading that identifies its content and the name of your nonprofit. The copies of your legal documents should have headings printed on their first page already—such as "Articles of (Name of Your Corporation)" or "Bylaws of (Name of Your Corporation)." Make sure to put identifying headings on all financial statements and other exhibits you prepare yourself, and to number each page if the document has multiple pages.

The sample below shows how the exhibit heading for a typical financial statement might look.

Heading for Exhibits

EXHIBIT A, *Blue Valley Education Foundation*
Proposed Budget for 20xx
Page 1

Make at least one copy of form FTB 3500 (from the appendix, CD-ROM, or online) and use this copy for your first draft, following the line-by-line instructions below. After making corrections to the draft form, copy your final responses to the final version of the form that you will mail to the FTB.

Instructions for Completing Form 3500

In this section, we go line by line through the Form FTB 3500, indicating the appropriate response or information you should provide. Each reference to a particular blank below corresponds to the same blank on the state exemption application.

If you have difficulty understanding the content or significance of certain responses, reread the previous chapters of this book. You may decide you need to consult with or give some of this work to a tax advisor or lawyer.

Background and Organizational Information (Blanks 1(a)–6(h))

Top of Form: You must file your articles of incorporation before you submit your state (and federal) tax exemption application. In the top left blank, insert your California corporation number. This is the number that appears above or to the left of the endorsed-filed stamp of the secretary of state in the upper right-hand corner of the first page of the articles. Typically, it starts with a letter followed by a seven-digit number. In the top-center blank "Federal employer identification number," type: "Number not yet assigned. Will indicate on first annual report." Of course, if you have applied for and received a federal employer number (see Chapter 9, "Prepare Your Tax Exemption Application," Part I, instructions for Line 4), you should show it here. Ignore the top-right blank, "Secretary of State file no." This item is for LLCs (limited liability companies) only. We assume you are applying for your tax exemption as a nonprofit corporation. (Nonprofit LLCs are unusual and require the help of an experienced lawyer and tax advisor to set up.)

On the next lines, write the full name of your corporation exactly as it appears in the heading of your articles of incorporation. Indicate the street and mailing address of the principal office of the corporation and the corporation's telephone number—you can use a private mailbox (PMB) number. The Franchise Tax Board will use this address as a mailing address to send forms to your organization.

Then fill in the name, street or mailing address (may be a PMB number), and telephone number of a representative who will be responsible for receiving communications from the Franchise Tax Board regarding your application. (This is usually one of the initial directors.)

If your nonprofit or your representative leases a private mailbox for the corporation's mail to be sent to, show the number as part of the address in the PMB no. item for the address.

Blank 1(a). Type "23701(d)" in the blank provided at the end of this line. This is the section of the California Revenue and Taxation Code that provides a state exemption for 501(c)(3) charitable, educational, religious, scientific, or literary groups.

If you fall under another category as listed in the Instructions for Form FTB 3500 (and are using this book to form a non-501(c)(3) tax exempt organization), indicate the appropriate subsection of Section 23701 that corresponds to the type of nonprofit corporation you are organizing. (For a further discussion of these special organizations, see the parallel federal tax exemption categories listed in Appendix B under *Special Nonprofit Tax-Exempt Organizations.*)

Blank 1(b). Enter the primary activity of your organization, using the keywords associated with your group's 501(c)(3) tax-exempt purposes. Use one or more of the following words to describe your activities: "charitable," "educational," "religious," "scientific," or "literary."

Sample Responses

Primary Activity of Organization:
Charitable Activities or
Charitable and Educational Activities or
Religious Activities

Blanks 2(a)–2(b). In 2(a), check "Corporation" and show the date you were incorporated as the "Date organized" in 2(a). This is the date the articles of incorporation were endorsed (filed) by the secretary of state. This date appears in the upper right-hand corner of the first page of the copies of the certified articles as part of the secretary of state's "endorsed-filed" stamp. It is not necessarily the date of the secretary of state's certification indicated on the facing certification page (containing the gold seal of California) attached to the front of each of the certified copies of the filed articles.

In response to 2(b): "If formed in another state..."), insert "N/A" in the blank (1), "Date qualified in California," to show that this information is not applicable to your California corporation.

Blanks 3(a)–3(c). Most groups should be able to indicate "No" to Question 3(a) and can skip the remaining questions under this item.

However, if you incorporated a preexisting nonprofit association that was granted a tax exemption for prior years, check "Yes" to 3(a) and provide the information requested under 3(b) through 3(c), attaching copies of the determination letter(s) received by the nonprofit association. Unincorporated associations that were granted tax-exempt status must file a new FTB 3500 to reapply for a tax exemption for their newly formed corporation.

SEE AN EXPERT

If your preexisting nonprofit association or your current corporation was previously denied an exemption, consult an attorney or tax specialist before preparing and filing your exemption application.

Blanks 4(a)–4(b). Check "No" to 4(a). However, if your preexisting nonprofit association or current nonprofit corporation filed federal income tax returns prior to the preparation of this state tax exemption application, indicate "Yes" and provide the additional information requested in 4(b).

Blank 5. State your annual accounting period. This is the same period as the fiscal year specified in Article 8 of the CD-ROM bylaws (for example, "January 1 to December 31"). The ending date of your accounting period must fall on the last day of a month.

TIP

Use attachment pages if necessary. If you answer "No" to Question 6(a) or "Yes" to Questions 6(b) – 6(h), you will need to use one or more attachment pages for your responses. Follow the instructions for preparing attachments for Question 7 below when providing the information required for Question 6(a). You can type more than one answer on one attachment page.

Blank 6(a). Indicate "Yes," unless you incorporated an existing nonprofit association. A "No" response is usually appropriate only for predecessor organizations whose activities your corporation will continue or whose property and other assets will be transferred to the new nonprofit corporation. Generally, only groups that adopted special articles of incorporation for an unincorporated association (as explained in "Prepare Articles of Incorporation" in Chapter 6) will answer "No" here.

If you check "No," attach a statement providing the information requested. As the reason for termination of the predecessor organization, you can simply state: "To incorporate the predecessor organization." You must also provide the Revenue and Taxation Code section number under which your preexisting group was tax-exempt (Revenue and Taxation Code § 23701(d) or another section).

If the predecessor group wasn't tax-exempt, the Franchise Tax Board will expect it to have filed state income tax returns. If the prior group did not file California income tax returns, then you need to see a tax specialist before proceeding. You may need to file a tax exemption application for the nonprofit association's years of activity prior to its conversion to a corporation. You can do this using the FTB 3500 form as explained in Item 7(b), below. Or you may decide that you should prepare and file income tax returns for the association for those prior years of activity. Of course, if you file income tax returns for the prior association and these returns show you owe taxes, you can expect to be hit with penalties and interest as well. The IRS will be notified of the state assessment, so you can expect to hear from it as well, if you didn't file federal income tax returns for those prior years of activity. If you are in this situation, consult a tax advisor to help you clear up the tax status of your prior association. You may find that it's easier to sort out than you think and can be done without too much time, trouble, or money. Then you can move on to get a nonprofit tax exemption for your new corporation.

Blank 6(b). If you have adopted nonmembership bylaws, check "No." If you have included membership provisions in your bylaws, check the "Yes" box and provide the information requested on an attachment page to your application. Indicate the qualifications for members contained in Article 12, Section 1, of your completed membership provisions on the CD-ROM. Most organizations will have used our suggested language for this provision and will show that "Any person is qualified to become a member of this corporation." If you have not modified the membership provisions in the CD-ROM form, write on the attachment page: "The corporation shall have only one class of members and all memberships have the same rights, privileges, restrictions, and conditions." Also indicate that "each member of the corporation is entitled to one vote on each matter submitted to a vote of the members and has no other rights or interest with respect to the assets or affairs of the corporation except as expressly provided by law." Unless you know the actual number of members who will be admitted to the corporation (which is unlikely), indicate that: "the number of members of the general public who will be admitted to the corporation is undetermined."

Blank 6(c). Check "No." If your proposed operations require a "Yes" response, you probably won't meet the requirements for obtaining nonprofit corporate status or receiving your tax exemptions. The applicable statutes, as previously discussed, require that no part of the net earnings of the corporation be distributed to members.

Blank 6(d). Mark "No." If your corporation plans to share space with any of the incorporators, mark "Yes" and provide the details of the arrangement on an attachment page. For example, when starting out you may want to use a room in a director's house as a corporate office, listing the house as the corporation's principal place of business. This kind of arrangement will usually not jeopardize your tax exemption if the director-landlord charges a reasonable rent (a "no rent" situation is preferable). If an incorporator benefits excessively by a shared-facilities arrangement, your exempt status may be imperiled.

Blank 6(e). Mark "No." If a "Yes" response is appropriate, provide the details on an attachment page. The example and discussion in 6(d) above apply to this blank also.

Blank 6(f). If, as is often the case, you plan to hire a promoter, incorporator (initial director), founder, or member as a salaried or compensated employee of the nonprofit corporation, indicate "Yes." Provide the information requested as to the employee's duties, responsibilities, qualifications, and compensation on the attachment page. At this point in the formation of your corporation, you may have decided that certain directors will be employed as salaried officers (for instance, president, treasurer, or secretary); or that these people will be salaried employees whose exact duties as employees and compensation have not yet been determined. In such cases, give as much information as you can and indicate how you'll determine their employee duties and their compensation. Remember: A majority of the board of directors of a California public benefit corporation cannot be paid (other than as a director) nor related to a person who is paid in a nondirector capacity. (See Blank 6(g), below, for a further discussion of this issue.)

Sample Responses to Blank 6(f)

A nonprofit corporation with ten directors wants to employ three of its initial directors as salaried officers and possibly as salaried employees for other services. The rate of compensation has not yet been determined. Assuming the nonprofit has adopted the bylaws included with this book (which contain a conflict-of-interest provision intended to help the group obtain a federal tax exemption—see Chapter 9, instructions to Part V), an appropriate response to this question on the attachment page might read as follows:

Blank 6(f). Three of the incorporators and first directors, **(names of directors)** , will be employed in the following officer capacities:

(name of director)	President
(name of director)	Vice President
(name of director)	Secretary/ Treasurer, Vice President

They also may be employed as regular employees. Their titled positions, job functions, and compensation for such regular employee status, as well as compensation for their officer positions, are, at present, undetermined, although total proposed budget figures have been determined for director and employee salaries (see Receipts and Expense Statement included as part of Side 6 of this application). Compensation will be reasonable and be paid in return for services rendered the nonprofit corporation in furtherance of its exempt purposes as required by the bylaws of the corporation and shall be fixed from time to time by resolution of the board of directors. Any compensation paid to directors or officers of this corporation shall be set in compliance with the corporation's conflict of interest and compensation approval policies set forth in Article 9 of the bylaws of this organization.

Blank 6(g). If any of your directors will be paid (other than for services performed as a director, such as attending board meetings), check the "Yes" box. You'll need to provide the requested information on an attachment page (instructions for preparing attachments are in "Attachments and Exhibits," above). The Franchise Tax Board is trying to determine if public benefit corporations meet the "disinterested director" rule contained in Section 5227 of the Nonprofit Corporation Law (see "Directors" in Chapter 2). You're asked to describe the relationship, if any, of unpaid board members to paid board members—that's because any person on the board related by blood or marriage to a paid director will be considered by the Franchise Tax Board to be an interested director (the Corporations Code has a more restrictive understanding of an interested director). If your response to this question shows that a majority of your public benefit corporation board is not disinterested per the Franchise Tax Board's rule, the board may deny (or at least question) your state tax exemption.

Blank 6(h). If your organization will conduct raffles or engage in other gaming activities, you will need to attach a statement explaining how you intend to conduct them. Cal. Penal Code § 320.5 exempts raffles held by certain nonprofit organizations from the general prohibition on lotteries provided several conditions are met.

If you answer "Yes" to this question, be sure to read Cal. Penal Code § 320.5 very carefully before you submit your answer. (You can find the statute online at www.leginfo.ca/calaw.

html. Select "Penal Code," then go to 320.5 from the index.) You'll see that there are very strict rules—for instance, charities must be in existence for one year before conducting a raffle, must register with the attorney general for a permit, and 90% of the gross receipts from the raffle must be used for the organization's charitable purposes (rather than to pay for operating the raffle).

Supporting Legal and Financial Documents (Item 7)

Item 7 asks for information about your group's finances, its funding sources, and its purpose and activities. Most of you will be able to prepare the material yourselves. However, if your operations will be financially complex, or if you are incorporating a predecessor organization, you may need to consult a tax specialist to assist you in preparing the financial data requested here. Submit the information required under Question 7 on attachment pages. These can be done as separate attachment pages or can be included as a continuation of any attachment pages you prepared under item 6.

Copies of Articles and Bylaws (Items 7(a) and 7(b))

The first items requested are copies of your articles and bylaws.

Item 7(a). This item requires that you attach a copy of your file-stamped, endorsed articles of incorporation, returned to you by the secretary of state as explained in Chapter 6. (An endorsed copy is one returned by the secretary of state that has a facing page containing the seal of the State of California.) On the attachment page for Blank 7, type:

7(a): Endorsed articles of incorporation attached, Exhibit A.

Staple a note or blank piece of paper to the first page of your endorsed-filed articles, and print or type the words "Exhibit A" on the note or paper.

Item 7(b). Type the following on the attachment page in response to this item:

7(b): Copy of proposed bylaws attached, Exhibit ___(letter, i.e., "B")___.

Make a copy of your bylaws and mark it as an exhibit. You can attach a note to the front of the bylaws and print or type "Exhibit B" on the note, or you simply can write "Exhibit B" across the top of the copy of your bylaws.

Required Financial Information (Item 7(c))

This portion of the application asks for information on your group's finances. Your answer will depend on how long your corporation has been doing business, and in what form. Your group will fit one of the situations described below.

Brand new nonprofits. If you have recently incorporated and have not yet begun operations (most groups using this book will fall in this category), respond to this question on an attachment page as follows:

7(c): ___(Name of corporation)___ is a new organization, recently incorporated, and has not yet commenced operations. See Receipts and Expense Statement, Side 8 of this application, below, for a proposed budget for the new organization for its first year.

We show you how to prepare a budget below. Brand new corporations do not need to prepare the statements of assets, liabilities, receipts, and expenditures requested in 7(c)(1) for past operations.

Nonprofits less than a year old. If your new corporation has been in existence for less than one year but has begun operations, you must submit financial statements (receipts and expenses, plus a balance sheet showing assets and liabilities) for your first partial year, plus a proposed budget for the entire first year. We explain how to prepare financial statements below. Respond on an attachment page as follows:

> 7(c): _____(name of corporation)_____ is a newly formed nonprofit corporation and has been operating for less than one year. Financial statements for period of operations, attached. For receipts and expenses for period of activity and proposed budget for entire first year, see Receipts and Expense Statement, Side 8 of this application.

Nonprofits more than a year old. If your corporation has been in existence for one year or more, you must give financial statements (statements of receipts and expenses, plus balance sheets showing assets and liabilities) for the periods for which you have been in existence and for which you want to obtain tax-exempt status. For example, if your corporation was formed three years ago and you want to receive tax-exempt status retroactively to the date your corporation was formed, you must submit financial statements for each of the three years. (We explain how to prepare financial statements below.) Respond to this item on an attachment page as follows: "7(c): Financial Statements for each accounting period corporation has been in existence and for which exemption is claimed are attached. For income statements, see Receipts and Expense Statement, Side 8 of this application."

EXAMPLE:

GoodWorks, Inc., a California nonprofit corporation, filed its articles on May 15, 2005. The group has a fiscal year and accounting period ending on December 31 of each year and is submitting its exemption application at the end of September, 2007. Like other groups, it wants to claim an exemption going back to the date the organization was formed. Therefore, GoodWorks submits three sets of financial statements for the following full or partial tax periods of the corporation. (Remember, you must submit financial statements for the periods for which you want an exemption):

1. May 15, 2005 to December 31, 2005 (This is the first [short] tax year of the corporation.)
2. January 1, 2006 to December 31, 2006 (the organization's second tax year)
3. January 1, 2007 to September 30, 2007 (the past portion of the current tax year).

Preexisting nonprofit associations. If you indicated "No" for Item 6(a) because you incorporated a preexisting nonprofit association, and if the association was not previously granted a tax-exemption by the Franchise Tax Board (as reported in Item 3(a)), you can seek to have your exemption effective for the prior years of operation of the association. Normally this is not necessary since most nonprofit associations do not make a profit in their early years and therefore rarely owe taxes for this period. Nonetheless, if you and your tax advisor decide you have a reason to do this, you must submit financial statements (statements of receipts and expenses plus balance sheets showing assets and liabilities) for the prior years during which the unincorporated association was in operation. (We explain how to prepare the financial statements below.)

Corporations that have been operating but have no financial activity. When nonprofits start operating, normally they have financial activity as part of their operations. For example, writing checks and making deposits is considered financial activity. Few nonprofit organizations that are operating have no financial activity. However, if your organization falls into this unusual category, respond to this item as follows on an attachment page:

7(c): The corporation has been operating but has not had any financial activity. Exhibit _____ is attached, which contains information substantiating operations during the years for which exemption is claimed. This information consists of (*fill in type of documentation you are providing, such as minutes of meeting of your board of directors*) and is attached. See Receipts and Expenses Statement, Side 8 of this application, for a proposed budget for the current and subsequent year.

Your minutes and other documents should substantiate that your nonprofit has been in operation pursuing its exempt purposes, but has not engaged in financial activity. You also need to submit a proposed budget for the current tax year, and a budget for the next (subsequent) tax year. We show you how to prepare a budget in "Special Instructions for New Corporations That Haven't Started Operations," below.

Preparing Financial Statements

Item 7c of your exemption application asks you to prepare financial statements. To do so, follow the instructions below and take a look at the sample at the end of this section.

Fill in the "Receipts and Expense Statement" on Side 8 of the FTB 3500 form for the current year and any prior year for which you are claiming an exemption. (This income and expense information is similar to the federal information you will prepare for your federal 1023 exemption application, but a little more

detailed. Don't expect to fill in all items—just put numbers in the items that apply to your past operations.) This statement has columns for you to go back only three years before the current year. If you want your state exemption to cover more than three prior years, make an additional copy of this form and supply income and expense information for any additional years beyond three (for example, the fourth year prior to the current one).

Special Instructions for New Corporations That Haven't Started Operations

New corporations that have not been in existence for one year and have not begun operations should fill in the "Receipts and Expense Statement" page of the state application as follows. Cross out the leftmost "Current year" column title and write in the following new heading, "Proposed budget for first year of operation." Write this new title above the chart—it won't fit in the heading space. List proposed figures for receipts and expenditures in the far left column. Proposed receipts and expenditures should be related to your exempt purposes. Don't try to be too precise; just give your most reasonable expectations.

New groups that haven't started operations will leave the preceding year columns blank. These groups do not have to prepare a balance sheet.

Special Instructions for New Corporations That Have Begun Operations

This is for corporations that have not been in existence for one year but have begun operations. In the far left column (the "Current Year" column), enter figures from your financial records from the date you incorporated to the ending date of the preceding month. In the column to the right of the "Current Year" column, insert your proposed figures for your entire first year of operations (from the date you incorporated to the upcoming end of your first tax year). Cross out the heading at the top of the chart, titled "3 preceding years for each year in existence," and write the following title across the top of the second column: "Proposed figures for entire first year." You can extend this new heading across the other columns to the right if you need the space. These figures should be larger than the figures in the far left column because the columns to the right include additional receipts and expenditures you expect from the time you prepare the form (the end of the month preceding the date you are filling in this statement) to the ending date of your first year of operation.

Submit a basic balance sheet (statement of assets and liabilities) for the same year (or years) for which you supplied financial information. New groups that have not begun operations do not need to prepare a balance sheet. All other groups should prepare a balance sheet for the current year and for each past year during which they were in operation and for which they are claiming an exemption.

To prepare a balance sheet for one or more years for your nonprofit organization, follow our sample form shown below or have an accountant or bookkeeper prepare these balance sheets for you. If yours is the typical nonprofit, you won't show many assets or liabilities, and your balance sheets will be brief.

You can design your own balance sheet, as we did; or you can get a more complete, ready-to-use balance sheet from Part IX, Section B, of the federal 1023 exemption application form. (It's on the CD-ROM for this book.)

For the special case of a nonprofit that has been in operation but has had no financial activity, you will need to do the following. You must provide program information for all the years you have been in operation and for

Balance Sheet

EXHIBIT __(letter)__   __(name of corporation or unincorporated association)__

Balance Sheet as of __(date of end of previous tax year or present date)__

Assets:

Cash	$_____
Equipment	$_____
Furniture and Fixtures	$_____
Accounts Receivable	$_____
Total Assets	$_____

Liabilities:

Accounts Payable	$_____
Loans Outstanding	$_____
Total Liabilities	$_____

Net Worth or Fund Balances:

Net Worth: (Total Assets – Total Liabilities)	$_____
Total Liabilities and Net Worth (Total Liabilities + Net Worth)	$_____

which you request an exemption, as explained above. You also need to submit proposed figures for the current and next year. To do this, fill in the appropriate receipts and expenses for the leftmost, current year column in the table on Side 8 of the FTB 3500 form. Use the next column for your next year's budget figures—cross out the heading at the top of the chart, titled "3 preceding years for each year in existence," and write the following title across the top of the second column: "Proposed figures for next year."

Purpose, Activities, Funding, and Other Information (Items 7(d)–7(i))

The rest of Item 7 concerns information on your nonprofit mission, program, and outreach activities. Your responses to this item go on attachment pages to your exemption application.

Item 7(d). This item requires a detailed statement about the specific purposes of your corporation. Don't quote from the "specific purpose" clause in your articles of incorporation. The concise statement in your articles will entitle you to tax exemptions under a category or categories of the tax exemption statutes. The statement here serves a different purpose—it should give the Franchise Tax Board a down-to-earth and more extensive picture of your corporation's purposes so that the tax board can really see how your nonprofit activities will benefit the public.

If you've already provided a detailed list of your primary objectives and purposes in Article 2, Section 1, of your bylaws, great! If it is thorough, use it here and don't worry about the form instructions to the contrary (they advise you not to quote the articles or bylaws, but if you followed our advice and wrote a detailed list in your bylaws, go ahead and use it). All you

need to do is to change the introductory clause to conform to the language of this item in the application. Specifically, respond to this item by stating:

> The specific purposes for which this nonprofit corporation was formed are _____ **(list your primary objectives and purposes from Article 2 of your bylaws)** _____.

If you didn't write a thorough and detailed list of your primary purposes and objectives for your bylaws, you'll have to do it now. Public benefit corporations should follow the instructions in Chapter 7, "Bylaws for a Public Benefit Corporation," special instruction ❹. Religious corporations should refer to Chapter 7, "Bylaws for a Religious Corporation," special instruction ❹.

Item 7(e). In this item, the Franchise Tax Board asks you to list what you will do (or, for corporations that have been operating, what they have done) to achieve the charitable, educational, literary, scientific, or religious purposes and objectives listed in response to Item 7(d).

For example, suppose you've said that one of your purposes is to educate the public on environmental issues. You might respond by saying that one way you'll accomplish this will be to disseminate brochures and other literature explaining how to set up solar energy heating systems as an alternative to traditional energy sources.

Many groups will have already given a complete, or partial, indication of the activities they will engage in to perform their specific purposes in Item 7(d). For example, groups often couch their purposes in language that describes the activities they will carry on—for instance, an educational group may have stated in 7(d) that one of its purposes is to operate a school or provide classes for members of the general public in subjects relevant to their educational purposes. These groups may respond to this item by simply referring to some or all of their responses to previous items as follows: "Refer to Item 7(d) for further information as to the programs and activities that will be carried on by the nonprofit corporation in order to accomplish the specific purposes of the organization."

Item 7(f). Here you'll list your present or proposed types and sources of funding, along with each fundraising activity and business enterprise you plan to engage in. Any activities should, of course, be related to your tax-exempt purposes. These activities may include performing services for a fee as long as the services are related to the tax-exempt purposes of the organization. Also include as exhibits copies of any agreements with outside groups relating to the production of income for the corporation. We suggest you don't use the phrase "business enterprises" unless your list includes revenue-raising activities that are unrelated to your exempt purposes.

EXAMPLE:

"On Your Toes," a group dedicated to dance instruction, might respond to this question as follows:

Proposed sources of funds and fundraising activities of the corporation consist of:

1. Maintaining a dance studio that will produce income derived from the public's enrollment in dance classes and other body movement art forms, such as tumbling and yoga, taught by the corporation's faculty.

2. Revenues received from public performances by the corporation's resident dance troupe as indicated in response to Item 7(e); and

3. Revenues received from sponsoring special events related to body movement (for example, dance performances) and other art forms (such as musical concerts) as indicated in response to Item 7(e).

References are made to information already furnished by the group in its response to Item 7(e) above.

As part of your answer to this item, refer to and attach copies of agreements your organization has entered into to conduct any of the listed activities. For example, an organization that will hold an annual book festival might attach a copy of their lease of festival space and copies of exhibition agreements that will be signed by bookstores that participate.

Item 7(g). For new groups, simply respond to this question on the attachment page by stating:

   __(name of corporation)__   is a newly formed corporation, with no discontinued activities.

If you incorporated a preexisting nonprofit organization and have discontinued activities previously engaged in, provide the information requested in response to this question.

Item 7(h). This item will not apply to most newly formed nonprofit corporations. If you have not entered into a lease or made other agreements for the development or use of property, respond on the attachment page as follows:

___(name of corporation)___ has not entered into a lease, nor does it own an interest in property, and has not entered into any agreement with other parties for the development of property.

If your organization has entered into a lease or an agreement relating to the use or development of property, say so in your response to this question and attach a copy of the lease to your application as an exhibit. Your answer could look like this:

Copy of lease, entered into between __(name of corporation)__ and __(name of lessor)__ with respect to the premises located at __(address of leased property)__ attached, Exhibit __(letter of exhibit)__.

Of course, your group should use the leased premises to carry out your exempt purposes, and using the leased premises for these purposes should already have been listed as one of your activities under Item 7(d), 7(e), or 7(f), above.

If you incorporated a preexisting nonprofit organization that currently leases property and your new corporation will continue to use the leased premises, state that the lease is currently held in the name of the predecessor organization. You will need to assign this lease to the new corporation or negotiate a new lease with the owner (see "Prepare Assignments of Leases and Deeds" in Chapter 10). If you plan to assign the lease to the corporation, state:

The lease will be assigned to the corporation upon its obtaining federal and state corporate income tax exemptions.

If you like, you can prepare an assignment of the lease now and attach it with your lease as an exhibit to your exemption application. The assignment should state that it is contingent upon the corporation attaining nonprofit corporate status and its federal and state tax exemptions. It should be given for minimal "consideration" (the payment of $1.00 is legally sufficient) and will, under the terms of most standard leases, require the written approval of the lessor to be effective. A sample Assignment of Lease that might be used for this purpose is shown below.

Item 7(i). The state and federal government like to see you actively solicit public participation in the activities of your nonprofit corporation by distributing promotional literature or arranging for space in newspapers and time on the radio as well as more modern methods of participation, such as hosting a public website. If you have copies or samples of literature that the corporation sells or will sell or distribute (such as publications, advertising copy, or promotional literature that you'll use to solicit contributions, obtain student enrollment in classes, and so on), include copies with your exemption application. Also include printouts of any Internet pages taken from your website. Explain on the attachment page that you are submitting this additional material in response to Item 7(j). If you do not have copies of promotional literature (which is true for most newly formed nonprofits), simply respond here as follows:

The corporation has not yet prepared promotional literature (*or, does not plan to distribute promotional literature*) or advertising.

Items 8, 9, and 10. Skip these items. They relate to other types of tax-exempt groups.

Assignment of Lease

__(name of original lessee, e.g., the predecessor nonprofit organization)__ , Lessee of those premises commonly known as __(address of leased property)__ , hereby assigns the attached Lease relating to the above premises, executed __(date original lease was signed)__ , and all rights, liabilities, and obligations thereunder, to __(name of corporation)__ , a California nonprofit corporation. This Assignment is given without consideration and no consideration will be required to effectuate this Assignment. This Assignment is, however, contingent upon said California corporation, __(name of corporation)__ , obtaining its exemption from payment of California corporate franchise taxes from the California Franchise Tax Board and exemption from payment of federal corporate income taxes from the Internal Revenue Service within one year from the date of execution of this Assignment of Lease.

Dated: _____

__(name of predecessor organization)__

By: __(signature of representative of above organization)__
    (typed name of representative)

The undersigned Lessor of the above premises hereby assents to this Assignment of Lease.

Dated: _____

__(signature of Lessor)__

(typed name of Lessor), Lessor

Specific Questions for 23701(d) Nonprofits (Item 11)

Item 11. All 501(c)(3) groups (religious, charitable, scientific, literary, or educational organizations) should answer Questions 11(a) through 11(d). Religious groups claiming an exemption as a church also must respond to the questions under 11(e) on an attachment page.

SEE AN EXPERT

Special purpose groups that do not plan to be exempt under 501(c)(3) of the Internal Revenue Code will have to circle and complete a different item on the exemption application. They should consult an attorney for help in forming their nonprofit corporation and obtaining the necessary tax exemptions.

Item 11(a). If your organization will receive 10% or more of its assets from any individual or from members of a family, check "Yes" and explain on an attachment page. Family includes brothers, sisters, spouses, grandparents, children, grandchildren, or any other "lineal descendants" (people in a direct line of descent from another person). There is nothing wrong with arrangements of this sort and now and then one person or family will provide substantial assets (such as a major cash contribution) to a newly formed nonprofit. The state will scrutinize your application more closely in this case to make sure the organization is not set up and operated to serve the interests of these individuals or family members.

SEE AN EXPERT

If you check "Yes" in Item 11(a) because your group will receive 10% or more of its assets from another group, or "Yes" in Item 11(d) because your group will own or hold a 10% voting interest in another corporation, you may be considered a member of an affiliated group of organizations or may encounter other problems. Consult a lawyer or tax advisor.

Item 11(b). This question concerns your group's plans for political action. If you answer "Yes" to 11(b), be prepared to show on an attachment page that your planned legislative activities will be "insubstantial" or that your lobbying and grassroots political activities will fall under and meet the requirements of the political expenditures election. Look ahead in Chapter 9 to "Prepare Your Tax Exemption Application," Part VIII, if you indicate "Yes." For more information on permissible lobbying activity by 501(c)(3) nonprofits, see "Limitation on Political Activities" in Chapter 3 and the CD-ROM.

Item 11(c). Here you're asked if your non-profit will participate in (for or against) political campaigns of candidates for public office. If you answer "Yes" to 11(c), you will not be able to obtain your state exemption under Section 23701(d) and will not be eligible for your federal tax exemption under Section 501(c)(3) of the Internal Revenue Code. (Remember, 501(c)(3)-type groups cannot participate in political campaigns of this sort.) For more detailed information on the prohibition against 501(c)(3)s participating in political campaigns, see "Limitation on Political Activities" in Chapter 3 and the CD-ROM.

Item 11(e). If you are setting up a church, provide the information requested in 11(e), (1) through (8), on a separate attachment page, keeping in mind the general guidelines and information contained in "Religious Purposes" in Chapter 3. Also refer to the church guidelines contained in IRS Publication 557 and see Chapter 9, "Prepare Your Tax Exemption Application," Part X, Line 5(a)—instructions for filling out the form for churches.

Items 12-25. Skip these items. They relate to other types of tax-exempt groups.

Sign and Mail Your Exemption Application

After filling in all the blanks and completing your attachment pages and exhibits, sign the application at the bottom of the first page. Write the date and have one of the people who signed the articles (one of the initial directors) sign as a representative, indicating his or her title as director.

To make sure you've completed everything you need to do, use the official checklist to the FTB 3500 form and make sure you've checked all items that apply to you.

Gather up your signed Form FTB 3500, plus any attachments and exhibits. Enclose your check —do not staple it to the 3500 form. Make a copy for your records. Enclose the originals, plus a $25 check made out to "Franchise Tax Board" (payable in U.S. dollars and drawn against a U.S. financial institution), and mail them to:

Exempt Organizations Section
Franchise Tax Board
P.O. Box 942857
Sacramento, CA 94257-4041

If all goes well, you should receive your tax exemption determination letter from the Franchise Tax Board within four to six weeks (the Franchise Tax Board says it can take up to 90 days, but normally you should not have to wait that long). If the Franchise Tax Board has questions, it will mail them to the representative of the organization listed in the FTB Form 3500.

SEE AN EXPERT

Seek help when you need it. If the Franchise Tax Board mails you questions that you cannot easily answer or your application is denied, you may wish to get expert help from a lawyer or tax advisor. See Chapter 12 for help in finding the right expert.

The determination letter will state that your organization is exempt from payment of state income taxes and give you information on the annual information return requirements (see "California Corporate Tax Returns and Reports" in Chapter 11). The state exemption normally is contingent upon your obtaining a federal income tax exemption within six months. When you get your federal exemption, mail a copy of the IRS determination letter to the Franchise Tax Board. Put the name of your corporation and its Employer Identification Number in a cover letter, and mail both to the Franchise Tax Board Exemption Organizations Section address shown above.

CAUTION

If you apply for your state tax exemption after you've gotten your federal 501(c)(3) tax exemption, include a copy of your federal tax exemption determination letter with your state tax exemption application (see "Mail IRS Letter to Franchise Tax Board" in Chapter 10). This will speed up the processing of your state form, and will eliminate the need for you to mail a copy of the IRS letter to the Franchise Tax Board later.

Same-Day Exemption Determination

Infrequently, the FTB allows applicants to hand deliver their exemption application to the Sacramento office, and to wait while the application is approved (if the FTB examiner decides it can quickly be approved). To get this type of personal service, you will have to have a very compelling reason (such as an unwaivable grant deadline), and the good luck to call the FTB at the right time to talk to the right person.

If you want to try this, call the FTB in Sacramento at 916-845-4171 and ask for the Exempt Organizations Unit. If your hand-carried request is approved, make an appointment to bring your application to the examiner at the Sacramento office. If it all goes extremely well in Sacramento, you may be able to walk away with your exemption—or at least walk away knowing that the examiner will start working on your application right away and make a determination as soon as possible. Again, don't expect to be able to get this type of expedited, personal service approved when you call the FTB—few do.

Apply for Your Federal 501(c)(3) Tax Exemption

Now that you've filed your articles and prepared your bylaws (and many of you will have also prepared your state tax exemption application), it's time to prepare your federal exemption application (IRS Form 1023). Obtaining your federal tax exemption is a critical step in forming your nonprofit organization, because most of the real benefits of being a nonprofit flow from 501(c)(3) tax-exempt status. You can submit your federal tax exemption application after or at the same time as you apply for your state tax exemption. To make your tax exemption retroactive to the date of your incorporation, your 1023 application must be postmarked within 27 months from the end of the month in which you filed your articles of incorporation.

The IRS revised the 1023 tax exemption application in 2004 to make it a gentler, friendlier form. However, it still remains a daunting task to understand and complete the application. The official instructions to Form 1023 say that it takes an average of approximately ten hours to complete the form (plus more time for each schedule), and almost another hour to assemble the material for mailing. Hopefully, by reading and following our line-by-line instructions below, you will accomplish this task in substantially less time. We provide a lot of handholding and suggestions for responses to make the task easier and less time consuming. And keep the following suggestion in mind: If you get stuck on a difficult question or run low on energy (as many do), take a break and return to it when you feel better able to follow and absorb the material. You will be well rewarded in the end for the time and effort you devote to this task.

> **CAUTION**
>
> **Special purpose nonprofits use a different IRS form.** If yours is a special purpose nonprofit group (formed for other than religious, educational, charitable, scientific, or literary purposes), you're likely to be exempt under subsections of Section 501(c) other than Subsection (3). To apply for your federal tax exemption, you'll need IRS Form 1024 instead of IRS Form 1023. Certain cooperative hospital service organizations and cooperative educational service organizations can use Form 1023—see the General Instructions to Form 1023, "Other Organizations that may file Form 1023."

Getting Started

Before diving into the task at hand, take a moment to read this section, which sets out the various tax forms and other IRS publications you'll encounter. We'll also give you tips on how to fill out the forms and deal with the additional information you may need to supply. Think of this portion of the chapter as your orientation.

Forms and Publications

You'll encounter several IRS forms as you make your way toward federal exempt status. We have provided copies of the following federal forms in tear-out form in Appendix B or on the CD-ROM at the back of this book, or both, as indicated below:

- IRS Form 1023. Package 1023: *Application for Recognition of Exemption* (June 2006) (CD-ROM and tear-out)
- *Instructions for Form 1023* (June 2006) (CD-ROM only)
- Form SS-4. *Application for Employer Identification Number* (February 2006) (CD-ROM and tear-out)

- *Instructions for Form SS-4* (February 2006) (CD-ROM only)
- Form 5768. *Election/Revocation of Election by an Eligible Section 501(c)(3) Organization to Make Expenditures to Influence Legislation* (February 2006) (CD-ROM and tear-out).

> **CAUTION**
>
> **Check that your IRS 1023 form is current.** If you are using the IRS 1023 form included with this book (whether in Appendix B or on the CD-ROM), check to see that the form is current. Go to the IRS website (www.irs.gov) and access the form online (see instructions below under "Ways to Complete the Exemption Application"). The heading on the form will tell you the revision date for the most current 1023 form. If the date of the online form is more recent than the version included with this book (February 2006), use the newer online version. You also can obtain the latest IRS forms by calling 800-TAX-FORM.

If you do prepare an IRS 1023 form that is newer than the one we provide with this book, the instructions below should still work since changes to the form usually consist of reorganization and format changes. If a newer form contains questions not covered in this chapter, call the IRS Exempt Organizations Customer Account Services (877-829-5500) and ask a tax-exempt organization specialist for help with the new material. This line often is busy, so you will need to be patient and persevere to get through. Or check Nolo's website for instructions for the new form (look for updates to this book). If the changes are minor or insignificant, Nolo won't provide any updates.

We have also included some federal tax publications on the CD-ROM. These publications are surprisingly readable and give a lot of practical information. You can get copies or updated versions by going online to www.irs.gov or by calling the IRS forms and publications request number, 800-TAX-FORM.

- Publication 557, *Tax-Exempt Status for Your Organization* (March 2005)
- Publication 4220, *Applying for 501(c)(3) Tax-Exempt Status* (September 2003)
- Publication 4221, *Compliance Guide for 501(c)(3) Tax-Exempt Organizations* (September 2003)
- Publication 1828, *Tax Guide for Churches and Religious Organizations* (September 2006).

> **TIP**
>
> **You can find additional helpful information, including articles on special exempt organization issues, from the IRS website at www.irs.gov.** Check the "Charities & Nonprofits" page.

Ways to Complete the Exemption Application

There are two ways to complete the federal tax exemption application:

- Use the tear-out form in the back of the book and fill it in by hand (print with a black ink pen) or typewriter (using a black ribbon).
- Use the IRS Form 1023 included on the CD-ROM file at the back of this book or go to the IRS website and obtain the form there.

Before you use the tear-out form from this book or the form on the CD-ROM, check the IRS website to make sure the revision date on the form you are using is the same as the date on the form available on the IRS website. To access the IRS form, go to the IRS website at www.irs.gov. In the search box, type "1023."

You should see links to both Form 1023 and the separate instructions to the form at the top of the list. The Form 1023 is provided in PDF format. Save and work with a backup copy of the form—you will fill in and save your responses on your working copy. You will need the latest version of Adobe's Reader program (available free from Adobe.com) to fill in and save your responses on the 1023 PDF form. For more information on installing and using PDF files, see Appendix A.

Preliminary Reading

Before starting your federal tax exemption application, read the Instructions for Form 1023 (available on the CD-ROM or from the IRS website). Also skim through Chapters 1, 2, and 3 of IRS Publication 557 and Publication 4220—the information there covers the basic requirements for obtaining a 501(c)(3) tax exemption.

If you find this reading a bit technical, don't let it bog you down. The information in this book, together with our line-by-line instructions for the forms, should be enough to get you through the process. If necessary, you can always refer back to the IRS publications and instructions when answering questions or filling out schedules.

Form 1023 Schedules, Attachments, and Exhibits

Form 1023 contains several schedules that only certain nonprofits (such as schools, churches, and hospitals) need to complete. Don't worry about these schedules—we will tell you if your group needs to complete a schedule as you go through the line-by-line instructions for Form 1023. We provide instructions for filling out the schedules below.

You may need to answer or continue your response to some questions on the form on an attachment page or pages. Use letter-sized paper (8 ½" x 11") and include the following information:

- the name and EIN (Employer Identification Number) of your corporation, at the top of each attachment page

- for each response, state the part and line number to which the response relates. Also provide a description, if appropriate (see the sample attachment page below).

- the page number in the header or footer of each page if you include more than one attachment page to your application. (Many groups will have multiple attachment pages.)

Attachment Page

GoodWorks, Inc.
EIN # XXXXXXX

Part IV, Narrative Description of Activities: The nonprofit organization also will engage in the following activities: …

Part V, Line 1a Names, titles, mailing addresses, and compensation of officers, directors, and trustees (continuation):

Name	Title	Mailing Address	Compensation (actual or proposed)

You do not need to have a separate attachment page for each response—just list your responses one after the other on your attachment pages (as shown on the sample below). The federal form has space under each question for your response, but often this space is insufficient. You can use attachment pages to continue any responses you start on the form.

You also can use attachments to indicate you are including additional information as exhibits. For example, you will need to attach documents, such as articles and bylaws, and other materials, such as copies of solicitations for financial support, to your application. Mark each document as an exhibit and label them in alphabetical order. You can write the exhibit letter at the top of the document, or you can staple a page or note to the first page of the document and write the exhibit reference (for example "Exhibit A") on the cover page or note. We recommend that you use a separate cover page or note for your certified copy of your articles of incorporation, since the articles you include as an exhibit should exactly match the articles you filed with the secretary of state. Make sure each document has a heading that identifies its content and the name and EIN of your nonprofit. The copies of your legal documents should have headings printed on the first page already, such as "Articles of [name of your corporation]" or "Bylaws of [name of your corporation]." Put similar identifying headings on all financial statements and other exhibits you prepare yourself and number each page if the document has multiple pages.

Public Inspection Rights

As you begin entering information on the federal form, keep in mind that your readership may at some point be members of the public, not just some unknown bureaucrat at the IRS. Your federal 1023 tax exemption application, any papers submitted with the application, and your tax exemption determination letter from the IRS must be made available by your organization for public inspection during regular business hours at your organization's principal office. However, any information that has been submitted to the IRS and approved by it as confidential is not required to be publicly disclosed (see "How to Keep Form 1023 Information Confidential," below), and you do not have to disclose the names and addresses of contributors if you qualify as a public charity—which we assume you will.

If your organization regularly maintains one or more regional or district offices having three or more employees (defined as offices that have a payroll consisting of at least 120 paid hours per week), you must make copies of the documents available for public inspection at each of these offices. Copies of your organization's three most recent annual information returns must also be available for public inspection at your principal office (and, if applicable, your regional or district office).

Members of the public can also make a written request for copies of your organization's tax exemption application and its tax returns for the last three years. You must comply within 30 days and are allowed to charge only reasonable copying and postage costs. The public also can request copies or public inspection of your organization's exemption application or its annual returns by calling IRS Exempt Organizations Customer Account Services at 877-829-5500. These public inspection requirements apply to 501(c)(3) public charities, not to 501(c)(3) private foundations—again, we expect most incorporators to qualify as public charities.

It's important to comply with inspection requests. If you don't permit public inspection, you could face a $20-per-day penalty. The IRS will impose an automatic $5,000 additional penalty if your failure to comply is willful. These penalties are not imposed on the organization—they are applied against "the person failing to meet (these) requirements." See IRS Publication 557 and IRC §§ 6104(e), 5562(c)(1)(C) and (D), and 6685 for further information on these rules.

CD-ROM

For additional information about IRS regulations on required disclosures by 501(c)(3) nonprofits, see the CD-ROM file: *Update: The Final Regulations on the Disclosure Requirements for Annual Information Returns and Applications for Exemption.*

How to Keep Form 1023 Information Confidential

Any information submitted with your 1023 is open to public inspection. However, if an attachment or response to your application contains information regarding trade secrets, patents, or other information that would adversely affect your organization if released to the public, you can clearly state "NOT SUBJECT TO PUBLIC INSPECTION" next to the material and include your reasons for requesting secrecy. If the IRS agrees, the information will not be open to public inspection.

IRS Regulation § 301.6104(a)-5 says that the IRS will agree if you convince them that "the disclosure of such information would adversely affect the organization."

CD-ROM

See the CD-ROM file, *Disclosure, FOIA and the Privacy Act,* for additional information on the restrictions applicable to the IRS and its employees regarding disclosures of information submitted to the IRS.

The Consequences of Filing Late

You should file your 1023 within 27 months after the end of the month in which you filed your articles of incorporation. In our experience, the most common problem faced by nonprofits is failing to file their Form 1023 on time. What happens if you file late?

First, if you file on time (within 27 months of incorporating) and the IRS grants your exemption, the exemption takes effect on the date on which you filed your articles. The same is true if you can show "reasonable cause" for your delay (this means you have convinced the IRS that your tardiness was understandable and excusable). If you file late and don't have reasonable cause (or the IRS doesn't buy your story), your tax-exempt status will begin as of the postmark date on your form. For more information, see "Prepare Your Tax Exemption Application," Part VII, below, and the instructions to Schedule E in "Filling Out the Schedules," below.

If your nonprofit has been organized for several years and you're just now getting around to filing your Form 1023, don't despair—you've got plenty of good company. The important point here is to persevere, complete your application, and mail it to the IRS as soon as possible.

Do You Need to File Form 1023?

Almost all nonprofit groups that want 501(c)(3) tax-exempt status will file Form 1023. Form 1023 serves two important purposes:

- It is used by nonprofit organizations to apply for 501(c)(3) tax-exempt status, and
- It serves as your notice to the IRS that your organization is a public charity, not a private foundation. Remember, as discussed earlier, the IRS will presume that 501(c)(3) nonprofit groups are private foundations unless you notify the IRS that you qualify for public charity status.

This said, there are a few groups that are not required to file a Form 1023. You aren't required to file if you are:

- a group that qualifies for public charity status and normally has gross receipts of not more than $5,000 in each tax year (the IRS uses a special formula to determine whether a group "normally" has annual gross receipts of not more than $5,000—for specifics, see IRS Publication 557, "Organizations Not Required to File Form 1023," "Gross Receipts Test")
- a church (a "church" includes synagogues, temples, and mosques), interchurch organization, local unit of a church, convention, or association of churches, or an integrated auxiliary of a church, or
- a subordinate organization covered by a group exemption letter (but only if the parent organization timely submits a notice to the IRS covering the subordinate organization—see the group exemption letter requirements in IRS Publication 557).

Even if one of the above exceptions applies to you, we recommend that you file a Form 1023 anyway. Why? First, it's risky to second-guess the IRS. If you're wrong and the IRS denies your claim to 501(c)(3) tax status several years from now, your organization may have to pay substantial back taxes and penalties. Second, the only way, on a practical and legal level, to assure others that you are a bona fide 501(c)(3) group is to apply for an exemption. If the IRS agrees and grants your tax exemption, then, and only then, can you assure contributors, grant agencies, and others that you are a qualified 501(c)(3) tax-exempt, tax-deductible organization listed with the IRS.

Prepare Your Tax Exemption Application

Now it's time to go through Form 1023, line by line and fill it in. The form is divided into numerous parts. As you go through the form, you will find out whether you need to complete any of the schedules included with the application. Instructions for the schedules are covered separately below.

Part I: Identification of Applicant

Line 1. Write the name of your corporation exactly as it appears in your articles of incorporation.

Line 2. If you have designated one person in your organization to receive return mail from the IRS regarding your 1023 application, such as one of the founders, list this person's name as the "c/o name." Otherwise, insert "not applicable."

Line 3. Provide the mailing address of the corporation. If you do not have a street address, provide a post office box address. The IRS wants you to include the full nine-digit zip code in your address. Include it if you know it. (Zip code information can be obtained online at the U.S. Postal Service Zip Code lookup page.)

Line 4. All nonprofit corporations (whether or not they have employees) must obtain a federal Employer Identification Number (EIN) prior to applying for 501(c)(3) tax exemption. You will insert this number here on your 1023 form and use this identification number on all your future nonprofit federal information, income, and employee tax returns. Even if your organization held an EIN prior to incorporation, you must obtain a new one for the nonprofit corporate entity. If your nonprofit corporation has not yet obtained an EIN, it should do so now.

The easiest and quickest way to get an EIN is to apply online from the IRS website. Go to www.irs.gov and type "EIN" in the upper search box. Then click Go to open a page that lists links to EIN-related Web pages. You should see a link to the online EIN application. The online form is an electronically fileable version of IRS Form SS4, *Application for Employer Identification Number.* Fill in the online version of the SS-4 form and submit the application to receive your EIN immediately.

Follow the instructions, below, when completing the SS-4 form:

- **Name and SSN of officer.** You will need to specify the name and Social Security Number of one of your principal officers. Normally the chief financial officer or treasurer will provide a name and SSN here.

- **Type of entity.** Check "church or church-controlled organization" if you are forming one; if not, check "other nonprofit organization" and specify its 501(c)(3) purpose (educational, charitable, and so on).

- **GEN number.** Most groups will ignore this item—it applies only to a group exemption application request. Members of an affiliated group of nonprofits can specify a previously assigned Group Exemption Number.

- **Reason for applying.** Check "started new business," then specify "formed nonprofit corporation" in the blank. If you are converting an existing unincorporated association (that has previously filed any appropriate tax returns for its association tax years with the IRS) to a nonprofit corporation, you can check "changed type of organization" instead, then insert "incorporation" in the blank.

- **Date Business Started.** The date you started your business is the date your articles were filed with the state filing office. Use the file-stamped date on the copy of your articles returned by the state office.

- **Employees.** You can enter zeros in the next item that asks the number of employees you expect to have in the next 12 months.

Make sure to write down your EIN number immediately before changing Web pages—you will not be able to back up and retrieve the EIN after you navigate away from the Web page. Print a copy of the online form (you can do this by clicking the "Print Form" button on the IRS Web page after receiving your EIN), write the assigned EIN in the upper-right of the printed form, then date and sign it and place the copy in your corporate records.

You also can apply for an EIN by phone. To do this, fill in the SS-4 form (included as a tear-out and on the CD-ROM, with separate instructions, or available on the IRS's website). Then call the IRS at 800-829-4933—be sure to complete the form before making the phone call. If you apply by phone, you will be assigned an EIN number immediately. Write this number in the upper right-hand box of a printed SS-4 form, then date and sign it, and keep a copy for your records. The IRS telephone representative may ask you to mail or fax a copy of your signed SS-4 form to the IRS.

You also can apply for an EIN by fax and get your EIN faxed back to you within four business days. See the instructions to Form SS-4 for more information on using the IRS Fax-TIN program.

Finally, you can get an EIN the slow way by simply mailing your SS-4 form to the IRS. Have an officer—typically the CFO or treasurer—sign the form, stating his or her title. Expect to wait at least four weeks. Remember, you can't complete line 4 of your 1023 form until you have your EIN.

Line 5. Specify the month your accounting period will end. Use the month number for your response. For example, if your accounting period will end December 31, insert "12." The accounting period must be the same as your corporation's tax year. Most nonprofits use a calendar year as their accounting period and tax year. If you choose to do the same, specify "12" here.

If you anticipate special seasonal cycles for your activities or noncalendar-year record-keeping or grant accountability procedures, you may wish to select a noncalendar accounting period for your corporation. For example, a federally funded school may wish to specify June ("6") in this blank, which reflects an accounting period of July 1 to June 30.

If you have any questions regarding the best accounting period and tax year for your group, check with your (probable) funding sources and consult your accountant or bookkeeper for further guidance.

Line 6(a) – 6(c). State the name of a director or officer the IRS can contact regarding your application, the phone number where this person can be contacted during business hours, and a fax number. The fax number is optional—if you don't want to provide one, insert "not applicable." We suggest you list the name and telephone number of the director

or officer who is preparing and will sign your tax exemption application (see Part XI, below). Nevertheless, don't expect the IRS to call to ask questions (or just to say "Hi"). If the IRS has questions about your application, it will usually contact you by mail.

Line 7. We assume you are filling in your 1023 form yourself, and will mark "No" to this item. However, if you are being helped by a lawyer, accountant, or other professional representative, mark "Yes" to allow the representative to talk on your behalf with the IRS about your 1023 application. If you mark "Yes," you will need to complete and attach an IRS Form 2848, *Power of Attorney and Declaration of Representative* (available from the IRS website) to your 1023 application.

Line 8. We assume most readers will answer "No" here. However, if you have paid or plan to pay an outside lawyer, accountant, or other professional or consultant to help you set up your nonprofit or advise you about its tax status, and the person is not acting as your formal representative (named in Form 2848 as explained in line 7 above) and the person is not a director, officer, or employee of your nonprofit, answer "Yes" and provide the requested information. Traditionally many nonprofits get professional guidance from unpaid lawyers and accountants who serve as volunteers to their board. If this is your situation, you can answer "No," since this item is asking about paid advice from an outsider. There is nothing wrong in paying an outsider for help. The purpose of this question is to require full disclosure of any paid relationships between your nonprofit and its advisors, to make sure the compensation arrangement is fair to the nonprofit, and to see that there is no obvious conflict of interest between the person's role and their paid status. An overriding concern of the IRS is to make sure that one person is not personally directing the organization and operation of your nonprofit to further their own personal financial interests and agenda.

Many professionals are being more careful these days and will shy away from providing professional advice on nonprofit boards unless they are indemnified and covered by Directors' Liability Insurance. Some paid advisors will automatically say "no" when asked to sit on a nonprofit board because they do not want to confuse their role as advisor to the nonprofit entity (their real client to whom they owe a professional duty) with the separate task of acting as an advisor to the board and its individual members.

Line 9(a) and 9(b). Insert the URL for your nonprofit's website, if you have one. Any website content should be consistent with your nonprofit purposes and program as described in your 1023 application. Also provide an email address to receive educational information from the IRS in the future. The email address is optional. If you leave either of these items blank, insert "not applicable" in the blank.

Line 10. Some nonprofits using this box will be eligible for an exemption from filing IRS Form 990, the annual information return for nonprofits or the shorter 990-EZ form for smaller groups—see "Federal Corporate Tax Returns" in Chapter 11. If you are reasonably sure you will be exempt—for example, if you are forming a church or know that you will have gross receipts of less than $25,000 per year—mark "yes" and state the reason why you are exempt on an attachment page. All other nonprofits using this book should mark "No" here.

We think it is wise to file 990 returns each year, even if you and the IRS initially agree that your group should be exempt from filing the returns. Why? Because you may fail to continue to meet the requirements for the exemption from filing, and may get hit with late-filing penalties if you have to go back and file your returns for prior years that you missed. By filing a return, even if not required, you normally start the running of the time frame during which the IRS can go back and audit your nonprofit tax returns. And your filed 990 can come in handy in many states for meeting your state income tax and any state attorney general filing requirements.

Line 11. Insert the date your articles were filed by the secretary of state in mm/dd/yyyy) format, such as 01/05/2008.

Line 12. We assume you will mark "No." If you are seeking an IRS 501(c)(3) tax exemption for a corporation formed abroad, mark "Yes," insert the name of the country, and seek additional help from an advisor who can assist you through your more complicated tax-exemption application process.

Part II: Organizational Structure

Line 1. Most tax-exempt nonprofits are formed as nonprofit corporate entities, and we expect you to follow the standard practice of forming a corporation too. Check "Yes" to indicate that your group is a corporation and attach a copy of your articles to your application. The copy should be a certified copy you received from the state filing office. It should show a file-date stamp on the first page or include a certification statement or page that states it was filed with the state and is a correct copy of the original filed document.

Line 2. We assume you will check "No" to indicate that you are not seeking a tax exemption for an LLC. Very few nonprofits are formed as limited liability companies. If this is what you are attempting to do, you should consult with an experienced lawyer.

Line 3. We assume you will check "No" here because we expect readers to form a traditional nonprofit tax exempt corporation, not an unincorporated association. An unincorporated association requires special paperwork (association charter or articles and association operating agreement), and it leaves the members potentially personally liable for the debts of and claims made against the association. If you are applying for a tax exemption for an unincorporated association, you should check with a lawyer before applying for your tax exemption.

Line 4(a) and 4(b). Check "No" to show that you are not applying for a tax exemption for a nonprofit trust. If you are interested in establishing a tax-exempt trust, see an expert.

Line 5. Check "Yes" and attach a copy of the bylaws you have prepared as part of Chapter 7. Make sure you have filled in all the blanks in your printed bylaws and include a completed Adoption of Bylaws page at the end of your bylaws. The adoption page should show the date of adoption and include the signatures of your initial directors.

Part III: Required Provisions in Your Organizing Document

Line 1. Your articles must contain a 501(c)(3) tax-exempt purpose clause (see Chapter 6, Instruction 6, in "Prepare Articles of Incorporation"). Check the box, and on the line provided insert the page, article, and paragraph where the 501(c)(3) purpose clause appears. Make sure you reference the 501(c)(3) purpose clause, not your state-required lawful purpose or specific purpose clause also included in your articles. (In the Sample Articles for a California Public Benefit Corporation in "Prepare Articles of Incorporation" in Chapter 6, the lawful purpose for state law requirements is specified in Article 2, and the 501(c)(3) required purpose clause is stated in Article 4.)

Line 2. Check the 2(a) box to indicate that your articles contain a 501(c)(3) asset dedication clause and fill in the blank in 2(b) to state the page, article, and paragraph where the dissolution clause appears in your articles. Leave the box in 2(c) unchecked—it applies to groups whose articles do not contain a dissolution clause and are instead relying on specific state law provision that requires all 501(c)(3)s formed in that state to dedicate their remaining assets upon dissolution to another 501(c)(3).

A requirement for 501(c)(3) tax exempt status is that any assets of a nonprofit that remain after the entity dissolves be distributed to another 501(c)(3) tax-exempt nonprofit—or to a federal, state, or local government for a public purpose (see "Limitation on Profits and Benefits" in Chapter 3). The articles in this book contain an explicit dedication clause that satisfies both federal and state tax exemption requirements.

For example, assume a nonprofit has the following asset dedication clause on page 2 of its articles:

SIX: The property of this corporation is irrevocably dedicated to ___[state one or more of your actual tax-exempt purposes, such as "charitable," "religious," "educational," "literary," and/or "scientific"]___ purposes and no part of the net income or assets of this corporation shall inure to the benefit of any director, officer, or member thereof or to the benefit of any private person.

On the dissolution or winding up of the corporation, its assets remaining after payment of, or provision for payment of, all debts and liabilities of this corporation shall be distributed to a nonprofit fund, foundation, or corporation which is organized and operated exclusively for

    [repeat the same purpose or purposes
stated in the first blank]   and which has
established its tax-exempt status under
Section 501(c)(3) of the Internal Revenue
Code.

It would check the box in 2(a), and insert the
following on the line in 2(b): "page 2, Article 6,
first paragraph." (This article provision is taken
from "Preparing Articles for a Public Benefit
Corporation" in Chapter 6, special instruction
number 8.)

Do not check the 2(c) box. To be thorough,
you can insert "Not Applicable" on the line at
the end of line 2(c).

The boxes that appear in line 2 will not apply
to most incorporators and should be ignored by
most groups.

Part IV: Narrative Description of Your Activities

You should be familiar with the material in
Chapter 3 concerning the basic requirements
for obtaining a 501(c)(3) tax exemption before
providing the information requested in this part
of the form. We will refer to earlier explanations
as we go along, but you may want to look over
Chapter 3 now before you proceed.

TIP

Tell it like it is. When you describe your
proposed activities, don't limit your narrative to only
those activities that fit neatly within the 501(c)(3)
framework if you're simply "gilding the lily" to gain
IRS approval. Sure, you'll probably get your tax
exemption, but you may not keep it. The IRS can
always decide later, after examining your sources of
support, that your actual activities go beyond the
scope of the activities disclosed in your application.
In short, it's a lot more painful and expensive to shut
down your nonprofit if it loses its tax exemption
rather than deciding at the outset not to apply for

501(c)(3) status because your proposed mission
does not qualify for tax exempt status.

On an attachment page, provide a detailed
description of *all* of your organization's
activities—past, present, and future—in their
order of importance (that is, in order of the
amount of time and resources devoted to each
activity). For each activity, explain in detail:

- the activity itself, how it furthers an exempt
  purpose(s) of your organization, and the
  percentage of time your group will devote
  to it
- when it was begun (or, if it hasn't yet begun,
  when it will begin)
- where and by whom it will be conducted,
  and
- how it will be funded (the financial information or projections you provide later in
  your application should be consistent
  with the funding methods or mechanisms
  you mention here). For example, if your
  application shows you will be obtaining
  the bulk of your tax-exempt revenue from
  providing program-related services, such
  as tuition or admission fees, and/or from
  grant funds, you will want to mention these
  sources of support here (see additional
  instructions on describing your financial
  support below).

Many new groups will be describing proposed
activities that are not yet operational, but you
must still provide very thorough information.

If you plan to conduct any unrelated business (business that doesn't directly further
your nonprofit goals), describe it here. Most
nonprofits will not have planned unrelated
business activities at this point. If you have, you
will not want to stress the importance or scope
of these incidental unrelated activities (for an
explanation of the tricky issues surrounding

unrelated business activities, see "Unrelated Business Activities" in Chapter 3).

Tempting though it might be, resist copying the language that already appears in the purpose clause in your articles—the IRS wants a narrative, not an abbreviated, legal description of your proposed activities. You may include a reference to, or repeat the language of, the longer statement of specific objectives and purposes included in Article 2, Section 2, of your bylaws. However, unless your bylaw language includes a detailed narrative of both your activities and purposes, we suggest you use it only as a starting point for a fuller response here. Generally, we recommend starting over with a fresh, straightforward statement of your group's nonprofit activities.

EXAMPLE 1:

A response by an environmental organization might read in part as follows: The organization's activities will consist primarily of educating the public on environmental issues with an emphasis on energy conservation. Since January 20___, the organization has published brochures promoting solar energy heating systems as an alternative to traditional energy sources. The price for the brochures is slightly above cost—see copies of educational material enclosed, Attachments A-D. The brochures are published in-house at [address of principal office]. Both paid and volunteer staff contribute to the research, writing, editing, and production process. This work constitutes approximately 80% of the group's activities. In addition to publishing, the organization's other activities include the following [list in order of importance other current, past, or planned activities and percentage of time devoted to each, where performed, and so on]...

EXAMPLE 2:

A nonprofit organization plans to sponsor activities for the purpose of supporting other nonprofit charities. It should describe both the activities in which it will engage to obtain revenue at special events and the manner in which this money will be spent to support other groups. Percentages of time and resources devoted to each should be given.

If you are forming an organization that automatically qualifies for public charity status (a church, school, hospital, or medical research organization) or has special tax exemption requirements, you will want to show that your organization meets the criteria that apply to your type of organization. See "Automatic Public Charity Status" in Chapter 4 for a discussion of each of these special types of nonprofits. In the 1023 form, you'll find schedules and instructions that apply to each type of special group (for example, Schedule A for churches, Schedule B for schools, and Schedule C for hospitals—see the table below). If you are forming one of these special types of nonprofits, skip ahead to "Filling Out the Schedules" and look over the instructions for the schedule you need to complete. That way, you'll have a better understanding of what the IRS is looking for in your statement about your nonprofit activities.

Schedules for Special Groups	
Type of Organization	**See Schedule**
Church	A
School, College, or University	B
Hospital and Medical Research Organization	C
Home for the Aged or Handicapped	F
Student Aid or Scholarship Benefit Organization	H

Your description should indicate your organization's anticipated sources of financial support—preferably in the order of magnitude (most money to least money). Here are a few tips to help you address this portion of your response:

- Your sources of support should be related to your exempt purposes—particularly if you plan to be classified as a public charity under the support test described in "Exempt Activities Support Test" in Chapter 4, where the group's primary support is derived from the performance of tax-exempt activities.

- If you plan to qualify as a publicly supported public charity (described in "Public Support Test" in Chapter 4), your responses here should show significant support from various governmental grants, private agency funding, or individual contributions.

- If you expect your principal sources of support to fluctuate substantially, attach a statement describing and explaining anticipated changes—see the specific instructions to Part II, line 2, in the 1023 package.

Your description should show how you will fund your activities. For example, if you will give classes, state how you will recruit instructors and attract students. If you will rely on grants, state your likely sources of grant support—for example, the particular or general categories of grant agencies you plan to approach. If your nonprofit expects to obtain funds through grant solicitations or other fundraising efforts—that is, by soliciting contributions from donors either directly or through paid fundraising—make sure you provide a narrative description of these efforts here, and also refer to Part VIII, line 4, of your application where you will provide additional information on your fundraising activities (see instructions to Part VIII below).

Include as exhibits any literature you plan to distribute to solicit support and indicate that this material is attached to your application.

Fundraising activities include unrelated business activities that will bring cash into your nonprofit. If you have concrete plans to engage in unrelated activities (which, of course, you should be able to clearly describe as an insubstantial part of your overall activities), include the details if you have not done so already in your response.

If your organization has or plans to have a website, provide information on the existing site (including its URL) or the planned site. The existing or proposed website content and any revenue it generates should be related to and further the exempt purposes of the group. If your website is used to solicit contributions or generate other revenue, explain how this is or will be done.

Finally, if your group intends to operate under a fictitious business name (an "aka"—also known as—or "dba"—doing-business-as—name) that differs from your formal corporate name as stated in your articles, make sure to mention the alternate name here, and why you want to use an alternate name.

Part V: Compensation and Financial Arrangements With Your Officers, Directors, Trustees, Employees, and Independent Contractors

The IRS has expanded this part of the application to try and prevent people from creating and operating nonprofits simply to benefit one or more of the nonprofit's founders, insiders, or major contributors. We've already explained the basic 501(c)(3) prohibition against private inurement and the excess benefit rules that penalize nonprofits and their managers if they pay unreasonable compensation to insiders and outsiders (see the discussion on the excess benefit rules in "Limitation on Profits and Benefits" in Chapter 3). In this part of the application, the IRS tries to find out if your nonprofit runs the risk of violating any of these rules. So if you have compensation or other financial arrangements with any of your founders, directors, officers, employees, contractors, contributors, and others, now is the time to disclose this information. It's better to find out ahead of time that the IRS objects to your proposed financial arrangements rather than pay hefty excess benefit taxes later and run the risk of losing your tax exemption.

Line 1(a). Provide the names, titles, mailing addresses, and proposed compensation of the initial directors named in your articles and your initial officers. You can ignore the instructions concerning trustees—your directors are the trustees of your nonprofit corporation. List your initial directors and your top-tier officer team, if you know who will fill these officer positions (such as President or Chief Executive Officer, Vice President, Secretary, and Treasurer or Chief Financial Officer, or any other title used in your organization). For director or officer mailing addresses, you can state the mailing address of the corporation.

At this stage in the organization of your nonprofit, you may not be absolutely certain what you will pay your initial directors and officers. However, if you have a good ballpark estimate or a maximum amount in mind, it's better to state it in your response instead of "unknown" or "not yet decided." In the sample bylaws included in this book, we say that directors will not be paid a salary but may be paid a per-meeting fee and reimbursed expenses (see Article 3, Section 6). Therefore, you may wish to respond along the following lines:

"Pursuant to Article 3, Section 6, of the corporation's bylaws, directors will not be paid a salary. They may be paid a reasonable fee for attending meetings of the board [you may mention a specific amount or a range if you have decided on a per-diem fee] and may be allowed reasonable reimbursement or advancement for expenses incurred in the performance of their duties." This response will not fit in the "Compensation amount" column, so you'll need to prepare your response as an attachment if you use this wording.

If you have decided on officers' salaries or a range or maximum compensation level for officers, you can state it in your response. If you are not sure who your board will appoint as initial officers and do not know the compensation level for your officers, you may wish to respond as follows: "The persons who will serve as officers and the compensation they will receive, if any, have not yet been determined by the board of directors. Any such compensation will be reasonable and will be paid in return for the performance of services related to the tax-exempt purposes of the corporation." This response will not easily fit in the space provided for your 1(a) response, so you'll probably need to prepare your response as an attachment if you use this wording.

If you have decided who will be elected to serve as officers, provide the details of these officer arrangements, including the amount of any salaries to be paid. Remember, though, that putting people on the payroll who are related to directors may cause you to run afoul of California's disinterested director rule—see "Directors" in Chapter 2.

Line 1(b). In this section, state the names, titles, mailing addresses, and compensation for your five top-paid employees who will earn more than $50,000 per year. You should include employer contributions made to employee benefit plans, 401(k)s, IRAs, expected bonus payments, and the like in computing the amount of compensation paid to your employees. You should only list employees who are not officers (all officer salaries should be reported in line 1(a) of this Part). It's best to anticipate who will be paid more than $50,000 by providing estimated compensation figures rather than leaving this information blank. However, if you really don't know yet which officers you will pay or how much you will pay them, you can respond as follows: "This corporation is newly formed and has not yet hired employees nor determined the amount of compensation to pay employees it may hire. However, all compensation will be reasonable and will be paid to employees in return for furthering the exempt purposes of this nonprofit corporation."

There is nothing special or suspect about paying an employee more than $50,000. In fact, compensation paid to employees who make less than $80,000 (a figure that is adjusted for cost of living increases) normally is not subject to scrutiny under the excess benefit rules. (See "Limitation on Profits and Benefits" in Chapter 3 for more on the excess benefit rules. If you are interested in the $80,000 category and how it fits within the excess

benefit rules, see IRS Regulation 53.4985-3(d)(3)(i) and IRC Section 414(q)(1)(B)(i).) For this line item, the IRS wants to see exactly how much your top five highest paid employees are getting paid if they make more than $50,000. Ignoring all the fine print of the excess benefit rules and regulations, just remember that the salary and other benefits you pay each employee should be no more than what a comparably paid person in a similar position in a similar organization would receive. With nonprofit symphony orchestra leaders getting paid over $2 million in annual salaries, plus lavish benefits and perks, it is questionable that using a comparability standard always produces the best or even reasonable results. And we're sure that readers of this book, who work long, hard hours getting paid less than they should in pursuit of their public purposes, should have little to worry about when it comes to the question of receiving unreasonably large salaries or other excess benefits from their nonprofit.

Line 1(c). Indicate the names of individuals (or names of businesses), titles (if individual), mailing addresses, and compensation for your five top-paid independent contractors who will earn more than $50,000 per year. Independent contractors are people and companies who provide nonemployee services to the nonprofit, such as a paid lawyer, accountant, outside bookkeeper, financial consultant, fundraiser, and other outside individuals and companies hired by the nonprofit who are not on the nonprofit's employee payroll. Typically, your nonprofit will have a separate contract for services with its independent contractors—particularly if it will pay them more than $50,000 per year. If your newly formed nonprofit has plans to contract for more than $50,000 with one or more outside individuals or companies, list them here and provide the expected amount of business you plan to do with each contractor annually. If, as is typical, your newly formed nonprofit does not have plans to contract for outside services, you can respond (in the blanks or on an attachment) as follows: "This newly formed nonprofit corporation has no current plans to contract for services with outside persons or companies. If and when it does, any such contracts will provide for payment in commercially reasonable amounts in return for services related to the exempt functions of this nonprofit."

Lines 2(a) – 9(a). The remaining questions in this Part V seek to determine if your nonprofit may run afoul of the excess benefit restrictions that apply to 501(c)(3) public charities—the type of nonprofit you are trying to establish. The excess benefit rules apply to "disqualified persons," as defined under the Internal Revenue Code, Section 4958. For these purposes, a disqualified person means anyone who exercises substantial influence over the nonprofit, such as founders, directors, officers, and substantial contributors. People who fall within the definition of disqualified persons are not prohibited from being paid by your nonprofit. Instead, their salaries and benefits are subject to scrutiny under the excess benefit rules. If the IRS finds that a disqualified person was overpaid—that is, the person received a salary, bonus, or benefits that exceeded the fair market value of the services provided or was excessive compared to amounts paid to similar people in other nonprofits—the disqualified person and the nonprofit and its managers can be subject to sanctions. The sanctions include being required to pay back previously paid salaries and stiff penalty taxes. (For more information on disqualified persons and the excess benefit rules, see "Limitation on Profits and Benefits" in Chapter 3.)

The IRS will review your answers in this section to see if there is any indication that an intentional or incidental purpose of your nonprofit is to financially benefit the private interests of any board members, officers, employees, or contractors. If the IRS determines that you are using nonprofit funds to excessively compensate any of these people, it will deny your tax exemption.

If you answer "Yes" to any of the remaining items in Part V, make sure to explain your response. Provide any additional information needed to show why you marked "Yes" on an attachment page.

TIP

There are numerous definitions of "Disqualified Persons" in the Internal Revenue Code. Don't get confused or concerned if you run up against different definitions of "disqualified persons" that apply to nonprofits. For example, a different definition of disqualified person (under IRC § 4946) is used to determine permitted sources of public support for 501(c)(3) public charity support tests and when applying the excise tax restrictions that apply to private foundations (see Chapter 4).

Line 2(a). Check "Yes" if any of your directors or officers are related to each other or have a business relationship with one another. A family relationship includes an individual's spouse, ancestors, children, brothers, and sisters (see the instructions to Form 1023 for a description of family and business relationships that must be disclosed). If you check "Yes," provide a list of names and a description of the family or business relationship between the individuals on an attachment page.

Line 2(b). Check "Yes" if your organization ("you" means your nonprofit) has an outside business relationship with its directors or officers (see the Form 1023 instructions for the types of business relationships that must be disclosed). Again, these relationships will not be an absolute bar to your obtaining a tax exemption, but the IRS will scrutinize payments made to these "related" parties to make sure they are being fairly, not excessively, compensated by your nonprofit (either through salaries and benefits or through separate business contracts with your nonprofit). Of course, it looks best if your board and officers do not have an outside business relationship with your nonprofit—and we expect, even just for appearances' sake, that most smaller nonprofits will not appoint board members or officers with whom the nonprofit plans to do outside business. If you check "Yes," disclose the names of the individuals and their business relationships with your nonprofit on an attachment page.

Line 2(c). This item asks if any of your directors or officers are related to the people listed in 1(b) or 1(c)—that is, related to your highest-paid employees or independent contractors who make more than $50,000. If you answer "Yes," specify the names of the directors and officers and their relationship to the highest-paid people. Again, it looks best if your board and officers are not related to your more highly compensated employees or contractors. But in the real world of small nonprofits, it may be impossible to start your nonprofit without getting Uncle Bill or Aunt Sally to provide their expertise by volunteering as an unpaid board member. As long as you disclose these arrangements and make sure to fairly pay—and not overpay—anyone, the IRS should conclude that your nonprofit is on the up-and-up and is entitled to its exemption if it meets all the substantive requirements.

Line 3(a). This item requests very important information (on an attachment page), which the IRS uses to determine if your nonprofit will pay excessive benefits to any insider or outsider. Specifically, it asks you to list the qualifications, average hours worked (or to

be worked), and duties of your directors and officers listed in 1(a) and highly compensated employees and contractors (listed in 1(b) and 1(c), respectively). Your responses here should justify any high salaries, benefits, or per diem amounts paid to your officers or directors. For example, if you plan to pay officers a significant salary that may raise IRS examiner eyebrows, make sure to list the extra qualifications and experience of the highly compensated officer. Don't hold back or be shy in touting the credentials (academic degrees, teaching positions, awards), experience (past associations as advisors or directors with other nonprofits), and other qualifications or community affiliations of your well-paid people. The IRS really wants to know why you pay people well (if, in fact, you are lucky enough to pay your officers and other employees a competitive wage, salary, or benefits). On the flip side, obviously, if you pay your part-time administrative aide, who just happens to be your cousin Joe, a lavish hourly wage plus full benefits, expect the IRS to balk. Unless Joe has special skills that are in high demand by other organizations and companies, the IRS will question this special arrangement.

Line 3(b). If any of the directors, officers, and highly paid people listed in 1(a) through 1(c) get paid by another organization or company that has common control with your nonprofit, you will need to mark "Yes" on this item and provide an explanation on an attachment page. As the instructions to Form 1023 explain, organizations with common control include those that have their boards or officers appointed or elected by the same parent or overseeing organization. In addition, if a majority of your board and/or officers and a majority of the board and/or officers of another organization consist of the same individuals, then you share common control. If common control between your nonprofit and another organization exists, expect the IRS to attribute the total compensation paid by both commonly controlled organizations to your board and officers, and also expect the IRS to judge the purposes and activities of your nonprofit in light of the control exercised or shared by the other organization. For example, if a majority of your officers are officers of another nonprofit, the IRS will want to know whether your nonprofit exists to serve the purposes or foster the activities of the related nonprofit. This may be fine if the other nonprofit is, itself, a 501(c)(3) tax-exempt nonprofit. But if it isn't, the common control aspect probably will adversely affect your ability to obtain your tax exemption—your nonprofit can't be formed to promote nonexempt purposes.

Line 4(a) – 4(g). This item asks whether your group has established the procedures and practices recommended under the safe harbor rules of the excess benefit provisions and regulations (see "Limitation on Profits and Benefits" in Chapter 3 for a brief summary of the safe harbor rules). These procedures are meant to minimize the risk that nonprofits will pay out excess benefits. You don't have to adopt and follow them, but you should if you want the IRS to look kindly on your tax exemption.

If you adopt the standard bylaws contained in this book, you can mark "Yes" to each question and provide the responses to each item shown below on an attachment page. The IRS instructions to this line do not ask you to give more information if you answer "Yes" to an item, but we think you should do so, stating in your response where the IRS can look in your bylaws to verify that you have adopted each practice (as explained for each item below).

Line 4(a). Check "Yes" and state on an attachment page: "This organization has adopted a conflict of interest policy that controls the approval of salaries to directors, officers, and other "disqualified persons" as defined in

Section 4958 of the Internal Revenue Code. See Article 9, as well as Article 3, Section 6, and Article 4, Section 10, of the bylaws attached to this application. Also, Article 9, Section 5, of this organization's bylaws applies additional conflict of interest requirements on the board and compensation committee when approving compensation arrangements."

Line 4(b). Check "Yes" and state on an attachment page: "Article 9, Section 3, of this organization's bylaws requires the approval of compensation of directors, officers, and any "disqualified person" as defined in Section 4958 of the Internal Revenue Code in advance after full disclosure of the surrounding facts and approval by disinterested members of the governing board or committee and prior to entering into the compensation agreement or arrangement. Further, Article 9, Section 5(a), of this organization's bylaws requires specific approval of compensation arrangements prior to the first payment of compensation under such arrangements."

Line 4(c). Check "Yes" and state on an attachment page: "Article 9, Section 4, of the organization's bylaws, which are attached to this application, require the taking of written minutes of meetings at which compensation paid to any director, officer, or other "disqualified person" as defined in Section 4958 of the Internal Revenue Code, are approved. The minutes must include the date and the terms of the approved compensation arrangements. Further, and specifically with respect to the approval by the board or compensation committee of compensation arrangements, Article 9, Section 5(d), of the organization's bylaws requires the recordation of the date and terms of compensation arrangements as well as other specific information concerning the basis for the approval of compensation arrangements."

Line 4(d). Check "Yes" and state on an attachment page: "Article 9, Section 4, of the organization's bylaws requires the written recordation of the approval of compensation and other financial arrangements between this organization and a director, officer, employee, contractor, and any other "disqualified person" as defined in Section 4958 of the Internal Revenue Code, including the names of the persons who vote on the arrangement and their votes. Further, and specifically with respect to the approval by the board or compensation committee of compensation arrangements, Article 9, Section 5(d), of the organization's bylaws requires the recordation of the board or committee who were present during discussion of the approval of compensation arrangements, those who voted on it, and the votes cast by each board or committee member."

Line 4(e). Check "Yes" and state on an attachment page: "Article 9, Section 5(c), of the organization's bylaws requires that the board or compensation committee considering the approval of a compensation arrangement obtain compensation levels paid by similarly situated organizations, both taxable and tax-exempt, for functionally comparable positions; the availability of similar services in the geographic area of this organization; current compensation surveys compiled by independent firms; and actual written offers from similar institutions competing for the services of the person who is the subject of the compensation arrangement. This article also provides that it is sufficient for these purposes to rely on compensation data obtained from three comparable organizations in the same or similar communities for similar services if this organization's three-years' average gross receipts are less than $1 million (as allowed by IRS Regulation 53.4958-6)."

Line 4(f). Check "Yes" and state on an attachment page: "Article 9, Section 5(d), of the organization's bylaws requires that the written minutes of the board or compensation committee meeting at which a compensation arrangement was discussed and approved include the terms of compensation and the basis for its approval. This bylaw provision includes a list of specific information that must be included in the required written minutes."

If you haven't adopted the bylaws included with this book or have deleted or changed the provisions in Article 9 of the bylaws, you may need to mark "No" to one or more of the items in line 4. And whether you mark "Yes" or "No," you will need to provide responses on an attachment page that explains your particular conflicts of interest and compensation approval standards and procedures. Your responses should be sufficient to convince the IRS that your directors, officers, employees, and contractors will be paid fairly for work done to further your organization's exempt purposes and that disinterested directors or compensation committee members—for example, nonpaid directors or committee members who are not related to anyone paid by your organization—set the salaries and other compensation of your officers, employees, and contractors.

Line 5(a) – 5(c). Mark "Yes" if you have adopted the bylaws included with this book. State on the attachment page for this item: "The board of directors of this organization has adopted bylaws that contain a conflicts of interest policy. The policy is set out in Article 9 of the attached bylaws. This policy is based on the sample conflict of interest policy contained in Appendix A of the official instructions to IRS Form 1023. The organization has added additional requirements in Article 9, Section 5, of its bylaws for the approval of compensation arrangements that are based on the additional requirements contained in IRS

Regulation Section 53.4958-6 to help ensure that all compensation arrangements are made by disinterested members of the organization's board or a duly constituted compensation committee of the board and are fair, reasonable, and in furtherance of the tax-exempt purposes of this organization."

If you mark "Yes" to 5(a), you can skip 5(b) and 5(c). If you marked "No" to 5(a) because you did not adopt the bylaws included with this book or changed them to adopt a different conflict-of-interest policy, include responses to questions 5(a) and 5(b) on an attachment page. Your responses should show that you will follow your own practices to make sure that your directors, officers, employees, and others who exert significant influence over your nonprofit cannot feather their own nests by setting their own salary levels and making their own self-serving business deals with your nonprofit.

Line 6(a) and 6(b). The IRS instructions to Form 1023 explain what the terms "fixed payment" and "non-fixed payment" mean. Essentially, question 6(a) asks if your organization will pay its directors, officers, highly paid employees, or highly paid contractors (those listed in this part, lines 1(a) through 1(c)) any discretionary amounts (such as bonuses) or amounts based on your organization's revenues (such as a salary kicker or bonus computed as a percentage of annual contributions received by your nonprofit). Question 6(b) asks this same question with respect to all the other employees of your nonprofit who receive compensation of more than $50,000 per year. Obviously, it looks best if your nonprofit's principals and employees do not receive these types of revenue-driven incentives, which are more typical in a business, not a nonprofit, setting. We assume most small nonprofits will be able to answer "No" to this question. If, however, you have an overriding need to pay directors,

officers, and employees discretionary bonuses or provide them with revenue- or performance-based compensation or commissions, you need to provide the information requested on an attachment page. Your response should show that these nonfixed payments will be fairly and reasonably paid as incentives to promote the nonprofit purposes of your organization (this may not be easy to show), and that it won't be used simply to pay out revenues to your principals. Remember—private inurement is a nonprofit no-no—so siphoning over revenue to nonprofit principals is not allowed, even in the guise of bonus or performance-based employee incentives.

Line 7(a) and 7(b). Question 7(a) asks if your organization will purchase goods, services, or assets from its directors, officers, highly paid employees, or highly paid contractors (those listed in this Part V, lines 1(a) through 1(c)). Question 7(b) asks if your organization will sell goods, services, or assets to these people.

Most nonprofits will be able to answer "No" to both these questions because they will want to stay clear of insider sales and purchase transactions, simply to avoid the appearance (if not the actuality) of self-dealing. That said, it's also a fact of life that some smaller nonprofits have to look to their directors, officers, and principal employees or contractors to buy or sell goods or services—these may be the only people willing to do business with the nonprofit at the start of its operations. Even more typically, a small nonprofit may want to buy goods at a special discount offered by a director or officer. If you answer "Yes" to one of these questions, provide the requested information in your response on an attachment page. Your response should make clear that any such purchases or sales will be arms-length—that is, your nonprofit will pay no more and sell at no less than the commercially competitive, fair market value price for the goods, services, or assets. If you plan to buy goods, services, or assets at a discount from a director, officer, employee, or contractor, make sure to say so, since this sort of bargain purchase is better than an arms-length deal from the perspective of the nonprofit.

The official instructions to Form 1023, line 7(a) and 7(b), indicate that you can ignore purchases and sales of goods and services in the normal course of operations that are available to the general public under similar terms or conditions. In other words, if you buy normal inventory items from a contractor listed in Part V, line 1(c), at standard terms paid by the general public for these inventory items, you do not have to mark "Yes" to 7(a). Frankly, if your organization plans to purchase any type of goods or services from a director, officer, or employee, we think it should be disclosed in your application, since deals of this sort may have the appearance of a self-dealing transaction. In such a case, you can check "Yes" to line 7(a), then make it clear in your response that your organization will pay the same price for the inventory or other standard items purchased from a director, officer, or employee as the price paid by the general public (the current commercially competitive fair market value price).

If you answer "Yes" to either question and have adopted the bylaws included with this book, you can add in your response that "Article 9, Section 3, of the organization's bylaws requires the approval of conflict-of-interest transactions or arrangements, such as the purchase or sale of goods, services, or assets between the organization and one of its directors, officers, or any other "disqualified person" as defined in Section 4958(f)(1) of the Internal Revenue Code and as amplified by Section 53.4958-3 of the IRS Regulations, by the vote of a majority of disinterested directors

or members of a board committee, only after a finding that a more advantageous transaction or arrangement is not available to the organization and that the proposed transaction or arrangement is in the organization's best interest, is for its own benefit, and is fair and reasonable."

Line 8(a)–8(f). Question 8(a) asks if your organization will enter into leases, contracts, or other agreements with its directors, officers, highly paid employees, or highly paid contractors (those listed in this part, lines 1(a) through (c)). If you answer "Yes," you must supply responses to items 8(b) through 8(f) on an attachment page.

To rephrase an observation made in the instructions to line 7 above, to avoid the appearance if not the actuality of self-dealing, it's best not to deal with nonprofit insiders when leasing property or contracting for goods, services, or making other business arrangements. Most nonprofits will shy away from doing this, and will answer "No" to 8(a).

However, newly formed nonprofits sometimes find it most practical (and economical) to lease or rent property owned by a founder, director, or officer, or may otherwise have to enter into a contract or arrangement with one of these people. There is nothing absolutely forbidden about doing so, but you will want to make sure that any lease, contract, or agreement between your nonprofit and one of these people reflects fair market value terms or better. For example, it looks best if a director leases property owned by the director to the nonprofit at a lower-than-market value rate (best of all, of course, is when the director lets the nonprofit use the lease premises rent-free).

If you answer "Yes" to 8(a), provide the information requested in 8(b) through 8(f) on an attachment page. If possible, attach a copy of any lease, rental, or other agreement as requested in 8(f). For a discussion of leases together with a sample assignment of lease, see "Prepare Assignment of Leases and Deeds" in Chapter 10. Also, if you have adopted the bylaws included with this book, you can add in your response to item 8(d) or 8(e) that "Article 9, Section 3, of the organization's bylaws requires the approval of conflict-of-interest transactions or arrangements, such as a lease, contract, or other agreement between this organization and any of its directors, officers, or any other "disqualified person" as defined in Section 4958(f)(1) of the Internal Revenue Code and as amplified by Section 53.4958-3 of the IRS Regulations, by the vote of a majority of disinterested directors or members of a board committee, only after a finding that a more advantageous transaction or arrangement is not available to the organization and that the proposed transaction or arrangement is in the organization's best interest, is for its own benefit, and is fair and reasonable."

Line 9(a) – 9(f). These questions are similar to those in 8(a) through 8(f) above, except they apply to leases, contracts, and agreements between your nonprofit and another business or organization associated with or controlled by your directors or officers. Specifically, these questions apply to business deals between your nonprofit and another company or organization in which one or more of your directors or officers also serves as a director or officer or one of your directors or officers owns a 35% or greater interest (for example, a 35% voting stock ownership interest in a profit-making corporation). You can ignore deals made between your corporation and another 501(c)(3) tax exempt nonprofit organization, even if one or more of your directors or officers also serves on the board or as an officer of the other 501(c)(3) tax exempt nonprofit organization.

EXAMPLE:

If one of your directors also serves as a board member on a nonprofit cooperative that is not tax-exempt under 501(c)(3) and your nonprofit enters in leases, contracts, or other agreements with the other nonprofit, answer "Yes" to 9(a) and provide the information requested in items 9(b) through 9(f).

EXAMPLE:

If one of your officers owns a 35% or greater stock interest in a business corporation, and your nonprofit buys goods and services from the business corporation (either through a formal contract or a verbal agreement), answer "Yes" to 9(a) and provide the information requested in items 9(b) through 9(f).

The discussion in line 8 above about leases and agreements between your nonprofit and individuals applies here to leases and agreements between your nonprofit and affiliated or controlled companies and organizations. If you answer "Yes," provide the information requested in items 9(b) through 9(f). Also, if you have adopted the bylaws included with this book, you can add in your response to item 9(d) or 9(e) that "Article 9, Section 3, of the organization's bylaws requires the approval of conflict-of-interest transactions or arrangements, such as a lease, contract, or other agreement between this organization and any "disqualified person" as defined in Section 4958(f)(1) of the Internal Revenue Code and as amplified by Section 53.4958-3 of the IRS Regulations, which includes thirty-five percent controlled entities, by the vote of a majority of disinterested directors or members of a board committee, only after a finding that a more advantageous transaction or arrangement is not available to the organization and that the proposed transaction or arrangement is in the organization's best interest, is for its own benefit, and is fair and reasonable."

Part VI: Your Members and Other Individuals and Organizations That Receive Benefits From You

Line 1(a). If you plan to implement programs that provide goods, services, or funds to individuals, check "Yes" and describe these programs on an attachment page. Many smaller nonprofits will provide goods or services as part of their exempt-purpose activities, such as a nonprofit dance studio (dance lessons or admissions to dance performances), formal and informal nonprofit schools (tuition or fees for classes and instructional services), hospitals (health care costs), and other educational or charitable groups. Of course, charitable-purpose groups often provide goods or services free to the public or at lower than market-rate cost—such as free or low-cost meals, shelter, and clothing. But educational-purpose groups often charge standard or slightly reduced rates for admissions, tuition, and services. Doing the latter is permissible. What the IRS wants to see is that your nonprofit is set up to provide goods and services as part of a valid nonprofit tax-exempt program, and that all members of the public—or at least a segment of the public that is not limited to particular individuals—will have access to your goods or services. What you can't do is set up a tax-exempt nonprofit that intends to benefit a private class or specific group of individuals, as individuals (such as your uncle Bob and Aunt Betty, or all your relatives and in-laws). The broader the class of people that your nonprofit benefits, the better. Making your nonprofit programs available to the public-at-large normally looks best to the IRS. And providing goods and services at rates below market rates also helps bolster

your credibility as a nonprofit, as opposed to revenue-driven, organization.

At this point in the process, most groups have not fully determined what they will charge for goods and services. If this is the case, explain in your response the services and benefits that will be provided to the public (or segment of the public) and explain generally how you will determine fees. For example, you may wish to indicate that "charges for the described benefits, products, and services are at present undetermined, but will be reasonable and related to the cost of the service to be provided." And again, if you plan to provide goods or services at a discount or free-of-charge, make sure you say so.

Line 1(b). If your nonprofit will provide goods or services to other organizations, check "Yes" and explain your program plans on an attachment page. If you donate or sell goods and services to another 501(c)(3) tax-exempt nonprofit at fair or discounted rates for use in their tax-exempt programs, your program should pass muster with the IRS. But if you simply plan to obtain revenue by selling goods and services provided to profit-making businesses, expect to have to justify this sort of commercial-looking activity. For example, an educational group may provide seminars to the human resource managers of business corporations on how to comply with federal and state fair employment regulations. This sort of program that serves the needs of employees should be fine with the IRS. But simply trafficking in goods and services for a profit with other organizations and companies will look like (and probably is in fact) a commercially driven, profit-making enterprise that won't qualify as a tax-exempt activity.

Indicate whether you are a membership organization. If you have included membership provisions in your bylaws or you have used the tear-out or CD-ROM membership provisions as explained in Chapter 7, you should check "Yes" and answer questions in lines 11(a), (b), and (c). If you have not formed a formal membership organization, check "No" and go on to line 12.

Line 2. Most groups will answer "No" to this question because the IRS frowns on groups that limit benefits, services, or funds to a specific individual or group of individuals. However, if the group of people benefited by the nonprofit is broad (not limited to specific individuals) and related to the exempt purposes of the nonprofit group, the IRS should have no objection (see the discussion to line 1(a) of this part above). If you answer "Yes," provide an explanation on an attachment page. You may be able to refer to information already provided in your response to line 1(a) of this part.

EXAMPLE:

A nonprofit musical heritage organization plans to provide programs and benefits to needy musicians residing in the community. If the overall tax-exempt purpose of the organization is allowed, the IRS will permit this limitation of benefits to a segment of the community.

Line 3. In this question, the IRS is looking for prohibited self-inurement—in this case, whether your nonprofit is set up primarily or directly to provide goods, services, or funds to individuals who have a family or business relationship with your directors, officers, or highest-paid employees or contractors listed in Part V, lines 1(a) through 1(c). Most groups will answer "No" here. However, if you think someone who fits in one of these categories may receive goods, products, or services incidentally from your nonprofit as a member of the public, check "Yes" and explain how these related

people will have access to your nonprofit's benefits. If your response makes it clear that these related people are not the focus of your nonprofit programs, but only coincidentally qualify as members of the general public, you should be okay.

Part VII: Your History

Line 1. Most groups will answer "No" to this question. However, if you are a successor to an incorporated or preexisting organization (such as an unincorporated association), mark "Yes."

"Successor" has a special technical meaning, which is explained in the official IRS instructions to this item. Basically, you are most likely to be a successor organization if your nonprofit corporation has:

- taken over the activities of a prior organization—this is presumably the case if your nonprofit corporation has appointed initial directors or officers who are the same people who served as the directors or officers of the prior association, and your nonprofit has the same purposes as the prior association

- taken over 25% or more of the assets of a preexisting nonprofit, or

- been legally converted from the previous association to a nonprofit—typically by filing special articles of incorporation to state the name of the prior association and a declaration by the prior officers of the association that the conversion to a nonprofit corporation was properly approved by the association.

We assume most readers will be starting new nonprofits, not inheriting the assets, people, and activities of a preexisting formal nonprofit association. We also assume most readers have not adopted special articles to legally convert a prior association to a nonprofit corporation. In the real world, this sort of conversion only occurs if the prior group was a highly organized and visible entity with a solid support base that it wants to leverage by formally converting the association to a nonprofit corporation. However, in most cases, small nonprofits that existed previously as informal nonprofit groups with few assets, little support, and hardly any formal infrastructure, normally start out fresh with a newly formed corporation that is not a successor to the prior nonprofit group. If you think your nonprofit corporation is a successor organization, we suggest you get help from a nonprofit expert to complete Schedule G and make sure all the paperwork for your new nonprofit as well as the prior group is in order.

If you are a successor to a prior nonprofit, mark "Yes," and complete Schedule G of the 1023 application. See "Filling Out the Schedules," below, for instructions on filling out Schedule G. The IRS will take the history, activities, and financial data of your prior association as well as your responses to Schedule G into account when deciding whether your nonprofit corporation is entitled to its tax exemption. It may also ask you to file tax returns for the prior association if it has not already done so for all preceding tax years during which the prior association was in operation.

Line 2. Most new groups will be able to answer "No" here because they will be submitting their exemption application within 27 months after the end of month when their nonprofit corporation was formed. The date of formation is the date the corporation's articles of incorporation were filed by the secretary of state and became effective. For example, if you filed your articles on January 12, 2007, you have until the end of April 2009 to submit (postmark) your exemption application.

If you are submitting your exemption application after this 27-month deadline, check

"Yes" and fill in and submit Schedule E with your 1023 exemption application.

Part VIII: Your Specific Activities

This part asks about certain types of activities, such as political activity and fundraising, that the IRS looks at more closely. These are activities that a 501(c)(3) is prohibited from engaging in or can only do within certain strict limitations—namely, without benefiting or catering to the special interests of particular individuals or organizations. Please read the official instructions to this Part in the 1023 instructions before reading our instructions below.

Line 1. A 501(c)(3) nonprofit organization may not participate in political campaigns (although some voter education drives and political debate activities are permitted—see "Limitation on Political Activities" in Chapter 3). The IRS may deny or revoke your tax-exempt status if you participate in or donate to a campaign. Most groups should answer "No" here.

If you think you should answer "Yes" to this question, check with a nonprofit lawyer or tax consultant—a "Yes" response means you do not qualify for a 501(c)(3) tax exemption. However, you may qualify for a 501(c)(4) tax exemption.

Line 2(a). This question concerns your group's plans, if any, to affect legislation. Most groups will answer "No" to this question. If you answer "No," you can move on to line 3.

If you plan to engage in efforts to influence legislation, check "Yes" and read "Limitation on Political Activities" in Chapter 3. Then complete 2(b).

Line 2(b). Check "Yes" if you plan to elect to fall under the alternate political expenditures test discussed in "Limitation on Political Activities" in Chapter 3, and attach a completed IRS Form 5768, *Election-Revocation of Election by an Eligible Section 501(c)(3) Organization To Make Expenditures To Influence Legislation.* We assume you have not already filed this form; if you have, attach a copy of the filed form. A copy of this simple, one-page consent form is included on the CD-ROM provided with this book. The political expenditures test is complicated, and you'll probably need the help of a seasoned nonprofit advisor to decide whether you will be able to meet the requirements and gain a benefit from electing this special test for political legislative activities. Before using the Form 5768 included on the CD-ROM, go to the IRS website at www.irs.gov and make sure it is the latest version of the form. If the IRS site has a more current version, use the website's form, not the form included on the CD-ROM.

If you checked "Yes" to line 2(a) and do not plan to elect the political expenditures test, check "No" to line 2(b). On an attachment, you must describe the extent and percentage of time and money you expect to devote to your legislative activities compared to your total activities. Be as specific as you can about the political activities you expect to promote and how you will promote them. If possible (and accurate), make it clear that your legislative activities will constitute an "insubstantial" part of your overall nonprofit programs and activities. If the IRS feels that your political program will be substantial, it will deny your 501(c)(3) tax exemption.

Line 3(a) – 3(c). Most 501(c)(3) nonprofits do not engage in bingo and gaming activities. If you plan to do so, read the IRS official instruction for this line as well as IRS Publication 3079, *Gaming Publication for Tax-Exempt Organizations,* before checking "Yes" to any of the questions in line 3 and providing the requested information.

Line 4(a). Read the official instructions to this line to learn the definition of fundraising and some of the different ways it may be conducted. Note that fundraising includes raising funds for your own organization, raising funds for other organizations, as well as having some other individual or organization raise funds for your group. If your nonprofit is one that will be obtaining revenue and operating funds only from the performance of its exempt functions— that is by providing services or goods related to your exempt purpose—you can check "No" here. Make sure that none of the specific fundraising activity boxes listed in 4(a) apply to your group. However, if you expect your nonprofit to do any type of fundraising, such as soliciting government grants, attracting private and public donations or contributions, or going whole hog and hiring a professional fundraiser, check "Yes" and then check each box that describes a fundraising activity that you plan to or may pursue in your quest for program funds and revenue. On an attachment page, describe each activity whose box you have checked. If your nonprofit plans to engage in a type of fundraising not listed under 4(a), check the "other" box and describe it in your attachment response. Be specific and as thorough as you can in your response about the people you will use, any compensation you will pay, the amount and type of support you hope to raise, and the use to which you will put raised funds for each fundraising activity. If you check "No" to 4(a), you can skip ahead to line 5.

Line 4(b). Mark "Yes" if you plan to hire paid fundraisers, and provide the financial and contract information requested on an attachment page. Any financial information should be actual or projected figures that cover the same periods as the financial information you will provide in Part IX (see the official 1023 Part IX instructions and our Part IX instructions below to determine the period for which you should provide financial information). Many beginning nonprofits will not plan to use paid fundraisers right away and can state: "This newly formed nonprofit has not entered into oral or written contracts with individuals or organizations for the raising of funds, and has no specific plans to do so in the foreseeable future."

Line 4(c). If your nonprofit will do fundraising for other organizations, state "Yes" and provide the information requested on an attachment page. Most nonprofit organizers using this book will not raise funds for other organizations even if they plan to raise funds for themselves and will mark "No" here.

Line 4(d). If you checked "Yes" to 4(a), provide the information requested for this item. You should provide this information for states or localities where you will raise funds for your organization or for other organizations, or where an individual or another organization, including a paid fundraiser, will raise funds for your organization.

Line 4(e). See the official instructions for this item—it concerns the special practice of soliciting and using "donor-advised" or "donor-directed" funds. Most nonprofits will not have plans to use this practice, but if you do, provide the information requested on an attachment page. The IRS will want to make sure that your organization does not use funds to meet the private needs of donors, but instead will use donor-directed funds for purposes that are consistent with the tax-exempt purposes of the nonprofit.

Here is a statement from the 2005 IRS Exempt Organization (EO) Report that explains why the IRS is concerned about donor-advised funds, and indicates that it will be keeping an eye out for abuse in this area:

Donor-advised funds allow private donors to provide input as to how their charitable contributions will be spent. A number of organizations have come to light through examinations, referrals from other parts of the IRS, and public scrutiny which appear to have abused the basic concepts underlying donor-advised funds. These organizations, while promoted as legitimate donor-advised funds, appear to be established for the purpose of generating questionable charitable deductions, providing impermissible economic benefits to the donors and their families (including tax-sheltered investment income for the donors), and providing management fees for the promoters. EO Examinations will identify organizations with a high potential for abuse in this area and commence examinations during FY 2005.

Line 5. This item is for special government-affiliated groups (see the instructions to the 1023 form). If you check "Yes," your nonprofit needs special assistance responding to this item and being able to meet the requirements for a 501(c)(3) tax exemption. If you check "Yes," consult a nonprofit legal advisor.

Line 6. See the 1023 instructions. If you are an economic development nonprofit and mark "Yes," you'll need expert help filling out your tax exemption to make sure your activities meet the 501(c)(3) requirements.

Below is a statement from the 2005 IRS Exempt Organization (EO) Report that explains why the IRS is applying special scrutiny to economic development nonprofits:

In response to referrals from HUD concerning abuse by individuals setting up exempt organizations for the purpose of participating in a number of HUD programs, EO initiated a compliance project in this area in FY 2004. Potential abuses include lack of charitable activity, personal use of program property, and most often, private benefit provided to for-profit construction contractors hired to complete the repairs to program properties. In these cases, contractors were usually related to the organizations' officers or board members, and were often the same individuals. Costs were over-stated and work was substandard or completely lacking. The project is currently focusing on abuses by exempt organizations in HUD's housing rehabilitation/resale and down payment assistance programs, and will expand to other HUD programs as staffing permits.

Line 7(a). Line 7 applies to nonprofits that will own or develop real estate, such as land or a building, in pursuit of its nonprofit activities. See the 1023 instructions for line 7(a) through 7(c) for more information. If you plan to develop or improve real estate, including land or buildings, mark "Yes" to 7(a) and provide the information requested on an attachment page, Mostly the IRS wants to make sure that your nonprofit is not planning to make any sweetheart real estate development deals that benefit people associated with your nonprofit and its directors and officers thorough family or business ties.

Line 7(b). If your nonprofit will maintain facilities, such as a building or office space or other physical address, and plans to use anyone other than employees or volunteers to manage the facilities—for example, if it plans to hire a management company to manage property—check "Yes" and provide the information requested on an attachment page. Again, the IRS wants you to show that the managers are not getting special breaks or excess payments because they are family members or business associates of the nonprofit's directors or officers.

Line 7(c). This line wants you to provide information on all developers and managers of real estate or facilities owned or used by your nonprofit if any of these developers or managers have a business or family relationship with your nonprofit directors or officers. If this question applies to your nonprofit, provide the information requested on an attachment page. If you have already provided the information in response to 7(a) and/or 7(b), you can refer to your previous response. The IRS will scrutinize any contracts you provide and negotiation processes you describe to make sure your nonprofit is not paying more than fair market value for real property development and management services.

Line 8. First read the 1023 instructions for this line. If your nonprofit plans to enter into joint ventures (business deals) with individuals or other nonprofits or commercial business entities, see a legal advisor before providing the information requested and completing your 1023 tax exemption application. Nonprofit organization joint ventures raise complex issues that require expert help to make sure they are structured properly to meet the requirements of the 501(c)(3) tax exemption

Line 9(a) – 9(d). if you are forming a child care organization, you may qualify for your tax exemption either under 501(k) of the Internal Revenue Code or 501(c)(3) as a school. Read the instructions before answering these questions. If you check "Yes" to 9(a), answer 9(b) through 9(d). If you answer "No," go on to line 10.

Line 10. This question asks if your nonprofit plans to publish, own, or have rights in intellectual property, such as art, books, patents, trademarks, and the like (see the 1023 instructions for definitions). If you answer "Yes," provide the information requested on an attachment page about ownership of the intellectual property, if and how you will derive revenue from the property, and generally how the property will be used as part of your nonprofit activities. In essence, the IRS wants to know whether your nonprofit plans to acquire and exploit copyrights, patents, and other forms of intellectual property and, if so, how. Examples of groups that would answer "Yes" include a visual arts exhibit studio, educational book publisher, scientific research center that engages in original (patentable) research, and any group that plans to market its trade name (a name used by the nonprofit and associated with its activities), trademark, or service (logos, words, and images used by the nonprofit to market its goods and services).

Nonprofits that conduct scientific research in the public interest are expected to make their patents, copyrights, processes, or formulae available to the public, not simply develop and exploit results of their research for their own use (see "Scientific Purposes" in Chapter 3). There is nothing wrong or underhanded, however, about a nonprofit owning and exploiting intellectual property related to its exempt purpose—for example, a qualified literary or education nonprofit owning and obtaining royalty revenue from the sale of its published educational works, or a nonprofit selling donated art to raise funds for its exempt purpose. Be careful though: If a nonprofit deals in intellectual property as a routine method of raising revenue operating revenue—for example, if a nonprofit licenses its trade name to obtain revenue—the IRS is likely to consider this income unrelated business income. If this unrelated income is clearly more than a small portion of the group's overall revenue, the IRS will likely question or deny the group's 501(c)(3) tax exemption.

The issue of copyright ownership sometimes is key to this issue. Remember: if copyrights in published works are owned by a 501(c)(3) nonprofit, this means that the copyrights, like all other assets owned by the nonprofit, are irrevocably dedicated to tax-exempt purposes and must be distributed (transferred) to another tax-exempt nonprofit when the organization dissolves. Hence, the IRS is apt to look more favorably on an educational nonprofit that holds copyrights in its published works. Conversely, if a nonprofit education group does not own the copyright to its published works, but instead publishes the works owned by others under the terms of standard commercial royalty contracts, the IRS may feel that the group is simply a commercial publisher that is not entitled to a 501(c)(3) educational tax exemption. However, if the group publishes education material written by volunteers or its employees or under "work for hire" contracts with outside authors, copyrights in the works are owned by the nonprofit, not by the authors. Publication of this material is clearly in the public interest and contains content related to the educational purpose of the nonprofit. Thus, the IRS is more likely agree that the group is entitled to a tax exemption.

The sale of art by nonprofits often piques the interest of IRS examiners. For example, if an educational nonprofit exhibits artwork owned by artists and collects a commission on each sale, the IRS may conclude that the organization runs a commercial art gallery that is not entitled to a tax exemption. There is no bright-line test for groups that deal in arts or sell goods and services. The IRS looks at all the facts and circumstances related to a group's activities and operations to determine if the group's primary purpose is a charitable, educational, or another 501(c)(3) purpose or, instead, represents a commercial enterprise. For examples of when the IRS has reached different conclusions after examining the activities of groups that sell art as part of their activities, see the summaries of selected IRS revenue rulings below:

TIP

How to find IRS revenue rulings. Each IRS revenue ruling is referenced with a two- or four-digit year prefix followed by a number—for example, revenue ruling 2004-98 is a 2004 ruling and revenue ruling 80-106 is a 1980 ruling, distinguished from other rulings during the year by the second sequential number. To read the ruling, go to TaxLinks.com. Click on the appropriate year in the heading (for example, 2006), then scroll through the numbered rulings for that year and select the appropriate ruling number (for example, 106).

- Rev. Rul. 80-106. Thrift shop; consignment sales. An organization operated a thrift shop that sold items that were either donated or received on consignment. Substantially all of the work in operating the thrift shop was performed without compensation, all transactions were at arm's length, and all profits were distributed to Section 501(c)(3) organizations. The organization qualified for exemption as an organization operated for charitable purposes.

- Rev. Rul. 76-152. Art gallery. A nonprofit educational organization, formed by art patrons to promote community under-standing of modern art trends by selecting for exhibit, exhibiting, and selling art works of local artists, and which retained a commission on sales that was less than customary commercial charges and was not sufficient to cover the cost of operating the gallery, did not qualify for exemption under Section 501(c)(3). The following statement in the ruling provides perhaps the best clue as to why the IRS rejected the group's application: "Since ninety percent of all sales proceeds are turned over to the individual artists, such direct benefits are substantial by any measure and the organization's provision of them cannot be dismissed as being merely incidental to its other purposes and activities."

- Rev. Rul. 71-395. A cooperative art gallery that was formed and operated by a group of artists for the purpose of exhibiting and selling their works, did not charge admission but received a commission from sales and rental of art sufficient to cover the cost of operating the gallery, did not qualify for exemption under Section 501(c)(3) as an educational organization.

- Rev. Rul. 66-178. A nonprofit organization was created to foster and develop the arts by sponsoring a public art exhibit at which the works of unknown but promising artists were selected by a panel of qualified judges for display. Artists eligible to have their works displayed were those who were not affiliated with art galleries and who had no medium for exhibiting their creations. The organization did not charge the artists any fees, nor did the organization sell or offer the displayed works for sale. For the exhibit, the organization prepared a catalogue which listed each work displayed, the name of its creator, and the artist's home or studio address. The catalogue was sold for a small fee to the public. The organization also received income from nominal admission fees to the exhibit and contributions. Funds were paid out for renting the exhibition hall, printing the catalogues, and administrative expenses. The organization qualified for a 501(c)(3) tax exemption.

If nothing else, the above rulings reinforce one fundamental fact about seeking and obtaining a tax exemption: The IRS looks at the full context of a nonprofit's operations—including its sources and uses of revenue—when deciding whether a group qualifies for 501(c)(3) tax exemption. Normally, no one fact is fatal or determinative. The more a group demonstrates that its operations are public rather than private or commercial interests, the better its chances of obtaining a tax exemption. And on a more subjective note, the above rulings also hint at the importance of couching your nonprofit activities in the most acceptable (least commercial) terms—for example, it may sound and look better to the IRS if your group collects "admission" or "consignment" fees rather than "commissions," since the latter term typically connotes overt commercial activity.

Below are two revenue rulings related to educational nonprofits that involve the publication of books and music. The first repeats the theme that the more a group looks and acts like a regular commercial venture, the less its chances of qualifying for 501(c)(3) tax-exempt status. The second shows that nonprofits that cater to a small, traditionally noncommercial, segment of public education stand a better chance of obtaining a tax exemption, at least partially because the nonprofit activity is, in fact, less likely to reap significant profits.

- Rev. Rul. 66-104. An education organization was created to meet the need for more satisfactory teaching materials and textbooks in economics and related fields. The organization contracted with commercial publishing firms for the publication of these materials which were used primarily by colleges and universities. The organization did not hold the copyright in its published material. The contracts between the organization and the publishers provided that the publishers pay all publication costs and a royalty to the organization on sales of the publication. In return, the publisher received the copyright, publishing, and selling rights. The agreement between the organization and the editors and authors provided that the royalty income would first be applied to pay for the costs of preparing the materials for publication, including funds to authors and editors. The remaining royalty was divided into specific percentages between the organization and the editors and authors. The IRS concluded that: "Although educational interests are served by the publication of better teaching materials, the facts in this case show only an enterprise conducted in an essentially commercial manner, in which all the participants expect to receive a monetary return." The IRS denied the organization's 501(c)(3) tax exemption.

- Rev. Rul. 79-369. The organization was created to stimulate, promote, encourage, and sustain interest in and appreciation of contemporary symphonic and chamber music. The organization records the new works of unrecognized composers as well as the neglected works of more established composers. The music selected for recording had a limited commercial market and was not generally produced by the commercial music publishing and recording industry for sale to the public. The organization sold its recordings primarily to libraries and educational institutions. Some records were provided free to radio stations operated by educational institutions. The organization also made sales to individuals. The records were not made available for sale through commercial record dealers except in a few specialty shops, but were sold through mail orders. The organization did not engage in any advertising, but relied upon those who were interested in this type of music to communicate the availability of the records. All sales were facilitated by the use of a catalogue published by the organization. The catalogue contents included information about the compositions and the composers. This information was retained in the catalogue so that the catalogue served as an archive with respect to these compositions and recordings. Copies of all recordings were maintained for availability in the future. The liner notes on the album covers contained a biography of the composer and a description of the composition by its composer. Composers received royalties from the sale of recordings as required by federal law. Due to the limited commercial market for this type of music, the royalties received by the composers were not significant. The group qualified for a 501(c)(3) tax exemption.

Line 11. This question asks if your nonprofit will accept contributions of various types of property, including works of art and automobiles. If you answer "Yes," provide the information requested. If you receive contributions of art, you may be able to refer to portions of your response to line 10, if you used line 10 to provide information on how you sell contributed art works. The IRS mostly wants to make sure your nonprofit is not simply setting up a contribution-conduit organization formed and operated primarily to generate income tax contributions for wealthy individuals associated with your group. See IRS Publication 526, *Charitable Contributions,* for the latest rules on the deductibility of contributions to qualified 501(c)(3) public charities.

Line 12(a) – 12(d). If your nonprofit plans to operate in one or more foreign countries, answer "Yes" to 12(a) and provide the information requested in 12(b) through 12(d) on an attachment page. Special tax-exemption and deductibility of contribution rules apply to

nonprofits created or operated abroad. If you answer "Yes," see a nonprofit advisor who has experience in advising nonprofits that operate in the foreign countries where you plan to operate for help in completing your 1023 application. Also see "Foreign Organizations in General" in the official 1023 instructions for basic information on nonprofits formed abroad. Finally, realize that a big part of the IRS's energies is now devoted to scrutinizing the operations of foreign-based nonprofits as part of the service's participation in antiterrorism. Here is an excerpt from the IRS 2005 EO (Exempt Organization) report:

> In FY 2005, EO will examine a sample of foreign grant making organizations; the primary focus of the examinations is to ensure that funds are used for their intended charitable purpose and not diverted for terrorist activity. The project will gather information about current practices, that is, the existence and effectiveness of controls put in place to monitor the distribution of overseas grants and other assistance. This committee will also address the need for possible guidance or other modifications to the laws in this area.

Line 13 (a) – 13(g). If your nonprofit will make grants or loans to other organizations or receive and disburse funds (for example as a fiscal agent) for other organizations, answer "Yes" to line 13(a), then answer 13(b) through 13(g). Most smaller nonprofits do not make grants or loans to other nonprofits, but may receive grant money as a fiscal agent for another nonprofit. If your group plans to do this, your responses should show that the groups you sponsor promote activities that are related to your tax-exempt purposes and that you exercise oversight in making sure the funds are accounted for and used properly by the groups you sponsor. If your responses demonstrate or imply that you disburse funds as a feeder group to promote regular commercial or nonexempt activities, the IRS will deny your exemption. The questions listed here should give you an indication of what the IRS is looking for—formal applications, grant proposals, fiscal reporting controls, and other procedures that you will use to select, monitor, and assess the groups that you sponsor.

Line 14(a) – 14(f). This question is similar to line 13, except it applies only to foreign groups that you assist or sponsor. If you answer "Yes" to 14(a), it asks additional questions (14(b) through 14(f)) to make sure you apply extra scrutiny to any foreign groups you sponsor (see the antiterrorism note in the line 12 instructions above—it is one of the drivers for this extra IRS scrutiny of groups that sponsor or assist foreign organizations).

Line 15. First read the instructions to this line in the official 1023 instructions. They provide a definition of what "close connection" means, and the definitions cover a lot of helpful material. If you answer "Yes," provide a thorough explanation on an attachment page of how your structure and/or operations are connected to those of another group. Obviously, if you do share space, people, programs, or other attributes or activities with another group, the IRS will want to see that you are not diverting your tax-exempt purposes or revenue to non-tax-exempt ends or purposes promoted by the group with which you are connected.

Line 16. See the instructions before answering this question. A cooperative hospital service organization is a very special type of organization that is tax-exempt under section 501(e) of the Internal Revenue Code, which like a 501(c)(3) group uses the 1023 application to apply for its tax exemption. You will need expert help completing your tax exemption

application if you answer "Yes" here.

Line 17. See the instructions before answering this question. A cooperative service organization of operating educational organizations is another special type of organization that is tax-exempt under Section 501(f) of the Internal Revenue Code. Like a 501(c)(3) group, it also uses the 1023 application to apply for its tax exemption. You will need expert help completing your tax exemption application if you answer "Yes" here.

Line 18. We assume readers of this book are not setting up a charitable risk pool under Section 501(n) of the Internal Revenue Code (see the instructions to the 1023 form). If you are, get help from an expert in this special field of nonprofit activity before completing your tax exemption application.

Line 19. As explained in the 1023 instructions to this line, a school is defined as an educational organization that has the primary function of presenting formal instruction, normally maintains a regular faculty and curriculum, normally has a regularly enrolled body of students, and has a place where its educational activities are carried on (for example, private primary or secondary schools and colleges). Check the "Yes" box and fill in Schedule B if one of your purposes, whether primary or otherwise, is operating a nonprofit school.

Line 20. If your nonprofit is setting up a hospital or medical care facility, including a medical research facility (see the definitions in the 1023 instructions), answer "Yes" and complete Schedule C. (See "Filling Out the Schedules," below, for instructions on completing Schedule C.)

Line 21. If you are forming a low-income housing facility or housing for the elderly or handicapped (see the 1023 instructions for definitions of these terms), check "Yes" and complete Schedule F.

Line 22. Refer to the 1023 instructions for definitions of terms before answering this question. If your nonprofit, whether it is a school or otherwise, will provide scholarships or other education or educational-related financial aid or assistance to individuals, check "Yes" and fill in Schedule H.

Part IX: Financial Data

All groups should complete the financial data tables in Section A (Statement of Revenues and Expenses) and Section B (Balance Sheet) of this Part IX. Start by reading the 1023 instructions for this part.

Statement of Revenues and Expenses

The financial data listed here includes your group's past and current receipts and expenses (many groups will need to show proposed receipts and expenses as explained below). The IRS will use this financial data to make sure that:

- your group's actual and/or proposed receipts and expenses correspond to the exempt-purpose activities and operational information you describe in your application
- you do not plan to engage substantially in unrelated business activities, and
- you do or most likely will meet the appropriate 501(c)(3) public charity support test (see our instructions to Part X, below).

The number of columns you use in Section A will depend on the number of full and partial tax years your group has been in existence. Most nonprofits will have a tax year that goes from January 1 to December 31, but some will have a tax year that ends on the last day of another month—see your response to Part 1, line 5, above.

New groups without prior tax years. If your nonprofit is newly formed, it probably has not been in existence for a full tax year. Put in projected numbers for the current year in column (a), and projections for the next two years in columns (b) and (c).

EXAMPLE:

You are a new nonprofit formed on February 15 of the current year, with a tax year that goes from January 1 to December 31, and you are applying for your tax exemption in June of the corporation's first tax year. The beginning "from" date of the period shown at the top of column (a) is the date you filed your articles—February 15 of the current year. The "to" date for this period should be December 31, the end of the current tax year. Use columns (b) and (c) to show projected figures for your next two tax years, going from January 1 to December 31 of each of the two years. Many new groups will repeat much of the information from their first tax year for the next two proposed tax years, unless they anticipate a major change in operations or sources of support.

Don't expect to fill in all the items. The IRS knows you've just commenced operations and that you are estimating possible sources of revenue and items of expense, and it expects to see a few blank lines. Also realize that some of your projected revenues and expenses may not neatly fit the categories shown in the printed revenue and expense table. You can use revenue item 7 (other income) and expense item 23 (other expenses) to list totals for these items, and attach a list that itemizes these additional items of revenue and expense on an attachment page. The IRS does not like to see large lump sum amounts, so break down these additional items of revenue and expense as much as possible.

Groups with prior tax years. If your nonprofit has been in existence for four or more prior tax years, show actual revenue and expense amounts for your last four completed tax years in columns (a) through (d). Note that the current year, column (a), will be your last completed tax year, not the partially completed current tax year. You will be supplying figures for four completed tax years, and no projected information.

Alternatively, if your nonprofit has been in existence more than one full tax year, but less than four tax years, you must show projected financial information for your current tax year in column (a), then show figures for your prior completed tax year(s) in the other column or columns. You also may need to show projected revenue and expense information in one of the columns for a future tax year depending on how many years you have been in existence. Here is how it works:

If your group has been existence one full prior tax year, show projected figures for the full current tax year in column (a), and your prior completed tax year in column (b). Then show projected figures for next year's revenues and expenses (the tax year after the current tax year) in column(c). This information represents three full tax years worth of information—one completed tax year and two projected tax years.

If your group has been in existence two full prior tax years, show projected figures for the full current tax year in column (a), your last completed tax year in column (b), and your first completed tax year in column (c). This information represents three full tax years worth of information—two completed tax years and one projected tax year.

Line 12 of the revenue and expense statement asks you to list any "unusual grant" revenue. This term is explained in the instructions for this line in the 1023 instructions, and we explain it in more detail in Chapter 4, in "Public Suport Test" (see the discussion under "Exceptions to the 2% Limit Rule") and "Exempt Activities Support Test" (see the discussion under "Unusual Grants Drop Out of the Computation"). Also see the specific rules on unusual grants contained in IRS Publication 557 (included on the CD-ROM).

Basically, unusual grants are permitted grants which can throw a kink in your public charity support computations because they come from one source, as opposed to several smaller grants from different sources. Remember, 501(c)(3) public support revenue is supposed to be spread out and come from a number of public sources, not just one or two. It is unlikely that you expect to receive an unusual grant this early in your nonprofit life—unusual grants normally happen only as a result of a sustained and successful outreach program that attracts one or two large grants that surprise the modest expectations of a small nonprofit. In effect, an unusual grant represents both good and bad news. The good news is the unusually large amount of the grant; the bad news is its potential damage to the group's ability to meet the technical public support requirements that apply to 501(c)(3) public charities. If you have received or expect to receive one or more unusual grants, insert the total number here on line 12 in the appropriate column (past, present, or future tax year), and list on an attachment page a description of each grant (what the grant was for, whether it was restricted to a specific use, and other terms of the grant), together with the donor's name, date, and amount of each unusual grant. If a large grant qualifies as an unusual grant, it will be disregarded by the IRS when it computes whether your support qualifies under the technical public charity support test rules (see Part X, below).

Balance Sheet

Prepare the balance sheet to show assets and liabilities of your corporation as of your last completed tax year, if any, or the current tax year if you have not yet completed one full tax year.

EXAMPLE:

You have organized a new nonprofit corporation, formed on April 1. You are preparing your 1023 application in November of the same year. Your tax year goes from January 1 to December 31. The current tax year period covered by column (a) of your Statement of Revenue and Expenses is from April 1 to December 31. Your balance sheet ending date will be the same ending date, December 31, the eventual ending date of your first tax year. This date should appear as the "year-end" date in the blank at the top right of the balance sheet page. Even though this is a future end date, you should base your statement of assets and liabilities on current information—that is on your organization's current assets and liabilities at the time of the preparation of your exemption application.

It's not uncommon for a small starting nonprofit without liabilities and accounts receivable to simply show a little cash as its only reportable balance sheet item. Other common items reported are line 8 depreciable assets—equipment owned by the corporation and used to conduct its exempt activities.

Line 17 of the balance sheet asks for fund balance or net asset information. Typically, this is the amount by which your assets exceed your liabilities—in other words, the net value of your assets. If you have difficulty preparing the financial information under this part, get the help of a tax or legal advisor.

Line 19 asks if there have been substantial changes in your assets and liabilities since the year-end date for your balance sheet. This question should be answered "No" by most groups. However, if your nonprofit is submitting a balance sheet for a prior completed period and your assets and liabilities have undergone significant change—as a result, perhaps of a sale or purchase of assets, a refinancing of debt, or other major structural change—answer "Yes" and provide an explanation on an attachment page.

Part X: Public Charity Status

You should be familiar with the material in Chapter 4 to answer the questions in this part of the form. This is where terms such as public charity and private foundation become important. We will refer to earlier explanations as we go along, but you may want to look over Chapter 4 now before you proceed. The questions in this part relate to whether you are seeking to be classified as a 501(c)(3) public charity or as a 501(c)(3) private foundation. As you know by now, we assume you want your nonprofit to qualify as a 501(c)(3) public charity, not as a 501(c)(3) private foundation.

Line 1(a) and (b). In Chapter 4, we discussed the distinction between the public charity and private foundation classifications and the reasons that you should try to meet one of the three primary tests for being classified as a public charity. The 1023 instructions provide a list of groups that qualify for public charity status, which lumps all publicly supported groups together ("groups that have broad financial support"). We use a different classification scheme in Chapter 4 that puts public charities into one of three categories:

1) Automatic Public Charity Status—groups that are set up for specific purposes or special

functions, such as churches, schools, hospitals, and public safety organizations, qualify as public charities (we say they automatically qualify because these groups, unlike the other two types of public charities listed below, do not have to meet public support tests).

2) Public Support Test Groups—these are groups that are supported by contributions and grants and that meet the ⅓ or ¹/₁₀ public support tests described in "Public Support Test" in Chapter 4.

3) Exempt Activities Support Test Groups— these are groups that obtain support through the performance of their exempt purposes, such as admissions, tuition, seminar fees, and receipts from goods and services related to the group's exempt purposes. We assume your nonprofit will either be setting up one of the special public charities that automatically qualify under (1) above, or a nonprofit that has or can reasonably expect to receive the type of support listed in (2), above.

Line 1(a). Check "Yes" or "No" on line 1(a) to indicate whether or not you are a private foundation. Again, we assume you expect to qualify as a public charity and will mark "No" to this question. If your response is "No," go on to line 5. If you are forming a 501(c)(3) private foundation, check "Yes" and go on to line 1(b).

Line1(b). This line only applies if you answered "Yes" to line 1(a). 1(b) asks you to check the box as a reminder that your private foundation requires special provisions in your articles or reliance on special provisions of state law. This book and its forms do not address these extra requirements, and you will need the help of a nonprofit advisor to form your 501(c)(3) private foundation and prepare your articles properly.

Lines 2 – 4. As with line 1(b) above, these lines only apply if you answered "Yes" to line 1(a)

indicating that you are applying for a tax exemption for a 501(c)(3) private foundation. These questions ask even more specific questions to help pigeonhole the private foundation into special subcategories—private operating and private nonoperating foundation categories. We assume you will get the help of an experienced legal or tax person who works with private foundations before answering these questions. After answering these questions, groups that are preparing their 1023 application for a private foundation skip the remaining lines in this part of the form and go on to Part XI.

All private foundations go on to Part XI, "User Fee Information."

Line 5. Check the box (letters (a)-(i)) that corresponds to the basis of your claim to public charity status. First, absorb what you can of the technical material given in the 1023 line 5 instructions. Then reread "How to Qualify for Public Charity Status" in Chapter 4—this section provides the names of these public charity organizations, the requirements they must meet, and the Internal Revenue Code sections that apply to them. Note that letter (i) is a special case that allows certain groups to have the IRS determine which public charity support test best suits their activities and sources of revenue. We cover this special choice in more detail in line (i), below.

The following chart shows how the different types of groups listed in this part of the application fit within the three different categories of public charity status discussed in "How to Qualify for Public Charity Status" in Chapter 4. If you concentrate on our basic division of these different groups into the three public charity categories, rather than focusing on the individual Internal Revenue Code sections, this part will go more smoothly.

IRS Line 5 Public Charities Covered in Chapter 4	
Line 5 (a) churches	Chapter 4, "Automatic Public Charity Status"
Line 5 (b) schools	Chapter 4, "Automatic Public Charity Status"
Line 5 (c) hospitals or medical research	Chapter 4, "Automatic Public Charity Status"
Line 5 (d) supporting organizations	Chapter 4, "Automatic Public Charity Status"
Line 5 (e) public safety organizations	Chapter 4, "Automatic Public Charity Status"
Line 5 (f) government organizations supporting colleges	Chapter 4, "Automatic Public Charity Status"
Line 5 (g) public support test groups	Chapter 4, "Public Support Test"
Line 5 (h) exempt activities support test groups	Chapter 4, "Exempt Activities Support Test"
Line 5 (i) either public support or exempt activities support test groups	Chapter 4, "Public Support Test" and "Exempt Activities Support Test"

Let's look a little more closely at each of the lettered boxes in line 5:

Line 5(a). If you seek to qualify automatically for public charity status as a church, see the 1023 instructions to this item. You will need to complete Schedule A and include it with your 1023 application. (See "Filling Out the Schedules," below, for instructions on completing Schedule A.)

Line 5(b). Check this box if your primary purpose is to set up and operate a formal school. If you check this box, make sure you have completed Schedule B. See the separate 1023 instructions to Schedule B in "Automatic Public Charity Status" in Chapter 4 (see the section "Schools"), and our instructions for filling out Schedule B, below.

If you will set up and operate a school, but operating the school is not your primary purpose, do not check this box—you will need to qualify as a public charity by checking one of the other line 5 boxes. However, you must complete Schedule B and attach it to your exemption application if you plan to operate a school, even if operating the school is not your primary purpose and the basis for your claim to public charity status—see the instruction to line 5(b) in the 1023 instructions.

Lines 5(c) – 5(f). Read the instructions for these lines in the 1023 instructions. Few groups will choose one of these boxes—each applies to a special type of organization such as a hospital, supporting organization, public safety organization, or government agency.

Line 5(c) hospitals and medical research groups will need to complete Schedule C—you should refer to the 1023 instructions for this schedule in "Automatic Public Charity Status" in Chapter 4 (see the section "Hospitals and Medical Research Organizations"), and our instructions for filling out Schedule C, below.

Line 5(d) supporting organizations are a special type of nonprofit set up to support other public charities. They are operated solely for the benefit of, or in connection with, any of the other public charity organizations (except one testing for public safety). A supporting organization must complete Schedule D. This information helps the IRS determine whether this type of organization supports other qualified public charities.

TIP

Get help when applying for an exemption for a special type of nonprofit. If you check one of the 5(c) through 5(f) boxes, the lawyer, accountant, or other advisor who is helping you organize one of these special corporations should help you with your application and any additional schedules you have to prepare and include with your application.

Line 5(g). First read the 1023 instructions for this line. This box is for organizations that receive a substantial part of their support from government agencies or from the general public. These are the public support test groups discussed in Chapter 4. If you believe this is the public charity best suited to your organization's sources of support, check the box on this line. If you are unsure whether this is the best support test to use for your group (that is, if you think that the exempt activities support test in line 5(h) also may apply to your organization), you may wish to let the IRS make this decision for you as explained in the line 5(i) instructions below.

As discussed in "Public Support Test" in Chapter 4, many groups will not want to fall under this public charity test because it does not allow your receipts from the performance of services related to the corporation's exempt purposes to be included as "qualified public support."

Groups checking line 5(g) go on to Part X, line 6.

Line 5(h). Start by reading the 1023 instructions for this line. This box is for organizations that normally receive ⅓ of their support from contributions, membership fees, and gross receipts from activities related to the exempt functions of the organization (subject to certain exceptions) but not more than ⅓ from unrelated trades and businesses or gross investment income. This exempt activities support test is discussed in Chapter 4. This is the most common and often the easiest way to qualify a new nonprofit organization as a public charity. So reread the requirements of this test and the definition of terms associated with it in Chapter 4. If you believe this public charity test best suits your expected sources of support, check this box. If you are unsure, see the instructions to line 5(i) just below.

Groups checking line 5(h), go on to Part X, line 6.

Line 5(i). If you feel that your group may qualify as a public charity either under line 5(g) or 5(h) but aren't sure which to choose, you can check this box. The IRS will decide which of these two public charity classifications best suits your organization based upon the financial data and other financial support information included in your 1023 application. For many new groups, line 5(i) is the best way to go. Rather than working through the math and the technical definitions necessary to approximate whether you will qualify as a public charity under line 5(g) or 5(h), by checking this box you let the IRS do the hard work for you.

Groups checking line 5(i), go on to Part X, line 6.

Here are some sample responses to line 5 by some typical, hypothetical nonprofit groups:

The First Fellowship Church, a religious organization that plans to maintain a space to provide weekly religious services to its congregation, checks line 5(a) to request automatic public charity status as a church.

The Workshop for Social Change, an educational group that plans to receive support from public and private grant funds and from individual and corporate contributions, checks line 5(g) to request public charity status as a publicly supported organization.

Everybody's Dance Studio and Dinner Theater—a group that expects to derive most of its operating revenue from student tuitions, special workshops, and ticket sales (as well as from other exempt-purpose activities)—selects line 5(h) to be classified as a group that meets the exempt activities support test discussed in Chapter 4.

The School for Alternative Social Studies—an accredited private postgraduate school with a formal curriculum, full-time faculty, and regularly enrolled student body—checks line 5(b) to request automatic public charity status as a formal private school.

The Elder Citizens' Collective and Information Exchange, which plans to derive support from contributions and grants as well as subscriptions to its weekly newsletter (and other exempt-purpose services and products made available to members and the public at large), checks line 5(i) to have the IRS decide whether line 5(g) or 5(h) is the appropriate public charity classification.

Line 6. Only groups that have checked line 5(g), 5(h), or 5(i) should respond to line 6(a) or 6(b). We call these groups that are seeking public charity status because of their sources of support "line 6 groups," and they must select whether they are seeking an advance or definitive ruling as to their public charity status by checking the box in line 6(a) or 6(b). For starters, read the official 1203 instructions for these lines, then read "What's Better—An Advance or a Definitive Ruling?" below, as well as "Advance and Definitive Rulings" in "Public Support Test" in Chapter 4. You have two mutually exclusive choices here: either (1) check the box in line 6(a) to request an advance ruling or (2) check the box in line 6(b) to request a definitive ruling. The first thing to realize is that you MUST request an advance ruling—that is you must check the line 6(a) box and cannot check the line 6(b) box, unless your nonprofit has completed a tax year consisting of at least eight months.

If you are not a line 6 group, you are done with Part X. You can move on to Part XI. By the way, although the IRS instructions and form do not say so explicitly, we assume that line 7 only applies to line 6 groups—those seeking to qualify as a 501(c)(3) public charity because of their sources of support. This is our best guess, and it's why we say that groups other than line 6 groups can move on to Part XI without answering line 7.

How to figure your first tax year. Most tax years of a nonprofit (or any other entity or person) are 12 months long, but the first tax years may be "short" tax years consisting of less than 12 months. The start of your first tax year is the date when your articles were filed. The end of your first tax year is the last day of the month when the nonprofit's accounting period ends, specified in Part I, line 5, of your 1023 exemption application.

EXAMPLE 1:

If a nonprofit files articles on February 10, and its tax year will end on December 31, it cannot request an advance ruling if it is preparing its exemption application in November of its first year. Even though it's been in operation for more than eight months, it has not completed its first tax year. Its first tax year will end on December 31.

EXAMPLE 2:

Let's assume that the same group prepares its exemption application in January of the next year after it was formed. It can request an advance ruling since it completed its first tax year, and this tax year consisted of at least eight months (the first tax year included the full months of March through December— ten full months).

EXAMPLE 3:

If the same group incorporated on May 15 and it applied for the exemption in January of the next year after it incorporated, it could not request an advance ruling. In this case, it would have completed one full tax year—its first short tax year from May 15 to December 31, but this tax year only included 7½ months.

There's another rule to keep in mind when deciding whether to request an advance or definitive ruling. As indicated in the 1023 instructions to line 6(a), if your nonprofit has completed more than five tax years, you cannot request an advance ruling—the IRS thinking here is that you've had enough prior tax years worth of operation for the IRS to definitely decide whether your group will receive enough public or exempt activity support to qualify for public charity status. In other words, if you are claiming a tax exemption going back five years or more, the IRS does not want you to wait any longer in testing your group's public sources of support to see if they qualify your group for public charity tax status.

So much for those groups that must request either an advance or definitive ruling. All other groups—those that are seeking an exemption and have been in operation for at least one tax year consisting of more than eight months but have not been operating for more than five prior tax years—can request either an advance ruling (by checking the line 6(a) box) OR a definitive ruling (by checking the line 6(b) box).

EXAMPLES:

Remember the Workshop for Social Change from the earlier example? This is a group that plans to qualify for public charity status as a line 5(g) publicly supported organization.

If the group has not completed one tax year of at least eight months, it must request an advance ruling by checking the line 6(a) box, then answering the remaining questions under line 6(a).

Everybody's Dance Studio and Dinner Theater is seeking public charity status as a line 5(h) group. It has completed its first tax year consisting of 11 months, and its support during this period qualifies it as a public charity under the exempt activities support test. It is reasonably confident that it will continue to meet this test in future years, so it checks the line 6(b) box to request a definitive ruling.

The Elder Citizens' Collective and Information Exchange, which checked line 5(i) to have the IRS decide which public charity support test worked best for the group, has completed one tax year of eight months or more, but its founders are unsure whether its exempt activities support will be sufficient to qualify it as a public charity over the next several years (under either the public support or the exempt activities support test). The founders decide to seek an advance ruling by checking the box in line 6(a), even though it is eligible to request a definitive ruling. At the end of its advance-ruling period, the IRS will make a final ruling whether the group qualifies as a public charity based upon the support the group actually received during the advance-ruling period. Further, because the group checked line 5(i), the IRS can choose to qualify the group as a public charity at the end of the advance-ruling period either under the public support test (line 5(g)) or the exempt activities support test (line 5(h)).

Now, Take a Break!

Completing the Public Charity Status part can be tricky. If you're feeling lost, overwhelmed, or just plain disgusted, take a break. When you come back and read our instructions to this part once or twice more, most of you will be able to successfully tackle this material and move on to the next (and last!) part of this federal form.

If you get stuck when choosing the proper public charity classification or, if applicable, an advance versus a definitive ruling, ask a board member, friend, or a friend of a friend with some legal or tax background to give you a hand. A little help will usually get you over this incorporation hurdle.

Line 6(a). If you are a line 6 group and have decided to request an advance ruling, check the line 6(a) box. Next, you must complete the consent form that appears below line 6(a).

By completing the consent, you allow the IRS to assess an additional year of excise taxes on investment income if your group is not granted public charity status at the end of its five-year advance-ruling period. By signing this form, you're not signing your life away. You are letting the IRS collect one excise tax from you for a limited, but longer than usual, period of time—only if the IRS determines that you are not a public charity at the end of the extended advance-ruling period and only if you are then liable for this particular excise tax because of your operations during the extended advance-ruling period. The IRS can assess this tax for any of the five years in the advance-ruling period at any time up to eight years, four months, and 15 days after the end of the first tax year in the advance-ruling period.

TIP

How to find more information on consent forms. If you want more information on what the consent form means in technical terms, see the explanation to line 6a on the 1023 form and the line 6a 1023 instructions. For general information on consents that extend the IRS limitations on assessments (which is what you are doing when you sign the 1023 consent), see IRS Publication 1035, *Extending the Tax Assessment Period*.

Complete the consent by filling in the top portion. Have a corporate director or officer (usually the same person who will sign your 1023 exemption application—see Part XI below) sign her name on the top left line, type her name and title on the middle top lines, then provide the date of signing on the top right line. Do not fill in the bottom lines under "For IRS Use Only" at the bottom of the consent. The IRS will complete these lines and then mail you a copy of the completed consent form when your exemption application is approved.

Line 6 groups that check the line 6(a) box and complete the consent form should go to line 7.

Line 6(b). If you are a line 6 group and have decided to request a definitive ruling, check the line 6(b) box and answer the remaining line 6(b) questions, as explained in the next several paragraphs. First read the official 1023 instructions to these additional line 6(b) items before following our instructions below.

6(b)(i)(a). Enter 2% (0.02) of the amount shown in Part IX-A (Revenues and Expenses), line 8, column (e)—this is 2% of your organization's total public support received over the tax years shown in Part IX-A. The IRS will use this number in computing whether your group meets the appropriate public charity support test.

What's Better—An Advance or a Definitive Ruling?

Broadly speaking, an advance ruling on your public charity status is tentative; a definitive ruling is for keeps. The IRS automatically makes a definitive ruling as to the public charity status of groups that are not required to fill in line 6. Line 6 groups—those that are seeking public charity status because of the nature of their support—can ask for a definitive ruling only if they have completed a tax year of at least eight months. If they haven't, line 6 groups must ask for an advance ruling. Even though an advance ruling is tentative and does not become final until the end of a five-year advance-ruling period, it does have a few advantages over a definitive ruling. Specifically, an advance ruling is likely to come sooner, and you risk less by asking for it. Here's why.

For a definitive ruling, the IRS will look at the actual support received to date by your group. If this support is not sufficient to qualify your group under the applicable public charity category, your public charity status will be denied (or, if you're lucky, the IRS will ask your permission to issue an advance, not a definitive, public charity ruling and wait to make a final determination on your qualification for public charity status at the end of the advance ruling period). Further, requesting a definitive ruling may take extra time and could require you to respond to additional IRS questions before your tax exemption is approved.

Obtaining an advance public charity ruling is easier. The IRS will issue an advance ruling if it appears from the financial statements and other information you submit with the 1023 application that the group's anticipated sources of support will qualify the organization for public charity status. Even better, the IRS will choose

for you the public charity support test that best matches your anticipated sources of support if you check line 5(i) as explained in the text. At the end of a five-year advance-ruling period, the IRS will look at the annual information returns of the organization. If actual support meets the requirements of the selected public charity category, the group will then receive final approval of its 501(c)(3) public charity status. If the group does not qualify for public charity status at the end of this period, it will be classified as a 501(c)(3) private foundation during succeeding tax years.

You probably know by now that classification as a private foundation at the end of your advance ruling period would not be a good turn of events. Your foundation and its managers will be subject to private foundation excise taxes. The group will not, however, be retroactively liable for most of the private foundation excise taxes during its advance-ruling period (see "Private foundation taxes" in "What to Expect From the IRS," below). And even if the IRS denies you public charity status at the end of the advance-ruling period, contributions made during the advance-ruling period by individual donors will still be treated as having been made to a valid public charity.

In our opinion, it often makes the most sense for line 6 groups to request an advance-ruling period for their public charity status even if they have completed one tax year of at least eight months at the time of their application (and can, therefore, request a definitive ruling if they want to). Generally, obtaining an advance ruling is quicker and easier, and it lets your actual sources of support during a five-year period speak for themselves. Of course, if your group is

What's Better—An Advance or a Definitive Ruling? (continued)

the exception and you can reasonably predict that its past support definitely (or most likely) qualifies it for public charity status, go ahead and request a definitive ruling.

Technical Note: Another downside of requesting a definitive ruling is that your group may have to transpose some of its financial information to meet IRS requirements. Specifically, as explained in the 1203 instruction to line 6(b), if you request a definitive ruling and your nonprofit has reported financial information using the accrual method of accounting—which means you

report income when you are entitled to receive it (even if you haven't been paid) and expenses when you are obligated to pay them (even if you haven't paid them)—you have to convert your numbers over to cash-basis numbers by using a special worksheet contained in IRS Form 990. In other words, if your nonprofit keeps its books on the accrual method of accounting, if you decide to request a definitive ruling, you'll probably need the help of a tax advisor to convert you financial data to a cash-basis format.

6(b)(i)(b). If any individual, organization, or company has contributed more than the 2% amount shown in 6(b)(i)(a) during the prior tax years covered in Part IX-A (Revenues and Expenses) of your application, supply the name(s) of the contributor(s) and the amount(s) contributed on an attachment page. Conversely, if no individual, organization, or company contributes more than this 2% amount, check the box at the right. Why does the IRS want this information? For line 5(g) public support test charities, the IRS generally does not count amounts that exceed 2% of the group's total support as qualified public support (for more on the 2% rule and its exceptions, see "Public Support Test" in Chapter 4 and IRS Publication 557, "Support From the General Public").

6(b)(ii)(a) and 6(b)(ii)(b). These questions require you to disclose sources of support that the IRS does not consider qualified public support for groups that are seeking public charity status under the exempt activities support test (the groups covered in Chapter 4 that rely on support received primarily from their exempt-purpose activities). We're

talking here about contributions from disqualified persons or gross receipts from other individuals that exceed the larger of 1% of the organization's total support or $5,000 in any tax year.

6(b)(ii)(a). For a definition of disqualified persons, including a "substantial contributor," see the official instructions to the form. We provide a somewhat friendlier set of definitions of these terms in "Who Are Disqualified Persons?" below. If a disqualified person provided gifts, grants, or contributions, membership fees, or payments for admissions, or other exempt-purpose services or products (these are the categories listed in lines 1, 2, and 9 of Part IX-A, Revenues and Expenses) during any tax year shown in Part IX-A, list the disqualified persons and amounts contributed or paid on an attachment page. If no disqualified person paid or contributed any of these amounts, check the box to the right.

6(b)(ii)(b). If any person (other than a disqualified person) has paid more than the larger of either $5,000 or 1% of the amount shown in line 9 of Part IX, Revenues and Expenses, (admissions or other exempt-purpose

Who Are Disqualified Persons?

People who are disqualified in the eyes of the IRS are not necessarily prohibited from participating in the operation of the 501(c)(3) nonprofit corporation. Instead, their contributions to the nonprofit may not count when figuring the public support received by public charities. (Note that the definitions of disqualified persons discussed here are different from the definitions of disqualified persons under IRC Section 4958 — see the instructions to Part V above for information on these separate set of definitions.) If the corporation is classified as a 501(c)(3) private foundation (we assume yours won't be), the corporation and the disqualified individual can be held liable for certain private foundation excise taxes. Disqualified persons for purposes of meeting the public charity support tests include:

1. Substantial contributors. These are donors who give more than $5,000, if the amount they contributed is more than 2% of the total contributions and bequests received by the organization. For example, suppose Ms. X makes a gift of $20,000 to your nonprofit corporation. If this gift exceeds 2% of all contributions and bequests made to your organization from the time it was created until the end of the corporate tax year in which Ms. X made the contribution, Ms. X is a substantial contributor.

To determine whether a substantial donor is a disqualified person, gifts and bequests made by that individual include all contributions and bequests made by the individual's spouse. Once a person is classified as a substantial contributor, he generally remains classified as one (regardless of future contributions made, or not made, by the individual, or future support received by the organization). However, if other conditions are met, a person will lose his status as a substantial

contributor if he makes no contribution to the organization for ten years.

2. All foundation managers. Directors, trustees, and officers (or people with similar powers or responsibilities), or any employee with final authority or responsibility to act on the matter in question, are disqualified as "foundation managers"—this is a buzzword that means the bigwigs in a nonprofit who exercise executive control. Officers include persons specifically designated as "officers" in the articles, bylaws, or minutes, and persons who regularly make administrative and policy decisions. Officers do not include independent contractors, such as accountants, lawyers, financial and investment advisors, and managers. Generally, any person who simply recommends action but cannot implement these recommendations will not qualify as an officer.

3. Owners and substantial players in entities that contribute. An owner of more than 20% of the total combined voting power of a corporation, the profits of a partnership, or the beneficial interest of a trust or unincorporated enterprise are all disqualified, if any of these entities is a substantial contributor.

4. Family members. A member of the family —including ancestors, spouse, and lineal descendants, such as children and grandchildren but not brothers and sisters—of any of the individuals described in 1, 2, or 3 above, is disqualified.

5. Other business entities. Corporations, partnerships, trusts, and so on in which the persons described in 1 through 4 above have at least a 35% ownership interest.

For further information on disqualified persons, see the "Private Foundation" link in the Public Charities & Non-Profits section of the IRS website at www.irs.gov.

services or products) during any completed tax year shown in Part IX-A, provide the name of the person or organization who made the payment and the amount of each payment on an attachment page. Our list should be broken down year-by-year. If no individual (other than a disqualified person) made such a payment for any of the completed tax years shown in Part IX-A, check the box to the right of this item.

Line 7. We assume this line applies only to line 6 groups—those that have checked either line 6(a) or 6(b). To answer this question, first refer to our instructions to Part IX-A above (Statement of Revenue and Expenses). If you have listed any unusual grants on line 12 of the Statement of Revenue and Expenses in any of the columns, check "Yes" and list them on an attachment page along with the donor's name, date, and amount and the nature of the grant (what the grant was for, whether it was restricted to a specific use, and other terms of the grant). If you provided this information in an attachment to Part IX-A, you can refer to your earlier response. For further explanation of what constitutes unusual grants, see "Unusual Grants," below. If you have not listed any unusual grants in the Part IX-A Revenue and Expense statement, check the "No" box.

Part XI: User Fee Information

You must pay a user fee when you submit your 1023 tax exemption application. This part of the application asks questions to determine the amount of the user fee you must include with your application. The fee is determined according to the amount of gross receipts your group has or expects to receive annually (averaged over a four-year period). See the 1023 instructions to this part first before reading our instructions below.

Unusual Grants

Unusual grants are contributions, bequests, or grants that your organization receives because it is publicly supported but which are so large that they could jeopardize your ability to meet your public support test The benefit of having a large grant qualify as an unusual grant is that it does not jeopardize the group's public charity status (as do other large sums received from a single source). It is unlikely that your beginning nonprofit has received sums that should be classified as unusual grants. For further information on this technical area, see the 1023 instructions to line 7 of Part X, the discussion and examples of unusual grants in "What Is Public Support?" in Chapter 4, (see "Money From Unusual Grants" and "Unusual Grants Drop Out of the Computation"), and the specific rules on unusual grants contained in IRS Publication 557.

! **CAUTION**

Always check that the fee amount is current. Your user fee check should be made payable to the "United States Treasury," and show "User fee Form 1023 [name of your group]" on the check memo line. Before writing your check, go to the IRS website at www.irs.gov to make sure you have the current fee amounts (fees were increased in 2006). Type "User Fee" in the keyword box to find fee amounts. Alternatively, call the IRS Exempt Organization Customer Service telephone number at 877-829-5500 to ask for current 1023 user fee amounts.

Line 1. Groups that qualify for a reduced user fee of $300 check "Yes." Your organization qualifies for this reduced fee if it is submitting its initial exemption application and:

- it is a new organization (in operation for less than four years) that anticipates annual gross receipts averaging not more than $10,000 during its first four tax years, or

- it has been in operation for four tax years or more and has had annual gross receipts averaging not more than $10,000 during the preceding four years.

Line 2. If you checked "Yes" in line 1, also check the line 2 box. If you did not check "Yes" to line 1, do not check box 2.

Line 3. If you did not check "Yes" to line 1, check the line 3 box and include a user fee check for $750. If you checked the line 1 box, do not check this box.

TIP

What happens if you guess incorrectly?
You may be concerned about what will happen if you estimate that your gross receipts will average no more than $10,000 during your first four tax years, but your actual gross receipts exceed this amount in one or more years. We don't know for sure, but if you make more than this threshold amount, it seems reasonable to assume that the IRS would monitor your annual information returns and ask you to pay the remaining balance later. Of course, if the financial information you submit with your 1023 exemption application shows that your group has, or expects to have, average gross receipts exceeding $10,000 for its first four years and you check the wrong box here, expect the IRS to return your exemption application due to insufficient payment or to send out a request for an additional payment before it continues processing your application.

Signature, Name, Title, and Date Lines. Have one of your initial directors or officers sign, type his name and title (director, president, chief operations officer, or the like), and insert the date on the lines provided at the bottom of Part XI.

Write a check payable to the United States Treasury for the amount of the user fee. Do not staple or otherwise attach your check to your application. You will simply place your check at the top of your assembled exemption application package as explained in the next section. The check does not have to be an organizational check. The person preparing the application or any other incorporator may write a personal check. The user fee is kept by the IRS in almost all circumstances, even if your application is denied. The only time it is refunded is if the IRS decides that it cannot issue a determination as to your exempt status one way or the other—because it has insufficient information or cannot resolve some of the issues associated with your tax exemption request. By the way, this rarely happens. For example, if you don't respond to any follow-up questions that the IRS may ask in response to your application, it normally denies your exemption (and keeps the check).

Whew! You're just about done. Follow the instructions below for assembling your entire federal exemption package.

Filling Out the Schedules

Certain groups must complete and submit schedules with their Form 1023 application. In the line-by-line instructions to the 1023 form, above, we let you know when you are required to complete a schedule. For example, in Part VII, line 1, of the application, we tell you that if you answered "Yes" to that item, you must complete Schedule G.

SKIP AHEAD

If you do not need to submit any schedules with your Form 1023, then you can skip this section.

Schedule A – Churches

See the separate instructions to Schedule A included in the last portion of the official 1023 instructions for help in filling out this schedule. We've discussed the requirements for churches in "Automatic Public Charity Status" in Chapter 4. The questions here seek to determine whether your organization possesses conventional, institutional church attributes—the more the better as far as the IRS is concerned. Some also relate to whether your organization unduly benefits, or was created to serve the personal needs of, your pastor, or the pastor's family and relatives. Obviously, doing so is an IRS no-no.

Schedule B – Schools, Colleges, and Universities

See the official 1023 instructions to Schedule B for help in completing this schedule. Your responses to this schedule should show that your operations are nondiscriminatory and in accordance with a nondiscrimination statement included in your bylaws and published in the community in which you serve (you must attach this bylaw resolution to Schedule B). For information on drafting and publishing this statement of nondiscrimination, see "Educational Purposes" in Chapter 3. Also see IRS Publication 557, "Private Schools" (included on the CD-ROM).

Schedule C – Hospitals and Medical Research Organizations

Make sure to check the appropriate boxes at the top of the schedule and fill out the appropriate section of the form. Generally this schedule seeks to determine two things:

- whether the hospital is charitable in nature and qualifies for 501(c)(3) tax-exempt status, and

- whether the hospital or medical research organization qualifies for automatic public charity status (see the Schedule C instructions in the official 1023 instructions and IRS Publication 557, "Hospitals and Medical Research Organizations").

A 501(c)(3) charitable hospital normally has many of the following characteristics:

- staff doctors selected from the community at large

- a community-oriented board of directors (directors come from the community served by the hospital)

- emergency room facilities open to the public

- a policy of allowing at least some patients to be treated without charge (on a charity basis)

- a nondiscrimination policy with respect to patient admissions (it doesn't pick and choose its patient population) and particularly does not discriminate against Medicare or Medicaid patients, and

- a medical training and research program that benefits the community.

Hospitals need to be careful when it comes to renting space to physicians who are members of the board—and carrying out a private practice that's unrelated to the community service programs of the hospital. The IRS will be particularly suspicious if such physicians are prior tenants and their rent is below fair market value. Section 1, question 7, of Schedule C addresses this issue.

Hospitals should adopt a suitable conflict-of-interest policy in their bylaws (see Schedule C, Section 1, line 14). Article 9 of the bylaws included with this book contains most of the provisions in the sample conflict-of-interest policy provided in Appendix A of the official 1023 instructions. However, it does not include the special bracketed provisions that apply specifically to hospitals. Make sure you insert these additional bracketed provisions. There are two, which are clearly marked in Appendix A of the 1023 instructions with the words "*[Hospital Insert — for hospitals that complete Schedule C...]*"—to the provisions in Article 9 of the bylaws included with this book.

Schedule D – Section 509(a)(3) Supporting Organizations

Refer to the 1023 instructions for this schedule, in "Automatic Public Charity Status" in Chapter 4 (see ""Supporting Organizations"), and Publication 557, "Section 509(a)(3) Organizations." This is a complicated schedule—you must meet a number of technical tests. Your nonprofit legal or tax advisor can help you qualify for this special type of public charity classification.

Schedule E – Organizations Not Filing Form 1023 Within 27 Months of Formation

Before filling in Schedule E, read the official IRS 1023 instructions to Schedule E, which are contained in the instructions for separate schedules at the end of the 1023 instructions. This material will give you some basic definitions and information that will help you work your way through the schedule.

Lines 1 – 3. Three groups are not required to file Form 1023: churches; public charities that normally have gross receipts of not more than $5,000 in each year (see the extra instructions for line 2(b) below); and subordinate organizations exempt under a group exemption letter (see "Do You Need to File Form 1023?" above). If you decide that you fall within one of these exceptions (after reading any additional instructions for the line below), check the "Yes" box or boxes on the appropriate line (either line

1, 2, or 3) and go on to Part VIII of the 1023 form. You do not need to complete the rest of Schedule E. If the IRS agrees that you qualify as one of these three special groups, your federal exemption will be effective retroactively from the date of your incorporation, even though you filed your exemption application late (after more than 27 months from the end of the month when you filed your articles).

If you fall within one of the three groups, you are filing an exemption application even though you believe you are not required to do so and even though you are filing more than 27 months after your nonprofit corporation was formed. As we said above, we agree that this is the best way to go, since by submitting your exemption application you are making sure the IRS agrees that your group is entitled to a tax exemption in one of these three special 501(c)(3) categories.

Line 2(a) and 2(b). The 2(a) exception is often applicable to new nonprofits. Your group qualifies if:

- it is a public charity rather than a private foundation (because one of the purposes of completing your 1023 application is to establish that you are eligible for public charity status, we assume that you meet this requirement), and

- it "normally" has gross receipts of not more than $5,000 in each tax year.

Groups that have been in existence for two tax years qualify if they had total gross receipts of $12,000 or less during the first two years. We assume your group has been in existence for at least two years since it is filing more than 27 months after it was formed. If you have been in existence for three or more tax years, your gross receipts over the three years must be $15,000 or less to qualify for the "normally $5,000" exception. Many new groups without outside sources of support can meet this gross receipts test during their beginning tax years. And, if you can't check "Yes" to line 2(a), there's a technical loophole in line 2(b): It says that groups that are filing their 1023 application within 90 days after the end of the tax year when they qualified for the "normally $5,000 gross receipts" test, also can file their application late.

EXAMPLE:

You form a new nonprofit corporation in January of 2005 and file your tax exemption application more than four years later—in February 2009. Your group had gross receipts of less than $5,000 for 2005 through 2007, but 2008 was a really good year so the total gross receipts for your organization over the three-tax-year period from January 2006 through December 2008 was $25,000. This is well over the three-year $15,000 cumulative total maximum amount. If you submit your 1023 application in February of 2009, which is within 90 days of the end of 2008, you can check box 2(b) and have the tax exemption extend all the way back to the date of incorporation, since it meets this special line 2(b) exception. Obviously, this 2(b) exception is intended for groups that file quickly after determining that their past three-year cumulative gross receipts put them over the $15,000 mark. Once they go over this mark, they become a group that is required to file a 1023 application—the IRS will let them have their tax exemption for all prior years, even though the last three-year cumulative total exceeded the $15,000 threshold, as long as the group files the 1023 within 90 days of the end of the high-receipts tax year.

Line 4. Here is where you end up if your group is filing the 1023 application more than 27 months from the date of your incorporation and you don't meet one of the three exceptions listed in lines 1 through 3 of this part. Groups formed on or before October 9, 1969 get a special break. Of course, we assume you were formed recently, and will check "No" and move on to line 5.

Line 5. Since your group is not one of the special groups listed in the previous lines on Schedule E, your group can only qualify for an exemption that extends back to its date of formation if it asks the IRS to qualify for late filing. To do this, check "Yes" and attach a statement giving the reasons why you failed to complete the 1023 application process within the 27-month period after your incorporation. Federal rules, contained in Treasury Regulations 301.9100-1 and 301.9100-3, also include a list of the acceptable reasons for late filing, as well as those that aren't. For example, acceptable reasons include the following: you relied on the advice of a lawyer, accountant, or an IRS employee, and received inaccurate information or were not informed of the deadline. These acceptable reasons are summarized in the 1023 instructions for this line. After attaching your statement, perhaps with the help of your tax advisor, go on to Part VIII of the 1023 application—you should not complete the rest of Schedule E.

If you don't think you can qualify for an extension (or if you decide not to bother—see "If You End Up on Schedule E, Line 5, Should You Ask for an Extension?" below), check "No" and go on to line 6.

If You End Up on Schedule E, Line 5, Should You Ask for an Extension?

Most groups will not end up on Schedule E, line 5—they will submit their 1023 application within 27 months from the date of their incorporation. If your group does end up here, you may decide not to bother seeking an extension and simply check "No" on line 5. This means that your 501(c)(3) exemption, if granted, will be effective only from the application's postmark date, not from the date of your incorporation. Is this so terrible? Often, it isn't. Here's why. Many nonprofits will not have any taxable income or contributions from donors during these early start-up months (the 27-plus months of operation prior to filing their 1023 application). Consequently, obtaining a tax exemption for these early months will not provide a tax benefit. However, if your group is facing tax liability for early operations, the need to provide donors with tax deductions for gifts contributed during the first 27-plus months, or the need to obtain 501(c)(3) tax-exempt status from the date of its creation for some other pressing reason, then it makes sense to prepare a special statement under line 5 as explained in the text. If you are unsure, check with your tax adviser.

Line 6 (a). If you checked "No" on line 5 (you don't want to qualify for an extension of time to file), you should check "Yes" to 6(a). This means that you agree that your 501(c)(3) exemption can be recognized only from its postmark date, not retroactively to the date of your incorporation. By the way, if you check "No" to 6(a), you are saying that you are applying for a tax exemption as a 501(c)(3) private foundation, not a public charity—this is something you definitely will not want to do. We assume all readers will want to form a 501(c)(3) public charity as mentioned earlier in this chapter and explained in more detail in Chapter 4. So check "Yes" to 6(a) and move on to 6(b).

Checking "Yes" to 6(a) means that you will have to request an advance ruling period for your public charity status, which you will do later in Part X of the application. We explain more about asking for an advance ruling for public charity status in our instructions to Part X, above. Also note that the financial data the IRS will use to decide whether to grant your request for an advance ruling period depends on how you answer line 6(b), just below.

Line 6(b). Since you checked "Yes" to line 6(a), you will be asking the IRS to grant an advance ruling on your public charity status. The IRS has two ways to decide whether your nonprofit sources of support qualify you for an advance ruling. It can either use the actual financial figures you submit in Part X of the 1023 for your past operations since you formed your nonprofit or, if you expect significant changes in your sources of financial support in the future, it can use projected financial figures. Most groups that are applying late for their tax exemption are not planning to substantially change how they get financial support, so they will check "No" to 6(a), and ignore the table in line 7—they will move on to line 8 of Schedule E. However, some groups that are applying late realize that their past operations and sources of financial support may or do not qualify them to meet one of the public charity support tests (as more fully explained in our instructions to Part X), and will want to change their plans for financial support now. If this is the case for your late-filing nonprofit, mark "Yes" to 6(b), then fill in the projected revenue table in line 7 to show your expected sources of future financial support.

Line 7. If you marked "Yes" to line 6(b), fill in projected sources of financial support for the next two full years following the current tax year. For example, if you are applying for your tax exemption late in July of 2004, and your nonprofit's tax year goes from January to December (the typical case), supply financial figures for the period from January 2005 to December 2007 in the table. You don't have to fill in items for all rows, but you should be able to supply figures that show that you expect your nonprofit to obtain support from sources that qualify it for public charity status under one of the two basic financial support categories discussed in Part X (check the instructions above, if you are filling out the line 7 table, to see what types of support you will be expected to have to qualify for one of the public charity support tests).

Line 8. If you are filing your 1023 application late and checked "Yes" to line 6(a) on Schedule E, you should complete line 8 of the Schedule, regardless of how you responded to 6(b). If you end up here, your application for 501(c)(3) status will be considered only from the date of its postmark. If you check "Yes" to line 8, you are asking the IRS to grant your group tax-exempt status as a 501(c)(4) organization—a social welfare group or a civic league—during your late filing period (the 27-month-plus period from the date your articles were filed up to the date your 1023 application postmark). What does this do for you? If your request for 501(c)(4) status is approved, your organization will be exempt from paying federal corporate income taxes as a 501(c)(4) organization from the date of its formation until the date of approval of your 501(c)(3) tax-exempt status (the 1023 postmark date). For most newly formed groups without taxable income during this initial period, obtaining this extra tax exemption will not be necessary and you can ignore this box.

However, if you or your tax advisor determines that your organization is subject to tax liability for this initial period, check this box and call 800-TAX-FORM to order IRS Publication 1024 (or go to www.irs.gov). Fill in the page 1 of Form 1024 and submit it with your exemption application. If you qualify as a 501(c)(4) social welfare group (as many 501(c)(3)s do—see "501(c)(4) Organizations," below), your 501(c)(3) tax determination letter will indicate that you qualify as a 501(c)(4) organization during your initial late filing (your pre-501(c)(3) period).

501(c)(4) Organizations

Internal Revenue Code Section 501(c)(4) provides a federal corporate income tax exemption for nonprofit social welfare groups and civic leagues (see *Special Nonprofit Tax-Exempt Organizations*, in Appendix B). Since the promotion of public welfare is defined as "promoting the common good and general welfare of the people of the community," many 501(c)(3) nonprofits also qualify as 501(c)(4) social welfare organizations. Although 501(c)(4) nonprofits are exempt from federal corporate income taxation, they are not eligible to receive tax-deductible contributions from donors. They also do not enjoy many of the other advantages associated with 501(c)(3) tax-exempt status, such as eligibility to receive public and private grant funds, participate in local, state, and federal nonprofit programs, obtain county real and personal property tax exemptions, and other benefits.

But 501(c)(4) organizations do enjoy one advantage not available to 501(c)(3) groups: They may engage in substantial legislative activities and may support or oppose candidates to public office. For further information on 501(c)(4) tax-exempt status, see IRS Publication 557.

Schedule F – Homes for the Elderly or Handicapped and Low-Income Housing

See the 1023 instructions for help in filling out this schedule. In part, this schedule attempts to determine whether elderly or handicapped housing facilities are made available to members of the public or the particular community at reasonable rates, whether provision is made for indigent residents, whether health care arrangements are adequate, and whether facilities are adequate to house a sufficient number of residents.

Schedule G – Successors to Other Organizations

Line 1(a). We assume your nonprofit is not a successor to a prior profit-making company, which is one such as a sole proprietorship, partnership, limited liability company, or a business corporation that allows its owners to have a proprietary (financial) interest in its assets. In the unlikely case that you check "Yes" to line 1(a) because you are a successor to a profit organization, we think you will need help from a nonprofit expert when filing out Schedule G and the rest of your tax exemption application to explain to the IRS why you decided to convert a prior profit-making activity to nonprofit corporate status, and why the new nonprofit is entitled to its tax exemption.

Successor groups that check "No" to line 1(a) will have to check "Yes" to line 2(a) to indicate that they are successors to a nonprofit groups (remember, a successor group is one that meets one of the successor tests listed above—if you are not a successor group, you shouldn't be filling in Schedule G). Even these groups may need help responding to Schedule G. For example, it asks for the prior tax status and

EIN of your predecessor group, and whether it has previously applied for a tax exemption. If the predecessor group was required to file tax returns and/or pay taxes but did not, expect the IRS to ask for these returns (and late filing and late payment penalties too). If the prior group was denied a tax exemption, you will need to clearly explain what has changed that makes you believe you qualify for an exemption now. The schedule also attempts to determine if the new nonprofit has been set up to benefit or serve the private interests of the people associated with the predecessor organization. If assets were transferred from the prior nonprofit association to the new nonprofit corporation, you are asked to provide a sales or transfer agreement (Schedule G, line 6(c)). If you have prepared this formal paperwork, attach a copy to your application. If you haven't (this is normally the case for a small nonprofits that are formally converting a prior nonprofit association to a nonprofit corporation), you should prepare (perhaps with help from someone with financial savvy associated with your nonprofit) and put together a simple term sheet that lists the assets and liabilities transferred to the new nonprofit and the terms of the transfer. This simple agreement should be signed by officers of the prior association and directors or officers of your new nonprofit, and attached to Schedule G.

If your nonprofit corporation will lease property or equipment previously owned or used by the predecessor organization or will lease property from people associated with the prior group, include an explanation and copies of any leases as requested in line 8. The IRS will scrutinize a lease to make sure that it does not provide for excessive rent payments to the people associated with the former organization. If a nonprofit corporation is a successor to a prior nonprofit association, it's usually best, if possible, for the prior association simply to assign any leases to the nonprofit corporation without payment (or for a $1 consideration to keep things legal) or have the corporation renegotiate the leases with the landlord. That way, the successor nonprofit corporation can deal with the landlord directly rather than have people from the former organization retain the lease and require rent payments from the successor nonprofit corporation. (For an example of an assignment of lease form, see "Prepare Assignments of Leases and Deeds" in Chapter 10.) If your successor nonprofit will lease property back to the people associated with the prior group, line 9 also asks for a copy of the lease agreement. Obviously, a lease-back of property will be strictly scrutinized by the IRS to see if the payments are reasonable—the IRS also will wonder why the new nonprofit transferred the assets in the first place, since after the transfer it decided to lease them back to the people associated with the prior group. Leaseback deals like this look fine in the normal business world, but raise IRS examiner eyebrows when they are disclosed on tax-exemption applications.

Schedule H – Organizations Providing Scholarships, Educational Loans, or Other Educational Grants

Schedule H is used by the IRS to determine whether your nonprofit will provide financial aid on a nondiscriminatory basis. The IRS wants to know that financial aid funds will not be set aside specifically to help put family and friends of people associated with your nonprofit through school and that the providing of funds in general will promote your group's tax-exempt public purposes, which typically will be charitable and/or educational. For further information on IRS guidelines, see IRS Publication 557, "Charitable Organization Supporting Education" and "Organization

Providing Loans." Section II of this schedule can be used to get IRS approval of your organization's grant-making procedures if your organization is classified as a private foundation (in the event your request for public charity classification under Part X is denied). If you wish to plan for this contingency, consult your tax advisor to help you select the appropriate IRC section on line 1(b) of Section II.

Assemble and Mail Your Application to the IRS

You've accomplished the most difficult part of your paperwork. The only task left is to gather up your application forms and papers and send them off to the IRS. Follow these steps:

- **Complete the checklist.** The IRS wants you to complete and include the checklist with your mailed materials. The checklist is included as the last two pages of the 1023 application form. To complete the checklist, check each box to show you completed all the checklist tasks. If you followed the previous steps in this chapter, you should be able to check each box and complete each checklist task as follows:

- **Assemble your application materials in order.** Put your materials together in the order shown in the checklist. Note that Forms 2848 and 8821, as well as amendments to articles of incorporation, nondiscriminatory school statement, and Form 5768, will not apply to most groups.

- **User fee.** Place your user fee check at the top of your materials. Do not staple it to your application papers.

- **EIN.** Make sure you have obtained an Employer Identification Number (it should be stated in Part I, line 4, of your application).

- **Completed Parts I through XI of your application.** We assume you can check this checklist box to show you have completed all parts of the 1023 form.

- **Schedules.** Check "Yes" or "No" to show which, if any, schedules you have completed and included with your application. Many groups will mark "No" to all schedules. Only submit schedules with your application that you have completed—do not include blank schedules.

- **Articles.** We assume you have included a file-stamped or certified copy of your articles in response to Part II, line 1, of the application. Fill in the two blanks here to show (1) your purpose clause (repeat the reference to your articles you inserted in response to Part III, line 1) and (2) your dissolution clause (repeat the reference to your articles you inserted in response to Part III, line 2(b)—we assume you did not refer to a state law provision in line 2(c); see our instructions to Part II above).

- **Signature.** Make sure a director or officer has signed, filled in the name and title lines, and dated the form at the bottom of Part XI (and, if applicable, completed and signed the Consent lines in Part X, line 6a—see our instructions to this line, above).

- **Name of organization.** The name you insert in Part 1, line 1, of the 1023 application must be the same as the name of your corporation in your articles of incorporation.

Make copies. After completing the checklist and including it as the first page of your exemption materials, make at least one photocopy of all pages and attachments to your application and file them in your corporate records book.

Mail your application. Mail your package to the IRS address listed in the checklist. You may want to send it certified mail, return receipt requested, to obtain proof of mailing

and/or of receipt by the IRS. At this writing, the address is:

Internal Revenue Service
P.O. Box 192
Covington, KY 41012-0192

As an alternative to regular mail, you may want to send your application papers to the IRS via an express mail service (see the approved list of private delivery services in the 1023 instructions, "Private Delivery Services"). The express mail address currently shown on the 1023 checklist is:

Internal Revenue Service
201 West Rivercenter Blvd.
Attn: Extracting Stop 312
Covington, KY 41011

Your next step is to wait. The IRS should inform you that it has received your application within three weeks of mailing. Although the IRS turnaround time to respond to your application is usually about two months, you may have to wait three to six months for a response to your exemption application.

You can request expedited filing of your 1023 application by submitting a written request along with your exemption application. The IRS may approve the request and speed up the processing of your application if your reason for the request is an impending grant deadline, your nonprofit provides disaster relief, or the IRS has already delayed a prior application or response to a previous application by the group. See "Expedite request" in the 1203 instructions for more information.

CAUTION

You must file annual federal and state information returns for your organization while your federal tax exemption application is pending (see "Annual Filing Requirements" in the 1023

instructions, and Chapter 11). Indicate on your annual returns that your federal 1023 application is pending approval by the IRS.

What to Expect From the IRS

After reviewing your application, the IRS will do one of three things:

- grant your federal tax exemption
- request further information, or
- issue a proposed adverse determination (a denial of tax exemption that becomes effective 30 days from the date of issuance).

If the IRS asks for more information and you are not sure what they want from you—or you just feel that you are in over your head—consult a nonprofit attorney or tax advisor. If you receive a proposed denial and you wish to appeal, see a lawyer immediately. For further information on appeal procedures, see IRS Publication 557, *Tax Exempt Status for your Organization,* and type "Appeal Procedures" in the Search box on the IRS website at www.irs.gov for links to other appeals procedure information

The Federal Determination Letter

The fortunate among you—and we trust it will be most of you—will get good news from the IRS. It will come in the form of a favorable determination letter, telling you that you are exempt from federal corporate income taxes under Section 501(c)(3) of the Internal Revenue Code, as a public charity. Unless you filed your application late and were not entitled to an extension, your tax exemption and public charity status will be effective retroactively to the date when your articles were filed with the secretary of state.

> **CAUTION**
>
> **If your determination letter tells you that you are exempt as a private foundation,** see a tax or legal advisor immediately. Most nonprofits will not want to maintain a nonprofit private foundation, and often decide to dissolve their nonprofit corporation immediately

Resist the natural temptation to file the letter without reading past the first sentences. In fact, the letter contains important information regarding the basis for your exemption and the requirements for maintaining it. Here's what to look for:

- **Are you properly classified?** Check to make sure that the public charity section listed by the IRS corresponds to the kind of public charity status you asked for. (You will find the various public charity code sections listed in Part X, line 5, of your copy of the 1023 form.) Some groups will have checked Part X, line 5(i), to let the IRS determine the proper public charity support test category support test for the organization.

- **Must you file a federal tax return?** The determination letter will tell you whether you must file a federal annual information return, IRS Form 990. Most 501(c)(3) groups must file this form (it's explained in Chapter 11).

- **Are you liable for excise taxes?** The determination letter also should state that you are not liable for excise taxes under Chapter 42 of the Internal Revenue Code. These are the taxes applicable to private foundations. With the exceptions noted below (for groups that have requested an advance public charity ruling), these excise taxes do not apply to you. The letter will also refer to other excise taxes for which you may be liable. These are the regular excise taxes applicable to all businesses that engage in certain activities, such as the sale of liquor, the manufacturing of certain products, and so on. For further information, see IRS Publication 510, *Excise Taxes.*

- **Information on deductions for donors.** Your letter will include information on the deductibility of charitable contributions made to your organization, and will refer to Internal Revenue Code sections that cover the deductibility of such donations.

- **Must you pay FUTA taxes?** Most groups will be told in their letter that they are exempt from federal unemployment (FUTA) taxes. You are, however, subject to filing nonprofit unrelated business income tax returns (Form 990-T). Nonprofits and their employees, however, are subject to Social Security (FICA) taxes—see "Federal and State Corporate Employment Taxes" in Chapter 11.

- **Advance ruling information.** If you requested an advance-ruling period for determining your public charity status, the letter will indicate that a final determination of your status will be made 90 days after the end of your advance-ruling period. Check to make sure that the IRS has the correct ending date of your annual accounting period. At the end of this period, the IRS will send you Form 8734, *Support Schedule for Advance Ruling Period,* which you will fill

out to show your actual sources of support during the advance ruling period. The IRS will review this form and your prior annual information returns and determine whether you have, in fact, met the public charity support requirements during the advance-ruling period.

> **CAUTION**
>
> **Make sure you receive Form 8734 from the IRS.** If you don't receive Form 8734 from the IRS shortly before the end of your advance ruling period, get it from their website and fill it in and mail in within 90 days of the end of your advance ruling period. If you don't file this form on time, the IRS will treat you as a private foundation—a result you definitely do not want.

- **Private foundation taxes.** The determination letter also may refer to IRC §§ 507(d) and 4940—these sections will apply to you if you are found to be a private foundation, not a public charity, at the end of your advance-ruling period. We have already mentioned the Section 4940 tax on investment income that may apply to you in such a case. Section 570(d) refers to an extra tax imposed on private foundations if they repeatedly engage in activities that give rise to the private foundation excise taxes discussed in Chapter 4.

Congratulations! You've just finished the most complicated, and indeed most crucial, part of your nonprofit incorporation process. The remaining formal incorporation steps are explained in the next chapter.

Final Steps in Organizing Your Nonprofit

Most of the hard work is over, but there are still a few important details to attend to. Don't be overwhelmed by the number of steps that follow—many will not apply to your nonprofit corporation and others are very simple.

To chart your way through the tasks that follow, we recommend you use the Incorporation Checklist included in Appendix B (and on the CD-ROM).

Mail IRS Letter to Franchise Tax Board

Your state determination of exemption letter will usually say that your state tax exemption is contingent on obtaining your federal tax exemption, and that you must file a copy of the federal determination letter with the Franchise Tax Board. If your letter includes this information, mail a copy of your federal determination letter to the Franchise Tax Board, to the address on the state determination of exemption letter.

Attach a brief cover letter stating that you are submitting the copy as instructed in your state exemption letter. Show the name of your corporation and your California corporate number in the heading of your letter. This is the six-digit number stamped at the top of the first page of each certified copy of your articles of incorporation.

Set Up a Corporate Records Book

Now take a few minutes to set up or order a corporate records book—this is an important part of your incorporation process.

Corporate Records Book

You will need a corporate records book to keep all your papers in an orderly fashion. These documents include articles of incorporation, bylaws, minutes of your first board meeting and ongoing director and shareholder meetings, tax exemption applications and determination letters, membership certificates (for those nonprofits with formal members), and any other related documents. You should keep your corporate records book at the principal office of your corporation at all times to make sure you always know where to find it.

To set up a corporate records book, you can simply place all your incorporation documents in a three-ring binder. If you prefer, you can order a custom-designed corporate records book through a legal stationery store.

Corporate Kits

You order a nonprofit corporate kit through a legal stationery store. These nonprofit corporate kits typically include:

- a corporate records book with minute paper and index dividers for charter (articles of incorporation), bylaws, minutes, and membership certificates

- a metal corporate seal (a circular stamp with the name of your corporation, the state's name, and year of incorporation), which you can use on important corporate documents

- membership certificates, printed with the name of your corporation.

Corporate Seals

Placing a corporate seal on a document is a formal way of showing that the document is the authorized act of the corporation. Nonprofits don't normally use a seal on everyday business papers (such as invoices and purchase orders), but they do use them for more formal documents, such as leases, membership certificates, deeds of trust, and certifications of board resolutions. A corporation is not legally required to have or use a corporate seal, but many find it convenient to do so.

A metal seal is usually included in the corporate kits or you can get a customized seal from a legal stationer for about $25 to $50.

Corporate Membership Certificates

If you have decided to adopt a formal membership structure with members entitled to vote for the board of directors, you may want to use membership certificates. Ten tear-out certificates are included in Appendix B. Unlike stock certificates used in profit corporations, membership certificates in nonprofit 501(c)(3) corporations do not represent an ownership interest in the assets of the corporation. They serve only as a formal reminder of membership status.

Each certificate that you issue should be numbered sequentially. Type the certificate number at the top of the form. Type the name of the corporation in the heading and the name of the member in the blank in the first paragraph. Have the certificate signed by your president and secretary, then place an impression of the seal of the corporation at the bottom. You should also record the name and address of the member and the number of the issued membership certificate in the membership list in your corporate records.

Prepare Offer to Transfer Assets From an Existing Business or Organization to Your Nonprofit

If you are incorporating an existing organization, we suggest you prepare an offer to transfer assets—this document will provide a formal record of the transfer and its terms. Your offer to transfer assets is a preliminary agreement. It will be accepted by the board of directors at the first meeting of the board and then formalized by a bill of sale. There are two basic types of offers, as we describe below.

Transfers From a For-Profit Business

If you are incorporating a preexisting for-profit business, you may want to prepare an offer to transfer the assets and liabilities of the predecessor organization to your nonprofit (to take effect after the corporation has obtained its federal tax exemption). An offer to transfer formalizes the transfer of assets and liabilities of the prior business to your nonprofit and provides documentation of the transfer.

> **CAUTION**
>
> There can be significant federal and state income tax consequences when the assets and liabilities of a prior business or organization are transferred to a new nonprofit corporation. Make sure to check with a knowledgeable tax advisor before transferring the assets and liabilities of a business or organization to your new nonprofit corporation.

When the people connected with the pre-existing business and the newly formed non-profit corporation are one and the same, the assets are usually donated without payment. However, when the nonprofit acquires assets from a preexisting profit-making business run by people different from those starting up the nonprofit, the nonprofit usually will agree to buy the assets. In either case, the offer will record the terms of the transfer (donation or sale of assets). You can prepare this offer (as we've explained in Chapter 9) when completing Schedule I, which you included with your federal tax exemption application. Refer to special instruction ❽, in "Prepare Your Offer to Transfer Form," below.

Transfers From an Informal Nonprofit Group

If you are incorporating a preexisting nonprofit association or another less formal type of nonprofit group, you might want to prepare a transfer form to document the details of the transfer of any assets and liabilities. Documentation of this type (who is transferring or contributing what to the new nonprofit) can avoid disputes or misunderstandings later on. In this case, you will need to modify the form to show that it is prepared by the trustees, officers, members, or organizers of the preexisting nonprofit organization or group.

Lots to Consider When Transferring Assets

Many practical and legal issues arise in a transfer of assets and liabilities from a prior business to a nonprofit. We suggest you consult an accountant to make sure you have considered:

- whether the preexisting business has retained sufficient assets to pay liabilities not assumed by the nonprofit
- whether real property should be kept by the prior business owners and leased to the nonprofit
- that payment by the prior business owners of liabilities not assumed by the nonprofit allows them a current, and sometimes necessary, tax deduction for the prior business, and
- that the transfer should be made on the date (the closing date referred to below) most advantageous for the prior owners of the profit business.

The new nonprofit corporation is not usually liable for the debts or liabilities of the prior business unless it assumes the debt or the transaction was fraudulent (with intent to frustrate and deceive the prior business creditors). In rare cases, the transfer must also comply with the Bulk Sales Law (the Bulk Sales Law is explained below in "Complying With the Bulk Sales Law").

The former business owners remain personally liable for debts or liabilities of the prior business incurred prior to the transfer of assets to the corporation (even if they are assumed by the corporation). They may also be held personally liable for debts incurred after the transfer, if credit is extended to the corporation by a creditor who believes and relies on the fact that she is still dealing with the prior profit business and hasn't been notified of the incorporation (see "Notify Others of Your Incorporation," below, for notification procedures).

Prepare Your Offer to Transfer Form

To transfer assets from a prior profit-making business or a nonprofit association to your nonprofit corporation, use the *Offer to Transfer Assets* form on the CD-ROM. Refer to the sample form as you follow the instructions below. The sample form below is written to apply to the transfer of a profit-making business to a nonprofit. We have included options in brackets for you to select either the word "business" or "organization" when preparing the form. Simply delete the inapplicable word as you prepare the offer with your word processor.

- The parenthetical blanks, "(_____)," in the sample form indicate information that you must supply.

- Optional information is enclosed in brackets, like this: "[**optional information**]."

- Corresponding blanks in the computer form are marked with a series of underlined characters.

- Replace the blanks in the computer form (each series of underlined characters) with the information indicated in the blanks in the sample form below.

Each circled number in the sample form (they look like this: ❶) refers to an instruction that helps you complete an item.

❶ Attach a copy of an assets and liabilities statement (Balance Sheet) that is current as of the date that is one business day before the date of sale. Insert this Balance Sheet date in the blank—it represents the "closing date of the offer," a date that is referred to throughout the remainder of the offer. As explained earlier, this date should be as advantageous as possible, tax-wise, to the prior business owners or organization (consult with your accountant if you need to). If you prepare this offer at the same time that you prepare your federal exemption application, keep in mind the three-to six-month time lag that usually occurs before the IRS approves your exemption. This means that you may want to hold off making the offer until you hear from the IRS that your federal tax exemption has been approved. This offer states that it is contingent upon your nonprofit corporation obtaining its tax exemption (see instruction ❼ below). Also, in the unlikely event that the Bulk Sales Law applies to you, make sure this date allows you enough time to comply with the appropriate presale notice requirements.

For an example, see the general format of the Balance Sheet provided in Part V of your federal exemption application. The bookkeeper or accountant of the prior business or organization can help you prepare this statement.

❷ If the nonprofit corporation will not assume any debts or liabilities of the preexisting business or organization, include these bracketed provisions in paragraph 3(b) and omit the bracketed provisions of paragraph 4(a).

❸ If the corporation is going to assume the debts and liabilities of the business or organization, include the bracketed provisions of paragraph 4(a) and omit the bracketed provisions in paragraph 3(b) as explained above. If the corporation is to assume some, but not all, debts and liabilities, indicate any exceptions in paragraph 4(a).

❹ Use paragraph 4(b) if you are transferring the business for a lump sum of cash to be paid by the corporation. If the assets will be donated, state $1 as the amount. This silly amount satisfies an age-old legal rule, namely, that there must be some consideration (money) for a contract to be valid, although the actual amount usually doesn't matter.

Offer to Transfer Assets

TO: __(name of corporation)__ , a California nonprofit __(public benefit__ __[or]   religious)__ corporation.

1. The undersigned is [are] the sole proprietor [partners] known as __"(name__ __of prior business)"__ , located at __(street address)__ , __(city)__ , __(county)__ , California.

2. A true and correct statement of the assets and liabilities of this business as of the close of business on __(date of statement)__ , _____ , is attached to this offer.❶

3. On the terms and conditions herein set forth, I [we] offer to sell and transfer to you at the close of business on __(closing date)__ , _____,❶ subject to such changes as may occur therein in the ordinary course of business between the date of this offer and the close of business on __(closing date)__ , _____:❶

    (a) All stock in trade, merchandise, fixtures, equipment, and other tangible assets of the business as shown on the financial statement attached to this offer [except ... __(indicate here any exceptions, e.g., real property to be__ __leased to the corporation, retained cash, etc.)   ;]__

    (b) The trade, business, name, goodwill, and other intangible assets of the business __[free and clear of all debts and liabilities of the business as shown__ __on the financial statement attached to this offer, and all such additional__ __liabilities as may be incurred by me (us) between the date of the financial__ __statement and the close of business on the   (closing date) ,   ].__❷

4. As consideration for the sale and transfer, you agree:

    __[(a) To assume and pay all debts and liabilities of the business as shown on__ __the financial statement attached to this offer, and all such additional__ __liabilities as may be reasonably incurred by me (us) between the date of__ __the financial statement and the close of business on   (closing date) ,__ _____ , except ... (indicate any unassumed debts or liabilities).]__❸

    (b) To pay an amount of $_____ [which represents the fair market value of the business as transferred to the above Corporation per the terms prescribed above], to be paid as follows: __(state terms of payment)__ .❹

[or]

(b) To execute a note in the amount of $_____, **[which amount represents the fair market value of the business as transferred to the above Corporation]**, incorporating the following provisions regarding payment under the note: **(state terms of loan)** .❺

5. If this offer is accepted by you and upon payment of $_____, per the terms of paragraph 4(b), above **[or "upon execution of a note per the terms of paragraph 4(b), above"]**,❻ I **[we]** shall:

(a) Deliver possession of the business and assets described in paragraph 3 of this offer to you at the close of business on   **(closing date)** , _____.

(b) Execute and deliver to you such instruments of transfer and other documents as may be required to fully perform my **[our]** obligations hereunder or as may be required for the convenient operation of said business thereafter by you.

[NOTE: It is clearly understood that this offer is contingent upon the above nonprofit corporation obtaining tax-exempt status with the State of California under Section 23701(d) of the Revenue and Taxation Code and with the IRS under Section 501(c)(3) of the Internal Revenue Code, and that failure to obtain either or both of these exemptions within   (number)   months shall allow me (us) to rescind this offer at any time thereafter, notwithstanding any of the other provisions of this offer contained above.]❼

Dated: _____, _____ ❽
  (signature of prior business owner[s])

[The blanks below are to be filled in later, after the first board meeting:].

The above Offer was accepted by the board of directors on   **(date of board meeting)** , _____, on behalf of   **(name of corporation)** , a California nonprofit   **(public benefit [or] religious)**   corporation.

By: _____
, President

_____
, Secretary

[When you have completed the form, you will wish to make several attachments as indicated in special instruction ❾.]

If you are transferring the business for its fair market value, write the dollar amount and include the language in brackets. If you are transferring the assets of a profit-making business, you can use the figure determined by the qualified expert in response to question 4(b) of Schedule I of your federal tax exemption application, unless this figure has changed. State the terms of the cash payment at the end of this paragraph (such as the date of payment).

❺ Use this paragraph 4(b) instead of the preceding paragraph 4(b) if the corporation will not immediately pay cash for the assets, but will instead sign a loan note and pay the amount in specified installments. The discussion above concerning fair market value applies here as well. Specify the terms of the loan—the amount and date of installment payments, the rate of interest, and maturity date, whether it's an interest-only loan with the principal amount paid at some future date, a noninterest note for the principal amount only, or payable on demand.

The terms of the loan should be commercially reasonable—a definite payback period and schedule, and a commercially reasonable rate of interest. This will help avoid a determination by the IRS that the prior business owners (who perhaps now are directors or officers of the nonprofit corporation) or organization are receiving some monetary advantage from the corporation, such as an above-market value payment or an excessive rate of interest paid by the nonprofit. Conversely, the more generous the terms to the nonprofit corporation, the less likely are your chances of having your exemption application denied or having problems with the IRS later upon an audit of your organization.

❻ Use the unbracketed sentence of paragraph 5 if the corporation will pay the full sum of money when the business is transferred to the corporation. Use the bracketed phrase if the amount will be paid off over time per the terms of a loan note.

❼ Include this bracketed NOTE paragraph if you are drafting the offer while preparing your federal exemption application. State how much time the corporation has to obtain its exemption before the prior business owner(s) can cancel the offer.

❽ Print the form and have the prior business owner(s) or one or more authorized managers or officers of the unincorporated organization sign and date the offer. If the offer is prepared for the transfer of assets of a prior nonprofit organization, we assume the transfer was properly approved by the prior nonprofit organization according to its charter or bylaws—see "Preparing Articles for an Unincorporated Association" in Chapter 6. Don't fill in the blanks at the bottom of the offer yet—do so after the first meeting of your board of directors. If you are preparing the offer for submission with your federal exemption application in response to Schedule I, question 4(a), your response to this item on an attachment page can state: "The offer is contingent upon the nonprofit corporation obtaining its federal tax exemption, at which time the offer will be submitted to the board of directors and, upon approval by the board, will be signed by the appropriate officers of the corporation."

❾ Attach a copy of the prepared financial statement to the offer and, if the lump sum or loan amount for the transfer of assets is the fair market value of a prior business, a copy of the appraisal that you prepared in response to Schedule I, question 4(b), of your federal exemption application. You don't need to attach the appraisal statement to your offer if you are preparing the offer for submission with your federal application (the appraisal schedule should be submitted separately as required by Schedule I).

If you are submitting this offer with your federal exemption application, make a copy of the form and all attachments, and submit these copies with your federal application. Place the originals of these papers in your corporate records book.

Prepare Minutes of Your First Board of Directors' Meeting

Now that you've prepared your articles and bylaws, obtained your state exemption, filed your articles with the secretary of state, and obtained your federal tax exemption (and possibly prepared an offer to transfer assets of a prior business or organization to your nonprofit corporation), your next step is to prepare minutes of your first board of directors' meeting. The purpose of this meeting is to transact the initial business of the corporation (elect officers, fix the legal address of the corporation, and so on) and to authorize the newly elected officers to take actions necessary to get your nonprofit corporation going (such as setting up bank accounts and admitting members, if appropriate). Although this meeting sometimes is a "paper meeting" (where the directors informally agree to the decisions reflected in the minutes without actually sitting down together and talking business), we suggest that you take this opportunity to meet in person and discuss any other steps you'll need to take to get your nonprofit corporation off the ground. Our minutes form assumes that your directors really did meet and approved the decisions reflected in the minutes.

Instructions for Preparing Minutes

Preparing minutes for your first meeting is not hard. Use the form on the CD-ROM (*Minutes of First Meeting of Board of Directors*) and consult the sample form below as you follow our instructions. We have flagged optional resolutions on the sample form and in the instructions. If an optional resolution does not apply to you, do not include it in your final minutes.

- The parenthetical blanks, "(_____)," in the sample form indicate information that you must complete on the form.
- Corresponding blanks in the computer form are marked with a series of underlined characters.
- Replace the blanks in the computer form (each series of underlined characters) with the information shown in the blanks in the sample form.
- Each circled number in the sample form (❶) refers to an instruction to help you complete an item.

❶ Normally, you must follow formal notice rules when holding special meetings (the first meeting of the board is a special meeting). This Waiver of Notice form allows you to dispense with that notice. Fill in this form as indicated, giving the time, date, and place of the meeting. Have all the directors sign the form and type the directors' names under their signature lines. It may be signed and dated before the actual meeting of the board.

❷ This is the first page of your minutes form. Fill in the blanks as indicated, entering the names of directors present and listing those, if any, who are absent (a quorum of the board, as specified in the bylaws, must be shown in attendance). Name one of the directors chairperson, and another as secretary of the meeting.

Minutes of First Meeting of Board of Directors
of
_____(name of corporation)_____

WAIVER OF NOTICE AND CONSENT TO HOLDING ❶
OF FIRST MEETING OF BOARD OF DIRECTORS
OF
_____(NAME OF CORPORATION)_____

a California Nonprofit __(Public Benefit [or] Religious)__ Corporation

We, the undersigned, being all the directors of __(name of corporation)__, a California nonprofit __(public benefit [or] religious)__ corporation, hereby waive notice of the first meeting of the board of directors of the corporation and consent to the holding of said meeting at __(principal place of business)__, California, on __(date)__, ____, at __(time)__ M., and consent to the transaction of any and all business by the directors at the meeting, including, without limitation, the adoption of bylaws, the election of officers, and the selection of the place where the corporation's bank account will be maintained.

Date: _____

__(signatures of director(s) listed in Article FIVE)__
(typed name) _____ , Director

_____ , Director

_____ , Director

_____ , Director

_____ , Director

MINUTES OF FIRST MEETING OF BOARD OF DIRECTORS ❷
OF
(NAME OF CORPORATION)

a California Nonprofit **(Public Benefit [or] Religious)** Corporation

The board of directors of **(name of corporation)** held its first meeting
on **(date)**, at **(principal office address)**, California. Written waiver of
notice was signed by all of the directors.

The following directors, constituting a quorum of the full board, were present at the
meeting:

(names of directors present at meeting)

_____

_____

_____

There were absent:

(names of absent directors, if any)

_____

_____

_____

On motion and by unanimous vote, **(name of director)** was elected temporary
chairperson and then presided over the meeting. **(name of director)** was
elected temporary secretary of the meeting.

The chairperson announced that the meeting was held pursuant to written waiver
of notice signed by each of the directors. Upon a motion duly made, seconded, and
unanimously carried, the waiver was made a part of the records of the meeting; it
now precedes the minutes of this meeting in the corporate records book.

BYLAWS ❸

There was then presented to the meeting for adoption a proposed set of bylaws of
the corporation. The bylaws were considered and discussed and, on motion duly
made and seconded, it was unanimously:

RESOLVED, that the bylaws presented to this meeting be and hereby are adopted as
the bylaws of the corporation;

RESOLVED FURTHER, that the secretary of this corporation be and hereby is
directed to execute a certificate of adoption of the bylaws, to insert the bylaws as
so certified in the corporate records book, and to see that a copy of the bylaws,
similarly certified, is kept at the corporation's principal office, as required by law.

CALIFORNIA AND FEDERAL TAX EXEMPTIONS ❹

The chairperson announced that, upon application previously submitted to the California Franchise Tax Board, the corporation was determined to be exempt from payment of state corporate franchise taxes as a/n __(tax-exempt classification, e.g., "educational," "charitable," "religious," etc.)__ organization under Section 23701(d) of the California Revenue and Taxation Code per Franchise Tax Board determination letter dated __(date of state determination letter)__ , _____. The chairperson also announced that, upon application previously submitted to the Internal Revenue Service, the corporation was determined to be exempt from payment of federal corporate income taxes as a/n __(tax-exempt classification, e.g., "educational," "charitable," "religious," etc.)__ organization under Section 501(c)(3) of the Internal Revenue Code per Internal Revenue Service determination letter dated __(date of federal determination letter)__ , _____, and, further, that the corporation has been classified as a public charity under Section __(IRC section or sections under which the corporation qualifies as a public charity)__ of the Internal Revenue Code.

The corporation has obtained an advance ruling of its federal public charity classification. The advance ruling period ends __(ending date of five-year advance ruling period)__ .

The chairperson then presented the originals of both state and federal tax exemption determination letters, and the secretary was instructed to insert these documents in the corporate records book.

ELECTION OF OFFICERS ❺

The chairperson then announced that the next item of business was the election of officers. Upon motion, the following persons were unanimously elected to the offices shown after their names:

_____(names of officers)_____	President
_____	Vice President
_____	Secretary
_____	Treasurer

COMPENSATION OF OFFICERS ❻

There followed a discussion concerning the compensation to be paid by the corporation to its officers. Upon motion duly made and seconded, it was unanimously:

RESOLVED, that the following annual salaries be paid to the officers of this corporation:

President	$_____
Vice President	$_____
Secretary	$_____
Treasurer	$_____

CORPORATE SEAL ❼

The Secretary presented to the meeting for adoption a proposed form of seal of the corporation. Upon motion duly made and seconded, it was:

RESOLVED, that the form of corporate seal presented to this meeting be and hereby is adopted as the seal of this corporation, and the secretary of the corporation is directed to place an impression thereof in the space next to this resolution.

(Impress seal here)

PRINCIPAL OFFICE ❽

After discussion as to the exact location of the corporation's principal office for the transaction of business in the county named in the bylaws, upon motion duly made and seconded, it was:

RESOLVED, that the principal office for the transaction of business of the corporation shall be at __(street address)__, in __(city)__, California.

BANK ACCOUNT ❾

Upon motion duly made and seconded, it was:

RESOLVED, that the funds of this corporation shall be deposited with __(name of bank)__.

RESOLVED FURTHER, that the treasurer of this corporation be and hereby is authorized and directed to establish an account with said bank and to deposit the funds of this corporation therein.

RESOLVED FURTHER, that any officer, employee, or agent of this corporation be and is authorized to endorse checks, drafts, or other evidences of indebtedness made payable to this corporation, but only for the purpose of deposit.

RESOLVED FURTHER, that all checks, drafts, and other instruments obligating this corporation to pay money shall be signed on behalf of this corporation by any __(number)__ of the following:

__(names of directors, officers, and/or staff)__

_____

_____

RESOLVED FURTHER, that said bank be and hereby is authorized to honor and pay all checks and drafts of this corporation signed as provided herein.

RESOLVED FURTHER, that the authority hereby conferred shall remain in force until revoked by the board of directors of this corporation and until written notice of such revocation shall have been received by said bank.

RESOLVED FURTHER, that the secretary of this corporation be and hereby is authorized to certify as to the continuing authority of these resolutions, the persons authorized to sign on behalf of this corporation, and the adoption of said bank's standard form of resolution, provided that said form does not vary materially from the terms of the foregoing resolutions.

· ·

CORPORATE CERTIFICATES (Optional) ❿

The secretary then presented to the meeting proposed director, sponsor, membership, or other forms of corporate certificates for approval by the board. Upon motion duly made and seconded, it was:

RESOLVED, that the form of certificates presented to this meeting are hereby adopted for use by this corporation and the secretary is directed to attach a copy of each form of certificate to the minutes of this meeting.

· ·

ISSUANCE OF MEMBERSHIPS (Optional) ⓫

The board next took up the matter of issuance of memberships in the corporation.

Upon motion duly made and seconded, it was unanimously:

RESOLVED, that upon __["making application therefor in writing" (or state other procedure as specified in the membership provisions in your bylaws)]____ ["and upon payment of an application fee" (and/or) "first annual dues in the amount(s) of $____,"]__ members shall be admitted to the corporation and shall be entitled to all rights and privileges and subject to all the obligations, restrictions, and limitations applicable to such membership in the corporation as set forth in the articles of incorporation and by-laws of the corporation and subsequent amendments and changes thereto, and subject to any further limitations as resolved from time to time by the board of directors.

RESOLVED FURTHER, that the secretary of the corporation shall record the name and address of each member in the membership book of the corporation and, upon the termination of any membership in accordance with the termination procedures specified in the bylaws of the corporation, the secretary shall record the date of termination of such membership in the membership book.

[RESOLVED FURTHER, that each person admitted to membership in the corporation shall be given a membership certificate, signed by the president and secretary of the corporation, and the secretary shall record the date of issuance of said certificate in the corporate membership book.]

ACCEPTANCE OF OFFER TO TRANSFER ASSETS AND ⓬ LIABILITIES OF PREDECESSOR ORGANIZATION (Optional)

Upon motion duly made and seconded, it was unanimously:

RESOLVED, that the corporation accept the written offer dated _____, ____, to transfer the assets and liabilities of the predecessor organization, __(name of predecessor organization)__, in accordance with the terms of said offer, a copy of which precedes the minutes of this meeting in the corporate records book.

RESOLVED FURTHER, that the appropriate officers of this corporation are authorized and directed to take such actions and execute such documents as they deem necessary or appropriate to effect the transfer of said business to this corporation.

Since there was no further business to come before the meeting, on motion duly made and seconded, the meeting was adjourned.

Dated:_____

_____⓭
, **Secretary**

❸ This resolution shows acceptance of the contents of the bylaws by your directors.

❹ This resolution recites the particulars of your federal and state tax exemption. Fill in the blanks as indicated, using information contained in your state and federal tax exemption determination letters. Indicate your tax-exempt classification with the state. This is the "Form of Organization" shown at the top of your state exemption letter—educational, religious, or charitable—and the date of your state determination letter. Provide the same information from your federal tax determination letter. Also show the Code section or sections under which you have obtained federal public charity status, as shown in your IRS exemption letter (for example, "a publicly supported organization of the type described in Section 509(a)(2)"). If you have requested and obtained an advance ruling period for your federal public charity status, check the box preceding the next to last paragraph in this resolution and type the date your advance ruling period ends (as specified in the heading of your IRS determination letter).

❺ Type the names of the persons you elect as officers of your corporation. Remember, directors may be officers and any one person may hold more than one officer position with the exception that the person(s) who serve(s) as the secretary and/or treasurer cannot also serve as the president (or chairperson of the board).

❻ If you decide to provide for officers' salaries, indicate each officer's salary in the blanks in this resolution. Of course, you may decide to omit one or more officer salaries here—if so, simply type a zero in the appropriate blank.

CAUTION

A majority of the directors of a California public benefit corporation cannot be paid (other than as directors of the corporation). See "Directors" in Chapter 2, for further information on this disinterested director rule for public benefit corporations.

Article 9, Section 5, of the bylaws included with this book contains compensation approval procedures that help your nonprofit meet the excess benefit avoidance rules under federal tax law (see "Limitation on Profits and Benefits" in Chapter 3 for more on these rules). These bylaw provisions require disinterested members of your board or a committee of the board (such as a compensation committee) to approve officer salaries, after obtaining comparable figures for compensation paid to similar officers in similar organizations. A safe harbor rule at the end of Article 9, Section 5c, allows smaller nonprofits to approve officer salaries if they have comparability data from three similar organizations showing that their officer salary levels are comparable to those organizations. Complying with this bylaw provision also should help you meet the special requirements under the California Nonprofit Integrity Act of 2004 for approving salaries paid to your chief executive officer and chief financial officer. (See "Limitation on Profits and Benefits" in Chapter 3, and the resources listed there that provide additional information about the special California compensation approval rules.)

If you fill in any of the officer salaries in this resolution, we suggest you add a paragraph to the resolution stating that you approved the salaries in compliance with Article 9, Section 5, of your bylaws, and that you document each of the applicable facts or items listed in Article 9, Section 5d, of the bylaws. For example, your additional language should include the following information:

- the name of the board committee that approved the salary and the members of the committee. This listing should show that only disinterested (unpaid) members voted for officer compensation

- the names and votes of each board or committee member

- the comparability data that justified the approval of the salary. Attach any written data to the minutes. The data should show specific salary levels paid by other organizations in your geographical and program area for similar officer positions, and

- the skills, experience, education, and other qualifications of all the officers that help justify each salary as reasonable.

❼ If you've ordered a corporate seal, impress your corporate seal in the space indicated on the printed form.

❽ So far, your formal documents have indicated only the county of the principal place of business of your corporation. Here you should provide the street address and city of this office. Do not use a post office box.

❾ It is important to keep corporate funds separate from any personal funds by depositing corporate funds into, and writing corporate checks out of, at least one corporate checking account. List the bank and branch office where you will maintain corporate accounts. In the fifth paragraph, say how many people must cosign corporate checks, giving the names of individuals allowed to cosign checks on the lines below this paragraph. As a minimal measure of fiscal control, specify the signature of two persons here. Many nonprofits list the president and treasurer, or the names of other supervisory officers who can be trusted with check-writing authority.

❿ This is an optional resolution for membership nonprofits. If you plan to use the tear-out membership certificates included with this book (or if you will order membership, director, or sponsor certificates from a legal stationer), include this page in your minutes. Attach to your printed minutes a sample of any certificates you plan to issue.

⓫ This resolution is for membership corporations, that must include it. State your procedure for admitting members in the first bracketed phrase, according to the membership provisions in your bylaws. If you have provided for application fees and/or annual dues in your bylaws, use the second bracketed phrase to describe the amount of such fees and/or dues provided for in your bylaws. If your membership corporation has no qualification requirements, annual fees, or dues, you can simply cross out the word "upon" just before the blank and leave the blank empty without filling in the blanks, or retype this paragraph to read: "RESOLVED that members shall be admitted to the corporation and shall be entitled to all rights and privileges and subject to all the obligations…" If you plan to issue membership certificates, add the bracketed paragraph shown on the sample form at the end of the resolution.

⓬ This is an optional resolution. If you have incorporated a preexisting profit-making business or other organization and have prepared an Offer to Transfer Assets, include this resolution in your final minutes, indicating the date of the offer and the name of the predecessor business or organization.

⓭ After printing your minutes, your secretary should date and sign the form at the bottom of the last page.

Place Your Minutes and Attachments in a Corporate Records Book

You are now through preparing your minutes. Place your minutes and all attachments in your corporate records book. Your attachments may include the following forms or documents:

- Waiver of notice and consent to holding of the first meeting
- Written offer (fill in the blanks at the end of the form and have your nonprofit corporation president and secretary sign the offer)
- Certified copy of your articles
- Copy of your bylaws, certified by the secretary of the corporation
- Original state and federal tax exemption determination letters, and
- Copy of any membership, director, and/or sponsor certificate that you plan to issue, certificate marked as a "Sample."

To certify your bylaws, have the corporate secretary date and sign the certificate section at the end of all copies of your bylaws.

Remember, you should continue to place an original or copy of all formal corporate documents in your corporate records book and keep this book at your principal office. For example, if you have prepared or ordered membership certificates, place any unissued certificates in the membership certificate section of your records book.

Complying With the Bulk Sales Law

A few nonprofits that have incorporated existing businesses may have to comply with California's Bulk Sales Law (Division 6 of the California Commercial Code, starting with Section 6101). You might have to comply, for example, if you have taken a preexisting retail or wholesale business, such as a charitable thrift shop, and incorporated it to obtain nonprofit corporate status. But compliance is required only if all of the following are true:

- The business being incorporated is a restaurant or one whose principal business is selling inventory from stock (such as a retail or wholesale business, including a business that manufactures what it sells).
- You are transferring more than half the value of the old business's inventory and equipment to your new corporation.
- The value of the business assets being transferred is $10,000 or more (an exemption from the provisions of the bulk sales law also applies if the value of the assets being transferred is more than $5 million).

If, as is true for most nonprofits, these three conditions do not apply to your incorporation, you can skip the rest of this section. For those of you who do, however, meet the test, take heart. Even if you are incorporating the type of business covered by this law, you may still be eligible for an exemption from most of the provisions of this law if your corporation:

- assumes the debts of the unincorporated business
- is not insolvent after the assumption of these debts; and
- publishes and files a notice to creditors within 30 days of the transfer of assets.

To comply with this exemption, call a local legal newspaper. The paper should be able to send you the proper form (see "Notify Others of Your Incorporation," below) to prepare and will publish and file this form with the county recorder's and tax collector's offices for a small fee.

There are various notice forms that fit specific provisions of the bulk sales law. To rely on the exemption above, prepare and have the newspaper publish and file a Notice to Creditors under Section 6013(c)(10) of the California Commercial Code. This notice will usually include a heading indicating that it is a Bulk Sale and Assumption form. In any case, it must include a clause stating that the buyer has assumed or will assume in full the debts that were incurred in the seller's business before the date of the bulk sale (you may see slightly different wording, but the sense should be the same).

For other exemptions from the Bulk Sales Law, see Division 6 of the California Commercial Code.

Prepare a Bill of Sale for Assets

If you have incorporated a preexisting business or organization, you may want to prepare a bill of sale to formally transfer the assets for the organization to the nonprofit corporation, according to the terms of the written offer. (The offer, which you prepared in "Prepare Offer to Transfer Assets From an Existing Business or Organization to Your Nonprofit" should have been accepted by the board at the first meeting and signed by the officers on behalf of the corporation after the meeting.) Prepare the bill of sale by completing the form on the CD-ROM that accompanies this book, following the sample form and special instructions below.

- The parenthetical blanks, "(_____)," in the sample form below indicate information that you must complete on the computer form on the CD-ROM.

- Optional information is enclosed in brackets, for example, "[**optional information**]."

- Corresponding blanks in the computer form are marked with a series of underlined characters.

- Replace the blanks in the computer form (each series of underlined characters) with the information indicated in the blanks in the sample form below.

- Each circled number in the sample form refers to a special instruction that will help you complete an item.

❶ Include this first bracketed phrase if your written offer specified an amount of money to be paid upon the transfer of the business. If appropriate, include the language that states that this amount represents the fair market value of the business or organization (if the assets were donated, you will just show $1 as the amount of payment without the statement concerning fair market value).

❷ Include this second bracketed phrase (instead of the first bracketed phrase referred to above) if the business or organization will be transferred in return for a promissory note. A sample promissory note is shown below. You may need to modify its terms to conform to the terms contained in your offer. In all cases, your note should state the date and place of its execution, the due date, amount to be paid, and rate of interest, if any.

❸ Attach an inventory to the offer, showing all tangible assets of the business—this can be copied from the schedule of assets and liabilities you've attached to your written offer. Add, in the blank provided, any nontransferred assets according to the terms of your offer.

❹ Include this paragraph if the corporation will assume liabilities of the prior business or organization, noting any exceptions.

❺ Include this paragraph if the business's or organization's accounts receivable will be transferred to the corporation, indicating any exceptions.

Bill of Sale

This is an agreement by ___(names of prior business owners)___, herein called "transferor(s)," and ___(name of corporation)___, herein called "the corporation."

1. In return for ___["payment of $_____ which represents the fair market value of the business transferred" (or state other amount to be paid per the terms of the written offer)]___ ❶ (or) ___["execution of a promissory note in the principal amount of $_____, with the terms as contained in said note, a copy of which is attached to this agreement"]___ ❷ by ___(name of corporation)___, a California nonprofit corporation, I [**we**] hereby sell, assign, and transfer to the corporation all my [**our**] right, title, and interest in the following property:

   All the tangible assets listed on the inventory attached to this bill of sale, and all stock in trade, trade, goodwill, leasehold interests, trade names, and other intangible assets ___["except ... (show nontransferred assets) of (name of prior business), located at (street address), (city), (county), California"].___ ❸

2. ___[In return for the transfer of the above property to it, the corporation hereby agrees to assume, pay, and discharge all debts, duties, and obligations that appear on the date of this agreement, on the books and owed on account of said business ["except ... (list any unassumed debts or liabilities) "]. The corporation agrees to indemnify and hold the transferor(s) of said business and their property free from any liability for any such debt, duty, or obligation and from any suits, actions, or legal proceedings brought to enforce or collect any such debt, duty, or obligation.]___ ❹

3. ___[The transferor(s) hereby appoint(s) the corporation as his (her, their) representative to demand, receive, and collect for itself, all debts and obligations now owing to said business ["except (list any exceptions) "]. The transferor(s) further authorize(s) the corporation to do all things allowed by law to recover and collect such debts and obligations and to use the transferor's(s') name(s) in such manner as it considers necessary for the collection and recovery of such debts and obligations, provided, however, without cost, expense, or damage to the transferor(s).]___ ❺

Dated:_____, _____

_____ ❻
, Transferor

_____
, Transferor

___(name of corporation)___
By:

_____
, President

_____
, Secretary

❻ Fill in the bottom portion of the bill of sale and print the form. Have the form signed by the prior business owners or the authorized manager(s) or officer(s) of the prior organization (the "transferors") and the president and secretary of the corporation. Place the completed form, together with the attachments (inventory and promissory note), in your corporate records book. Give copies to the prior business owners or representatives of the prior nonprofit organization. The business or organization is now officially transferred.

Prepare Assignments of Leases and Deeds

If you have transferred a prior business or organization to your corporation, the prior owners or nonprofit organization may want to prepare assignments of leases or deeds if they are transferring real property interests to the corporation. Under an assignment, you step into the shoes of the old tenant—the terms and conditions of the lease don't change. For an example of an assignment of lease form, see Chapter 8, instructions to item 7(h). (You won't want to include the clause making the assignment of lease contingent on the corporation's obtaining its federal tax exemption, since you've already obtained it.)

Promissory Note

For value received, the undersigned California nonprofit corporation promises to pay to **(names of prior business owners or name of prior unincorporated nonprofit association)** the principal amount of $_____, together with interest at the rate of ___% per annum with a total amount due under this note of $ **(principal + interest)** , to be paid in full by **(due date)** , with payment to be made in **(number)** equal monthly installments of $_____ each payable on the _____ day of each month, with the first installment being due on **(date)** [or state other provisions per the terms of the written Offer regarding rate of interest, if any, due date, and manner of payment].

Executed this _____ day of _____, ____, at _____, _____, County of _____, California.

_____**(name of corporation)**_____

By:

_____, President

_____, Secretary

> **TIP**
> **To avoid going through a reassignment, ask the landlord to terminate the old lease and renegotiate a new lease between the landlord and your new corporation.** Use this approach if you think you can hammer out a better deal than the old lease gave the old tenants.

If you prepare an assignment, the terms of the lease itself will normally require you to get the landlord's consent. It is particularly important to communicate with the landlord if the nonprofit corporation expects to obtain an exemption from local real property taxes on the leased premises from the county tax assessor (see "Apply for Your Property Tax Exemption," below). Nonprofit groups that obtain the exemption will want a clause in their new lease that gives them a credit against rent payments for the amount of any decrease in the landlord's property tax bill.

A real estate broker can help you obtain and prepare forms to transfer property in which the prior owners have an ownership interest. If a mortgage or deed of trust is involved, you may well need the permission of the lender, too.

File Final Papers for the Prior Organization

If you have incorporated a prior business or other organization, you may need to file final sales tax and other returns for the preexisting organization. You will also want to cancel any permits or licenses issued to the prior business or its principals. If you need new licenses, get them in the name of the new nonprofit corporation.

Notify Others of Your Incorporation

If a preexisting group has been incorporated, notify creditors and other interested parties, in writing, of the termination and dissolution of the prior organization and its transfer to the new corporation. This is advisable as a legal precaution and as a courtesy to those who have dealt with the prior organization.

To notify past creditors, suppliers, organizations, and businesses of your incorporation, send a friendly letter that shows the date of your incorporation, your corporate name, and its principal office address. Make a copy of each letter and put it in your corporate records book.

If the prior group was organized as a partnership, have a local legal newspaper publish a Notice of Dissolution of Partnership in the county where the partnership office or property was located. Then file the form with the local county clerk's office according to the instructions on the form, or pay the newspaper to file it for you.

Apply for a Mailing Permit

Most 501(c)(3) tax-exempt nonprofit corporations will qualify for and want to obtain a third-class nonprofit mailing permit from the U.S. Post Office. This permit entitles you to lower rates on mailings, an important advantage for many groups since the nonprofit rate is considerably lower than the regular third-class rate.

To obtain your permit, bring to your local or main post office branch:

- a file-stamped or certified copy of your articles
- a copy of your bylaws

- a copy of your federal and state tax-exemption determination letters, and

- copies of program literature, newsletters, bulletins, and any other promotional materials.

The post office clerk will ask you to fill out a short application and take your papers. If your local post office branch doesn't handle this, the clerk will send you to a classifications office at the main post office. You'll pay a one-time fee and an annual permit fee. The clerk will forward your papers to the classification office at the regional post office for a determination. In a week or so, you will receive notice of the post office's determination.

Once you have your permit, you can mail letters and parcels at the reduced rate by affixing stamps to your mail; by taking the mail to your post office and filling out a special mailing form; or by using the simpler methods of either stamping your mail with an imprint stamp (made by a stampmaker) or leasing a mail-stamping machine that shows your imprint information. Ask the classifications clerk for further information.

Apply for Your Property Tax Exemption

As a nonprofit corporation, you can obtain an exemption from local (county) property taxes on the corporation's personal and real property, whether it's owned or leased. Reread "California Welfare Exemption" in Chapter 5, which explains the welfare exemption, before deciding whether to apply for it. Most groups that meet the requirements will want it.

If you lease from an organization that, itself, is exempt under the welfare exemption, you should prepare and submit the application

to be exempt from personal property taxes and to reduce your rent payments to your landlord once you qualify for a real property tax exemption on the portion of the premises that you rent (you should agree with your landlord to reduce your rent once you qualify for the welfare exemption on the leased premises). Both the nonprofit tenant and the nonprofit owner of the property must apply for and obtain the welfare exemption to qualify for a real property welfare tax exemption on the leased premises.

Timing Your Application

You need not have your federal or state tax exemption to apply for the welfare exemption. Even if you have not yet filed your articles with the secretary of state (but are sure that you will do so), go ahead and file if the February 15 property tax assessment deadline is approaching.

It's a good idea to file for this exemption early, before you've even obtained your state and federal tax exemptions. When you do become a tax-exempt nonprofit corporation, you will be able to obtain a complete, partial, or prorated refund on any applicable real or personal property taxes associated with real property you buy or rent or personal property you acquire during the fiscal year after you submit the copies of your state and federal exemptions to complete your welfare exemption application information.

In your application, explain how far along you are in your incorporation process. For example, you might write, "nonprofit corporation, preparing to apply for state corporate franchise tax exemption"; or "proposed nonprofit corporation to be exempt from corporate taxation under Section 23701(d) of the California Revenue and Taxation Code and Section 501(c)(3) of the Internal Revenue Code" in the appropriate blanks. Answer the questions on the application and provide attachments as best you can (for instance, you can attach filed or unfiled articles or proposed financial statements). Note on the form that you will supply additional appropriate documents (such as filed articles, exemption letters, financial data, and descriptions of real and/or personal property) during the fiscal year, when available.

If you are seeking an exemption for real property owned by the nonprofit corporation, the grant deed for the property should be filed in the county recorder's office before March 1 (15 days before you file your claim). If you are seeking an exemption on leased property, your lease or assignment of lease should be dated before March 1.

Applying for an Exemption

Applying for the welfare exemption isn't difficult. Follow these steps:

- Call the local county assessor's office and request a welfare exemption claim form. A list of county assessors with contact information is provided on the State Board of Equalization's website at www. boe.ca.gov/proptaxes/assessors.htm. When you contact the county assessor, ask for the welfare exemption form for first-time filers, Form BOE-267, *Welfare Exemption (First Filing)*. Complete the claim form, using the accompanying instruction sheet. Fill in all of the blanks on the form. If a particular item doesn't apply, mark it as "Not Applicable."

- Assemble copies of your certified articles, federal and state exemption determination letters (if you have obtained them), and the requested financial statements. These statements are your operating statement and balance sheet—you should be able to use the financial information submitted with your federal exemption application. Include any other appropriate attachments (such as a copy of a lease).

- Assemble all the papers together—the completed claim form and all documents. They do not need to be stapled or fastened together. Make two copies of all the papers.

- File two (duplicate) sets of your claim form and attachments with the county assessor. Keep one copy to place in your corporate records book. File your papers before February 15 of the fiscal year for which you are seeking the exemption (the property tax fiscal year goes from July 1 to June 30). If you submit it after this date and before January 1 of the following year, you will only be allowed a 90% exemption if your claim is approved. If you file even later than this during the fiscal year, you will be allowed an 85% exemption, except that the maximum amount in taxes you will have to pay is $250.

The assessor will go out and inspect your property, to determine if the uses to which it is being put meet the requirements of the welfare exemption. The inspector will prepare a field inspection report and send it, together with one copy of your claim and attachments, to the State Board of Equalization in Sacramento. The Board will review the documents and make a decision, sending a copy of the decision to you and one copy to the local assessor. If you've been granted the exemption, the local assessment roll will be updated and a tax "bill" showing your exemption will be sent to you. If you are renting, the updated tax bill will go to your landlord.

TIP

Religious corporations may be able to avail themselves of the streamlined application and renewal procedures of the religious exemption under Section 207 of the Revenue and Taxation Code—call your local county tax assessor's office (Exemption Division).

RESOURCE

For more information on the welfare exemption and how to apply for it, consult the *Assessor's Handbook—Welfare Exemption*, publication number AH-267, a pamphlet for local tax assessors written by the Board of Equalization. The handbook is included in the file listed below. If you want to check if a newer edition has come out since the publication of this book, go to the California State Board of Equalization website at www.boe.ca.gov/ahcont.htm. Select "AH-267, Welfare, Church, and Religious Exemptions" from the link list to view the handbook in your browser.

CD-ROM

The following file is included on the CD-ROM at the back of this book: *Assessors' Handbook Section 267*, "Welfare, Church, and Religious Exemptions."

File a Domestic Corporation Statement

Shortly after you file your articles of incorporation, you will receive a *Statement of Information for a Domestic Nonprofit Corporation* (Form SI-200) from the secretary of state's office. This form requests basic organizational information (which will be a matter of public record and can be obtained by anyone for a small fee), including the address of your principal office, the names and addresses of your officers, and your agent for service of process. (Your initial agent is designated in your articles of incorporation and is the person authorized to receive legal documents on behalf of your corporation.) This form must be filled out and sent back to the secretary of state within 90 days of the date your articles are filed. You may want to retain some anonymity for your officers by listing the principal office of the corporation as their business address.

Every two years, the secretary of state will send you a new statement to prepare and file. Failure to file this statement when required can result in penalties and can, eventually, lead to suspension of corporate powers by the secretary of state. The California Secretary of State's website allows you to fill in and file the domestic corporation statement online from your browser—if you use this online form preparation and filing method, you do not need to mail in your initial or biennial statements. Go to the state site at www.ss.ca.gov/business/hpd_forms.htm, click the link to the Statement of Information - Domestic Nonprofit Corporation (SI-100), then select the link to the form online.

File an Initial Report With the Attorney General

Most California public benefit corporations must register by filing an initial report and thereafter file annual reports with the California Attorney General, Charitable Trusts Section. Some California nonprofit corporations, however, are exempt from registration and reporting requirements—these include California religious nonprofit corporations and California public benefit nonprofits organized as hospitals or schools. All other 501(c)(3)

California nonprofit corporations must file an initial and annual reports with the Attorney General's Charitable Trusts Section. When a public benefit corporation files its articles, the secretary of state forwards a copy of the articles to the attorney general. The attorney general will send nonexempt groups an initial report form (Form CT-1) to complete and file, and an annual reporting form (RRF-1) to complete and file for the second and subsequent years of the corporation. For more information on filing initial and annual reports, see "Attorney General Annual Periodic Report" Chapter 11.

As noted above, in addition to religious groups, the following types of 501(c)(3) nonprofits should be exempt from initial and annual reporting with the attorney general. If you think you fit in one of these categories but have received a CT-1 form, call the attorney general's office in Sacramento to see if you can establish your attorney general exemption.

- **Schools.** Educational organizations set up as formal schools with the institutional attributes (such as a regular faculty and curriculum, enrolled body of students, and established place of instruction) don't have to file form CT-1 with the attorney general. Notice that this definition is more restrictive than the one used for qualifying for your federal tax exemption, and is basically the same as that which applies to schools for purposes of obtaining public charity status.

- **Hospitals.** The attorney general has a restrictive definition of hospitals. In addition to being the kind of charitable hospital that made it eligible for the federal tax exemption and public charity status, the hospital must be operated on a 24-hour-a-day basis and have a round-the-clock medical staff. Day or outpatient clinics or those that don't have licensed practitioners regularly working at the clinic will not, in most cases, qualify for the exemption.

RESOURCE

The *Attorney General's Guide for Charities* is a helpful guide for California nonprofits, as well as a source of information on the attorney general's reporting and filing requirements. It also contains excellent summaries of the legal responsibilities and liabilities of nonprofit directors under California law, as well as practical information on fundraising, fiscal management, and other important nonprofit issues. We recommend all California nonprofits obtain a copy of this valuable sourcebook. This guide is available for viewing and downloading from the Attorney General's Division of Charitable Trusts website located at http://ag.ca.gov/charities/publications.php. The site also contains other informative publications of the Attorney General's Office, including the *Attorney General's Guide to Charitable Solicitations* plus the initial (CT-1) and ongoing (RRF-1) registration and reporting forms required to be filed with the Attorney General's Office.

CD-ROM

The *Attorney General's Guide for Charities* (2005) is included on the CD-ROM.

Issue Membership Certificates

If you have set up a membership corporation and have membership certificates, you will want to issue them to members after they have applied for membership in the corporation and paid any fees required by the membership provisions in your bylaws. The corporate president and secretary should sign each certificate before giving it to the member.

If you have ordered membership materials as part of a corporate kit, record each member's name and address, together with the number of the certificate, in the membership roll in your corporate records book.

If you are using the tear-out membership certificate included in Appendix B, complete each certificate by typing the number of the certificate, the name of the corporation, and the name of the member on the certificate. Then execute the certificate by filling in the date and having the president and secretary sign at the bottom (if you have a seal, impress it at the bottom of each certificate). Give the certificate to the member, then record the member's name, address, certificate number, and date of issuance on a separate page in your corporate records book. The information on these pages, kept in the corporate records book, constitutes the membership book of the corporation.

File Your Articles With the County Recorder

Unincorporated associations that have just incorporated (see "Preparing Articles for an Unincorporated Association" in Chapter 6) and that owned real property prior to incorporating should file a certified copy of their articles of incorporation with the county recorder of the county or counties in which the previous unincorporated association owned property. This will show legal ownership by the new nonprofit corporation of the preexisting unincorporated association's real property.

When filing these copies of your articles, send the county recorder two copies, together with the required fee. Request that one copy be file-stamped by the county recorder and returned to you. Place this copy in the articles section of your corporate records book.

Register With the Fair Political Practices Commission

If your nonprofit corporation plans to lobby for legislation, hire a lobbyist, or otherwise be politically active (for example, by supporting or opposing state, county, or city measures to be voted on by the public), you must comply with registration and reporting requirements for lobbying activity administered by the California Fair Political Practices Commission. Call the office in Sacramento for further information if you think these registration and reporting requirements apply to the activities of your nonprofit corporation. (Request a copy of the *Information Manual for Lobbying Disclosure Provisions of the Political Reform Act*, or read this manual at your county law library.)

Check State and Local Solicitation Requirements

If you plan to solicit contributions directly (by mail, the Internet, or door-to-door) or through paid fundraisers or consultants, make sure your organization and the people it hires comply with state and local solicitation laws, regulations, and ordinances. For tips on how to learn about state laws that may apply to your organization and its fundraisers and consultants, see "State Solicitation Laws and Requirements" in Chapter 5.

After Your Corporation Is Organized

You have now incorporated your non-profit and have handled many initial organizational details. But before you close this book, read just a little more. After incorporating, you need to become familiar with the formalities of corporate life, such as filing tax returns, paying employment taxes, and preparing minutes of formal corporate meetings. In this chapter, we look at some tax and other routine filings required by federal, state, and local governmental agencies. At the end, we give you an overview of what's involved in dissolving a nonprofit corporation.

The information presented here won't tell you everything you will need to know about these subjects, but will provide some of the basics and indicate some of the major areas that you (or your tax advisor) will need to go over in more detail.

Piercing the Corporate Veil— If You Want to Be Treated Like a Corporation, It's Best to Act Like One

After you've set up a corporation of any kind, your organization should act like one. Although filing your articles of incorporation with the secretary of state brings the corporation into existence as a legal entity, this is not enough to ensure that a court or the IRS will treat your organization as a corporation. What we are referring to here is not simply maintaining your various tax exemptions or even your nonprofit status with the state—we are talking about being treated as a valid corporate entity in court and for tax purposes. Remember, it is your legal corporate status that allows your organization to be treated as an entity apart from its directors, officers, and employees and allows it to be taxed (or not taxed), sue, or be sued, on its own. It is

the corporate entity that insulates the people behind the corporation from taxes and lawsuits.

Courts and the IRS do, on occasion, scrutinize the organization and operation of a corporation, particularly if it is directed and operated by a small number of people who wear more than one hat (such as those who fill both director and officer positions). If you don't take care to treat your corporation as a separate legal entity, a court may decide to disregard the corporation and hold the principals (directors and officers) personally liable for corporate debts. This might happen if the corporation doesn't have adequate money to start with, making it likely that creditors or people who have claims against the corporation won't be able to be paid; if corporate and personal funds are commingled; if the corporation doesn't keep adequate corporate records (such as minutes of meetings); or generally doesn't pay much attention to the theory and practice of corporate life. Also, the IRS may assess taxes and penalties personally against those connected with managing the affairs of the corporation if it concludes that the corporation is not a valid legal or tax entity. In legal jargon, holding individuals responsible for corporate deeds or misdeeds is called "piercing the corporate veil."

To avoid problems of this type, be careful to operate your corporation as a separate legal entity. Hold regular and special meetings of your board and membership as required by your bylaws and as necessary to take formal corporate action. It is critical that you document formal corporate meetings with neat and thorough minutes. Also, it is wise to have enough money in your corporate account to pay foreseeable debts and liabilities that may arise in the course of carrying out your activities—even nonprofits should start with a small cash reserve. Above all, keep corporate funds separate from the personal funds of the individuals who manage or work for the corporation.

Federal Corporate Tax Returns

In this section, we list and briefly discuss the main IRS tax paperwork you can expect to face as a 501(c)(3) nonprofit corporation.

> **CAUTION**
>
> **IRS forms, instructions, fees, and penalties are subject to constant change.** Make sure to get the most current information (on return deadlines, tax rates, penalties, and so on) when you file. You can download the federal tax forms discussed in this section from the IRS website at www.irs.gov.

Public Charities: Annual Exempt Organization Return

Nonprofit corporations exempt from federal corporate income tax under Section 501(c)(3) and qualified (under an advance or definitive ruling) as public charities must file IRS Form 990, *Annual Return of Organization Exempt From Income Tax* (together with Form 990, Schedule A). The filing deadline is on or before the 15th day of the fifth month (within four and a half months) following the close of their accounting period (tax year). You should file this even if your 1023 federal application for exemption is still pending.

Some groups may be eligible to file IRS Form 990-EZ instead of Form 990. This is a short-form annual return that can be used by small tax-exempt public charities—those with gross receipts of less than $100,000 and total assets of less than $250,000.

> **CAUTION**
>
> **Watch out for short deadlines.** Your first 990 return deadline may come up on you sooner than you expect if your first tax year is a short year— a tax year of less than 12 months.

EXAMPLE:

If your accounting period as specified in your bylaws runs from January 1 to December 31 and your articles were filed on December 1, your first tax year consists of one month, from December 1 to December 31. In this situation, your first Form 990 would have to be filed within four and a half months of December 31 (by May 15 of the following year), only five and a half months after your articles were filed. It is likely that your federal tax exemption application would still be pending at this time.

Groups Exempt From Filing Form 990

The Internal Revenue Code exempts certain public charities from filing Form 990, including certain churches, schools, mission societies, religious activity groups, state institutions, corporations organized under an Act of Congress, tax-exempt private foundations, certain trusts, religious and apostolic organizations, and public charities. In general, these groups cannot normally have more than $25,000 in gross receipts in each taxable year. See the official instructions to IRS Form 990 for the details of these exemptions.

Your federal exemption determination letter should state whether you must file Form 990. Most public charities will be publicly supported organizations or receive a majority of their support from exempt-purpose revenue (see "Public Support Test" and "Exempt Activities

Support Test" in Chapter 4). Because these groups are not institutional public charities falling under one of the automatic exemptions to filing listed above, they will have to file Form 990 unless they meet the normally not more than $25,000 gross receipts exemption. To rely on this exemption, fill in the top portion of the 990 form and check the box indicating that you are eligible for this exemption.

If your nonprofit corporation makes the political expenditures election by filing Federal Election Form 5768 (discussed in "Limitation on Political Activities" in Chapter 3), indicate on Form 990, Schedule A, that you made this election and fill in the appropriate part of the schedule showing your actual lobbying expenditures during the year.

> **TIP**
>
> **990 returns as financial disclosure.** Most California public benefit corporations must report annually to the California Attorney General. A copy of the nonprofit's federal Form 990 must be included with the attorney general annual report form.

> **CAUTION**
>
> **New IRS e-Postcard annual filing requirement for small nonprofits.** Beginning in 2008, small tax-exempt organizations that previously were not required to file returns with the IRS will be required to file an annual electronic notice with the IRS—Form 990-N, *Electronic Notice (e-Postcard) for Tax-Exempt Organizations not Required To File Form 990 or 990-EZ*. The IRS will send informational letters in July 2007 notifying small nonprofits about the new filing requirement and the electronic filing procedures. This new filing requirement will apply to tax periods beginning after December 31, 2006. Organizations that do not file the e-Postcard or an information return Form 990 or 990-EZ for three consecutive years will have their tax-exempt status revoked.

If you want more information about this new filing requirement, including notification about when the filing system is ready, you can subscribe to Exempt Organization's EO Update on the Charities pages of www.irs.gov.

Private Foundations: Annual Exempt Organization Return

Very few 501(c)(3) nonprofits will be classified as private foundations. If you are one, however, you must file a *Federal Annual Return of Private Foundation Exempt From Income Tax*, Form 990-PF, within four and one-half months of the close of your tax year. You file this Form 990-PF instead of Form 990 discussed above. You'll provide information on receipts and expenditures, assets and liabilities, and other information that will help the IRS determine whether you are liable for private foundation excise taxes. You should receive the form and separate instructions for completing it close to the end of your accounting period. Again, watch out for a short first year and an early deadline for filing your Form 990-PF.

The foundation manager(s) must publish a notice telling the public that they may see the annual report. Do so in a local county newspaper before the filing deadline for the 990-PF. The notice must state that the annual report is available for public inspection, at the principal office of the corporation, within 180 days after the publication of the inspection notice. A copy of the published notice must be attached to the 990-PF.

Unrelated Business Income: Annual Exempt Organization Tax Return

With a few minor exceptions, Section 501(c)(3) federal tax-exempt corporations that have gross incomes of $1,000 or more during the year from an unrelated trade or business must file an *Exempt Organization Business Income Tax Return*

(Form 990-T). The form is due within two and a half months after the close of their tax year. For a definition and discussion of unrelated trades and businesses, see "Federal Unrelated Business Income Tax" in Chapter 5, and obtain Federal Publication 598, *Tax on Business Income of Exempt Organizations*. Use booklet 598 and the separate instructions to Form 990-T to prepare this form.

The taxes imposed on unrelated business income are the same rates applied to normal federal corporate income. Remember that too much unrelated business income may indicate to the IRS that you are engaging in nonexempt activities to a substantial degree and may jeopardize your tax exemption.

File Your Returns on Time

The IRS and the state are notoriously efficient in assessing and collecting late filing and other penalties. So, while it's generally true that your nonprofit corporation does not have to worry about paying taxes, you should worry a bit about filing your annual information returns on time (including your employment tax returns and payments). Too many nonprofit corporations have had to liquidate when forced to pay late filing penalties for a few years' worth of simple informational returns that they inadvertently forgot to file.

Another important aspect of late filing penalties and delinquent employment taxes is that the IRS (and state) can, and often do, try to collect these often substantial amounts from individuals associated with the corporation if the corporation doesn't have sufficient cash to pay them. Remember, one of the exceptions to the concept of limited liability is liability for unpaid taxes and tax penalties. The IRS and state can go after the person (or persons) associated with the corporation who are responsible for reporting and/or paying taxes.

More Information on Taxes

We suggest all nonprofits obtain IRS Publication 509, *Tax Calendars,* prior to the beginning of each year. This pamphlet contains tax calendars showing the dates for corporate and employer filings during the year.

Information on withholding, depositing, reporting, and paying federal employment taxes can be found in IRS Publication 15, Circular E, *Employer's Tax Guide,* and the Publication 15-A and 15-B Supplements.

Other helpful IRS publications are Publication 542, *Tax Information on Corporations,* and Publication 334, *Tax Guide for Small Business.*

Helpful information on accounting methods and bookkeeping procedures is contained in IRS Publication 538, *Accounting Period and Methods,* and Publication 583, *Starting a Business and Keeping Records.*

You can get IRS publications online at www .irs.gov. You can also pick them up at your local IRS office (or order them by phone—call your local IRS office or try the toll-free IRS forms and publications request telephone number, 800-TAX-FORM). California tax forms and information are available at www.ftb. ca.gov/index.html. California employment tax information can be downloaded from www. edd.cahwnet.gov.

For information on withholding, contributing, paying, and reporting California employment, unemployment, and disability taxes, get the *California Employer's Tax Guide* (Publication DE 44), available online at www.edd.cphwnet.gov/ taxrep/taxform.htm#publications.

California Corporate Tax Returns and Reports

In this section, we list some of the California tax reporting forms and paperwork you will need to tackle as a tax-exempt nonprofit corporation.

Public Charities: Annual Exempt Organization Return

Nonprofit corporations exempt from tax under 23701(d) of the California Revenue and Taxation Code (the state parallel exemption to the federal 501(c)(3) exemption) and classified by the IRS as public charities must file a *California Exempt Organization Annual Information Return*, Form 199. The form is due within four and a half months of the close of their tax year. Some groups are allowed to file Form 199-B. The state exemptions from the filing requirements for this form are similar to the IRS exemptions from filing Form 990.

Even if you are exempt from filing state annual returns, you may have to file an annual statement giving the name and address of your corporation, its major activities, its sources of income, and the section of the Internal Revenue Code under which you are exempt (plus, in some cases, information concerning gross receipts and assets). Check the instructions to Form 199 for further information on these rules.

If you've made a political expenditures election with the state (by submitting a copy of your federal 5768 election form to the Franchise Tax Board within the year), attach Form FTB-3509, *Political or Legislative Activities by Section 23701(d) Organizations*, to your 199 or 199-B annual state return.

There are penalties for not filing Form 199 on time. A failure to file Form 199 or 199-B can result in a suspension of corporate rights, powers, and privileges; or a revocation of the corporation's state tax exemption.

Private Foundations: Annual Exempt Organization Return

California corporations exempt under Section 23701(d) of the Revenue and Taxation Code and classified as private foundations must file Form 199. Private foundations must provide some additional information not required of public charities that file the same form. Instead of filling out Part II of this form, you can (and should, to avoid extra paperwork) provide a copy of your annual report to the attorney general (Form RRF-1—see "Attorney General Annual Periodic Report," below), or furnish a copy of IRS Form 990-PF and its schedules instead (see "Groups Exempt From Filing Form 990," above).

Unrelated Business Income Tax Return and Quarterly Estimated Tax Payments

All corporations that are exempt from state corporate franchise taxes under Section 23701(d) (except those formed to carry out a state function) must file an annual *Exempt Organization Business Income Tax Return*, Form 109, if their gross income during the year from an unrelated trade or business is $1,000 or more. They'll pay an 8.84% state tax (the normal corporate tax rate) on their taxable unrelated business income.

This return must be filed within four and a half months of the end of the tax year. Paying the tax, unlike paying the federal unrelated business income tax, is done periodically during the year for which the tax is due, by estimating your expected income from unrelated trade or business activities during the current year.

Twenty-five percent of the estimated tax must be paid within three and a half months of the beginning of the tax year. The balance of the tax is payable in three equal installments on or before the 15th day of the sixth, ninth, and 12th months of the tax year. If you've underestimated, at the end of the year you'll pay any additional amount with your annual return.

The state doesn't usually send you forms and instructions for paying this tax during your first year. You won't receive it for later years, either, unless a prior annual information return shows that the corporation is likely to have unrelated business income. If the state does send you a form, it will be Form 100-ES.

Form 100-ES is the same form that regular profit corporations use. The normal minimum franchise tax that profit corporations must pay with their first annual estimated tax payment does not apply to tax-exempt nonprofits. Nonprofits pay a simple 8.84% rate on their estimated taxable unrelated business income. Because you must make estimated unrelated business tax payments if this tax applies to you (whether or not the Franchise Tax Board sends you the forms), make sure you pay attention to this often overlooked aspect of nonprofit corporate taxation. Penalties apply to underpayment of this estimated tax and to late filing of the return referred to above.

Attorney General Annual Periodic Report

Subject to a few exceptions, 501(c)(3) and 23701(d) tax-exempt public benefit nonprofit corporations must file an annual report with the California Attorney General (Form RRF-1). However, religious organizations, nonprofit schools, and hospitals are exempt from the annual RRF-1 filing requirement (see the instructions to the RRF-1 form, included on the CD-ROM as noted below). The attorney general should mail the Form RRF-1 to you, along with a Form 990. Groups with total assets or gross receipts over $25,000 must also file a federal 990 or 990-PF annually with the attorney general (with the required schedules and attachments). Failure to make these required annual filings on time can result in late filing penalties. Groups with total assets or gross receipts of $100,000 or more must pay a Form RRF-1 filing fee of $25.

CD-ROM

The RRF-1 Form and instructions are included on the CD-ROM in the following files:

- *Registration/Renewal Fee Report to the Attorney General of California*
- *Instructions for Filing Form RRF-1.*

Be sure to check that these are the most current forms. Go to the Attorney General's website at http://ag.ca.gov and type "RRF-1" in the search box.

Public Benefit Corporations' Annual Corporate Report

Nonmembership public benefit corporations must furnish all directors with an annual report containing financial information, including a statement of assets, liabilities, receipts, and expenditures. The report is due within 120 days after the close of the fiscal year. (See Article 7, Section 6, of the public benefit corporation bylaws.) Membership public benefit corporations must also submit this annual report within the same time period to any member who requests it. The annual report (or a separate statement sent to all directors and members) must also disclose the details of certain indemnification or self-dealing transactions (see "Directors" in Chapter 2, and Article 7, Section 7, of the public benefit corporation bylaws).

It should not be very difficult to compile the financial information required for this annual report. The corporation will have already prepared most of the information needed in order to comply with the state and federal annual tax return requirements discussed above. Keep in mind that this annual report to insiders must be furnished within approximately four months—120 days—after the close of the fiscal year. This is a little sooner than most of the annual state and federal tax returns, which must be submitted within four and one-half months of the close of the tax year.

Federal and State Corporate Employment Taxes

You must pay employment taxes on behalf of the people who work for your nonprofit corporation. Directors, with certain exceptions, are not considered employees if they are paid only for attending board meetings. However, if they are paid for other services or are salaried employees of the corporation, they will be considered employees whose wages are subject to the employment taxes. Nonprofit tax-exempt corporations are often exempt from having to pay certain employment taxes for their employees (for example, federal unemployment insurance).

Independent contractors (such as consultants) who are not subject to the full control of the corporation (for example, how the work is to be performed) are generally not considered employees. Wages paid to these outsiders are not subject to the employment taxes discussed below.

Of course, it goes without saying that corporate directors, officers, and other compensated corporate personnel must report employment compensation on their individual annual federal and state income tax returns (IRS Form 1040; California Form 540).

In addition to reading this material, we recommend you get the publications listed in "More Information on Taxes," above. This will give you more detailed and the most current information to help you compute your withholding and employer contribution payments. Also, check with the IRS and your local state employment tax district office if you need more information.

CAUTION

Be careful when classifying people as independent contractors. The law in this area is fuzzy, and the IRS (as well as the California Employment Development Department, which oversees state unemployment taxes) is obstinate about trying to prove that outsiders really work for the corporation (and must be covered by payroll taxes). For more information, see IRS Publication 937. An excellent legal guide to the ins and outs of independent contractor status is *Working for Yourself: Law & Taxes for Contractors, Freelancers & Consultants*, by Stephen Fishman (Nolo).

Federal Employment Taxes and Forms

This section summarizes the federal payroll tax paperwork and payment obligations that will apply to your 501(c)(3) nonprofit. It's not meant to give you all the details, just a heads-up so you can go online and figure out more for yourself. (See the online payroll tax resources listed above in "More Information on Taxes.")

Employee's Withholding Certificate

Each employee of the corporation must fill out and give the corporation an *Employee's Withholding Allowance Certificate* (IRS Form W-4), on or before commencing employment. This form indicates the marital status and number of allowances claimed by the employee, and is used in determining the amount of income taxes withheld from the employee's wages.

Income Tax Withholding

The corporation must withhold federal income tax from wages paid to employees based upon the wage level, marital status, and number of allowances claimed on the employee's W-4. These, as well as other employment taxes, are withheld and reported on a calendar year basis (January 1 to December 30), regardless of the tax year of the corporation. You'll submit returns on a quarterly basis and deposit withheld tax in an authorized bank on a quarterly (or more frequent) basis; or you can pay with the quarterly return—see IRS Publication 15.

Social Security Tax Withholding

Employees who work in a 501(c)(3) nonprofit corporation are subject to Social Security (FICA) tax withholding. Employers withhold FICA taxes from the employee's wages, and must match the tax, too. The combined amount is reported quarterly and paid either with the quarterly return or deposited in an authorized bank. See the next section below and IRS Publication 15 for specifics.

Quarterly Withholding Returns and Deposits

On or before the last day of the month immediately following the end of each calendar quarter, the corporation must file an *Employer's Quarterly Federal Tax Return*, Form 941. This is a consolidated return, including both withheld income taxes and Social Security taxes, and has specific payment and deposit rules.

Deposits of income and Social Security taxes must be made on a quarterly, monthly,

or more frequent basis. You will want to pay careful attention to withholding, depositing, paying, and reporting these taxes to avoid costly penalties. Again, consult IRS Publication 15 for details.

Federal Unemployment Tax

Your 501(c)(3) tax-exempt nonprofit corporation should be exempt from federal unemployment (FUTA) taxes. Your federal exemption letter should tell you that you are exempt from these taxes.

Annual Wage and Tax Statement

Your nonprofit corporation must furnish two copies of the *Wage and Tax Statement* (IRS Form W-2) to each employee from whom income tax has been withheld (or would have been withheld if the employee had claimed no more than one withholding allowance on his W-4). This form must show total wages paid and amounts deducted for income and Social Security taxes. A special six-part W-2 should be used in California to show state income tax and disability insurance contributions, in addition to the required federal withholding information. Give W-2s to employees no later than January 21.

The corporation must submit each employee's previous year's W-2 form and an annual *Transmittal of Income and Tax Statement* (Form W-3) to the Social Security Administration on or before the last day of February.

State Employment Taxes and Forms

This section summarizes the state payroll tax requirements that will apply to your 501(c)(3) nonprofit. Again, see "More Information on Taxes," above, to obtain more information online and forms.

Employer Registration Form

Nonprofit corporations with employees must register with the California Employment Development Department within 15 days of becoming subject to either the California Unemployment Insurance Code or to California personal income tax withholding provisions. Because this usually happens once wages in excess of $100 in a calendar quarter are paid, you should register right away if you plan to have any employees. Do this by preparing and submitting *Employer's Registration Form* DE-1, available from the local Employment Tax District offices listed in the state DE-44 publication. If you plan to apply for a sales tax permit, your permit application can also serve as your employer registration form.

Personal Income Tax Withholding

The corporation must withhold California personal income taxes from employees' wages according to the tax tables in Publication DE-44. The tables take into account the marital status, claimed allowances, and wage level of the employee. These tables automatically allow for applicable exemptions and the state's standard deduction.

California Unemployment and Disability Insurance

Most nonprofit 501(c)(3) tax-exempt corporations are subject to California unemployment and disability insurance tax contributions and withholding. Certain churches or religious nonprofit corporations and schools that are a part of a church or religious nonprofit corporation are not subject to unemployment and disability insurance taxes. Rates change constantly. For further information, consult the DE-44 publication listed in "More Information on Taxes," above. If you have any questions, call your local employment tax office.

Also, certain types of services performed for 501(c)(3) tax-exempt nonprofit groups are not subject to state unemployment and disability coverage unless elected (the criterion here is the type of services, not the type of nonprofit). The California Employment Development Department should mail Form DE-1-NP, which lists these excluded services and allows you to elect coverage for any which apply to you.

California unemployment insurance can be paid by 501(c)(3) groups in one of two ways: (1) the regular contribution rate method, or (2) a prorated cost of benefits paid. Form DE-1-NP, referred to above, allows you to select which payment method you want to use.

Under the regular contribution rate method, unemployment insurance contributions are paid by the corporation at its "employer contribution rate" shown on the *Quarterly Withholding Return* (DE-3) discussed below.

Under the prorated cost of benefits method, the corporation pays the actual amount of unemployment benefits received by ex-employees who receive such benefits, to the extent that such benefits are attributable to base period wages paid by the corporation to the ex-employee. Ask the local employment tax office for Form DE-1378-F, which contains examples of your potential liability under this method.

Disability insurance contributions are paid by the employee and withheld, reported, and submitted to the state by the corporation. Again, rates change—check your DE-44 pamphlet.

Withholding Returns

A corporation is required in most cases to file monthly returns with the state, reporting and paying personal income tax withholding and disability and unemployment tax contributions for each employee.

The corporation must file a quarterly return, reporting the employment taxes mentioned above for the previous quarter and pay any balance not already paid with monthly returns. For specifics, consult the DE-44 pamphlet.

> **CAUTION**
>
> **Officers can be personally liable.** Under Section 1735 of the California Unemployment Insurance Code, officers and other persons in charge of corporate affairs are personally liable for taxes, interest, and penalties owed by the corporation.

Annual Wage and Tax Statement

The corporation should prepare a six-part combined federal/state *Wage and Tax Statement*, IRS Form W-2. This form indicates total annual state personal income tax and state disability insurance withholding. Copies of this form should be provided to the employee.

Annual Reconciliation of Income Tax Withholding Form

The corporation must prepare and file a completed *Reconciliation of Income Tax Withheld*, Form DE-43, with the Employment Development Department annually, before February 28, attaching one copy of each employee's W-2 and a totaled listing of the California personal income tax amounts withheld as shown on the attached W-2s.

Sales Tax Forms and Exemption From Sales Tax

Many nonprofits sell goods to the public and therefore are subject to collecting, depositing, and reporting sales tax. We cover some of the basic rules and exceptions in this section. For more information on the sales tax and forms, go online to the main sales tax page on the State Board of Equalization's website.

Sales Tax

Subject to a few exceptions, as noted in "Exempt Transactions" below, every nonprofit corporation that has gross receipts from the sale of tangible personal property in California (for example, merchandise sold to customers) must apply for a sales tax seller's permit. You can file the application (Form BT-400) with the nearest office of the California Board of Equalization. Even groups exempt from collecting sales tax, as described below, must obtain a seller's permit. This application can also serve as an employer registration form with the Employment Development Department.

There's no fee for applying for or obtaining a sales tax (seller's) permit. Some applicants, however, may be required to post a bond or other security for payment of future sales taxes. A separate permit is required for each place of business at which transactions relating to sales tax are customarily entered into with customers. Sales tax is added to the price of certain goods and is collected from the purchaser.

Wholesalers, as well as retailers, must obtain a permit. A wholesaler, however, is not required to collect sales tax from a retailer who holds a valid seller's permit and who buys items for resale to customers, provided a resale certificate is completed in connection with the transaction.

> **EXAMPLE:**
>
> If your nonprofit sells supplies to another nonprofit with its own seller's permit, you are exempt from collecting sales tax on the transaction—the nonprofit buyer will collect the sales tax on the supplies when it sells them to the public.

Sellers must file periodic sales and use tax returns, reporting and paying sales tax collected from customers. A seller must keep complete records of all business transactions, including sales, purchases, and other expenditures; and have them available for inspection by the Board of Equalization at any time.

Exempt Transactions

Certain transactions entered into by any kind of organization (profit or nonprofit) are not subject to the collection of sales tax. Examples are sales of personal property shipped out of state, certain sales incidental to the performance of services, and purchases of art that will be loaned by certain nonprofits. Call a Board of Equalization office for further information.

Groups Exempt From Collecting and Submitting Sales Tax

A few tax-exempt nonprofit corporations are exempt from collecting sales tax and preparing the quarterly report. To be eligible for the exemption, a nonprofit corporation must meet all of the following stringent requirements:

- The organization must be formed and operated for charitable purposes, and must qualify for the welfare exemption from property taxation provided by Section 214 of the California Revenue and Taxation Code. If the corporation owns the retail location, it must have obtained the welfare exemption for the real property at this location. If it leases the premises, it must have obtained the welfare exemption on the personal property (such as inventory and furnishings) at this location.

- The organization must be engaged in the relief of poverty and distress and the sales must be made principally as a matter of assistance to purchasers in a distressed financial condition. These conditions are fulfilled if the corporation sells its goods at reduced prices so as "to be of real assistance to purchasers." Incidental sales to persons other than low income consumers will not prevent the organization from obtaining the sales tax exemption.

- The property sold must have been made, prepared, assembled, or manufactured by the organization. This condition will be satisfied when the property is picked up at various locations and assembled at one or more locations for purposes of sale, even though nothing other than assembling needs to be done to place it in salable condition. Property is considered prepared when it is made ready for sale by such processes as cleaning, repairing, or reconditioning.

A nonprofit corporation seeking to obtain this exemption from sales tax collection and reporting must, as we've said, still apply for a seller's permit by filing Form BT-400, attaching to it a *Certificate of Exemption—Charitable Organizations*, Form BT-719, also available at the nearest board of equalization office. Applicants should also request an information sheet relating to the exemption, Form BT-719-A.

Other sales tax exemptions exist for special nonprofit groups (for example, certain nonprofit cooperative nursery schools are exempt).

Licenses and Permits

Many businesses, whether operating as profit or nonprofit corporations, partnerships, limited liability companies, or sole proprietorships, must obtain state licenses and permits before commencing business. While you may not be subject to the usual kind of red tape applicable to strictly profit-making enterprises (for example, contractors and real estate brokers), you should check with your local department of consumer affairs office for information concerning any state licensing requirements for your activities or type of organization. If one of the boards does not regulate your activities, they may be able to refer you to the particular state agency that oversees your operations.

Many nonprofit institutions (for example, schools or hospitals) will, of course, need to comply with a number of registration and reporting requirements administered by the state and, possibly, the federal government. A local business license or permit may also be required for your activities. Check with your city business license department.

Newly incorporated groups that have held licenses or permits for previous activities or operations should check to see if special corporate licensing requirements apply to their activities. In some cases, a separate corporate license must be taken out in the corporate name; in others a corporate license must be obtained in the name of supervisory corporate personnel.

You should also check to see if the city and county where your principal place of business is located (and other places where you plan to conduct activities) require you to obtain a permit for soliciting funds for charitable purposes. Many cities and counties have enacted permit (or other) requirements of this type.

RESOURCE

The California License Handbook, published by the California Trade and Commerce Agency, is a comprehensive guide to California license requirements, as well as a thorough sourcebook on California's regulatory agencies and the red tape involved in doing business in California. Call the department in Sacramento to obtain ordering information or download it from the Trade and Commerce Agency's website at http://commerce. ca.gov/state/ttca/ttca_homepage.jsp. Click Permits & Licenses; the page that opens lists various resources for learning more about permits and licenses, including a link to view and download the *License Handbook*.

Workers' Compensation

With some exceptions, employees of a nonprofit corporation, whether officers or otherwise, must be covered by workers' compensation insurance. Rates vary depending on the salary level and risk associated with an employee's job. If directors are paid only for travel expenses for attending meetings, they may be exempt from coverage (although flat per-meeting payments will generally make them subject to coverage). This is a blurry area, so check with your insurance agent or broker (or your local State Compensation Insurance Commission) for names of carriers, rates, and the extent of required coverage.

For online information, go to the California Department of Insurance website at www. insurance.ca.gov and click the link for Workers' Compensation Information or enter "Workers' Compensation" in the search box to find the link.

Private Insurance Coverage

Nonprofit corporations, like other organizations, should carry the usual kinds of commercial insurance to help protect against losses in the event of an accident, fire, theft, and so on. Remember, although being incorporated can help insulate directors, officers, and others from personal liability and loss, it won't protect against losses to corporate assets. Look into coverage for general liability, product liability, and fire and theft. You should also consider liability insurance for directors and officers, particularly if your nonprofit corporation wants to reassure any passive directors that they will be protected from personal liability in the event of a lawsuit (see "Directors" in Chapter 2). To take advantage of California's volunteer director and officer immunity provisions, adequate director and officer liability insurance must be obtained (or be proven to be unobtainable)— see "Directors" in Chapter 2.

Dissolving a Nonprofit Corporation

We'll end our discussion of the housekeeping details affecting California nonprofit corporations with a short summary of the Nonprofit Corporation Law provisions related to dissolving (ending) the corporation. The primary point to keep in mind here is that a California nonprofit corporation may be dissolved by mutual consent (in a voluntary dissolution) with a minimum of formality. The forms and instructions you'll need to dissolve a nonprofit voluntarily are available online from the Secretary of State's Business Programs Division website. Go to www.ss.ca.gov/business/bpd_forms.htm. Then click the "Corporations" link to locate and download *Certificate of Election to Wind Up and Dissolve* and *Certificate of Dissolution* forms for nonprofit corporations.

Don't let our discussion of dissolution, court filings, and attorney general supervision scare you into thinking that this will be your fate. In fact, the great majority of small, sensibly run nonprofit corporations will never face any

major problems. Of course, you should use good judgment as to when and why to pay a financial or legal advisor to answer important questions related to your individual problems. The fact that you can competently do many things on your own doesn't mean that you will never need to see an accountant or lawyer.

Voluntary Dissolution

Any nonprofit corporation may, on its own and out of court, decide to voluntarily wind up and dissolve, for any reason. In a nonmembership corporation, you'll need the board's approval; in a membership corporation, the approval of a majority of the members is needed.

The board of directors of a public benefit corporation may elect to dissolve the corporation, without membership approval, if any of the following conditions apply (the rules are essentially the same for religious corporations):

- the corporation has no members
- the corporation has not commenced business and has not issued any memberships
- the corporation has been adjudged bankrupt
- the corporation has disposed of all its assets and hasn't conducted any activity for the past five years, or
- a subsidiary corporation must dissolve because its charter from a head organization has been revoked.

Occasionally, the court will supervise a corporation's voluntary dissolution. This can happen upon the request of the corporation itself, or by request of 5% or more of the members or three or more creditors.

Involuntary Dissolution

An involuntary dissolution is one that happens in court against the wishes of the nonprofit board. One-third of the membership votes of a nonprofit corporation, one-half of the directors, or the attorney general can force a dissolution as explained below. The attorney general can also trigger a dissolution for the separate reasons discussed below. The petition for dissolution must be filed in the superior court of the county of the corporation's principal office.

Dissolution Triggered by Directors, Members, or Attorney General

One-third of the members, one-half of the directors, or the attorney general can force an involuntary dissolution by filing a court petition based on one or more of the following grounds:

- The nonprofit corporation has abandoned its activities for more than one year.

- The nonprofit corporation has an even number of directors who are equally divided and cannot agree to the management of its affairs, so that the corporation's business cannot be conducted to advantage, or so that there is danger that its property and business (exempt-purpose activities) will be impaired and lost, and the members are so divided into factions that they cannot elect an odd-numbered board.

- The members have been unable, at two consecutive meetings (or in two written ballots), where full voting power has been exercised, or during a four-year period, whichever period is shorter, to elect successors to directors whose term has expired or would have expired upon election of their successors.

- There is internal dissension and two or more factions of members are so deadlocked that the corporation's activities can no longer be conducted to advantage.

- Those in control of the nonprofit corporation (the directors) have been guilty of or knowingly allowed persistent and pervasive fraud, mismanagement, or abuse of authority, or the corporation's property is being misapplied or wasted by its directors or officers.

- Liquidation is reasonably necessary because the corporation is failing and has continuously failed to carry out its purposes.

- The limited period (if this applies) for which the corporation was formed has terminated without extension of such period (one member alone can file a court petition for involuntary dissolution on this basis).

- In the case of a subordinate corporation created under the authority of a head organization, the articles of incorporation of the subordinate corporation require it to dissolve because its charter has been surrendered to, taken away, or revoked by the head organization.

Additional Grounds for Dissolution in Actions Brought by Attorney General

In addition to the grounds mentioned above, the attorney general can bring an action for involuntary dissolution of the corporation based on its own information or upon another party's complaint, for any of the following reasons:

- The corporation has seriously violated any provision of the statutes regulating corporations or charitable organizations.

- The corporation has fraudulently abused or usurped corporate privileges or powers.

- The corporation has, by action or default, violated any provision of law that authorizes the forfeiture of corporate existence for noncompliance.

- The corporation has failed for five years to pay to the California Franchise Tax Board any tax for which it is liable.

In certain situations, the corporation may take corrective action to avoid a dissolution initiated by the attorney general.

Religious Corporations

The California Nonprofit Corporation Law doesn't directly provide for the involuntary winding up of a religious corporation. However, the attorney general may go to court and, following Section 9230 of the Religious Corporation Law and the procedures of Section 803 of the Code of Civil Procedure, ask a judge to rule on whether the corporation is properly qualified or classified as a religious corporation. If the judge decides that the corporation is improperly qualified, the attorney general can ask the Franchise Tax Board and IRS to revoke the corporation's religious tax exemptions.

Winding Up Corporate Business and Distribution of Assets

Once a voluntary or involuntary dissolution process begins (by vote of the board and/or members to start a voluntary winding up or upon the filing of an involuntary dissolution court petition), the corporation must stop doing business, except to the extent necessary to wind up its affairs pending a distribution of its assets. All corporate debts and liabilities must be paid or provided for (to the extent that corporate assets can do so). If any corporate assets remain after paying corporate debts, a 501(c)(3) tax-exempt nonprofit corporation must distribute them to another 501(c)(3) group.

If the corporation has obtained personal and real property tax exemptions by complying with Section 214 of the California Revenue and Taxation Code, it must distribute any remaining tax-exempt property to the particular type of 501(c)(3) group specified in the "irrevocable dedication" clause of its articles.

If your involuntary or voluntary dissolution is subject to superior court supervision, you'll have to publish a notice to creditors of the corporation (a standard formality handled by newspapers that publish legal notices). Creditors who don't file claims within a specified period of time after you've published your notice will be barred from participating in any distribution of the corporation's assets.

Lawyers, Legal Research, and Accountants

While we believe you can take care of the bulk of the work required to organize and operate your nonprofit corporation, you may need to consult a lawyer or accountant on complicated or special issues. It also makes sense to have a lawyer or accountant experienced in forming nonprofits and preparing tax exemption applications look over your papers. Reviewing your incorporation papers with an attorney or accountant is a sensible way to ensure that all of your papers are up to date and meet your needs. Besides, making contact with a legal and tax person early in your corporate life is often a sensible step. As your group grows and its programs expand, you'll be able to consult these professionals for help with ongoing legal and tax questions.

The professionals you contact should have experience in nonprofit incorporations and tax exemption applications. They should also be prepared to help you help yourself—to answer your questions and review, not rewrite, the forms you have prepared.

The next sections provide a few general suggestions on how to find the right lawyer or tax adviser and, if you wish to do your own legal research, how to find the law.

Lawyers

Finding the right lawyer is not always easy. Obviously, the best lawyer to choose is someone you personally know and trust, who has lots of experience advising smaller nonprofits. Of course, this may be a tall order. The next best is a nonprofit advisor whom a friend, another nonprofit incorporator, or someone in your nonprofit network recommends. A local nonprofit resource center, for example, may be able to steer you to one or more lawyers who maintain active nonprofit practices. With patience and persistence (and enough phone calls), this second word-of-mouth approach almost always brings positive results.

Another approach is to locate a local non-profit legal referral panel. Local bar associations or another nonprofit organization typically run panels of this sort. A referral panel in your area may be able to give you the names of lawyers who are experienced in nonprofit law and practice and who offer a discount or free consultation as part of the referral panel program. Ask about (and try to avoid) referral services that are operated on a strict rotating basis. With this system, you'll get the name of the next lawyer on the list, not necessarily one with nonprofit experience.

You can also try the lawyer directory at www .nolo.com. The directory is new but lawyers are being added regularly, so check whether your local area is included. You can search lawyers by practice area.

When you call a prospective lawyer, speak with the lawyer personally, not just the reception desk. You can probably get a good idea of how the person operates by paying close attention to the way your call is handled. Is the lawyer available, or is your call returned promptly? Is the lawyer willing to spend at least a few minutes talking to you to determine if she is really the best person for the job? Does the lawyer seem sympathetic to, and compatible with, the nonprofit goals of your group? Do you get a good personal feeling from your conversation? Oh, and one more thing: Be sure to get the hourly rate the lawyer will charge set in advance. If you are using this book, you will probably want to eliminate lawyers who charge $200 per hour to support an office on top of the tallest building in town.

What About Low-Cost Law Clinics?

Law clinics advertise their services regularly on TV and radio. Can they help you form a nonprofit organization? Perhaps, but usually at a rate well above their initial low consultation rate. Because the lawyer turnover rate at these clinics is high and the degree of familiarity with nonprofit legal and tax issues is usually low, we recommend you spend your money more wisely by finding a reasonably priced nonprofit lawyer elsewhere.

Legal Research

Many incorporators may want to research legal information on their own. You can browse the nonprofit laws online (go to www.leginfo.ca.gov /calaw.html; check the Corporations Code box; click the search button at the bottom of the page; then scroll down to the section you want to view). Most county law libraries are open to the public (you need not be a lawyer to use them) and are not difficult to use once you understand how the information is categorized and stored. They are an invaluable source of corporate and general business forms, federal and state corporate tax procedures, and information. Research librarians will usually go out of their way to help you find the right statute, form, or background reading on any corporate or tax issue.

Finding the Law You Need

Whether you are leafing through your own copy of the nonprofit corporation law or browsing corporate statutes online or at your local county law library, finding a particular corporate provision is usually a straightforward process. First define and, if necessary, narrow down the subject matter of your search to essential key words associated with your area of interest. For example, if one of the directors on your board resigns and you want to determine whether there are any statutory rules for filling vacancies on the board, you will define and restrict your search to the key areas of "directors" and "resignation" or "vacancies."

The laws governing nonprofits in California (the Nonprofit Corporation Law) are contained in Division 2 of the California Corporations Code. If you want information on filling a director vacancy in your nonprofit (a public benefit corporation), you would start with the Nonprofit Corporation Law. There is a section in the Nonprofit Corporation Law (Part 2) that covers nonprofit public benefit corporations. One of the topics in the public benefit corporations section is "Directors and Management." Within that section, there is a subsection for "Selection, Removal and Resignation of Directors," followed by a range of code sections devoted to this subject area. If you read through those code sections, you would find the information you were looking for.

Another search strategy is to simply start at the beginning of the Nonprofit Corporations Law and leaf through all the major and minor headings. Eventually—usually after just a few minutes or so—you will hit upon your area of interest or will satisfy yourself that the area in question is not covered by the corporate statutes. By the way, after going through the nonprofit law this way once or twice, you should become acquainted with most of its major headings. This will help you locate specific nonprofit subject areas and statutes quickly when searching this material in the future.

Legal Shorthand and Definitions

Many rules in the corporate statutes are given in legal shorthand—short catchwords and phrases that are defined elsewhere in the code. For example, a common requirement in corporate statutes is that a matter or transaction be "approved by the board" or "approved by a majority of the board." But what do these phrases mean—how much approval is enough? An alphabetical listing of definitions that apply to California nonprofit corporations is contained in California Corporations Code §§ 5030–5080. Read this definition section before you go on to search for a particular rule, so that you'll understand any legal shorthand you might encounter. (By the way, the first phrase usually means approval by a majority of directors present at a meeting at which a quorum of directors is present; the second usually means approval by a majority of the full board.)

Annotated Codes

When you look up a nonprofit statute, whether online or in a book, you might want to use an annotated version of the codes. Annotated codes include not only the text of the statutes themselves, but also brief summaries of court cases that discuss each statute. After you find a relevant statute, you may want to scan these case summaries—and perhaps even read some of the cases—to get an idea of how courts have interpreted the language of the statute.

RESOURCE

If you are interested in doing your own legal research, an excellent source of information is *Legal Research: How to Find & Understand the Law*, by Stephen Elias and Susan Levinkind (Nolo). To browse the California Corporations Code, go to www.leginfo.ca.gov. Then check the "Corporations Code" box and click /calaw.html. You'll see the list of linked headings to the California Nonprofit Statutes, starting at Section 5002.

Accountants and Tax Advice

As you already know, organizing and operating a nonprofit corporation involves a significant amount of financial and tax work. While much of it is easy, some of it requires a nit-picking attention to definitions, cross-references, formulas, and other elusive or downright boring details, particularly when preparing your federal 1023 tax exemption application. As we often suggest in the book, you may find it sensible to seek advice or help from an accountant or other tax advisor when organizing your nonprofit corporation.

For example, you may need help preparing the income statements, balance sheets, and other financial and tax information submitted with your IRS tax exemption application. Also, if your organization will handle any significant amount of money, you will need an accountant or bookkeeper to set up your double-entry accounting books (cash receipts and disbursement journals, general ledger, and so on). Double-entry accounting techniques are particularly important to nonprofits that receive federal or private grant or program funds—accounting for these "restricted funds" usually requires the assistance of a professional.

Nonprofit corporation account books should be designed to allow for easy transfer of financial data to state and federal nonprofit corporate tax returns and disclosure statements. It should be easy to use the books to determine, at any time, whether receipts and expenditures fall into the categories proper for maintaining your 501(c)(3) tax exemption, public charity status, and grant or program eligibility. You will also want to know whether your operations are likely to subject you to an unrelated business income tax under federal and state rules.

Once your corporation is organized and your books are set up, corporate personnel with experience in bookkeeping and nonprofit tax matters can do the ongoing work of keeping the books and filing tax forms. Whatever your arrangement, make sure to at least obtain the tax publications listed in "More Information on Taxes" in Chapter 11. These pamphlets contain essential information on preparing and filing IRS corporation and employment tax returns.

When you select an accountant or book-keeper, the same considerations apply as when selecting a lawyer. Choose someone you know or whom a friend or nonprofit contact recommends. Be as specific as you can regarding the services you want performed. Make sure the advisor has had experience with nonprofit taxation and tax exemption applications, as well as regular payroll, tax, and accounting procedures. Many nonprofit bookkeepers work part-time for several nonprofit organizations. Again, calling people in your nonprofit network is often the best way to find this type of person.

How to Use the CD-ROM

The tear-out forms in Appendix B are included on a CD-ROM in the back of the book. This CD-ROM, which can be used with Windows computers, installs files that you use with software programs that are already installed on your computer. It is *not* a stand-alone software program. Please read this appendix and the README.TXT file included on the CD-ROM for instructions on using the Forms CD.

Note to Mac users: This CD-ROM and its files should also work on Macintosh computers. Please note, however, that Nolo cannot provide technical support for non-Windows users.

How to View the README File

If you do not know how to view the file README.TXT, insert the Forms CD-ROM into your computer's CD-ROM drive and follow these instructions:

- **Windows 2000, XP, and Vista:** (1) On your PC's desktop, double click the My Computer icon; (2) double click the icon for the CD-ROM drive into which the Forms CD-ROM was inserted; (3) double click the file README.TXT.

- **Macintosh:** (1) On your Mac desktop, double click the icon for the CD-ROM that you inserted; (2) double click on the file README.TXT.

While the README file is open, print it out by using the Print command in the File menu.

Installing the Form Files Onto Your Computer

Before you can do anything with the files on the CD-ROM, you need to install them onto your hard disk. In accordance with U.S. copyright laws, remember that copies of the CD-ROM and its files are for your personal use only.

Insert the Forms CD and do the following:

Windows 2000, XP, and Vista Users

Follow the instructions that appear on the screen. (If nothing happens when you insert the Forms CD-ROM, then (1) double click the My Computer icon; (2) double click the icon for the CD-ROM drive into which the Forms CD-ROM was inserted; and (3) double click the file WELCOME.EXE.)

By default, all the files are installed to the \CA Nonprofit Forms folder in the \Program Files folder of your computer. A folder called "CA Nonprofit Forms" is added to the "Programs" folder of the Start menu.

Macintosh Users

Step 1: If the "CA Nonprofit Forms CD" window is not open, open it by double clicking the "CA Nonprofit Forms CD" icon.

Step 2: Select the "CA Nonprofit Forms" folder icon.

Step 3: Drag and drop the folder icon onto the icon of your hard disk.

Using the Word Processing Files to Create Documents

This section concerns the files for forms that can be opened and edited with your word processing program.

All word processing forms come in rich text format. These files have the extension ".RTF." For example, the form for the Bill of Sale for Assets discussed in Chapter 10 is on the file BILLSALE.RTF. All forms, their file names, and file formats are listed at the end of this appendix.

RTF files can be read by most recent word processing programs including all versions of MS Word for Windows and Macintosh, WordPad for Windows, and recent versions of WordPerfect for Windows and Macintosh.

To use a form from the CD to create your documents you must: (1) open a file in your word processor or text editor; (2) edit the form by filling in the required information; (3) print it out; and (4) rename and save your revised file.

The following are general instructions. However, each word processor uses different commands to open, format, save, and print documents. Please read your word processor's manual for specific instructions on performing these tasks.

Do not call Nolo's technical support if you have questions on how to use your word processor or your computer.

Step 1: Opening a File

There are three ways to open the word processing files included on the CD-ROM after you have installed them onto your computer.

- Windows users can open a file by selecting its "shortcut" as follows: (1) Click the Windows "Start" button; (2) open the "Programs" folder; (3) open the "Corporate Records Forms" subfolder; (4) open the "RTF" subfolder; and (5) click on the shortcut to the form you want to work with.

- Both Windows and Macintosh users can open a file directly by double clicking on it. Use My Computer or Windows Explorer (Windows 2000, XP, or Vista) or the Finder (Macintosh) to go to the folder you installed or copied the CD-ROM's files to.

Then, double click on the specific file you want to open.

- You can also open a file from within your word processor. To do this, you must first start your word processor. Then, go to the File menu and choose the Open command. This opens a dialog box where you will tell the program (1) the type of file you want to open (*.RTF); and (2) the location and name of the file (you will need to navigate through the directory tree to get to the folder on your hard disk where the CD's files have been installed).

Where Are the Files Installed?

Windows Users

- RTF files are installed by default to a folder named \CA Nonprofit Forms\RTF in the \Program Files folder of your computer.

Macintosh Users

- RTF files are located in the "RTF" folder within the "CA Nonprofit Forms" folder.

Step 2: Editing Your Document

Fill in the appropriate information according to the instructions and sample agreements in the book. Underlines are used to indicate where you need to enter your information, frequently followed by instructions in brackets. Be sure to delete the underlines and instructions from your edited document. You will also want to make sure that any signature lines in your completed documents appear on a page with at least some text from the document itself.

Editing Forms That Have Optional or Alternative Text

Some of the forms have optional or alternate text:

- With optional text, you choose whether to include or exclude the given text.
- With alternative text, you select one alternative to include and exclude the other alternatives.

When editing these forms, we suggest you do the following:

Optional text

If you don't want to include optional text, just delete it from your document.

If you do want to include optional text, just leave it in your document.

In either case, delete the italicized instructions.

Alternative text

First delete all the alternatives that you do not want to include, then delete the italicized instructions.

Step 3: Printing Out the Document

Use your word processor's or text editor's "Print" command to print out your document.

Step 4: Saving Your Document

After filling in the form, use the "Save As" command to save and rename the file. Because all the files are "read-only," you will not be able to use the "Save" command. This is for your protection. *If you save the file without renaming it, the underlines that indicate where you need to enter your information will be lost, and you will not be able to create a new document with this file without recopying the original file from the CD-ROM.*

Using Government Forms

Electronic copies of useful government forms are included on the CD-ROM in Adobe Acrobat PDF format. You must have the Adobe Reader installed on your computer to use these forms. Adobe Reader is available for all types of Windows and Macintosh systems. If you don't already have this software, you can download it for free at www.adobe.com.

All forms, their file names, and file formats are listed at the end of this appendix. These form files were created by the government, not by Nolo.

Some of these forms have fill-in text fields. To create your document using these files, you must: (1) open a file; (2) fill in the text fields using either your mouse or the tab key on your keyboard to navigate from field to field; and (3) print it out.

Saving a filled-in form: Newer government forms are enabled with "document rights" that allow you to save your filled-in form to your hard disk. Version 5.1 or later of Adobe Reader is required. When you open these government forms in Reader, you'll see a document rights message box if this feature is available. If you are using an earlier version of Adobe Reader, you will be prompted to download a newer version that will allow you to save. You will *not* be able to save government forms that do not have document rights enabled, but you can still print out completed versions of these forms.

Forms without fill-in text fields cannot be filled out using your computer. To create your document using these files, you must: (1) open the file; (2) print it out; and (3) complete it by hand or typewriter.

Step 1: Opening a Form

PDF files, like the word processing files, can be opened one of three ways.

- Windows users can open a file by selecting its "shortcut" as follows: (1) Click the Windows "Start" button; (2) open the "Programs" folder; (3) open the "CA Nonprofit Forms" subfolder; (4) open the "PDF" folder; and (5) click on the shortcut to the form you want to work with.

- Both Windows and Macintosh users can open a file directly by double clicking on it. Use My Computer or Windows Explorer (Windows 2000, XP, or Vista) or the Finder (Macintosh) to go to the folder you created and copied the CD-ROM's files to. Then, double click on the specific file you want to open.

- You can also open a PDF file from within Adobe Reader. To do this, you must first start Reader. Then, go to the File menu and choose the Open command. This opens a dialog box where you will tell the program the location and name of the file (you will need to navigate through the directory tree to get to the folder on your hard disk where the CD's files have been installed).

Step 2: Filling in a Form

Use your mouse or the Tab key on your keyboard to navigate from field to field within these forms.

- If document rights are enabled, you can save your completed form to disk using Adobe Reader 5.1 or higher.

- If document rights are not enabled, be sure to have all the information you will need to complete a form on hand, because you will not be able to save a copy of the filled-in form to disk. You can, however, print out a completed version.

NOTE: This step is only applicable to forms that have been created with fill-in text fields. Forms without fill-in fields must be completed by hand or typewriter after you have printed them out.

Step 3: Printing a Form

Choose Print from the Acrobat Reader File menu. This will open the Print dialog box. In the "Print Range" section of the Print dialog box, select the appropriate print range, then click OK.

Where Are the PDF Files Installed?

Windows Users

- PDF files are installed by default to a folder named \CA Nonprofit Forms\PDF in the \Program Files folder of your computer.

Macintosh Users

- PDF files are located in the "PDF" folder within the "CA Nonprofit Forms" folder.

List of Files Included on the Forms CD

The following files are in rich text format (RTF):

File Name	Form/Document Title
BILLSALE.RTF	Bill of Sale for Assets
CHECKLST.RTF	Incorporation Checklist
COVERLET.RTF	Cover Letter for Filing Articles
MEMCERT.RTF	Membership Certificate
MINUTES.RTF	Minutes of First Meeting of the Board of Directors
OFFER.RTF	Offer to Transfer Assets
PUBARTS.RTF	Articles for Public Benefit Corporation
PUBBYLAW.RTF	Bylaws for Public Benefit Corporation
PUBMEM.RTF	Membership Bylaw Provisions for Public Benefit Corporation
RELARTS.RTF	Articles of Incorporation for Religious Corporation
RELBYLAW.RTF	Bylaws for Religious Corporation
RELMEM.RTF	Membership Bylaw Provisions for Religious Corporation
UNINC.RTF	Special Article Provisions for an Unincorporated Association
IRS7550.RTF	IRS Revenue Procedure 75-50
IRS4598.RTF	IRC Section 4958, Taxes on excess benefit transactions
IRS4958R.RTF	IRS Regulations Section 53.4598-0, Table of Contents

The following files are in Adobe Acrobat PDF Format (asterisks indicate forms with fill-in text fields):

File Name	Form/Document Title
naavinquiryform.pdf	*Name Availability Inquiry Letter (2005)
naavreservform.pdf	*Name Reservation Request Form (2005)
04_3500bk.pdf	*California Exemption Application (Form 3500) (2006)
f1023.pdf	*Form 1023: Application for Recognition of Exemption (2006)
i1023.pdf	Instructions for Form 1023 (2006)
fss4.pdf	*Form SS-4: Application for Employer Identification Number (2006)
iss4.pdf	Instructions for Form SS-4 (2006)
f5768.pdf	*Form 5768: Election/Revocation To Make Expenditures To Influence Legislature (2004)
p557.pdf	Publication 557: Tax Exempt Status for Your Organization (2005)
p1828.pdf	Publication 1828: Tax Guide for Churches and Religious Organizations (2006)
p4220.pdf	Publication 4220: Applying for 501(c)(3) Tax-Exempt Status (2003)
p4221.pdf	Publication 4221: Compliance Guide for 501(c)(3) Tax-Exempt Organizations (2003)
rrf1_form.pdf	*Form RRF-1: Registration/Renewal Fee Report to Attorney General (2005)
rrf1_instructs.pdf	Instructions for Form RRF-1 (2005)

gfc.pdf	Attorney General's Guide for Charities (2005)
99char.pdf	Guide to Charitable Solicitation 1999
ah267.pdf	Assessors' Handbook Section 267, Welfare, Church, and Religious Exemptions (2004)
eotopicb03.pdf	Public Charity or Private Foundation Status Issues under IRC 509(a)(1)-(4), 4942(j)(3), and 507
eotopicc03.pdf	Disclosure, FOIA and the Privacy Act
topico00.pdf	Update: The Final Regulations on the Disclosure Requirements for Annual Information Returns and Applications for Exemption
eotopich97.pdf	Education, Propaganda, and the Methodology Test
eotopici02.pdf	Election Year Issues
topic-p.pdf	Lobbying Issues
topicn00.pdf	Private School Update
topic-o.pdf	UBIT: Current Developments
eotopice03.pdf	Intermediate Sanctions (IRC 4958) Update

Information and Tear-Out Forms

California Secretary of State Contact Information

*Incorporation Checklist

Special Nonprofit Tax-Exempt Organizations

*Name Availability Inquiry Letter

*Name Reservation Request Form

*California FTB 3500 Exemption Application (2006)

*IRS Package 1023: Application for Recognition of Exemption (6/2006)

*IRS Form SS-4: Application for Employer Identification Number (2/2006)

*IRS Form 5768: Election/Revocation of Election by an Eligible Section 501(c)(3) Organization To Make Expenditures To Influence Legislation (12/2004)

Member Register

Membership Certificates

(* Asterisks indicate forms are also included on the CD-ROM—see Appendix A.)

CALIFORNIA SECRETARY OF STATE CONTACT INFORMATION

Office hours for all locations are Monday through Friday
8:00 a.m. to 5:00 p.m.

Sacramento Office

1500 11th Street
Sacramento, CA 95814
916-657-5448*

- Name Availability Unit
  (*recorded information on how to obtain)
- Document Filing Support Unit
- Legal Review Unit
- Information Retrieval and Certification Unit
- Status
  (*recorded information on how to obtain)
- Statement of Information Unit
  (filings only)
  P.O. Box 944230
  Sacramento, CA 94244-2300
- Substituted Service of Process
  (must be hand delivered to the Sacramento office)

San Francisco Regional Office

455 Golden Gate Avenue, Suite 14500
San Francisco, CA 94102-7007
415-557-8000

Fresno Regional Office

1315 Van Ness Ave., Suite 203
Fresno, CA 93721-1729
559-445-6900

Los Angeles Regional Office

300 South Spring Street, Room 12513
Los Angeles, CA 90013-1233
213-897-3062

San Diego Regional Office

1350 Front Street, Suite 2060
San Diego, CA 92101-3609
619-525-4113

Chapter	Page	New* Groups	Existing* Groups	Optional**	Step Name	My Group	Done
How to Form a Nonprofit Corporation in California **Incorporation Checklist**							
6	105	✓	✓		Choose a Corporate Name		
	117	✓	✓		Prepare Articles of Incorporation		
	127		✓	✓	Prepare Articles for an Unincorporated Association		
	130	✓	✓		Make Copies of Articles		
	133	✓	✓		File Your Articles		
7		✓	✓		Prepare Bylaws		
8		✓	✓		Prepare State Tax Exemption Application		
9		✓	✓		Prepare and File Your Federal Tax Exemption Application		
10	252	✓	✓		Mail IRS Letter to Franchise Tax Board		
	252	✓	✓		Set Up a Corporate Records Book		
	253		✓	✓	Prepare Offer to Transfer Assets		
	259		✓		Prepare Minutes of First Board Meeting		
	268	✓	✓		Place Minutes and Attachments in Corporate Records Book		
	268		✓	✓	Comply with Bulk Sales Law		
	269		✓	✓	Prepare Bill of Sale for Assets		
	271		✓	✓	Prepare Assignments of Leases and Deeds		
	271		✓	✓	File Final Papers for Prior Organization		
	271		✓	✓	Notify Others of Your Incorporation		
	272	✓	✓	✓	Apply for Nonprofit Mailing Permit		
	272	✓	✓	✓	Apply for Property Tax Exemption		
	274	✓	✓		File Domestic Corporation Statement		
	275	✓	✓	✓	Register with Attorney General (Public Benefit Corps.)		
	276	✓	✓	✓	Issue Membership Certificates		
	276		✓	✓	File Articles With County Recorder		
	276	✓	✓	✓	Register With Fair Political Practices Commission		

* New = Groups starting operations as newly formed corporations.
* Existing = Groups in operation prior to incorporation.
** Optional = 1) Optional step may be elected by new or existing groups; or
                 2) Step must be followed by some (but not all) new or existing groups to which step applies.

	Special Nonprofit Tax-Exempt Organizations			
IRC §	**Organization and Description**	**Application Form**	**Annual Return**	**Deductibility of Contributions[1]**
501(c)(1)	**Federal Corporations:** corporations organized under an Act of Congress as federal corporations specifically declared to be exempt from payment of federal income taxes.	No Form	None	Yes, if made for public purposes
501(c)(2)	**Corporations Holding Title to Property for Exempt Organizations:** corporations organized for the exclusive purpose of holding title to property, collecting income from property, and turning over this income, less expenses, to an organization which, itself, is exempt from payment of federal income taxes.	1024	990	No
501(c)(4)	**Civil Leagues, Social Welfare Organizations, or Local Employee Associations:** civic leagues or organizations operated exclusively for the promotion of social welfare, or local associations of employees, the membership of which is limited to the employees of a particular employer within a particular municipality, and whose net earnings are devoted exclusively to charitable, educational, or recreational purposes. Typical examples of groups which fall under this category are volunteer fire companies, homeowners or real estate development associations, or employee associations formed to further charitable community service.	1024	990	Generally, No[2]
501(c)(5)	**Labor, Agricultural, or Horticultural Organizations:** organizations of workers organized to protect their interests in connection with their employment (e.g., labor unions) or groups organized to promote more efficient techniques in production or the betterment of conditions for workers engaged in agricultural or horticultural employment.	1024	990	No
501(c)(6)	**Business Leagues, Chambers of Commerce, Etc.:** business leagues, chambers of commerce, real estate boards, or boards-of-trade organized for the purpose of improving business conditions in one or more lines of business.	1024	990	No
501(c)(7)	**Social and Recreational Clubs:** clubs organized for pleasure, recreation, and other nonprofit purposes, no part of the net earnings of which inure to the benefit of any member. Examples of such organizations are hobby clubs and other special interest social or recreational membership groups.	1024	990	No
501(c)(8)	**Fraternal Beneficiary Societies:** groups which operate under the lodge system for the exclusive benefit of their members, which provide benefits such as the payment of life, sick, or accident insurance to members.	1024	990	Yes, if for certain 501(c)(3) purposes
501(c)(9)	**Volunteer Employee Beneficiary Associations:** associations of employees which provide benefits to their members, enrollment in which is strictly voluntary and none of the earnings of which inure to the benefit of any individual members except in accordance with the association's group benefit plan.	1024	990	No
501(c)(10)	**Domestic Fraternal Societies:** domestic fraternal organizations operating under the lodge system which devote their net earnings to religious, charitable, scientific, literary, educational, or fraternal purposes and which do not provide for the payment of insurance or other benefits to members.	1024	990	Yes, if for certain 510(c)(3) purposes

Special Nonprofit Tax-Exempt Organizations (continued)

IRC §	Organization and Description	Application Form	Annual Return	Deductibility of Contributions[1]
501(c)(11)	**Local Teacher Retirement Fund Associations:** associations organized to receive amounts received from public taxation, from assessments on the teaching salaries of members, or from income from investments, to devote solely to providing retirement benefits to its members.	No Form[3]	990	No
501(c)(12)	**Benevolent Life Insurance Associations, Mutual Water and Telephone Companies, Etc.:** organizations organized on a mutual or cooperative basis to provide the above and similar services to members, 85% of whose income is collected from members, and whose income is used solely to cover the expenses and losses of the organization.	1024	990	No
501(c)(13)	**Cemetery Companies:** companies owned and operated exclusively for the benefit of members solely to provide cemetery services to their members.	1024	990	Generally, Yes
501(c)(14)	**Credit Unions:** credit unions and other mutual financial organizations organized without capital stock for nonprofit purposes.	1024	990	No
501(c)(15)	**Mutual Insurance Companies:** certain mutual insurance companies whose gross receipts are from specific sources and are within certain statutory limits.	1024	990	No
501(c)(16)	**Farmers' Cooperatives:** associations organized and operated on a cooperative basis for the purpose of marketing the products of members or other products.	1024	990	No
501(c)(19)	**War Veteran Organizations:** posts or organizations whose members are war veterans and which are formed to provide benefits to their members.	1024	990	Generally, No
501(c)(20)	**Group Legal Service Organizations:** organizations created for the exclusive function of forming a qualified group legal service plan.	1024	990	No
510(d)	**Religious and Apostolic Organizations:** religious associations or corporations with a common treasury which engage in business for the common benefit of members. Each member's share of the net income of the corporation is reported on his individual tax return. This is a rarely used section of the Code used by religious groups which are ineligible for 501(c)(3) status because they engage in a communal trade or business.	No Form	1065	No
521(a)	**Farmers' Cooperative Associations:** farmers, fruit growers, and like associations organized and operated on a cooperative basis for the purpose of marketing the products of members or other producers, or for the purchase of supplies and equipment for members at cost.	1028	990-C	No

For specific information on the requirements of several of these special-purpose tax exemption categories, see IRS publication 557, *Tax-Exempt Status for Your Organization.*

[1]An organization exempt under a subsection of IRC Section 501 other than (c)(3)—the types listed in this table—may establish a fund exclusively for 510(c)(3) purposes, contributions to which are deductible. Section 501(c)(3) tax-exempt status should be obtained for this separate fund of a non-501(c)(3) group. See IRS publication 557 for further details.

[2]Contributions to volunteer fire companies and similar organizations are deductible, but only if made for exclusively public purposes.

[3]Application is made by letter to the key District Director.

Name Availability Inquiry Letter
Corporations, Limited Partnerships, Limited Liability Companies

To inquire as to the availability of a corporation, limited partnership or limited liability company name, complete the order form below, listing up to three names to be checked. Submit your request by mail, along with a self-addressed envelope, to:

Secretary of State
Name Availability Unit
1500 11th Street, 3rd Floor
Sacramento, CA 95814

Email and/or online inquiries regarding name availability cannot be accepted at this time.

REQUESTOR'S INFORMATION	
YOUR NAME:	
FIRM NAME, IF ANY:	
ADDRESS:	
CITY/STATE/ZIP:	
TELEPHONE #:	FAX #:

SELECT ENTITY TYPE (choose only one)

[ ] Corporation   [ ] Limited Partnership   [ ] Limited Liability Company

NAME(S) TO BE CHECKED

1st Choice	
FOR OFFICE USE ONLY	( ) is available. ( ) is not available. We have:
2nd Choice	
FOR OFFICE USE ONLY	( ) is available. ( ) is not available. We have:
3rd Choice	
FOR OFFICE USE ONLY	( ) is available. ( ) is not available. We have:

Note: Checking the availability of a corporation, limited partnership or limited liability company name does not reserve the name and has no binding effect on the Secretary of State, nor does it confer any rights to a name. A name reservation request can be made over-the-counter at any Secretary of State office location or can be addressed in writing to the Sacramento office. Fees and instructions for reserving a name are included on the Name Reservation Request Form.

THE SPACE BELOW IS RESERVED FOR OFFICE USE ONLY

Date:	I #	By:

Secretary of State
Business Programs Division

1500 11ᵗʰ Street, 3ʳᵈ Floor
Sacramento, CA 95814

Business Entities
(916) 657-5448

Name Reservation Request
Corporations, Limited Partnerships, and Limited Liability Companies

To request the reservation of a corporation, limited partnership or limited liability company name, complete the Name Reservation Request Form on the following page and attach a check in the amount of $10.00 (made payable to the Secretary of State) and submit the request:

- **By mail**, along with a self-addressed envelope, to Secretary of State, Name Availability Unit, 1500 11ᵗʰ Street, 3ʳᵈ Floor, Sacramento, CA 95814. Please refer to Business Entities Mail Processing Times for current mail processing times.

- **In person** (over-the-counter) at the Secretary of State's office in Sacramento. *Corporation* names can also be reserved, in person, at any of the Secretary of State's regional offices. Please refer to Contact Information for regional office locations and addresses. A special handling fee of $10.00 is applicable for each name reserved in person. The special handling fee must be remitted by separate check (made payable to the Secretary of State) as it will be retained whether the proposed name is accepted or denied for reservation. The special handling fee is not applicable to requests submitted by mail.

Only one reservation will be made per request form. You may list up to three names, in order of preference, and the first available name will be reserved for a period of 60 days. The remaining names will not be researched.

A name reservation is made for a period of 60 days, and can be renewed, but not for consecutive periods, to the same applicant or for the benefit of the same party.

Email and/or online requests for name reservations cannot be accepted at this time. Please complete the Name Reservation Request Form on the following page.

Name Reservation Request Form
Corporations, Limited Partnerships, and Limited Liability Companies

THE PROPOSED NAME IS TO BE RESERVED FOR USE BY:	
YOUR NAME:	
FIRM NAME (IF ANY):	
ADDRESS:	
CITY/STATE/ZIP:	
TELEPHONE #:	FAX #:

TYPE OF ENTITY (choose only one)

[ ] Corporation   [ ] Limited Partnership   [ ] Limited Liability Company

NAME TO BE RESERVED

Enter the name to be reserved. Only one reservation will be made per name reservation request form. You may list up to three names, in order of preference, and the first available name will be reserved for a period of 60 days. The remaining names will not be researched.

1st Choice:

FOR OFFICE USE ONLY   ( ) is available.   ( ) is available only with consent from * :   ( ) is not available. We have * :

    *

2nd Choice:

FOR OFFICE USE ONLY   ( ) is available.   ( ) is available only with consent from ** :   ( ) is not available. We have ** :

    **

3rd Choice:

FOR OFFICE USE ONLY   ( ) is available.   ( ) is available only with consent from *** :   ( ) is not available. We have *** :

    ***

SUSPENDED/FORFEITED CORPORATION

[ ] If the proposed name is being reserved for the purpose of reviving a suspended/forfeited corporation, check the box and include the corporate number.	CORPORATION NUMBER

MAIL BACK RESPONSE

[ ] If the name reservation request form is submitted in person and if you would like the reservation to be mailed back, check the box and include a self-addressed envelope.

FEES
Make check(s) payable to the Secretary of State.

Reservation Fee: The fee for reserving a corporation, limited partnership or limited liability company name is $10.00 (per reserved name).

Special Handling Fee: A $10.00 special handling fee is applicable for processing requests delivered in person to the Secretary of State's office. The $10.00 special handling fee must be remitted by separate check for each submittal and will be retained whether the proposed name is accepted or denied for reservation. The special handling fee does not apply to name reservation requests submitted by mail.

THE SPACE BELOW IS RESERVED FOR OFFICE USE ONLY

Date:	Amt Rec'd:	R #:	By:

NAME RESERVATION REQUEST FORM (REV 07/2005)

Exemption Application

California corporation number	Federal employer identification number	Secretary of State file no.

Name of organization as shown in the organization's creating document

Address including Suite, Room, or PMB no.	Daytime telephone number

City	State	ZIP Code

Name of representative to be contacted regarding additional requirements or information	Daytime telephone number

Representative's mailing address including Suite, Room, or PMB no.

City	State	ZIP Code

ALL applicants must complete item 1 through item 7i. Also furnish the information requested in item 8 through item 25, as applicable.

1 a Enter the California Revenue and Taxation Code (R&TC) section under which exemption is claimed_____.See General Information C.

b Primary activity of organization:_____

2 a What is the legal form of the organization? ☐ Corporation ☐ Unincorporated association ☐ Trust ☐ Limited Liability Company
Date formed _____

b If formed in another state, furnish the following information:
(1) Date qualified in California _____ **(2)** State in which formed _____

3 a Has this organization or its predecessor(s) previously applied for exemption? ☐ Yes ☐ No

Enclose, but do not staple, any payments.

b If "Yes," check the appropriate box(es) below and enter either "Granted" or "Denied" and the date exemption was "Granted" or "Denied."
☐ California _____ Date _____ ☐ Federal _____ Date _____ ☐ Other State _____ Date _____ .

c Enter the R&TC section number under which the organization previously filed with the Franchise Tax Board _____ .
Furnish copies of any determination letters received.

4 a Has the organization filed federal tax returns? ☐ Yes ☐ No

b If "Yes," state type of returns and years filed. _____

5 Annual accounting period (must end on last day of the month)._____

		Yes	No
6 a	Is this a new organization? If "No," attach a statement indicating the name of the California predecessor(s), the period during which it was in existence, the reasons for its termination, and the R&TC section number under which it previously filed with the FTB.....		
b	Is this a membership organization? If "Yes," attach a statement that fully explains the qualifications for members, the different classes of membership, the number of members in each class, and the voting rights and privileges accorded each class.......		
c	Has the organization made, or are there plans to make, any distribution of its property or surplus to officers or members? If "Yes," attach a detailed statement.................		
d	Will any of the incorporators share any facilities with the organization? If "Yes," attach a detailed explanation................		
e	Will any property be rented, purchased, or transferred in any way from any of the incorporators? If "Yes," attach a detailed explanation.................		
f	Will any promoter, incorporator, founder, or member be employed by the organization? If "Yes," furnish complete details, including duties, responsibilities, qualifications, and compensation.................		
g	Will any member of the board of directors be compensated for services other than services performed as a board member, e.g., officer, and/or employee? If "Yes," furnish the name(s) of the director(s), and the amount(s) of compensation for each. Also list the name(s) of the other director(s), indicating their blood or marriage relationship, if any, to the compensated director(s).....		
h	Does the organization plan to conduct raffles or other gaming activities? If so, attach a statement describing how they will be conducted and how the organization will use the funds..........		

Continue to Item 7.

Be sure to include the $25 application fee. Make the check or money order payable to the "Franchise Tax Board." Do not send cash. Allow 90 calendar days for processing. **Note:** Make all checks or money orders payable in U.S. dollars and drawn against a U.S. financial institution.

Under penalties of perjury, I declare that I have examined this application, including accompanying schedules and statements, and to the best of my knowledge and belief, it is true, correct, and complete.

DATE	SIGNATURE OF OFFICER OR REPRESENTATIVE	TITLE

7 **TO ENSURE THAT THE FTB WILL PROCESS THE ORGANIZATION'S EXEMPTION APPLICATION, ATTACH THE FOLLOWING INFORMATION TO THE APPLICATION.** Failure to provide the following documents may delay our determination as to whether the organization qualifies for exemption.

a A copy of the creating document. The type of document to be submitted depends upon the way in which the organization was created. If the organization is:

- A California corporation, submit a copy of the endorsed articles of incorporation and all subsequent endorsed amendments. "Endorsed" means the articles bear the stamps of the California Secretary of State (SOS).
- A foreign corporation that is qualified through the SOS, submit a copy of the endorsed articles of incorporation and all subsequent endorsed amendments from the state or country in which incorporated. "Endorsed" means the articles bear the stamps of the SOS.
- An unincorporated association, submit either: a copy of the constitution, articles of association, bylaws, or other document that contains the language required as shown in the samples on page 8 of the instructions AND which is signed by the board of directors or other governing body.
- A trust, submit a copy of the trust document and any subsequent modifications to it.
- A California limited liability company, submit a copy of the endorsed articles of organization.
- A limited liability company formed in another state and qualified in California, submit a copy of the endorsed Application for Registration (Form LLC-5), a copy of the certificate of good standing from the home state, and a copy of the articles of organization from the home state.

b A copy of the bylaws, proposed bylaws, operating agreement, or other code of regulations.

c Financial documents. The documents to be provided depend upon whether the organization has been operating or has not yet started to operate. If the organization has:

1. Been operating, furnish complete statements of receipts and expenditures, assets and liabilities for each accounting period that it has been in existence and **for which exemption is requested.** See the Receipts and Expense Statement on Side 8 of this form. Do not send bank statements or monthly reports. However, bank statements or monthly reports should be retained as support for items on the income and expense statement.

2. Been operating but has not had any financial activity, provide information substantiating operations during the years for which you are requesting exemption. Example, minutes from meetings of board of directors. In addition, furnish a proposed budget showing sources of income and areas of expenditures for the current year and subsequent year. The proposed budget is required and the organization should base it upon the most reasonable expectations.

3. Not yet started to operate, furnish a proposed budget showing the sources of income and areas of expenditures for the first year of operation. The budget is required before the FTB will process the application and should be based upon the most reasonable expectations. Refer to the Receipts and Expenses Statement on Side 8 of this form.

d A statement describing the specific purposes for which the organization was formed. A general nonprofit purpose statement will not be acceptable, and do not quote the articles of incorporation or bylaws.

e A statement describing in detail the programs and activities that the organization presently conducts or will conduct and how it will accomplish its specific purposes.

f A statement describing in detail each type or source of funding, each fund raising activity, and each business enterprise the organization has engaged in or plans to engage in either alone or with other parties (accompanied by copies of all agreements, if any, for the conduct of each fund raising activity or business enterprise).

g A statement that fully explains any discontinued specific activities that the organization engaged in or sponsored. Give dates of commencement and termination and the reasons for discontinuance. (Omit if this is a new organization.)

h A copy of each lease, if any, in which the organization is the lessee or lessor of property (real, personal, gas, oil, or mineral), or in which an interest is owned under such lease, together with copies of all agreements with other parties for development of the property.

i Summary of any literature that the organization sells or distributes and summary of any organizational advertising.

Each item listed below refers to a separate California Revenue and Taxation Code (R&TC) section. Provide the information for the section under which the organization claims exemption.

8 R&TC Section 23701a – Labor, agricultural, or horticultural organization: Submit an explanation of any services to be performed for members. Cooperative organizations applying for exemption under R&TC Section 23701a must submit a copy of the federal exemption letter showing exemption under IRC Section 501(c)(5).

9 R&TC Section 23701b – Fraternal beneficiary societies, etc.:

  a State whether the organization operates, or plans to operate, under the lodge system or for the exclusive benefit of the members of a lodge system. Operating under the lodge system means carrying on activities under a form of organization that comprises local branches (called lodges, chapters, or the like) that are largely self-governing and chartered by a parent organization.

  b If the organization is a subordinate or local lodge, etc., attach a certificate signed by the secretary of the parent organization certifying that the subordinate lodge is a duly constituted body operating under the jurisdiction of the parent body.

  c If the organization is a parent or grand lodge, attach a statement showing the number of subordinate lodges in active operation and whether periodic meetings are actually held.

  d Attach a statement describing the types of benefits (life, sick, accident, or other benefits) paid, or to be paid, to members.

10 R&TC Section 23701c – Cemetery company or corporation chartered solely for burial purposes:

  a Attach these statements and/or documents:

    (1) Complete copy of the sales contract or other document involved in the organization's acquisition of cemetery property.

    (2) Complete copy of any contract designating an agent to sell the cemetery plots.

    (3) Name(s) of officer(s) and director(s) of the organization from the date of incorporation to the present date, and the period for which each held office.

    (4) Appraised value of cemetery property as of the date acquired (the appraisal should be obtained from sources other than the parties in interest).

  b Does the organization have or plan to have a perpetual care fund? ☐ Yes ☐ No

    If "Yes," furnish a copy of the federal exemption letter, a copy of the fund agreement, and a statement explaining the nature of such fund (cash, securities, unsold land, etc.). Also attach a statement that fully explains the manner in which the fund is or will be administered, the specific purposes for which the fund is to be used, and the name(s) of the person(s) administering the fund.

  c Does the organization operate a crematorium? ☐ Yes ☐ No

11 R&TC Section 23701d – Religious, charitable, scientific, literary, or educational organization: Attach a statement explaining all "Yes" answers in item 11a through item 11d.

	Yes	No
a Has the organization received, or does it expect to receive, 10% or more of its assets from any organization or group of affiliated organizations (affiliated through stockholding, common ownership, or otherwise), any individual, or members of a family group (brother or sister whether whole or half blood, spouse, ancestor, or lineal descendant)?.		
b Is the organization now, has it ever been, or does it plan to be engaged in carrying on propaganda, or otherwise advocating or opposing pending or proposed legislation (this includes dissemination of such information to the general public while representing the organization)?.		
c Has the organization participated in, or does it plan to participate or intervene in, any political campaign (including the publishing or distributing of statements) on behalf of, or in opposition to, any candidate for public office?.		
d Does the organization hold, or plan to hold, 10% or more of any class of stock or 10% or more of the total combined voting power of stock in any corporation?.		

  e If claiming exemption as a church, **attach a statement including the information requested in item (1) through item (8) below:**

    (1) Has a permanent place of worship been established? At what address? Who is the legal owner of this property? Describe the physical characteristics of the organization's church buildings. Explain to what extent these buildings are used for purposes other than religious worship.

    (2) Does the organization have a regular congregation or conduct religious services on a regular basis? How many usually attend the regular worship services? Attach samples of worship service programs and newspaper announcements of the organization's activities. Where and how often are religious services held?

    (3) Furnish information regarding the religious background and formal religious training of the religious leaders. Furnish a copy of each religious leader's certificate of ordination.

    (4) What amount of the annual gross income will be received from incorporators, ministers, officers, directors, or their families?

    (5) What amount of the organization's proposed expenditures will be used for the personal living expenses of the individuals mentioned in item (4) above?

(Item 11 continues on Side 4.)

(6) How many hours per week will the religious or spiritual leader(s) devote to organizational activities? Will this person(s) engage in employment unrelated to the activities of the organization? If so, indicate the number of hours per week and describe the employment activity.

(7) List all the officers, directors, trustees, etc., of the organization and describe their qualifications for such office. Are any of the officers or directors related by blood or marriage? If "Yes," explain.

(8) Will any founder, member, or officer:

(a) Take a vow of poverty?

(b) Transfer personal assets to this organization, like a home, automobile, furnishings, business, or recreational assets, etc., that will be made available for the personal use of the donor(s)?

(c) Assign or donate to the organization income that will be used in part or whole to pay the donor(s) as salary, stipend, or living allowance (such as food, medical expenses, clothing, insurance, etc.)?

12 R&TC Section 23701e – Business league, chamber of commerce, etc.: Has the organization performed, or does it plan to perform, particular services for members, shareholders, or others, such as furnishing credit reports or collection accounts, inspecting products, conducting advertising, purchasing merchandise, or other similar undertakings? ☐ Yes ☐ No   If "Yes," attach a detailed statement, including income realized and expenses incurred in such activities. If engaged in advertising, attach samples of material.

13 R&TC Section 23701f – Civic leagues, social welfare organizations, and local associations of employees:

a If the organization is applying as a civic league or social welfare organization, attach a statement explaining how the organization will promote the common good or welfare of an entire community.

b If the organization is applying as a local association of employees, attach a statement giving the names and addresses of employers that have employees who are eligible for membership in the association. If an employer has employees (who are eligible for membership) located in more than one plant or office, give the address of each plant or office.

14 R&TC Section 23701g – Social and recreational organization:

		Yes	No
a	Has the organization solicited, or does it plan to solicit, public patronage of the facilities by advertisement or otherwise? If "Yes," attach sample copies of such advertisements or other solicitations.		
b	Are nonmembers, other than bona fide guests of members, permitted, or will they be permitted, to use the club facilities or participate in or attend any functions or activities conducted by the organization? If "Yes," attach a statement describing the functions or activities in which nonmembers have participated or will participate, or to which they have been or will be admitted. If nonmembers have participated in or have been admitted to any functions or activities, state the amount received from nonmembers. Provide a schedule in the statement detailing the expenses attributable to such nonmembers, the expenses attributable to such functions, and the disposition made of net profits, if any, derived from the functions		
c	Has the organization rented or leased, or does it plan to rent or lease, any part of the club's property to others? If "Yes," attach a statement indicating the reason for such action, or proposed action, and the amount received, or to be received. Also attach copies of the rental agreements or leases		
d	Has the organization derived or will it derive any income from nonmembers not explained above? If "Yes," explain in detail.		

e Furnish a statement separating the member and nonmember income for the past three years and a proposed budget separating member and nonmember income for the next period of operation.

f Enter the total number of club members: _____ . If there are different classes of membership, attach a statement explaining the dues and privileges of each class.

g Provide copies of:

(1) House rules;

(2) All other documents used in considering or granting memberships, including agreements or contracts, if any; and

(3) Corporate resolutions demonstrating adoption of policy or change of policy regarding membership or use of facilities.

15 R&TC Section 23701h – Title holding corporation:

a Attach a statement giving the complete names and addresses of organizations for which title to property is held, the number of shares of capital stock held and whether shares of stock have ever been held by persons other than such organizations. If stock was so held, include the years held and the total number of shares of each class of stock.

Note: R&TC Section 23701h requires turning over net income to a parent organization periodically. Organizations with members, incorporating as a nonprofit corporation under the California Corporations Code, are precluded from exempt status under R&TC Section 23701h. California Corporations Code Sections 5410 and 7411 prohibit any distribution to members of nonprofit public benefit corporations or nonprofit mutual benefit corporations unless the organization dissolves.

Incorporated organizations seeking exemption under R&TC Section 23701h that have members must incorporate under the for profit provisions of the California Corporations Code.

(Item 15 continues on Side 5.)

b State whether the annual income (less expenses) is, or will be, turned over to the organization for which title to property is held. Explain what disposition will be made of income that will not be turned over to the organization.

c Attach a copy of an exemption letter (federal or California) for each organization for which property will be held. If property will be held for organization(s) located in California, the organization must furnish a California exemption letter.

16 R&TC Section 23701i – Voluntary employees' beneficiary organization: Furnish a copy of the federal determination letter showing exemption under IRC Section 501(c)(9).

17 R&TC Section 23701l - Fraternal society, etc.:

a State whether the organization operates, or plans to operate, under the lodge system or for the exclusive benefit of the members of a lodge system. Operating under the lodge system means carrying on activities under a form of organization that comprises local branches (called lodges, chapters, or the like) that are largely self-governing and chartered by a parent organization.

b If the organization is a subordinate or local lodge, etc., attach a certificate signed by the secretary of the parent organization certifying that the subordinate lodge is a duly constituted body operating under the jurisdiction of the parent body.

c If the organization is a parent or grand lodge, attach a statement showing the number of subordinate lodges in active operation and whether periodic meetings are actually held.

18 R&TC Section 23701n – Supplemental unemployment compensation trust: Attach a copy of the supplemental unemployment benefit plan and pertinent agreements and a copy of the federal determination letter.

19 R&TC Section 23701t – Homeowners' association:

a Furnish a copy of the recorded Declaration of Covenants, Conditions, and Restrictions.

b Will any of the individual units/lots owned by the organization or its members be occupied for other than personal residential purposes? ☐Yes ☐No If "Yes," provide the following information:

　(1) What percentage of the units/lots will be used for nonresidential purposes? _____

　(2) If the organization claims exemption as a condominium management association, enter square footage of all units and square footage devoted to residential purposes. All units _____ Residential _____

　(3) If the organization claims exemption as a residential real estate management association, enter the local real property zoning for lots within the association. Total number of lots _____ Number of lots zoned residential _____

　(4) What percentage of the organization's total gross income will be derived from dues, fees, or assessments from nonresidential members?_____

c Will this organization own, maintain, or operate a mutual water company, well, electrical generating facility, or other utility? ☐Yes ☐No If "Yes," describe in detail and answer these questions:

　(1) Are the members/shareholders: ☐the actual users of the utility or ☐simply investors?

　(2) Is this organization furnishing utilities to (check applicable box[es]): ☐residential homes, ☐commercial businesses (including agricultural enterprises)? If both, indicate what percent of this organization's total income will be derived from sale of utilities for nonresidential usage
_____

　(3) How are members/shareholders assessed for utilities usage? Are they assessed equally or on the basis of square footage/acreage?

　(4) Are meters utilized to determine charges to members/stockholders? ☐Yes ☐No
If "Yes," provide a detailed breakdown on how rates are determined and the amount of revenue received.

d Will any of the units/lots be rented by a person, or series of persons, for periods of less than 30 days that, when added together, equal more than half of the association's taxable year? ☐Yes ☐No If "Yes," what percentage of the units/lots are rented in this manner? _____

e What date was the first unit sold, or when will the first unit be available for sale? _____

f What date did the association become active? _____ Provide details of these activities.

_____

_____

g When were (will) dues first collected? month _____day _____year _____

20 R&TC Section 23701u – Public facility financial corporation:

a Attach samples of all certificates of participation or other securities to be issued.

b Attach copies of all leases, contracts, trust agreements, or other agreements that have been, or will be, entered into by this corporation.

21 R&TC Section 23701v – Mobile home park acquisition association:

  a Are all members of the organization owners of manufactured homes or mobile home tenants of the mobile home park? ☐ Yes ☐ No
     If "No," explain the circumstances under which other individuals can become members of the organization.

  b Describe the mobile home park in which owner/tenant members reside.

  c Are all lots within the park rented or leased to mobile home or manufactured home owners? ☐ Yes ☐ No   If "No," explain.

  d Does the rent paid by each owner include rental for the lot occupied by the mobile home or manufactured home? ☐ Yes ☐ No   If "No,"
     explain.

  e Will the organization carry on activities other than purchasing or preparing to purchase the mobile home park in which members
     reside? ☐ Yes ☐ No   If "Yes," describe in detail the other activities and indicate the percentage of total operations represented by such
     activities.

22 R&TC Section 23701w – War Veterans' organization:

  To be completed by a post or organization of past or present members of the Armed Forces of the United States.

  a What is the total membership of your post or organization? _____

  b How many members are present or former members of the Armed Forces of the United States? _____

  c How many members are cadets (include students in college, university, or armed services academies)? _____ How many are spouses,
     widows, or widowers of cadets, or of past or present members of the Armed Forces of the United States? _____

  d Does the organization have a membership category other than the ones set out above? ☐ Yes ☐ No   If "Yes," explain in detail and enter the
     number of members in this category.

  To be completed by an auxiliary unit or society of a post or organization of past or present members of the Armed Forces of the United States.

  e Is the organization affiliated with and organized according to the bylaws, and regulations formulated by such an exempt post or
     organization? ☐ Yes ☐ No

  f How many members does the organization have? _____

  g How many members are past or present members of the Armed Forces of the United States, or have spouses or persons related to them within
     two degrees of blood relationship (grandparents, brothers, sisters, and grandchildren are the most distant relationships allowable) that are past
     or present members of the Armed Forces of the United States (enter total)? _____

  h Are all of the members themselves members of a post or organization, past or present members of the Armed Forces of the United States,
     or spouses of members of such a post or organization, or related to members of such a post or organization within two degrees of blood
     relationship? ☐ Yes ☐ No   If "No," explain in detail.

23 R&TC Section 23701x – Title holding organization:

  a Attach a statement giving the complete names and addresses of organizations or trusts for which title to property is being held, and the number
     of shares of capital stock held by each entity.

  b State whether the annual income (less expenses) is, or will be, turned over to the organizations for which title to property is held. Explain what
     disposition will be made of the income that is not or, will not be, turned over to the organizations.

  c Furnish a copy of a federal determination letter for each organization or trust for which property is, or will be, held.

  d For those organizations of trust for which property is, or will be, held and which do not have a federal determination letter, provide detailed
     information to show that each shareholder is:

     (1) A governmental plan described in IRC Section 414(d); or

     (2) The United States, any state or political subdivision thereof, or any agency or instrumentality of the foregoing.

  e State the total number of stockholders or beneficiaries.

  f Describe in detail each class of stock or beneficial interest.

  Note: R&TC Section 23701x requires turning over net income to specified parent organizations periodically. Organizations with members
  incorporating as a nonprofit corporation under the California Corporations Code are precluded from exempt status under that section. California
  Corporations Code Sections 5410 and 7411 prohibit any distribution to members of nonprofit public benefit corporations or nonprofit mutual
  benefit corporations unless the organization dissolves.

  Incorporated organizations seeking exemption under R&TC Section 23701x that have members must incorporate under the for profit provisions
  of the California Corporations Code.

24 R&TC Section 23701y – Credit Unions:

  a Provide a copy of the organization's license to operate a credit union.

  b What is the total number of members of the organization? _____

25 R&TC Section 23701z – Self-Insurance pools for charitable organizations:

  a Provide a list of names, California corporation numbers, and federal employer identification numbers (FEINs) for all participants in the pool.

  b Describe in detail the activities of each participating corporation.

  c Furnish a copy of the latest federal determination letter showing exemption under IRC Section 501 for each participating corporation.

  d Describe in detail all insurance services to be provided to members of the pool.

Receipts and Expenses Statement

Complete information is required to adequately respond to Item 7c on Side 2. The statement below represents the basic financial details necessary to complete the organization's request for exemption. The organization may substitute its own receipts and expenses statement, or statements, but the details **must** be complete as indicated in this statement. Failure to provide complete financial information may result in denial of the organization's exemption application.

- For each year exempt status is requested, provide the financial information represented in the statement below.
- If the organization has had financial activities for less than one year, provide a financial statement for the period of activities, and a projected budget for the entire first year.
- If this is the organization's first year of operation, and/or the organization has no prior financial activity, provide a proposed budget for the entire first year of operation. The proposed budget should be based on the organization's most reasonable expectations.

Calendar or Fiscal Year Ending

RECEIPTS	Current year	Three preceding years for each year in existence			Total
Gifts.					
Grants					
Contributions received.					
Fundraising					
Membership income					
Nonmembership income (R&TC Section 23701g).					
Membership dues and assessments (R&TC Section 23701t)					
Other business income					
Gross investment income					
Gross royalty income.					
Gross rental income					
Gross receipts from admissions					
Gross receipts from commissions.					
Gross receipts from sale of merchandise					
Gross receipts from services provided					
Gross receipts from furnishing of facilities					
Gain or loss from sale of capital assets.					
Other income (attach sheet itemizing each type).					
TOTAL RECEIPTS					
EXPENSES					
Fundraising					
Contributions, gifts, grants, and similar amounts paid					
Disbursements to or for member benefit.					
Compensation of officers.					
Compensation of directors					
Compensation of trustees					
Rental expenses					
Other salaries and wages.					
Occupancy (rents).					
Other (including all operational and administrative expenses – attach sheet)					
TOTAL EXPENSES					
Excess of receipts over expenses					

Procedural Checklist

Has the organization:

_____ Completed Side 1, including item 1a through item 6h?

Note: Attach a statement if the organization needs to clarify an answer to any of these questions.

_____ Included the information and documents requested on Side 2, item 7a through item 7i?

_____ Completed the appropriate lines for the organization's needs on Side 3, item 8 through Side 7, item 25d?

_____ Included the $25 application fee?

_____ Signed the application?

(The application must be signed by an officer or an authorized representative of the organization. The signature must be the original, not a copy.)

Make sure the organization's application is complete.

If the organization does not complete all applicable parts of form FTB 3500, Exemption Application, or does not provide all required attachments, additional correspondence will be necessary in order to complete the review of its application. This will delay the determination of exempt status or result in denial of the application.

Note: Retain a copy of the completed form FTB 3500 and all attachments for the organization's permanent records.

How to Get California Tax Information   (Keep this page for future use.)

Automated Toll-Free Phone Service

Use our Automated Toll-Free Phone Service to get recorded answers to many of your questions about California taxes and to order current year California Business Entity tax forms and publications. This service is available in English and Spanish to callers with touch-tone telephones. Have paper and pencil ready to take notes.

Call from within the
United States. . . . . (800) 338-0505

Call from outside the
United States. . . . . (916) 845-6600
(not toll-free)

Where to get General Tax Information

By Internet – You can get answers to Frequently Asked Questions from our Website at **www.ftb.ca.gov**.

By Phone – You can hear recorded answers to Frequently asked Questions 24 hours a day, 7 days a week. Call our automated phone service at the number listed above. Select "Business Entity Information," then select "General Tax Information." Enter the 3-digit code, listed below, when prompted.

Code – Prefiling Assistance
715 – If my actual tax is less than the minimum franchise tax, what figure do I put on line 23 of Form 100 or Form 100W?
717 – What are the current tax rates for corporations?
718 – How do I get an extension of time to file?
722 – When does my corporation file a short period return?
734 – Is my corporation subject to a franchise tax or income tax?

S corporations
704 – Is an S corporation subject to the minimum franchise tax?
705 – Are S corporations required to file estimated payments?
706 – What forms do S corporations file?
707 – The tax for my S corporation is less than the minimum franchise tax. What figure do I put on line 22 of Form 100S?

Exempt Organizations
709 – How do I get tax-exempt status?
710 – Does an exempt organization have to file Form 199?
736 – I have exempt status. Do I need to file Form 100 or Form 109 in addition to Form 199?

Minimum Tax and Estimate Tax
712 – What is the minimum franchise tax?
714 – My corporation is not doing business; does it have to pay the minimum franchise tax?

Billings and Miscellaneous Notices
723 – I received a bill for $250. What is this for?

Tax Clearance
724 – How do I dissolve my corporation?

Miscellaneous
700 – Who do I need to contact to start a business?
701 – I need a state Employer ID number for my business. Who do I contact?
703 – How do I incorporate?
737 – Where do I send my payment?

Letters

If you write to us, be sure your letter includes the California corporation number, or FEIN, your daytime and evening telephone numbers, and a copy of the notice. Send your letter to:

EXEMPT ORGANIZATIONS UNIT MS F-120
FRANCHISE TAX BOARD
PO BOX 1286
RANCHO CORDOVA CA 95741-1286

We will respond to your letter within ten weeks. In some cases we may need to call you for additional information. Do not attach correspondence to your tax return unless it relates to an item on the return.

Your Rights As A Taxpayer

FTB's goals include making certain that your rights are protected so that you have the highest confidence in the integrity, efficiency, and fairness of our state tax system. FTB Pub. 4058, California Taxpayers' Bill of Rights, includes information on your rights as a California taxpayer, the Taxpayers' Rights Advocate Program, and how you request written advice from the FTB on whether a particular transaction is taxable. See "Where To Get Income Tax Forms and Publications," on this page.

Where to Get Tax Forms and Publications

By Internet – You can download, view, and print California tax forms and publications from our Website at **www.ftb.ca.gov**.

By phone – You can order current year California Business Entity tax forms between 6 a.m. and 8 p.m. Monday through Friday. Call our automated phone service at the number listed above. Select "Business Entity Information," then select "Forms and Publications." Follow the recorded instructions and enter the 3-digit code, listed below, when prompted. To order prior year forms, call the number listed under "Assistance," and select option five to speak with a representative.

Allow two weeks to receive your order. If your corporation's mailing address is outside California, allow three weeks.

Code
817 – California Corporation Tax Forms and Instructions. This booklet includes: Form 100, California Corporation Franchise or Income Tax Return
814 – Form 109, California Exempt Organization Business Income Tax Return
815 – Form 199, Exempt Organization Return
818 – Form 100-ES, Corporation Estimated Tax
802 – FTB 3500, Exemption Application

In person – Many libraries and post offices provide free California tax booklets during the filing season. Most libraries have forms and schedules to photocopy (a nominal fee may apply).

Note: Employees at libraries and post offices cannot provide tax information or assistance.

By mail – Write to:

TAX FORMS REQUEST UNIT
FRANCHISE TAX BOARD
PO BOX 307
RANCHO CORDOVA CA 95741-0307

Assistance

Telephone assistance is available year-round from 7 a.m. until 6 p.m. Monday through Friday, except holidays.

Call from within the
United States. . . . . (800) 852-5711

Call from outside the
United States . . . . (916) 845-6500
(not toll-free)

Assistance for persons with disabilities
We comply with the Americans with Disabilities Act. Persons with hearing or speech impairments please call:

From TTY/TDD: . . . . (800) 822-6268

Asistencia bilingüe en español
Asistencia telefónica esta disponible todo el año durante las 7 a.m. y las 6 p.m. lunes a viernes, excepto días festivos.

Dentro de los Estados Unidos,
llame al . . . . (800) 852-5711
Fuera de los Estados Unidos,
llame al (cargos aplican) . . . . . . (916) 845-6500

Pagina Electronica: **www.ftb.ca.gov**

Recycled Recyclable

Application for Recognition of Exemption
Under Section 501(c)(3) of the Internal Revenue Code

OMB No. 1545-0056

Note: *If exempt status is approved, this application will be open for public inspection.*

*Use the instructions to complete this application and for a definition of all **bold** items.* For additional help, call IRS Exempt Organizations Customer Account Services toll-free at 1-877-829-5500. Visit our website at **www.irs.gov** for forms and publications. If the required information and documents are not submitted with payment of the appropriate user fee, the application may be returned to you.

Attach additional sheets to this application if you need more space to answer fully. Put your name and EIN on each sheet and identify each answer by Part and line number. Complete Parts I - XI of Form 1023 and submit only those Schedules (A through H) that apply to you.

Part I	**Identification of Applicant**

1 Full name of organization (exactly as it appears in your **organizing document**)

2 c/o Name (if applicable)

3 **Mailing address** (Number and street) (see instructions) | Room/Suite

4 Employer Identification Number (EIN)

City or town, state or country, and ZIP + 4

5 Month the annual accounting period ends (01 – 12)

6 Primary contact (officer, director, trustee, or **authorized representative**)

a Name:

b Phone:

c Fax: (optional)

7 Are you represented by an authorized representative, such as an attorney or accountant? If "Yes," provide the authorized representative's name, and the name and address of the authorized representative's firm. Include a completed Form 2848, *Power of Attorney and Declaration of Representative,* with your application if you would like us to communicate with your representative. ☐ Yes ☐ No

8 Was a person who is not one of your officers, directors, trustees, employees, or an authorized representative listed in line 7, paid, or promised payment, to help plan, manage, or advise you about the structure or activities of your organization, or about your financial or tax matters? If "Yes," provide the person's name, the name and address of the person's firm, the amounts paid or promised to be paid, and describe that person's role. ☐ Yes ☐ No

9a Organization's website:

b Organization's email: (optional)

10 Certain organizations are not required to file an information return (Form 990 or Form 990-EZ). If you are granted tax-exemption, are you claiming to be excused from filing Form 990 or Form 990-EZ? If "Yes," explain. See the instructions for a description of organizations not required to file Form 990 or Form 990-EZ. ☐ Yes ☐ No

11 Date incorporated if a corporation, or formed, if other than a corporation. (MM/DD/YYYY) / /

12 Were you formed under the laws of a **foreign country?** If "Yes," state the country. ☐ Yes ☐ No

---

For Paperwork Reduction Act Notice, see page 24 of the instructions.   Cat. No. 17133K   Form **1023** (Rev. 6-2006)

Part II   Organizational Structure

You must be a corporation (including a limited liability company), an unincorporated association, or a trust to be tax exempt. (See instructions.) **DO NOT file this form unless you can check "Yes" on lines 1, 2, 3, or 4.**

1 Are you a **corporation**? If "Yes," attach a copy of your articles of incorporation showing **certification of filing** with the appropriate state agency. Include copies of any amendments to your articles and be sure they also show state filing certification. ☐ **Yes** ☐ **No**

2 Are you a **limited liability company (LLC)**? If "Yes," attach a copy of your articles of organization showing certification of filing with the appropriate state agency. Also, if you adopted an operating agreement, attach a copy. Include copies of any amendments to your articles and be sure they show state filing certification. Refer to the instructions for circumstances when an LLC should not file its own exemption application. ☐ **Yes** ☐ **No**

3 Are you an **unincorporated association**? If "Yes," attach a copy of your articles of association, constitution, or other similar organizing document that is dated and includes at least two signatures. Include signed and dated copies of any amendments. ☐ **Yes** ☐ **No**

4a Are you a **trust**? If "Yes," attach a signed and dated copy of your trust agreement. Include signed and dated copies of any amendments. ☐ **Yes** ☐ **No**

b Have you been funded? If "No," explain how you are formed without anything of value placed in trust. ☐ **Yes** ☐ **No**

5 Have you adopted **bylaws**? If "Yes," attach a current copy showing date of adoption. If "No," explain how your officers, directors, or trustees are selected. ☐ **Yes** ☐ **No**

Part III   Required Provisions in Your Organizing Document

The following questions are designed to ensure that when you file this application, your organizing document contains the required provisions to meet the organizational test under section 501(c)(3). Unless you can check the boxes in both lines 1 and 2, your organizing document does not meet the organizational test. **DO NOT file this application until you have amended your organizing document.** Submit your original and amended organizing documents (showing state filing certification if you are a corporation or an LLC) with your application.

1 Section 501(c)(3) requires that your organizing document state your exempt purpose(s), such as charitable, religious, educational, and/or scientific purposes. Check the box to confirm that your organizing document meets this requirement. Describe specifically where your organizing document meets this requirement, such as a reference to a particular article or section in your organizing document. Refer to the instructions for exempt purpose language. Location of Purpose Clause (Page, Article, and Paragraph): _____ ☐

2a Section 501(c)(3) requires that upon dissolution of your organization, your remaining assets must be used exclusively for exempt purposes, such as charitable, religious, educational, and/or scientific purposes. Check the box on line 2a to confirm that your organizing document meets this requirement by express provision for the distribution of assets upon dissolution. If you rely on state law for your dissolution provision, do not check the box on line 2a and go to line 2c. ☐

2b If you checked the box on line 2a, specify the location of your dissolution clause (Page, Article, and Paragraph). Do not complete line 2c if you checked box 2a. _____

2c See the instructions for information about the operation of state law in your particular state. Check this box if you rely on operation of state law for your dissolution provision and indicate the state: _____ ☐

Part IV   Narrative Description of Your Activities

Using an attachment, describe your *past, present,* and *planned* activities in a narrative. If you believe that you have already provided some of this information in response to other parts of this application, you may summarize that information here and refer to the specific parts of the application for supporting details. You may also attach representative copies of newsletters, brochures, or similar documents for supporting details to this narrative. Remember that if this application is approved, it will be open for public inspection. Therefore, your narrative description of activities should be thorough and accurate. Refer to the instructions for information that must be included in your description.

Part V   Compensation and Other Financial Arrangements With Your Officers, Directors, Trustees, Employees, and Independent Contractors

1a List the names, titles, and mailing addresses of all of your officers, directors, and trustees. For each person listed, state their total annual **compensation**, or proposed compensation, for all services to the organization, whether as an officer, employee, or other position. Use actual figures, if available. Enter "none" if no compensation is or will be paid. If additional space is needed, attach a separate sheet. Refer to the instructions for information on what to include as compensation.

Name	Title	Mailing address	Compensation amount (annual actual or estimated)

Part V **Compensation and Other Financial Arrangements With Your Officers, Directors, Trustees, Employees, and Independent Contractors** *(Continued)*

b List the names, titles, and mailing addresses of each of your five highest compensated employees who receive or will receive compensation of more than $50,000 per year. Use the actual figure, if available. Refer to the instructions for information on what to include as compensation. Do not include officers, directors, or trustees listed in line 1a.

Name	Title	Mailing address	Compensation amount (annual actual or estimated)

c List the names, names of businesses, and mailing addresses of your five highest compensated **independent contractors** that receive or will receive compensation of more than $50,000 per year. Use the actual figure, if available. Refer to the instructions for information on what to include as compensation.

Name	Title	Mailing address	Compensation amount (annual actual or estimated)

The following "Yes" or "No" questions relate to *past, present, or planned* relationships, transactions, or agreements with your officers, directors, trustees, highest compensated employees, and highest compensated independent contractors listed in lines 1a, 1b, and 1c.

2a Are any of your officers, directors, or trustees **related** to each other through **family** or **business relationships**? If "Yes," identify the individuals and explain the relationship. ☐ Yes ☐ No

b Do you have a business relationship with any of your officers, directors, or trustees other than through their position as an officer, director, or trustee? If "Yes," identify the individuals and describe the business relationship with each of your officers, directors, or trustees. ☐ Yes ☐ No

c Are any of your officers, directors, or trustees related to your highest compensated employees or highest compensated independent contractors listed on lines 1b or 1c through family or business relationships? If "Yes," identify the individuals and explain the relationship. ☐ Yes ☐ No

3a For each of your officers, directors, trustees, highest compensated employees, and highest compensated independent contractors listed on lines 1a, 1b, or 1c, attach a list showing their name, qualifications, average hours worked, and duties.

b Do any of your officers, directors, trustees, highest compensated employees, and highest compensated independent contractors listed on lines 1a, 1b, or 1c receive compensation from any other organizations, whether tax exempt or taxable, that are related to you through **common control**? If "Yes," identify the individuals, explain the relationship between you and the other organization, and describe the compensation arrangement. ☐ Yes ☐ No

4 In establishing the compensation for your officers, directors, trustees, highest compensated employees, and highest compensated independent contractors listed on lines 1a, 1b, and 1c, the following practices are recommended, although they are not required to obtain exemption. Answer "Yes" to all the practices you use.

a Do you or will the individuals that approve compensation arrangements follow a conflict of interest policy? ☐ Yes ☐ No
b Do you or will you approve compensation arrangements in advance of paying compensation? ☐ Yes ☐ No
c Do you or will you document in writing the date and terms of approved compensation arrangements? ☐ Yes ☐ No

Part V Compensation and Other Financial Arrangements With Your Officers, Directors, Trustees, Employees, and Independent Contractors *(Continued)*

d Do you or will you record in writing the decision made by each individual who decided or voted on compensation arrangements? ☐ Yes ☐ No

e Do you or will you approve compensation arrangements based on information about compensation paid by **similarly situated** taxable or tax-exempt organizations for similar services, current compensation surveys compiled by independent firms, or actual written offers from similarly situated organizations? Refer to the instructions for Part V, lines 1a, 1b, and 1c, for information on what to include as compensation. ☐ Yes ☐ No

f Do you or will you record in writing both the information on which you relied to base your decision and its source? ☐ Yes ☐ No

g If you answered "No" to any item on lines 4a through 4f, describe how you set compensation that is **reasonable** for your officers, directors, trustees, highest compensated employees, and highest compensated independent contractors listed in Part V, lines 1a, 1b, and 1c.

5a Have you adopted a **conflict of interest policy** consistent with the sample conflict of interest policy in Appendix A to the instructions? If "Yes," provide a copy of the policy and explain how the policy has been adopted, such as by resolution of your governing board. If "No," answer lines 5b and 5c. ☐ Yes ☐ No

b What procedures will you follow to assure that persons who have a conflict of interest will not have influence over you for setting their own compensation?

c What procedures will you follow to assure that persons who have a conflict of interest will not have influence over you regarding business deals with themselves?

Note: A conflict of interest policy is recommended though it is not required to obtain exemption. Hospitals, see Schedule C, Section I, line 14.

6a Do you or will you compensate any of your officers, directors, trustees, highest compensated employees, and highest compensated independent contractors listed in lines 1a, 1b, or 1c through **non-fixed payments**, such as discretionary bonuses or revenue-based payments? If "Yes," describe all non-fixed compensation arrangements, including how the amounts are determined, who is eligible for such arrangements, whether you place a limitation on total compensation, and how you determine or will determine that you pay no more than reasonable compensation for services. Refer to the instructions for Part V, lines 1a, 1b, and 1c, for information on what to include as compensation. ☐ Yes ☐ No

b Do you or will you compensate any of your employees, other than your officers, directors, trustees, or your five highest compensated employees who receive or will receive compensation of more than $50,000 per year, through non-fixed payments, such as discretionary bonuses or revenue-based payments? If "Yes," describe all non-fixed compensation arrangements, including how the amounts are or will be determined, who is or will be eligible for such arrangements, whether you place or will place a limitation on total compensation, and how you determine or will determine that you pay no more than reasonable compensation for services. Refer to the instructions for Part V, lines 1a, 1b, and 1c, for information on what to include as compensation. ☐ Yes ☐ No

7a Do you or will you purchase any goods, services, or assets from any of your officers, directors, trustees, highest compensated employees, or highest compensated independent contractors listed in lines 1a, 1b, or 1c? If "Yes," describe any such purchase that you made or intend to make, from whom you make or will make such purchases, how the terms are or will be negotiated at **arm's length**, and explain how you determine or will determine that you pay no more than **fair market value**. Attach copies of any written contracts or other agreements relating to such purchases. ☐ Yes ☐ No

b Do you or will you sell any goods, services, or assets to any of your officers, directors, trustees, highest compensated employees, or highest compensated independent contractors listed in lines 1a, 1b, or 1c? If "Yes," describe any such sales that you made or intend to make, to whom you make or will make such sales, how the terms are or will be negotiated at arm's length, and explain how you determine or will determine you are or will be paid at least fair market value. Attach copies of any written contracts or other agreements relating to such sales. ☐ Yes ☐ No

8a Do you or will you have any leases, contracts, loans, or other agreements with your officers, directors, trustees, highest compensated employees, or highest compensated independent contractors listed in lines 1a, 1b, or 1c? If "Yes," provide the information requested in lines 8b through 8f. ☐ Yes ☐ No

b Describe any written or oral arrangements that you made or intend to make.

c Identify with whom you have or will have such arrangements.

d Explain how the terms are or will be negotiated at arm's length.

e Explain how you determine you pay no more than fair market value or you are paid at least fair market value.

f Attach copies of any signed leases, contracts, loans, or other agreements relating to such arrangements.

9a Do you or will you have any leases, contracts, loans, or other agreements with any organization in which any of your officers, directors, or trustees are also officers, directors, or trustees, or in which any individual officer, director, or trustee owns more than a 35% interest? If "Yes," provide the information requested in lines 9b through 9f. ☐ Yes ☐ No

Part V	**Compensation and Other Financial Arrangements With Your Officers, Directors, Trustees, Employees, and Independent Contractors** *(Continued)*

b Describe any written or oral arrangements you made or intend to make.

c Identify with whom you have or will have such arrangements.

d Explain how the terms are or will be negotiated at arm's length.

e Explain how you determine or will determine you pay no more than fair market value or that you are paid at least fair market value.

f Attach a copy of any signed leases, contracts, loans, or other agreements relating to such arrangements.

Part VI	**Your Members and Other Individuals and Organizations That Receive Benefits From You**

The following "Yes" or "No" questions relate to goods, services, and funds you provide to individuals and organizations as part of your activities. Your answers should pertain to *past, present,* and *planned* activities. (See instructions.)

1a In carrying out your exempt purposes, do you provide goods, services, or funds to individuals? If "Yes," describe each program that provides goods, services, or funds to individuals. ☐ **Yes** ☐ **No**

b In carrying out your exempt purposes, do you provide goods, services, or funds to organizations? If "Yes," describe each program that provides goods, services, or funds to organizations. ☐ **Yes** ☐ **No**

2 Do any of your programs limit the provision of goods, services, or funds to a specific individual or group of specific individuals? For example, answer "Yes," if goods, services, or funds are provided only for a particular individual, your members, individuals who work for a particular employer, or graduates of a particular school. If "Yes," explain the limitation and how recipients are selected for each program. ☐ **Yes** ☐ **No**

3 Do any individuals who receive goods, services, or funds through your programs have a family or business relationship with any officer, director, trustee, or with any of your highest compensated employees or highest compensated independent contractors listed in Part V, lines 1a, 1b, and 1c? If "Yes," explain how these related individuals are eligible for goods, services, or funds. ☐ **Yes** ☐ **No**

Part VII	**Your History**

The following "Yes" or "No" questions relate to your history. (See instructions.)

1 Are you a **successor** to another organization? Answer "Yes," if you have taken or will take over the activities of another organization; you took over 25% or more of the fair market value of the net assets of another organization; or you were established upon the conversion of an organization from for-profit to non-profit status. If "Yes," complete Schedule G. ☐ **Yes** ☐ **No**

2 Are you submitting this application more than 27 months after the end of the month in which you were legally formed? If "Yes," complete Schedule E. ☐ **Yes** ☐ **No**

Part VIII	**Your Specific Activities**

The following "Yes" or "No" questions relate to specific activities that you may conduct. Check the appropriate box. Your answers should pertain to *past, present,* and *planned* activities. (See instructions.)

1 Do you support or oppose candidates in **political campaigns** in any way? If "Yes," explain. ☐ **Yes** ☐ **No**

2a Do you attempt to **influence legislation**? If "Yes," explain how you attempt to influence legislation and complete line 2b. If "No," go to line 3a. ☐ **Yes** ☐ **No**

b Have you made or are you making an **election** to have your legislative activities measured by expenditures by filing Form 5768? If "Yes," attach a copy of the Form 5768 that was already filed or attach a completed Form 5768 that you are filing with this application. If "No," describe whether your attempts to influence legislation are a substantial part of your activities. Include the time and money spent on your attempts to influence legislation as compared to your total activities. ☐ **Yes** ☐ **No**

3a Do you or will you operate bingo or **gaming** activities? If "Yes," describe who conducts them, and list all revenue received or expected to be received and expenses paid or expected to be paid in operating these activities. **Revenue and expenses** should be provided for the time periods specified in Part IX, Financial Data. ☐ **Yes** ☐ **No**

b Do you or will you enter into contracts or other agreements with individuals or organizations to conduct bingo or gaming for you? If "Yes," describe any written or oral arrangements that you made or intend to make, identify with whom you have or will have such arrangements, explain how the terms are or will be negotiated at arm's length, and explain how you determine or will determine you pay no more than fair market value or you will be paid at least fair market value. Attach copies or any written contracts or other agreements relating to such arrangements. ☐ **Yes** ☐ **No**

c List the states and local jurisdictions, including Indian Reservations, in which you conduct or will conduct gaming or bingo.

Part VIII　Your Specific Activities *(Continued)*

4a　Do you or will you undertake **fundraising**? If "Yes," check all the fundraising programs you do or will conduct. (See instructions.)　　　　　　　　　☐ **Yes**　　☐ **No**

☐ mail solicitations

☐ email solicitations

☐ personal solicitations

☐ vehicle, boat, plane, or similar donations

☐ foundation grant solicitations

☐ phone solicitations

☐ accept donations on your website

☐ receive donations from another organization's website

☐ government grant solicitations

☐ Other

　　Attach a description of each fundraising program.

b　Do you or will you have written or oral contracts with any individuals or organizations to raise funds for you? If "Yes," describe these activities. Include all revenue and expenses from these activities and state who conducts them. Revenue and expenses should be provided for the time periods specified in Part IX, Financial Data. Also, attach a copy of any contracts or agreements.　　☐ **Yes**　　☐ **No**

c　Do you or will you engage in fundraising activities for other organizations? If "Yes," describe these arrangements. Include a description of the organizations for which you raise funds and attach copies of all contracts or agreements.　　☐ **Yes**　　☐ **No**

d　List all states and local jurisdictions in which you conduct fundraising. For each state or local jurisdiction listed, specify whether you fundraise for your own organization, you fundraise for another organization, or another organization fundraises for you.

e　Do you or will you maintain separate accounts for any contributor under which the contributor has the right to advise on the use or distribution of funds? Answer "Yes" if the donor may provide advice on the types of investments, distributions from the types of investments, or the distribution from the donor's contribution account. If "Yes," describe this program, including the type of advice that may be provided and submit copies of any written materials provided to donors.　　☐ **Yes**　　☐ **No**

5　Are you **affiliated** with a governmental unit? If "Yes," explain.　　☐ **Yes**　　☐ **No**

6a　Do you or will you engage in **economic development**? If "Yes," describe your program.　　☐ **Yes**　　☐ **No**

b　Describe in full who benefits from your economic development activities and how the activities promote exempt purposes.

7a　Do or will persons other than your employees or volunteers **develop** your facilities? If "Yes," describe each facility, the role of the developer, and any business or family relationship(s) between the developer and your officers, directors, or trustees.　　☐ **Yes**　　☐ **No**

b　Do or will persons other than your employees or volunteers **manage** your activities or facilities? If "Yes," describe each activity and facility, the role of the manager, and any business or family relationship(s) between the manager and your officers, directors, or trustees.　　☐ **Yes**　　☐ **No**

c　If there is a business or family relationship between any manager or developer and your officers, directors, or trustees, identify the individuals, explain the relationship, describe how contracts are negotiated at arm's length so that you pay no more than fair market value, and submit a copy of any contracts or other agreements.

8　Do you or will you enter into **joint ventures**, including partnerships or **limited liability companies** treated as partnerships, in which you share profits and losses with partners other than section 501(c)(3) organizations? If "Yes," describe the activities of these joint ventures in which you participate.　　☐ **Yes**　　☐ **No**

9a　Are you applying for exemption as a childcare organization under section 501(k)? If "Yes," answer lines 9b through 9d. If "No," go to line 10.　　☐ **Yes**　　☐ **No**

b　Do you provide child care so that parents or caretakers of children you care for can be **gainfully employed** (see instructions)? If "No," explain how you qualify as a childcare organization described in section 501(k).　　☐ **Yes**　　☐ **No**

c　Of the children for whom you provide child care, are 85% or more of them cared for by you to enable their parents or caretakers to be gainfully employed (see instructions)? If "No," explain how you qualify as a childcare organization described in section 501(k).　　☐ **Yes**　　☐ **No**

d　Are your services available to the general public? If "No," describe the specific group of people for whom your activities are available. Also, see the instructions and explain how you qualify as a childcare organization described in section 501(k).　　☐ **Yes**　　☐ **No**

10　Do you or will you publish, own, or have rights in music, literature, tapes, artworks, choreography, scientific discoveries, or other **intellectual property**? If "Yes," explain. Describe who owns or will own any copyrights, patents, or trademarks, whether fees are or will be charged, how the fees are determined, and how any items are or will be produced, distributed, and marketed.　　☐ **Yes**　　☐ **No**

Part VIII Your Specific Activities *(Continued)*

11 Do you or will you accept contributions of: real property; conservation easements; closely held securities; intellectual property such as patents, trademarks, and copyrights; works of music or art; licenses; royalties; automobiles, boats, planes, or other vehicles; or collectibles of any type? If "Yes," describe each type of contribution, any conditions imposed by the donor on the contribution, and any agreements with the donor regarding the contribution. ☐ Yes ☐ No

12a Do you or will you operate in a **foreign country** or **countries?** If "Yes," answer lines 12b through 12d. If "No," go to line 13a. ☐ Yes ☐ No
  b Name the foreign countries and regions within the countries in which you operate.
  c Describe your operations in each country and region in which you operate.
  d Describe how your operations in each country and region further your exempt purposes.

13a Do you or will you make grants, loans, or other distributions to organization(s)? If "Yes," answer lines 13b through 13g. If "No," go to line 14a. ☐ Yes ☐ No
  b Describe how your grants, loans, or other distributions to organizations further your exempt purposes.
  c Do you have written contracts with each of these organizations? If "Yes," attach a copy of each contract. ☐ Yes ☐ No
  d Identify each recipient organization and any **relationship** between you and the recipient organization.
  e Describe the records you keep with respect to the grants, loans, or other distributions you make.
  f Describe your selection process, including whether you do any of the following:
  (i) Do you require an application form? If "Yes," attach a copy of the form. ☐ Yes ☐ No
  (ii) Do you require a grant proposal? If "Yes," describe whether the grant proposal specifies your responsibilities and those of the grantee, obligates the grantee to use the grant funds only for the purposes for which the grant was made, provides for periodic written reports concerning the use of grant funds, requires a final written report and an accounting of how grant funds were used, and acknowledges your authority to withhold and/or recover grant funds in case such funds are, or appear to be, misused. ☐ Yes ☐ No
  g Describe your procedures for oversight of distributions that assure you the resources are used to further your exempt purposes, including whether you require periodic and final reports on the use of resources.

14a Do you or will you make grants, loans, or other distributions to foreign organizations? If "Yes," answer lines 14b through 14f. If "No," go to line 15. ☐ Yes ☐ No
  b Provide the name of each foreign organization, the country and regions within a country in which each foreign organization operates, and describe any relationship you have with each foreign organization.
  c Does any foreign organization listed in line 14b accept contributions earmarked for a specific country or specific organization? If "Yes," list all earmarked organizations or countries. ☐ Yes ☐ No
  d Do your contributors know that you have ultimate authority to use contributions made to you at your discretion for purposes consistent with your exempt purposes? If "Yes," describe how you relay this information to contributors. ☐ Yes ☐ No
  e Do you or will you make pre-grant inquiries about the recipient organization? If "Yes," describe these inquiries, including whether you inquire about the recipient's financial status, its tax-exempt status under the Internal Revenue Code, its ability to accomplish the purpose for which the resources are provided, and other relevant information. ☐ Yes ☐ No
  f Do you or will you use any additional procedures to ensure that your distributions to foreign organizations are used in furtherance of your exempt purposes? If "Yes," describe these procedures, including site visits by your employees or compliance checks by impartial experts, to verify that grant funds are being used appropriately. ☐ Yes ☐ No

Form **1023** (Rev. 6-2006)

Part VIII Your Specific Activities *(Continued)*

15	Do you have a **close connection** with any organizations? If "Yes," explain.	☐ **Yes**	☐ **No**
16	Are you applying for exemption as a **cooperative hospital service organization** under section 501(e)? If "Yes," explain.	☐ **Yes**	☐ **No**
17	Are you applying for exemption as a **cooperative service organization of operating educational organizations** under section 501(f)? If "Yes," explain.	☐ **Yes**	☐ **No**
18	Are you applying for exemption as a **charitable risk pool** under section 501(n)? If "Yes," explain.	☐ **Yes**	☐ **No**
19	Do you or will you operate a **school**? If "Yes," complete Schedule B. Answer "Yes," whether you operate a school as your main function or as a secondary activity.	☐ **Yes**	☐ **No**
20	Is your main function to provide **hospital** or **medical care**? If "Yes," complete Schedule C.	☐ **Yes**	☐ **No**
21	Do you or will you provide **low-income housing** or housing for the **elderly** or **handicapped**? If "Yes," complete Schedule F.	☐ **Yes**	☐ **No**
22	Do you or will you provide scholarships, fellowships, educational loans, or other educational grants to individuals, including grants for travel, study, or other similar purposes? If "Yes," complete Schedule H.	☐ **Yes**	☐ **No**

Note: Private foundations may use Schedule H to request advance approval of individual grant procedures.

Part IX   Financial Data

For purposes of this schedule, years in existence refer to completed tax years. If in existence 4 or more years, complete the schedule for the most recent 4 tax years. If in existence more than 1 year but less than 4 years, complete the statements for each year in existence and provide projections of your likely revenues and expenses based on a reasonable and good faith estimate of your future finances for a total of 3 years of financial information. If in existence less than 1 year, provide projections of your likely revenues and expenses for the current year and the 2 following years, based on a reasonable and good faith estimate of your future finances for a total of 3 years of financial information. (See instructions.)

A. Statement of Revenues and Expenses

	Type of revenue or expense	Current tax year	3 prior tax years or 2 succeeding tax years			
		(a) From .... To	(b) From .... To	(c) From .... To	(d) From .... To	(e) Provide Total for (a) through (d)
Revenues	1 Gifts, grants, and contributions received (do not include unusual grants)					
	2 Membership fees received					
	3 Gross investment income					
	4 Net unrelated business income					
	5 Taxes levied for your benefit					
	6 Value of services or facilities furnished by a governmental unit without charge (not including the value of services generally furnished to the public without charge)					
	7 Any revenue not otherwise listed above or in lines 9–12 below (attach an itemized list)					
	8 Total of lines 1 through 7					
	9 Gross receipts from admissions, merchandise sold or services performed, or furnishing of facilities in any activity that is related to your exempt purposes (attach itemized list)					
	10 Total of lines 8 and 9					
	11 Net gain or loss on sale of capital assets (attach schedule and see instructions)					
	12 **Unusual grants**					
	13 Total Revenue Add lines 10 through 12					
Expenses	14 Fundraising expenses					
	15 Contributions, gifts, grants, and similar amounts paid out (attach an itemized list)					
	16 Disbursements to or for the benefit of members (attach an itemized list)					
	17 Compensation of officers, directors, and trustees					
	18 Other salaries and wages					
	19 Interest expense					
	20 Occupancy (rent, utilities, etc.)					
	21 Depreciation and depletion					
	22 Professional fees					
	23 Any expense not otherwise classified, such as program services (attach itemized list)					
	24 Total Expenses Add lines 14 through 23					

Part IX   Financial Data (Continued)

B. Balance Sheet (for your most recently completed tax year)

Year End:

Assets

(Whole dollars)

1	Cash	1
2	Accounts receivable, net	2
3	Inventories	3
4	Bonds and notes receivable (attach an itemized list)	4
5	Corporate stocks (attach an itemized list)	5
6	Loans receivable (attach an itemized list)	6
7	Other investments (attach an itemized list)	7
8	Depreciable and depletable assets (attach an itemized list)	8
9	Land	9
10	Other assets (attach an itemized list)	10
11	Total Assets (add lines 1 through 10)	11

Liabilities

12	Accounts payable	12
13	Contributions, gifts, grants, etc. payable	13
14	Mortgages and notes payable (attach an itemized list)	14
15	Other liabilities (attach an itemized list)	15
16	Total Liabilities (add lines 12 through 15)	16

Fund Balances or Net Assets

17	Total fund balances or net assets	17
18	Total Liabilities and Fund Balances or Net Assets (add lines 16 and 17)	18

19 Have there been any substantial changes in your assets or liabilities since the end of the period shown above? If "Yes," explain.   ☐ Yes   ☐ No

Part X   Public Charity Status

Part X is designed to classify you as an organization that is either a **private foundation** or a **public charity**. Public charity status is a more favorable tax status than private foundation status. If you are a private foundation, Part X is designed to further determine whether you are a **private operating foundation**. (See instructions.)

1a Are you a private foundation? If "Yes," go to line 1b. If "No," go to line 5 and proceed as instructed. If you are unsure, see the instructions.   ☐ Yes   ☐ No

  b As a private foundation, section 508(e) requires special provisions in your organizing document in addition to those that apply to all organizations described in section 501(c)(3). Check the box to confirm that your organizing document meets this requirement, whether by express provision or by reliance on operation of state law. Attach a statement that describes specifically where your organizing document meets this requirement, such as a reference to a particular article or section in your organizing document or by operation of state law. See the instructions, including Appendix B, for information about the special provisions that need to be contained in your organizing document. Go to line 2.   ☐

2 Are you a private operating foundation? To be a private operating foundation you must engage directly in the active conduct of charitable, religious, educational, and similar activities, as opposed to indirectly carrying out these activities by providing grants to individuals or other organizations. If "Yes," go to line 3. If "No," go to the signature section of Part XI.   ☐ Yes   ☐ No

3 Have you existed for one or more years? If "Yes," attach financial information showing that you are a private operating foundation; go to the signature section of Part XI. If "No," continue to line 4.   ☐ Yes   ☐ No

4 Have you attached either (1) an affidavit or opinion of counsel, (including a written affidavit or opinion from a certified public accountant or accounting firm with expertise regarding this tax law matter), that sets forth facts concerning your operations and support to demonstrate that you are likely to satisfy the requirements to be classified as a private operating foundation; or (2) a statement describing your proposed operations as a private operating foundation?   ☐ Yes   ☐ No

5 If you answered "No" to line 1a, indicate the type of public charity status you are requesting by checking one of the choices below. You may check only one box.

   The organization is not a private foundation because it is:

  a 509(a)(1) and 170(b)(1)(A)(i)—a church or a convention or association of churches. Complete and attach Schedule A.   ☐

  b 509(a)(1) and 170(b)(1)(A)(ii)—a **school**. Complete and attach Schedule B.   ☐

  c 509(a)(1) and 170(b)(1)(A)(iii)—a **hospital**, a cooperative hospital service organization, or a medical research organization operated in conjunction with a hospital. Complete and attach Schedule C.   ☐

  d 509(a)(3)—an organization supporting either one or more organizations described in line 5a through c, f, g, or h or a publicly supported section 501(c)(4), (5), or (6) organization. Complete and attach Schedule D.   ☐

| **Part X** | **Public Charity Status** *(Continued)* |

e 509(a)(4)—an organization organized and operated exclusively for testing for public safety. ☐

f 509(a)(1) and 170(b)(1)(A)(iv)—an organization operated for the benefit of a college or university that is owned or operated by a governmental unit. ☐

g 509(a)(1) and 170(b)(1)(A)(vi)—an organization that receives a substantial part of its financial support in the form of contributions from publicly supported organizations, from a governmental unit, or from the general public. ☐

h 509(a)(2)—an organization that normally receives not more than one-third of its financial support from gross **investment income** and receives more than one-third of its financial support from contributions, membership fees, and gross receipts from activities related to its exempt functions (subject to certain exceptions). ☐

i A publicly supported organization, but unsure if it is described in 5g or 5h. The organization would like the IRS to decide the correct status. ☐

6 If you checked box g, h, or i in question 5 above, you must request either an **advance** or a **definitive ruling** by selecting one of the boxes below. Refer to the instructions to determine which type of ruling you are eligible to receive.

a **Request for Advance Ruling:** By checking this box and signing the consent, pursuant to section 6501(c)(4) of the Code you request an advance ruling and agree to extend the statute of limitations on the assessment of excise tax under section 4940 of the Code. The tax will apply only if you do not establish public support status at the end of the 5-year advance ruling period. The assessment period will be extended for the 5 advance ruling years to 8 years, 4 months, and 15 days beyond the end of the first year. You have the right to refuse or limit the extension to a mutually agreed-upon period of time or issue(s). Publication 1035, *Extending the Tax Assessment Period,* provides a more detailed explanation of your rights and the consequences of the choices you make. You may obtain Publication 1035 free of charge from the IRS web site at *www.irs.gov* or by calling toll-free 1-800-829-3676. Signing this consent will not deprive you of any appeal rights to which you would otherwise be entitled. If you decide not to extend the statute of limitations, you are not eligible for an advance ruling. ☐

Consent Fixing Period of Limitations Upon Assessment of Tax Under Section 4940 of the Internal Revenue Code

For Organization

---   --   ------------------------
(Signature of Officer, Director, Trustee, or other   (Type or print name of signer)   (Date)
authorized official)

                                                            (Type or print title or authority of signer)

For IRS Use Only

---   ------------------------
IRS Director, Exempt Organizations   (Date)

b **Request for Definitive Ruling:** Check this box if you have completed one tax year of at least 8 full months and you are requesting a definitive ruling. To confirm your public support status, answer line 6b(i) if you checked box g in line 5 above. Answer line 6b(ii) if you checked box h in line 5 above. If you checked box i in line 5 above, answer both lines 6b(i) and (ii). ☐

(i) **(a)** Enter 2% of line 8, column (e) on Part IX-A. Statement of Revenues and Expenses. _____

   (b) Attach a list showing the name and amount contributed by each person, company, or organization whose gifts totaled more than the 2% amount. If the answer is "None," check this box. ☐

(ii) **(a)** For each year amounts are included on lines 1, 2, and 9 of Part IX-A. Statement of Revenues and Expenses, attach a list showing the name of and amount received from each **disqualified person.** If the answer is "None," check this box. ☐

   (b) For each year amounts are included on line 9 of Part IX-A. Statement of Revenues and Expenses, attach a list showing the name of and amount received from each payer, other than a disqualified person, whose payments were more than the larger of (1) 1% of line 10, Part IX-A. Statement of Revenues and Expenses, or (2) $5,000. If the answer is "None," check this box. ☐

7 Did you receive any unusual grants during any of the years shown on Part IX-A. Statement of Revenues and Expenses? If "Yes," attach a list including the name of the contributor, the date and amount of the grant, a brief description of the grant, and explain why it is unusual.   ☐ **Yes**   ☐ **No**

Part XI   User Fee Information

You must include a user fee payment with this application. It will not be processed without your paid user fee. If your average annual gross receipts have exceeded or will exceed $10,000 annually over a 4-year period, you must submit payment of $750. If your gross receipts have not exceeded or will not exceed $10,000 annually over a 4-year period, the required user fee payment is $300. See instructions for Part XI, for a definition of **gross receipts** over a 4-year period. Your check or money order must be made payable to the United States Treasury. *User fees are subject to change. Check our website at www.irs.gov and type "User Fee" in the keyword box, or call Customer Account Services at 1-877-829-5500 for current information.*

1 Have your annual gross receipts averaged or are they expected to average not more than $10,000?   ☐ **Yes**   ☐ **No**
   If "Yes," check the box on line 2 and enclose a user fee payment of $300 (Subject to change—see above).
   If "No," check the box on line 3 and enclose a user fee payment of $750 (Subject to change—see above).

2 Check the box if you have enclosed the reduced user fee payment of $300 (Subject to change).   ☐

3 Check the box if you have enclosed the user fee payment of $750 (Subject to change).   ☐

I declare under the penalties of perjury that I am authorized to sign this application on behalf of the above organization and that I have examined this application, including the accompanying schedules and attachments, and to the best of my knowledge it is true, correct, and complete.

Please Sign Here ▶

_____   _____   _____
(Signature of Officer, Director, Trustee, or other   (Type or print name of signer)   (Date)
authorized official)

_____
(Type or print title or authority of signer)

Reminder: Send the completed Form 1023 Checklist with your filled-in-application.   Form **1023** (Rev. 6-2006)

Schedule A. Churches

1a Do you have a written creed, statement of faith, or summary of beliefs? If "Yes," attach copies of relevant documents. ☐ **Yes** ☐ **No**

b Do you have a form of worship? If "Yes," describe your form of worship. ☐ **Yes** ☐ **No**

2a Do you have a formal code of doctrine and discipline? If "Yes," describe your code of doctrine and discipline. ☐ **Yes** ☐ **No**

b Do you have a distinct religious history? If "Yes," describe your religious history. ☐ **Yes** ☐ **No**

c Do you have a literature of your own? If "Yes," describe your literature. ☐ **Yes** ☐ **No**

3 Describe the organization's religious hierarchy or ecclesiastical government.

4a Do you have regularly scheduled religious services? If "Yes," describe the nature of the services and provide representative copies of relevant literature such as church bulletins. ☐ **Yes** ☐ **No**

b What is the average attendance at your regularly scheduled religious services? _____

5a Do you have an established place of worship? If "Yes," refer to the instructions for the information required. ☐ **Yes** ☐ **No**

b Do you own the property where you have an established place of worship? ☐ **Yes** ☐ **No**

6 Do you have an established congregation or other regular membership group? If "No," refer to the instructions. ☐ **Yes** ☐ **No**

7 How many members do you have? _____

8a Do you have a process by which an individual becomes a member? If "Yes," describe the process and complete lines 8b–8d, below. ☐ **Yes** ☐ **No**

b If you have members, do your members have voting rights, rights to participate in religious functions, or other rights? If "Yes," describe the rights your members have. ☐ **Yes** ☐ **No**

c May your members be associated with another denomination or church? ☐ **Yes** ☐ **No**

d Are all of your members part of the same **family**? ☐ **Yes** ☐ **No**

9 Do you conduct baptisms, weddings, funerals, etc.? ☐ **Yes** ☐ **No**

10 Do you have a school for the religious instruction of the young? ☐ **Yes** ☐ **No**

11a Do you have a minister or religious leader? If "Yes," describe this person's role and explain whether the minister or religious leader was ordained, commissioned, or licensed after a prescribed course of study. ☐ **Yes** ☐ **No**

b Do you have schools for the preparation of your ordained ministers or religious leaders? ☐ **Yes** ☐ **No**

12 Is your minister or religious leader also one of your officers, directors, or trustees? ☐ **Yes** ☐ **No**

13 Do you ordain, commission, or license ministers or religious leaders? If "Yes," describe the requirements for ordination, commission, or licensure. ☐ **Yes** ☐ **No**

14 Are you part of a group of churches with similar beliefs and structures? If "Yes," explain. Include the name of the group of churches. ☐ **Yes** ☐ **No**

15 Do you issue church charters? If "Yes," describe the requirements for issuing a charter. ☐ **Yes** ☐ **No**

16 Did you pay a fee for a church charter? If "Yes," attach a copy of the charter. ☐ **Yes** ☐ **No**

17 Do you have other information you believe should be considered regarding your status as a church? If "Yes," explain. ☐ **Yes** ☐ **No**

Schedule B. Schools, Colleges, and Universities

If you operate a school as an activity, complete Schedule B

Section I   Operational Information

1a Do you normally have a regularly scheduled curriculum, a regular faculty of qualified teachers, a regularly enrolled student body, and facilities where your educational activities are regularly carried on? If "No," do not complete the remainder of Schedule B. ☐ Yes ☐ No

b Is the primary function of your school the presentation of formal instruction? If "Yes," describe your school in terms of whether it is an elementary, secondary, college, technical, or other type of school. If "No," do not complete the remainder of Schedule B. ☐ Yes ☐ No

2a Are you a public school because you are operated by a state or subdivision of a state? If "Yes," explain how you are operated by a state or subdivision of a state. Do not complete the remainder of Schedule B. ☐ Yes ☐ No

b Are you a public school because you are operated wholly or predominantly from government funds or property? If "Yes," explain how you are operated wholly or predominantly from government funds or property. Submit a copy of your funding agreement regarding government funding. Do not complete the remainder of Schedule B. ☐ Yes ☐ No

3 In what public school district, county, and state are you located?

4 Were you formed or substantially expanded at the time of public school desegregation in the above school district or county? ☐ Yes ☐ No

5 Has a state or federal administrative agency or judicial body ever determined that you are racially discriminatory? If "Yes," explain. ☐ Yes ☐ No

6 Has your right to receive financial aid or assistance from a governmental agency ever been revoked or suspended? If "Yes," explain. ☐ Yes ☐ No

7 Do you or will you contract with another organization to develop, build, market, or finance your facilities? If "Yes," explain how that entity is selected, explain how the terms of any contracts or other agreements are negotiated at arm's length, and explain how you determine that you will pay no more than fair market value for services. ☐ Yes ☐ No

Note. Make sure your answer is consistent with the information provided in Part VIII, line 7a.

8 Do you or will you manage your activities or facilities through your own employees or volunteers? If "No," attach a statement describing the activities that will be managed by others, the names of the persons or organizations that manage or will manage your activities or facilities, and how these managers were or will be selected. Also, submit copies of any contracts, proposed contracts, or other agreements regarding the provision of management services for your activities or facilities. Explain how the terms of any contracts or other agreements were or will be negotiated, and explain how you determine you will pay no more than fair market value for services. ☐ Yes ☐ No

Note. Answer "Yes" if you manage or intend to manage your programs through your own employees or by using volunteers. Answer "No" if you engage or intend to engage a separate organization or independent contractor. Make sure your answer is consistent with the information provided in Part VIII, line 7b.

Section II   Establishment of Racially Nondiscriminatory Policy

Information required by **Revenue Procedure 75-50.**

1 Have you adopted a racially nondiscriminatory policy as to students in your organizing document, bylaws, or by resolution of your governing body? If "Yes," state where the policy can be found or supply a copy of the policy. If "No," you must adopt a nondiscriminatory policy as to students before submitting this application. See Publication 557. ☐ Yes ☐ No

2 Do your brochures, application forms, advertisements, and catalogues dealing with student admissions, programs, and scholarships contain a statement of your racially nondiscriminatory policy? ☐ Yes ☐ No

a If "Yes," attach a representative sample of each document.

b If "No," by checking the box to the right you agree that all future printed materials, including website content, will contain the required nondiscriminatory policy statement. ▶ ☐

3 Have you published a notice of your nondiscriminatory policy in a newspaper of general circulation that serves all racial segments of the community? (See the instructions for specific requirements.) If "No," explain. ☐ Yes ☐ No

4 Does or will the organization (or any department or division within it) discriminate in any way on the basis of race with respect to admissions; use of facilities or exercise of student privileges; faculty or administrative staff; or scholarship or loan programs? If "Yes," for any of the above, explain fully. ☐ Yes ☐ No

Schedule B. Schools, Colleges, and Universities *(Continued)*

5 Complete the table below to show the racial composition for the current academic year and projected for the next academic year, of: (a) the student body, (b) the faculty, and (c) the administrative staff. Provide actual numbers rather than percentages for each racial category.

If you are not operational, submit an estimate based on the best information available (such as the racial composition of the community served).

Racial Category	(a) Student Body		(b) Faculty		(c) Administrative Staff	
	Current Year	Next Year	Current Year	Next Year	Current Year	Next Year
Total						

6 In the table below, provide the number and amount of loans and scholarships awarded to students enrolled by racial categories.

Racial Category	Number of Loans		Amount of Loans		Number of Scholarships		Amount of Scholarships	
	Current Year	Next Year	Current Year	Next Year	Current Year	Next Year	Current Year	Next Year
Total								

7a Attach a list of your incorporators, founders, board members, and donors of land or buildings, whether individuals or organizations.

  b Do any of these individuals or organizations have an objective to maintain segregated public or private school education? If "Yes," explain.   ☐ **Yes**   ☐ **No**

8 Will you maintain records according to the non-discrimination provisions contained in Revenue Procedure 75-50? If "No," explain. (See instructions.)   ☐ **Yes**   ☐ **No**

Schedule C. Hospitals and Medical Research Organizations

Check the box if you are a **hospital**. See the instructions for a definition of the term "hospital," which includes an organization whose principal purpose or function is providing **hospital** or **medical care**. Complete Section I below. ☐

Check the box if you are a **medical research organization** operated in conjunction with a hospital. See the instructions for a definition of the term "medical research organization," which refers to an organization whose principal purpose or function is medical research and which is directly engaged in the continuous active conduct of medical research in conjunction with a hospital. Complete Section II. ☐

Section I   Hospitals

1a Are all the doctors in the community eligible for staff privileges? If "No," give the reasons why and explain how the medical staff is selected. ☐ **Yes** ☐ **No**

2a Do you or will you provide medical services to all individuals in your community who can pay for themselves or have private health insurance? If "No," explain. ☐ **Yes** ☐ **No**

b Do you or will you provide medical services to all individuals in your community who participate in Medicare? If "No," explain. ☐ **Yes** ☐ **No**

c Do you or will you provide medical services to all individuals in your community who participate in Medicaid? If "No," explain. ☐ **Yes** ☐ **No**

3a Do you or will you require persons covered by Medicare or Medicaid to pay a deposit before receiving services? If "Yes," explain. ☐ **Yes** ☐ **No**

b Does the same deposit requirement, if any, apply to all other patients? If "No," explain. ☐ **Yes** ☐ **No**

4a Do you or will you maintain a full-time emergency room? If "No," explain why you do not maintain a full-time emergency room. Also, describe any emergency services that you provide. ☐ **Yes** ☐ **No**

b Do you have a policy on providing emergency services to persons without apparent means to pay? If "Yes," provide a copy of the policy. ☐ **Yes** ☐ **No**

c Do you have any arrangements with police, fire, and voluntary ambulance services for the delivery or admission of emergency cases? If "Yes," describe the arrangements, including whether they are written or oral agreements. If written, submit copies of all such agreements. ☐ **Yes** ☐ **No**

5a Do you provide for a portion of your services and facilities to be used for charity patients? If "Yes," answer 5b through 5e. ☐ **Yes** ☐ **No**

b Explain your policy regarding charity cases, including how you distinguish between charity care and bad debts. Submit a copy of your written policy.

c Provide data on your past experience in admitting charity patients, including amounts you expend for treating charity care patients and types of services you provide to charity care patients.

d Describe any arrangements you have with federal, state, or local governments or government agencies for paying for the cost of treating charity care patients. Submit copies of any written agreements.

e Do you provide services on a sliding fee schedule depending on financial ability to pay? If "Yes," submit your sliding fee schedule. ☐ **Yes** ☐ **No**

6a Do you or will you carry on a formal program of medical training or medical research? If "Yes," describe such programs, including the type of programs offered, the scope of such programs, and affiliations with other hospitals or medical care providers with which you carry on the medical training or research programs. ☐ **Yes** ☐ **No**

b Do you or will you carry on a formal program of community education? If "Yes," describe such programs, including the type of programs offered, the scope of such programs, and affiliation with other hospitals or medical care providers with which you offer community education programs. ☐ **Yes** ☐ **No**

7 Do you or will you provide office space to physicians carrying on their own medical practices? If "Yes," describe the criteria for who may use the space, explain the means used to determine that you are paid at least fair market value, and submit representative lease agreements. ☐ **Yes** ☐ **No**

8 Is your board of directors comprised of a majority of individuals who are representative of the community you serve? Include a list of each board member's name and business, financial, or professional relationship with the hospital. Also, identify each board member who is representative of the community and describe how that individual is a community representative. ☐ **Yes** ☐ **No**

9 Do you participate in any joint ventures? If "Yes," state your ownership percentage in each joint venture, list your investment in each joint venture, describe the tax status of other participants in each joint venture (including whether they are section 501(c)(3) organizations), describe the activities of each joint venture, describe how you exercise control over the activities of each joint venture, and describe how each joint venture furthers your exempt purposes. Also, submit copies of all agreements. ☐ **Yes** ☐ **No**
Note. Make sure your answer is consistent with the information provided in Part VIII, line 8.

Schedule C. Hospitals and Medical Research Organizations *(Continued)*

Section I	Hospitals *(Continued)*

10 Do you or will you manage your activities or facilities through your own employees or volunteers? If "No," attach a statement describing the activities that will be managed by others, the names of the persons or organizations that manage or will manage your activities or facilities, and how these managers were or will be selected. Also, submit copies of any contracts, proposed contracts, or other agreements regarding the provision of management services for your activities or facilities. Explain how the terms of any contracts or other agreements were or will be negotiated, and explain how you determine you will pay no more than fair market value for services. ☐ **Yes** ☐ **No**

Note. Answer "Yes" if you do manage or intend to manage your programs through your own employees or by using volunteers. Answer "No" if you engage or intend to engage a separate organization or independent contractor. Make sure your answer is consistent with the information provided in Part VIII, line 7b.

11 Do you or will you offer recruitment incentives to physicians? If "Yes," describe your recruitment incentives and attach copies of all written recruitment incentive policies. ☐ **Yes** ☐ **No**

12 Do you or will you lease equipment, assets, or office space from physicians who have a financial or professional relationship with you? If "Yes," explain how you establish a fair market value for the lease. ☐ **Yes** ☐ **No**

13 Have you purchased medical practices, ambulatory surgery centers, or other business assets from physicians or other persons with whom you have a business relationship, aside from the purchase? If "Yes," submit a copy of each purchase and sales contract and describe how you arrived at fair market value, including copies of appraisals. ☐ **Yes** ☐ **No**

14 Have you adopted a **conflict of interest policy** consistent with the sample health care organization conflict of interest policy in Appendix A of the instructions? If "Yes," submit a copy of the policy and explain how the policy has been adopted, such as by resolution of your governing board. If "No," explain how you will avoid any conflicts of interest in your business dealings. ☐ **Yes** ☐ **No**

Section II	Medical Research Organizations

1 Name the hospitals with which you have a relationship and describe the relationship. Attach copies of written agreements with each hospital that demonstrate continuing relationships between you and the hospital(s).

2 Attach a schedule describing your present and proposed activities for the direct conduct of medical research; describe the nature of the activities, and the amount of money that has been or will be spent in carrying them out.

3 Attach a schedule of assets showing their fair market value and the portion of your assets directly devoted to medical research.

Form **1023** (Rev. 6-2006)

Schedule D. Section 509(a)(3) Supporting Organizations

Section I   Identifying Information About the Supported Organization(s)

1 State the names, addresses, and EINs of the supported organizations. If additional space is needed, attach a separate sheet.

Name	Address	EIN
		−
		−

2 Are all supported organizations listed in line 1 public charities under section 509(a)(1) or (2)? If "Yes," go to Section II. If "No," go to line 3. ☐ Yes ☐ No

3 Do the supported organizations have tax-exempt status under section 501(c)(4), 501(c)(5), or 501(c)(6)? ☐ Yes ☐ No

If "Yes," for each 501(c)(4), (5), or (6) organization supported, provide the following financial information:

- Part IX-A. Statement of Revenues and Expenses, lines 1–13 and
- Part X, lines 6b(ii)(a), 6b(ii)(b), and 7.

If "No," attach a statement describing how each organization you support is a public charity under section 509(a)(1) or (2).

Section II   Relationship with Supported Organization(s)—Three Tests

To be classified as a supporting organization, an organization must meet one of three relationship tests:

Test 1: "Operated, supervised, or controlled by" one or more publicly supported organizations, or
Test 2: "Supervised or controlled in connection with" one or more publicly supported organizations, or
Test 3: "Operated in connection with" one or more publicly supported organizations.

1 Information to establish the "operated, supervised, or controlled by" relationship (Test 1)

Is a majority of your governing board or officers elected or appointed by the supported organization(s)? If "Yes," describe the process by which your governing board is appointed and elected; go to Section III. If "No," continue to line 2. ☐ Yes ☐ No

2 Information to establish the "supervised or controlled in connection with" relationship (Test 2)

Does a majority of your governing board consist of individuals who also serve on the governing board of the supported organization(s)? If "Yes," describe the process by which your governing board is appointed and elected; go to Section III. If "No," go to line 3. ☐ Yes ☐ No

3 Information to establish the "operated in connection with" responsiveness test (Test 3)

Are you a trust from which the named supported organization(s) can enforce and compel an accounting under state law? If "Yes," explain whether you advised the supported organization(s) in writing of these rights and provide a copy of the written communication documenting this; go to Section II, line 5. If "No," go to line 4a. ☐ Yes ☐ No

4 Information to establish the alternative "operated in connection with" responsiveness test (Test 3)

a Do the officers, directors, trustees, or members of the supported organization(s) elect or appoint one or more of your officers, directors, or trustees? If "Yes," explain and provide documentation; go to line 4d, below. If "No," go to line 4b. ☐ Yes ☐ No

b Do one or more members of the governing body of the supported organization(s) also serve as your officers, directors, or trustees or hold other important offices with respect to you? If "Yes," explain and provide documentation; go to line 4d, below. If "No," go to line 4c. ☐ Yes ☐ No

c Do your officers, directors, or trustees maintain a close and continuous working relationship with the officers, directors, or trustees of the supported organization(s)? If "Yes," explain and provide documentation. ☐ Yes ☐ No

d Do the supported organization(s) have a significant voice in your investment policies, in the making and timing of grants, and in otherwise directing the use of your income or assets? If "Yes," explain and provide documentation. ☐ Yes ☐ No

e Describe and provide copies of written communications documenting how you made the supported organization(s) aware of your supporting activities.

Schedule D. Section 509(a)(3) Supporting Organizations *(Continued)*

Section II	**Relationship with Supported Organization(s)—Three Tests** *(Continued)*

5 Information to establish the "operated in connection with" integral part test (Test 3)

Do you conduct activities that would otherwise be carried out by the supported organization(s)? If "Yes," explain and go to Section III. If "No," continue to line 6a. ☐ Yes ☐ No

6 Information to establish the alternative "operated in connection with" integral part test (Test 3)

a Do you distribute at least 85% of your annual **net income** to the supported organization(s)? If "Yes," go to line 6b. (See instructions.) ☐ Yes ☐ No

If "No," state the percentage of your income that you distribute to each supported organization. Also explain how you ensure that the supported organization(s) are attentive to your operations.

b How much do you contribute annually to each supported organization? Attach a schedule.

c What is the total annual revenue of each supported organization? If you need additional space, attach a list.

d Do you or the supported organization(s) **earmark** your funds for support of a particular program or activity? If "Yes," explain. ☐ Yes ☐ No

7a Does your organizing document specify the supported organization(s) by name? If "Yes," state the article and paragraph number and go to Section III. If "No," answer line 7b. ☐ Yes ☐ No

b Attach a statement describing whether there has been an historic and continuing relationship between you and the supported organization(s).

Section III	**Organizational Test**

1a If you met relationship Test 1 or Test 2 in Section II, your organizing document must specify the supported organization(s) by name, or by naming a similar purpose or charitable class of beneficiaries. If your organizing document complies with this requirement, answer "Yes." If your organizing document does not comply with this requirement, answer "No," and see the instructions. ☐ Yes ☐ No

b If you met relationship Test 3 in Section II, your organizing document must generally specify the supported organization(s) by name. If your organizing document complies with this requirement, answer "Yes," and go to Section IV. If your organizing document does not comply with this requirement, answer "No," and see the instructions. ☐ Yes ☐ No

Section IV	**Disqualified Person Test**

You do not qualify as a supporting organization if you are **controlled** directly or indirectly by one or more **disqualified persons** (as defined in section 4946) other than **foundation managers** or one or more organizations that you support. Foundation managers who are also disqualified persons for another reason are disqualified persons with respect to you.

1a Do any persons who are disqualified persons with respect to you, (except individuals who are disqualified persons only because they are foundation managers), appoint any of your foundation managers? If "Yes," (1) describe the process by which disqualified persons appoint any of your foundation managers, (2) provide the names of these disqualified persons and the foundation managers they appoint, and (3) explain how control is vested over your operations (including assets and activities) by persons other than disqualified persons. ☐ Yes ☐ No

b Do any persons who have a family or business relationship with any disqualified persons with respect to you, (except individuals who are disqualified persons only because they are foundation managers), appoint any of your foundation managers? If "Yes," (1) describe the process by which individuals with a family or business relationship with disqualified persons appoint any of your foundation managers, (2) provide the names of these disqualified persons, the individuals with a family or business relationship with disqualified persons, and the foundation managers appointed, and (3) explain how control is vested over your operations (including assets and activities) in individuals other than disqualified persons. ☐ Yes ☐ No

c Do any persons who are disqualified persons, (except individuals who are disqualified persons only because they are foundation managers), have any influence regarding your operations, including your assets or activities? If "Yes," (1) provide the names of these disqualified persons, (2) explain how influence is exerted over your operations (including assets and activities), and (3) explain how control is vested over your operations (including assets and activities) by individuals other than disqualified persons. ☐ Yes ☐ No

Schedule E. Organizations Not Filing Form 1023 Within 27 Months of Formation

Schedule E is intended to determine whether you are eligible for tax exemption under section 501(c)(3) from the postmark date of your application or from your date of incorporation or formation, whichever is earlier. If you are not eligible for tax exemption under section 501(c)(3) from your date of incorporation or formation, Schedule E is also intended to determine whether you are eligible for tax exemption under section 501(c)(4) for the period between your date of incorporation or formation and the postmark date of your application.

1 Are you a church, association of churches, or integrated auxiliary of a church? If "Yes," complete Schedule A and stop here. Do not complete the remainder of Schedule E.   ☐ Yes   ☐ No

2a Are you a public charity with annual **gross receipts** that are normally $5,000 or less? If "Yes," stop here. Answer "No" if you are a private foundation, regardless of your gross receipts.   ☐ Yes   ☐ No

b If your gross receipts were normally more than $5,000, are you filing this application within 90 days from the end of the tax year in which your gross receipts were normally more than $5,000? If "Yes," stop here.   ☐ Yes   ☐ No

3a Were you included as a subordinate in a group exemption application or letter? If "No," go to line 4.   ☐ Yes   ☐ No

b If you were included as a subordinate in a group exemption letter, are you filing this application within 27 months from the date you were notified by the organization holding the group exemption letter or the Internal Revenue Service that you cease to be covered by the group exemption letter? If "Yes," stop here.   ☐ Yes   ☐ No

c If you were included as a subordinate in a timely filed group exemption request that was denied, are you filing this application within 27 months from the postmark date of the Internal Revenue Service final adverse ruling letter? If "Yes," stop here.   ☐ Yes   ☐ No

4 Were you created on or before October 9, 1969? If "Yes," stop here. Do not complete the remainder of this schedule.   ☐ Yes   ☐ No

5 If you answered "No" to lines 1 through 4, we cannot recognize you as tax exempt from your date of formation unless you qualify for an extension of time to apply for exemption. Do you wish to request an extension of time to apply to be recognized as exempt from the date you were formed? If "Yes," attach a statement explaining why you did not file this application within the 27-month period. Do not answer lines 6, 7, or 8. If "No," go to line 6a.   ☐ Yes   ☐ No

6a If you answered "No" to line 5, you can only be exempt under section 501(c)(3) from the postmark date of this application. Therefore, do you want us to treat this application as a request for tax exemption from the postmark date? If "Yes," you are eligible for an advance ruling. Complete Part X, line 6a. If "No," you will be treated as a private foundation.   ☐ Yes   ☐ No

Note. Be sure your ruling eligibility agrees with your answer to Part X, line 6.

b Do you anticipate significant changes in your sources of support in the future? If "Yes," complete line 7 below.   ☐ Yes   ☐ No

Schedule E. Organizations Not Filing Form 1023 Within 27 Months of Formation *(Continued)*

7   Complete this item only if you answered "Yes" to line 6b. Include projected revenue for the first two full years following the current tax year.

Type of Revenue	Projected revenue for 2 years following current tax year		
	(a) From .... To	**(b)** From .... To	**(c)** Total
1 Gifts, grants, and contributions received (do not include unusual grants)			
2 Membership fees received			
3 Gross investment income			
4 Net unrelated business income			
5 Taxes levied for your benefit			
6 Value of services or facilities furnished by a governmental unit without charge (not including the value of services generally furnished to the public without charge)			
7 Any revenue not otherwise listed above or in lines 9–12 below (attach an itemized list)			
8 Total of lines 1 through 7			
9 Gross receipts from admissions, merchandise sold, or services performed, or furnishing of facilities in any activity that is related to your exempt purposes (attach itemized list)			
10 Total of lines 8 and 9			
11 Net gain or loss on sale of capital assets (attach an itemized list)			
12 Unusual grants			
13 Total revenue. Add lines 10 through 12			

8   According to your answers, you are only eligible for tax exemption under section 501(c)(3) from the postmark date of your application. However, you may be eligible for tax exemption under section 501(c)(4) from your date of formation to the postmark date of the Form 1023. Tax exemption under section 501(c)(4) allows exemption from federal income tax, but generally not deductibility of contributions under Code section 170. Check the box at right if you want us to treat this as a request for exemption under 501(c)(4) from your date of formation to the postmark date.   ▶ ☐

Attach a completed Page 1 of Form 1024, Application for Recognition of Exemption Under Section 501(a), to this application.

Schedule F. Homes for the Elderly or Handicapped and Low-Income Housing

Section I	General Information About Your Housing

1 Describe the type of housing you provide.

2 Provide copies of any application forms you use for admission.

3 Explain how the public is made aware of your facility.

4a Provide a description of each facility.
  b What is the total number of residents each facility can accommodate?
  c What is your current number of residents in each facility?
  d Describe each facility in terms of whether residents rent or purchase housing from you.

5 Attach a sample copy of your residency or homeownership contract or agreement.

6 Do you participate in any joint ventures? If "Yes," state your ownership percentage in each joint venture, list your investment in each joint venture, describe the tax status of other participants in each joint venture (including whether they are section 501(c)(3) organizations), describe the activities of each joint venture, describe how you exercise control over the activities of each joint venture, and describe how each joint venture furthers your exempt purposes. Also, submit copies of all joint venture agreements.   ☐ **Yes**   ☐ **No**

  Note. Make sure your answer is consistent with the information provided in Part VIII, line 8.

7 Do you or will you contract with another organization to develop, build, market, or finance your housing? If "Yes," explain how that entity is selected, explain how the terms of any contract(s) are negotiated at arm's length, and explain how you determine you will pay no more than fair market value for services.   ☐ **Yes**   ☐ **No**

  Note. Make sure your answer is consistent with the information provided in Part VIII, line 7a.

8 Do you or will you manage your activities or facilities through your own employees or volunteers? If "No," attach a statement describing the activities that will be managed by others, the names of the persons or organizations that manage or will manage your activities or facilities, and how these managers were or will be selected. Also, submit copies of any contracts, proposed contracts, or other agreements regarding the provision of management services for your activities or facilities. Explain how the terms of any contracts or other agreements were or will be negotiated, and explain how you determine you will pay no more than fair market value for services.   ☐ **Yes**   ☐ **No**

  Note. Answer "Yes" if you do manage or intend to manage your programs through your own employees or by using volunteers. Answer "No" if you engage or intend to engage a separate organization or independent contractor. Make sure your answer is consistent with the information provided in Part VIII, line 7b.

9 Do you participate in any government housing programs? If "Yes," describe these programs.   ☐ **Yes**   ☐ **No**

10a Do you own the facility? If "No," describe any enforceable rights you possess to purchase the facility in the future; go to line 10c. If "Yes," answer line 10b.   ☐ **Yes**   ☐ **No**

  b How did you acquire the facility? For example, did you develop it yourself, purchase a project, etc. Attach all contracts, transfer agreements, or other documents connected with the acquisition of the facility.

  c Do you lease the facility or the land on which it is located? If "Yes," describe the parties to the lease(s) and provide copies of all leases.   ☐ **Yes**   ☐ **No**

Schedule F. Homes for the Elderly or Handicapped and Low-Income Housing *(Continued)*

Section II   Homes for the Elderly or Handicapped

1a Do you provide housing for the elderly? If "Yes," describe who qualifies for your housing in terms of age, infirmity, or other criteria and explain how you select persons for your housing. ☐ **Yes**   ☐ **No**

 b Do you provide housing for the handicapped? If "Yes," describe who qualifies for your housing in terms of disability, income levels, or other criteria and explain how you select persons for your housing. ☐ **Yes**   ☐ **No**

2a Do you charge an entrance or founder's fee? If "Yes," describe what this charge covers, whether it is a one-time fee, how the fee is determined, whether it is payable in a lump sum or on an installment basis, whether it is refundable, and the circumstances, if any, under which it may be waived. ☐ **Yes**   ☐ **No**

 b Do you charge periodic fees or maintenance charges? If "Yes," describe what these charges cover and how they are determined. ☐ **Yes**   ☐ **No**

 c Is your housing affordable to a significant segment of the elderly or handicapped persons in the community? Identify your **community**. Also, if "Yes," explain how you determine your housing is affordable. ☐ **Yes**   ☐ **No**

3a Do you have an established policy concerning residents who become unable to pay their regular charges? If "Yes," describe your established policy. ☐ **Yes**   ☐ **No**

 b Do you have any arrangements with government welfare agencies or others to absorb all or part of the cost of maintaining residents who become unable to pay their regular charges? If "Yes," describe these arrangements. ☐ **Yes**   ☐ **No**

4 Do you have arrangements for the healthcare needs of your residents? If "Yes," describe these arrangements. ☐ **Yes**   ☐ **No**

5 Are your facilities designed to meet the physical, emotional, recreational, social, religious, and/or other similar needs of the elderly or handicapped? If "Yes," describe these design features. ☐ **Yes**   ☐ **No**

Section III   Low-Income Housing

1 Do you provide low-income housing? If "Yes," describe who qualifies for your housing in terms of income levels or other criteria, and describe how you select persons for your housing. ☐ **Yes**   ☐ **No**

2 In addition to rent or mortgage payments, do residents pay periodic fees or maintenance charges? If "Yes," describe what these charges cover and how they are determined. ☐ **Yes**   ☐ **No**

3a Is your housing affordable to low income residents? If "Yes," describe how your housing is made affordable to low-income residents. ☐ **Yes**   ☐ **No**

   Note. Revenue Procedure 96-32, 1996-1 C.B. 717, provides guidelines for providing low-income housing that will be treated as charitable. (At least 75% of the units are occupied by low-income tenants or 40% are occupied by tenants earning not more than 120% of the very low-income levels for the area.)

 b Do you impose any restrictions to make sure that your housing remains affordable to low-income residents? If "Yes," describe these restrictions. ☐ **Yes**   ☐ **No**

4 Do you provide social services to residents? If "Yes," describe these services. ☐ **Yes**   ☐ **No**

Schedule G. Successors to Other Organizations

1a Are you a **successor** to a **for-profit organization**? If "Yes," explain the relationship with the **predecessor** organization that resulted in your creation and complete line 1b.   ☐ **Yes**   ☐ **No**

  b Explain why you took over the activities or assets of a for-profit organization or converted from for-profit to nonprofit status.

2a Are you a successor to an organization other than a for-profit organization? Answer "Yes" if you have taken or will take over the activities of another organization; or you have taken or will take over 25% or more of the fair market value of the net assets of another organization. If "Yes," explain the relationship with the other organzation that resulted in your creation.   ☐ **Yes**   ☐ **No**

  b Provide the tax status of the predecessor organization.

  c Did you or did an organization to which you are a successor previously apply for tax exemption under section 501(c)(3) or any other section of the Code? If "Yes," explain how the application was resolved.   ☐ **Yes**   ☐ **No**

  d Was your prior tax exemption or the tax exemption of an organization to which you are a successor revoked or suspended? If "Yes," explain. Include a description of the corrections you made to re-establish tax exemption.   ☐ **Yes**   ☐ **No**

  e Explain why you took over the activities or assets of another organization.

3 Provide the name, last address, and EIN of the predecessor organization and describe its activities.
    Name: _____   **EIN:** ___−_____
    Address: _____

4 List the owners, partners, principal stockholders, officers, and governing board members of the predecessor organization. Attach a separate sheet if additional space is needed.

Name	Address	Share/Interest (If a for-profit)

5 Do or will any of the persons listed in line 4, maintain a working relationship with you? If "Yes," describe the relationship in detail and include copies of any agreements with any of these persons or with any for-profit organizations in which these persons own more than a 35% interest.   ☐ **Yes**   ☐ **No**

6a Were any assets transferred, whether by gift or sale, from the predecessor organization to you?   ☐ **Yes**   ☐ **No**
    If "Yes," provide a list of assets, indicate the value of each asset, explain how the value was determined, and attach an appraisal, if available. For each asset listed, also explain if the transfer was by gift, sale, or combination thereof.

  b Were any restrictions placed on the use or sale of the assets? If "Yes," explain the restrictions.   ☐ **Yes**   ☐ **No**

  c Provide a copy of the agreement(s) of sale or transfer.

7 Were any debts or liabilities transferred from the predecessor for-profit organization to you?   ☐ **Yes**   ☐ **No**
    If "Yes," provide a list of the debts or liabilities that were transferred to you, indicating the amount of each, how the amount was determined, and the name of the person to whom the debt or liability is owed.

8 Will you lease or rent any property or equipment previously owned or used by the predecessor for-profit organization, or from persons listed in line 4, or from for-profit organizations in which these persons own more than a 35% interest? If "Yes," submit a copy of the lease or rental agreement(s). Indicate how the lease or rental value of the property or equipment was determined.   ☐ **Yes**   ☐ **No**

9 Will you lease or rent property or equipment to persons listed in line 4, or to for-profit organizations in which these persons own more than a 35% interest? If "Yes," attach a list of the property or equipment, provide a copy of the lease or rental agreement(s), and indicate how the lease or rental value of the property or equipment was determined.   ☐ **Yes**   ☐ **No**

Schedule H. Organizations Providing Scholarships, Fellowships, Educational Loans, or Other Educational Grants to Individuals and Private Foundations Requesting Advance Approval of Individual Grant Procedures

Section I   *Names of individual recipients are not required to be listed in Schedule H.*
Public charities and private foundations complete lines 1a through 7 of this section. See the instructions to Part X if you are not sure whether you are a public charity or a private foundation.

1a   Describe the types of educational grants you provide to individuals, such as scholarships, fellowships, loans, etc.

  b   Describe the purpose and amount of your scholarships, fellowships, and other educational grants and loans that you award.

  c   If you award educational loans, explain the terms of the loans (interest rate, length, forgiveness, etc.).

  d   Specify how your program is publicized.

  e   Provide copies of any solicitation or announcement materials.

  f   Provide a sample copy of the application used.

2   Do you maintain case histories showing recipients of your scholarships, fellowships, educational loans, or other educational grants, including names, addresses, purposes of awards, amount of each grant, manner of selection, and relationship (if any) to officers, trustees, or donors of funds to you? If "No," refer to the instructions.   ☐ **Yes**   ☐ **No**

3   Describe the specific criteria you use to determine who is eligible for your program. (For example, eligibility selection criteria could consist of graduating high school students from a particular high school who will attend college, writers of scholarly works about American history, etc.)

4a   Describe the specific criteria you use to select recipients. (For example, specific selection criteria could consist of prior academic performance, financial need, etc.)

  b   Describe how you determine the number of grants that will be made annually.

  c   Describe how you determine the amount of each of your grants.

  d   Describe any requirement or condition that you impose on recipients to obtain, maintain, or qualify for renewal of a grant. (For example, specific requirements or conditions could consist of attendance at a four-year college, maintaining a certain grade point average, teaching in public school after graduation from college, etc.)

5   Describe your procedures for supervising the scholarships, fellowships, educational loans, or other educational grants. Describe whether you obtain reports and grade transcripts from recipients, or you pay grants directly to a school under an arrangement whereby the school will apply the grant funds only for enrolled students who are in good standing. Also, describe your procedures for taking action if the terms of the award are violated.

6   Who is on the selection committee for the awards made under your program, including names of current committee members, criteria for committee membership, and the method of replacing committee members?

7   Are relatives of members of the selection committee, or of your officers, directors, or **substantial contributors** eligible for awards made under your program? If "Yes," what measures are taken to ensure unbiased selections?   ☐ **Yes**   ☐ **No**

    Note. If you are a private foundation, you are not permitted to provide educational grants to **disqualified persons.** Disqualified persons include your substantial contributors and foundation managers and certain family members of disqualified persons.

Section II   Private foundations complete lines 1a through 4f of this section. Public charities do not complete this section.

1a   If we determine that you are a private foundation, do you want this application to be considered as a request for advance approval of grant making procedures?   ☐ **Yes**   ☐ **No**   ☐ **N/A**

  b   For which section(s) do you wish to be considered?
- 4945(g)(1)—Scholarship or fellowship grant to an individual for study at an educational institution   ☐
- 4945(g)(3)—Other grants, including loans, to an individual for travel, study, or other similar purposes, to enhance a particular skill of the grantee or to produce a specific product   ☐

2   Do you represent that you will (1) arrange to receive and review grantee reports annually and upon completion of the purpose for which the grant was awarded, (2) investigate diversions of funds from their intended purposes, and (3) take all reasonable and appropriate steps to recover diverted funds, ensure other grant funds held by a grantee are used for their intended purposes, and withhold further payments to grantees until you obtain grantees' assurances that future diversions will not occur and that grantees will take extraordinary precautions to prevent future diversions from occurring?   ☐ **Yes**   ☐ **No**

3   Do you represent that you will maintain all records relating to individual grants, including information obtained to evaluate grantees, identify whether a grantee is a disqualified person, establish the amount and purpose of each grant, and establish that you undertook the supervision and investigation of grants described in line 2?   ☐ **Yes**   ☐ **No**

Schedule H. Organizations Providing Scholarships, Fellowships, Educational Loans, or Other Educational Grants to Individuals and Private Foundations Requesting Advance Approval of Individual Grant Procedures *(Continued)*

Section II	Private foundations complete lines 1a through 4f of this section. Public charities do not complete this section. *(Continued)*

4a Do you or will you award scholarships, fellowships, and educational loans to attend an educational institution based on the status of an individual being an *employee of a particular employer?* If "Yes," complete lines 4b through 4f.　　☐ **Yes**　☐ **No**

　b Will you comply with the seven conditions and either the percentage tests or facts and circumstances test for scholarships, fellowships, and educational loans to attend an educational institution as set forth in Revenue Procedures 76-47, 1976-2 C.B. 670, and 80-39, 1980-2 C.B. 772, which apply to inducement, selection committee, eligibility requirements, objective basis of selection, employment, course of study, and other objectives? (See lines 4c, 4d, and 4e, regarding the percentage tests.)　　☐ **Yes**　☐ **No**

　c Do you or will you provide scholarships, fellowships, or educational loans to attend an educational institution to employees of a particular employer?　　☐ **Yes**　☐ **No**　☐ **N/A**

　　If "Yes," will you award grants to 10% or fewer of the eligible applicants who were actually considered by the selection committee in selecting recipients of grants in that year as provided by Revenue Procedures 76-47 and 80-39?　　☐ **Yes**　☐ **No**

　d Do you provide scholarships, fellowships, or educational loans to attend an educational institution to children of employees of a particular employer?　　☐ **Yes**　☐ **No**　☐ **N/A**

　　If "Yes," will you award grants to 25% or fewer of the eligible applicants who were actually considered by the selection committee in selecting recipients of grants in that year as provided by Revenue Procedures 76-47 and 80-39? If "No," go to line 4e.　　☐ **Yes**　☐ **No**

　e If you provide scholarships, fellowships, or educational loans to attend an educational institution to children of employees of a particular employer, will you award grants to 10% or fewer of the number of employees' children who can be shown to be eligible for grants (whether or not they submitted an application) in that year, as provided by Revenue Procedures 76-47 and 80-39?　　☐ **Yes**　☐ **No**　☐ **N/A**

　　If "Yes," describe how you will determine who can be shown to be eligible for grants without submitting an application, such as by obtaining written statements or other information about the expectations of employees' children to attend an educational institution. If "No," go to line 4f.

　　Note. Statistical or sampling techniques are not acceptable. See Revenue Procedure 85-51, 1985-2 C.B. 717, for additional information.

　f If you provide scholarships, fellowships, or educational loans to attend an educational institution to *children of employees of a particular employer* without regard to either the 25% limitation described in line 4d, or the 10% limitation described in line 4e, will you award grants based on facts and circumstances that demonstrate that the grants will not be considered compensation for past, present, or future services or otherwise provide a significant benefit to the particular employer? If "Yes," describe the facts and circumstances that you believe will demonstrate that the grants are neither compensatory nor a significant benefit to the particular employer. In your explanation, describe why you cannot satisfy either the 25% test described in line 4d or the 10% test described in line 4e.　　☐ **Yes**　☐ **No**

Form 1023 Checklist

(Revised June 2006)

Application for Recognition of Exemption under Section 501(c)(3) of the Internal Revenue Code

Note. *Retain a copy of the completed Form 1023 in your permanent records. Refer to the* General Instructions *regarding Public Inspection of approved applications.*

Check each box to finish your application (Form 1023). Send this completed Checklist with your filled-in application. If you have not answered all the items below, your application may be returned to you as incomplete.

☐ Assemble the application and materials in this order:
- Form 1023 Checklist
- Form 2848, *Power of Attorney and Declaration of Representative* (if filing)
- Form 8821, *Tax Information Authorization* (if filing)
- Expedite request (if requesting)
- Application (Form 1023 and Schedules A through H, as required)
- Articles of organization
- Amendments to articles of organization in chronological order
- Bylaws or other rules of operation and amendments
- Documentation of nondiscriminatory policy for schools, as required by Schedule B
- Form 5768, Election/Revocation of Election by an Eligible Section 501(c)(3) Organization To Make Expenditures To Influence Legislation (if filing)
- All other attachments, including explanations, financial data, and printed materials or publications. Label each page with name and EIN.

☐ User fee payment placed in envelope on top of checklist. DO NOT STAPLE or otherwise attach your check or money order to your application. Instead, just place it in the envelope.

☐ Employer Identification Number (EIN)

☐ Completed Parts I through XI of the application, including any requested information and any required Schedules A through H.
- You must provide specific details about your past, present, and planned activities.
- Generalizations or failure to answer questions in the Form 1023 application will prevent us from recognizing you as tax exempt.
- Describe your purposes and proposed activities in specific easily understood terms.
- Financial information should correspond with proposed activities.

☐ Schedules. Submit only those schedules that apply to you and check either "Yes" or "No" below.

Schedule A   Yes ___ No ___   Schedule E   Yes ___ No ___

Schedule B   Yes ___ No ___   Schedule F   Yes ___ No ___

Schedule C   Yes ___ No ___   Schedule G   Yes ___ No ___

Schedule D   Yes ___ No ___   Schedule H   Yes ___ No ___

☐ An exact copy of your complete articles of organization (creating document). Absence of the proper purpose and dissolution clauses is the number one reason for delays in the issuance of determination letters.

- Location of Purpose Clause from Part III, line 1 (Page, Article and Paragraph Number)_____
- Location of Dissolution Clause from Part III, line 2b or 2c (Page, Article and Paragraph Number) or by operation of state law _____

☐ Signature of an officer, director, trustee, or other official who is authorized to sign the application.
- Signature at Part XI of Form 1023.

☐ Your name on the application must be the same as your legal name as it appears in your articles of organization.

Send completed Form 1023, user fee payment, and all other required information, to:

Internal Revenue Service
P.O. Box 192
Covington, KY 41012-0192

If you are using express mail or a delivery service, send Form 1023, user fee payment, and attachments to:

Internal Revenue Service
201 West Rivercenter Blvd.
Attn: Extracting Stop 312
Covington, KY 41011

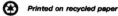 *Printed on recycled paper*

Form **SS-4**

(Rev. February 2006)

Department of the Treasury
Internal Revenue Service

Application for Employer Identification Number

(For use by employers, corporations, partnerships, trusts, estates, churches, government agencies, Indian tribal entities, certain individuals, and others.)

▶ See separate instructions for each line.   ▶ Keep a copy for your records.

OMB No. 1545-0003

EIN

Type or print clearly.

1 Legal name of entity (or individual) for whom the EIN is being requested

2 Trade name of business (if different from name on line 1)

3 Executor, administrator, trustee, "care of" name

4a Mailing address (room, apt., suite no. and street, or P.O. box)

5a Street address (if different) (Do not enter a P.O. box.)

4b City, state, and ZIP code

5b City, state, and ZIP code

6 County and state where principal business is located

7a Name of principal officer, general partner, grantor, owner, or trustor

7b SSN, ITIN, or EIN

8a **Type of entity** (check only one box)
- ☐ Sole proprietor (SSN) _____
- ☐ Partnership
- ☐ Corporation (enter form number to be filed) ▶ _____
- ☐ Personal service corporation
- ☐ Church or church-controlled organization
- ☐ Other nonprofit organization (specify) ▶ _____
- ☐ Other (specify) ▶
- ☐ Estate (SSN of decedent) _____
- ☐ Plan administrator (SSN) _____
- ☐ Trust (SSN of grantor) _____
- ☐ National Guard   ☐ State/local government
- ☐ Farmers' cooperative   ☐ Federal government/military
- ☐ REMIC   ☐ Indian tribal governments/enterprises
- Group Exemption Number (GEN) ▶ _____

8b If a corporation, name the state or foreign country (if applicable) where incorporated

State

Foreign country

9 **Reason for applying** (check only one box)
- ☐ Started new business (specify type) ▶ _____
- ☐ Hired employees (Check the box and see line 12.)
- ☐ Compliance with IRS withholding regulations
- ☐ Other (specify) ▶
- ☐ Banking purpose (specify purpose) ▶ _____
- ☐ Changed type of organization (specify new type) ▶ _____
- ☐ Purchased going business
- ☐ Created a trust (specify type) ▶ _____
- ☐ Created a pension plan (specify type) ▶ _____

10 Date business started or acquired (month, day, year). See instructions.

11 Closing month of accounting year

12 First date wages or annuities were paid (month, day, year). **Note.** If applicant is a withholding agent, enter date income will first be paid to nonresident alien. (month, day, year) . . . . ▶

13 Highest number of employees expected in the next 12 months (enter -0- if none).

Do you expect to have $1,000 or less in employment tax liability for the calendar year? ☐ **Yes** ☐ **No**. (If you expect to pay $4,000 or less in wages, you can mark yes.)

Agricultural	Household	Other

14 Check **one** box that best describes the principal activity of your business.
- ☐ Construction   ☐ Rental & leasing   ☐ Transportation & warehousing
- ☐ Real estate   ☐ Manufacturing   ☐ Finance & insurance
- ☐ Health care & social assistance   ☐ Wholesale–agent/broker
- ☐ Accommodation & food service   ☐ Wholesale–other   ☐ Retail
- ☐ Other (specify)

15 Indicate principal line of merchandise sold, specific construction work done, products produced, or services provided.

16a Has the applicant ever applied for an employer identification number for this or any other business? . . . . ☐ **Yes**   ☐ **No**
Note. If "Yes," please complete lines 16b and 16c.

16b If you checked "Yes" on line 16a, give applicant's legal name and trade name shown on prior application if different from line 1 or 2 above.
Legal name ▶   Trade name ▶

16c Approximate date when, and city and state where, the application was filed. Enter previous employer identification number if known.
Approximate date when filed (mo., day, year)   City and state where filed   Previous EIN

Third Party Designee	Complete this section **only** if you want to authorize the named individual to receive the entity's EIN and answer questions about the completion of this form.	
	Designee's name	Designee's telephone number (include area code) ( )
	Address and ZIP code	Designee's fax number (include area code) ( )

Under penalties of perjury, I declare that I have examined this application, and to the best of my knowledge and belief, it is true, correct, and complete.

Name and title (type or print clearly) ▶

Applicant's telephone number (include area code) (   )

Signature ▶   Date ▶

Applicant's fax number (include area code) (   )

For Privacy Act and Paperwork Reduction Act Notice, see separate instructions.   Cat. No. 16055N   Form **SS-4** (Rev. 2-2006)

Do I Need an EIN?

File Form SS-4 if the applicant entity does not already have an EIN but is required to show an EIN on any return, statement, or other document.[1] See also the separate instructions for each line on Form SS-4.

IF the applicant...	AND...	THEN...
Started a new business	Does not currently have (nor expect to have) employees	Complete lines 1, 2, 4a–8a, 8b (if applicable), and 9–16c.
Hired (or will hire) employees, including household employees	Does not already have an EIN	Complete lines 1, 2, 4a–6, 7a–b (if applicable), 8a, 8b (if applicable), and 9–16c.
Opened a bank account	Needs an EIN for banking purposes only	Complete lines 1–5b, 7a–b (if applicable), 8a, 9, and 16a–c.
Changed type of organization	Either the legal character of the organization or its ownership changed (for example, you incorporate a sole proprietorship or form a partnership)[2]	Complete lines 1–16c (as applicable).
Purchased a going business[3]	Does not already have an EIN	Complete lines 1–16c (as applicable).
Created a trust	The trust is other than a grantor trust or an IRA trust[4]	Complete lines 1–16c (as applicable).
Created a pension plan as a plan administrator[5]	Needs an EIN for reporting purposes	Complete lines 1, 3, 4a–b, 8a, 9, and 16a–c.
Is a foreign person needing an EIN to comply with IRS withholding regulations	Needs an EIN to complete a Form W-8 (other than Form W-8ECI), avoid withholding on portfolio assets, or claim tax treaty benefits[6]	Complete lines 1–5b, 7a–b (SSN or ITIN optional), 8a–9, and 16a–c.
Is administering an estate	Needs an EIN to report estate income on Form 1041	Complete lines 1, 2, 3, 4a–6, 8a, 9-11, 12-15 (if applicable), and 16a–c.
Is a withholding agent for taxes on non-wage income paid to an alien (i.e., individual, corporation, or partnership, etc.)	Is an agent, broker, fiduciary, manager, tenant, or spouse who is required to file Form 1042, Annual Withholding Tax Return for U.S. Source Income of Foreign Persons	Complete lines 1, 2, 3 (if applicable), 4a–5b, 7a–b (if applicable), 8a, 9, and 16a–c.
Is a state or local agency	Serves as a tax reporting agent for public assistance recipients under Rev. Proc. 80-4, 1980-1 C.B. 581[7]	Complete lines 1, 2, 4a–5b, 8a, 9, and 16a–c.
Is a single-member LLC	Needs an EIN to file Form 8832, Entity Classification Election, for filing employment tax returns, **or** for state reporting purposes[8]	Complete lines 1–16c (as applicable).
Is an S corporation	Needs an EIN to file Form 2553, Election by a Small Business Corporation[9]	Complete lines 1–16c (as applicable).

[1] For example, a sole proprietorship or self-employed farmer who establishes a qualified retirement plan, or is required to file excise, employment, alcohol, tobacco, or firearms returns, must have an EIN. A partnership, corporation, REMIC (real estate mortgage investment conduit), nonprofit organization (church, club, etc.), or farmers' cooperative must use an EIN for any tax-related purpose even if the entity does not have employees.

[2] However, do not apply for a new EIN if the existing entity only (a) changed its business name, (b) elected on Form 8832 to change the way it is taxed (or is covered by the default rules), or (c) terminated its partnership status because at least 50% of the total interests in partnership capital and profits were sold or exchanged within a 12-month period. The EIN of the terminated partnership should continue to be used. See Regulations section 301.6109-1(d)(2)(iii).

[3] Do not use the EIN of the prior business unless you became the "owner" of a corporation by acquiring its stock.

[4] However, grantor trusts that do not file using Optional Method 1 and IRA trusts that are required to file Form 990-T, Exempt Organization Business Income Tax Return, must have an EIN. For more information on grantor trusts, see the Instructions for Form 1041.

[5] A plan administrator is the person or group of persons specified as the administrator by the instrument under which the plan is operated.

[6] Entities applying to be a Qualified Intermediary (QI) need a QI-EIN even if they already have an EIN. See Rev. Proc. 2000-12.

[7] See also *Household employer* on page 3. **Note.** State or local agencies may need an EIN for other reasons, for example, hired employees.

[8] Most LLCs do not need to file Form 8832. See *Limited liability company (LLC)* on page 4 for details on completing Form SS-4 for an LLC.

[9] An existing corporation that is electing or revoking S corporation status should use its previously-assigned EIN.

Form **5768**

(Rev. December 2004)

Department of the Treasury
Internal Revenue Service

Election/Revocation of Election by an Eligible Section 501(c)(3) Organization To Make Expenditures To Influence Legislation

(Under Section 501(h) of the Internal Revenue Code)

For IRS
Use Only ▶

Name of organization	Employer identification number

Number and street (or P.O. box no., if mail is not delivered to street address)	Room/suite

City, town or post office, and state	ZIP + 4

1 Election—As an eligible organization, we hereby elect to have the provisions of section 501(h) of the Code, relating to expenditures to influence legislation, apply to our tax year ending_____and all subsequent tax years until revoked.

(Month, day, and year)

Note: *This election must be signed and postmarked within the first taxable year to which it applies.*

2 Revocation—As an eligible organization, we hereby revoke our election to have the provisions of section 501(h) of the Code, relating to expenditures to influence legislation, apply to our tax year ending_____

(Month, day, and year)

Note: *This revocation must be signed and postmarked before the first day of the tax year to which it applies.*

Under penalties of perjury, I declare that I am authorized to make this (check applicable box) ▶ ☐ election ☐ revocation
on behalf of the above named organization.

_____   _____   _____
(Signature of officer or trustee)   (Type or print name and title)   (Date)

General Instructions

Section references are to the Internal Revenue Code.

Section 501(c)(3) states that an organization exempt under that section will lose its tax-exempt status and its qualification to receive deductible charitable contributions if a substantial part of its activities are carried on to influence legislation. Section 501(h), however, permits certain eligible 501(c)(3) organizations to elect to make limited expenditures to influence legislation. An organization making the election will, however, be subject to an excise tax under section 4911 if it spends more than the amounts permitted by that section. Also, the organization may lose its exempt status if its lobbying expenditures exceed the permitted amounts by more than 50% over a 4-year period. For any tax year in which an election under section 501(h) is in effect, an electing organization must report the actual and permitted amounts of its lobbying expenditures and grass roots expenditures (as defined in section 4911(c)) on its annual return required under section 6033. See Schedule A (Form 990 or Form 990-EZ). Each electing member of an affiliated group must report these amounts for both itself and the affiliated group as a whole.

To make or revoke the election, enter the ending date of the tax year to which the election or revocation applies in item **1** or **2,** as applicable, and sign and date the form in the spaces provided.

Eligible Organizations.—A section 501(c)(3) organization is permitted to make the election if it is not a disqualified organization (see below) and is described in:

1. Section 170(b)(1)(A)(ii) (relating to educational institutions),
2. Section 170(b)(1)(A)(iii) (relating to hospitals and medical research organizations),
3. Section 170(b)(1)(A)(iv) (relating to organizations supporting government schools),
4. Section 170(b)(1)(A)(vi) (relating to organizations publicly supported by charitable contributions),
5. Section 509(a)(2) (relating to organizations publicly supported by admissions, sales, etc.), or
6. Section 509(a)(3) (relating to organizations supporting certain types of public charities other than those section 509(a)(3) organizations that support section 501(c)(4), (5), or (6) organizations).

Disqualified Organizations.—The following types of organizations are not permitted to make the election:

a. Section 170(b)(1)(A)(i) organizations (relating to churches),

b. An integrated auxiliary of a church or of a convention or association of churches, or

c. A member of an affiliated group of organizations if one or more members of such group is described in **a** or **b** of this paragraph.

Affiliated Organizations.—Organizations are members of an affiliated group of organizations only if **(1)** the governing instrument of one such organization requires it to be bound by the decisions of the other organization on legislative issues, or **(2)** the governing board of one such organization includes persons (i) who are specifically designated representatives of another such organization or are members of the governing board, officers, or paid executive staff members of such other organization, and (ii) who, by aggregating their votes, have sufficient voting power to cause or prevent action on legislative issues by the first such organization.

For more details, see section 4911 and section 501(h).

Note: *A private foundation (including a private operating foundation) is not an eligible organization.*

Where To File.—Mail Form 5768 to the Internal Revenue Service Center, Ogden, UT 84201-0027.

Member Register

Certificate Number	Date of Issuance			Member's Name and Address
	Month	Day	Year	

Member Register

Certificate Number	Date of Issuance			Member's Name and Address
	Month	Day	Year	

Certificate Number _____

A CALIFORNIA NONPROFIT CORPORATION

MEMBERSHIP CERTIFICATE

*THIS IS TO CERTIFY THAT _____
is a member of the above Corporation incorporated under the laws of this state and is
entitled to the full rights and privileges of such membership, subject to the duties and
restrictions, as more fully set forth in the Corporation's Articles of Incorporation and Bylaws.*

*IN WITNESS WHEREOF, the Corporation has caused this Certificate to be executed by its
duly authorized officers, and its corporate seal to be hereunto affixed.*

Dated _____

_____ , President

_____ , Secretary

Certificate Number ______________

For one membership

Issued To:

____

____

Date ______________________, ______

MEMBERSHIPS IN THIS
NONPROFIT CORPORATION
ARE NONTRANSFERABLE

Received Certificate Number ______________

For one membership

This ______ day of ____________, ______

____

SIGNATURE OF MEMBER

Certificate Number ______

____

A CALIFORNIA NONPROFIT CORPORATION

MEMBERSHIP CERTIFICATE

THIS IS TO CERTIFY THAT ______________________________________
is a member of the above Corporation incorporated under the laws of this state and is entitled to the full rights and privileges of such membership, subject to the duties and restrictions, as more fully set forth in the Corporation's Articles of Incorporation and Bylaws.

IN WITNESS WHEREOF, the Corporation has caused this Certificate to be executed by its duly authorized officers, and its corporate seal to be hereunto affixed.

Dated ______________________

______________________, *President*

______________________, *Secretary*

A CALIFORNIA NONPROFIT CORPORATION

MEMBERSHIP CERTIFICATE

Certificate Number _____

THIS IS TO CERTIFY THAT _____
*is a member of the above Corporation incorporated under the laws of this state and is
entitled to the full rights and privileges of such membership, subject to the duties and
restrictions, as more fully set forth in the Corporation's Articles of Incorporation and Bylaws.*

*IN WITNESS WHEREOF, the Corporation has caused this Certificate to be executed by its
duly authorized officers, and its corporate seal to be hereunto affixed.*

Dated _____

_____ , *President*

_____ , *Secretary*

MEMBERSHIPS IN THIS
NONPROFIT CORPORATION
ARE NONTRANSFERABLE

Certificate Number _____
For one membership

Issued To: _____

Date _____, _____

Received Certificate Number _____
For one membership

This _____ day of _____, _____

SIGNATURE OF MEMBER

A CALIFORNIA NONPROFIT CORPORATION

MEMBERSHIP CERTIFICATE

Certificate Number _____

THIS IS TO CERTIFY THAT _____
is a member of the above Corporation incorporated under the laws of this state and is entitled to the full rights and privileges of such membership, subject to the duties and restrictions, as more fully set forth in the Corporation's Articles of Incorporation and Bylaws.

IN WITNESS WHEREOF, the Corporation has caused this Certificate to be executed by its duly authorized officers, and its corporate seal to be hereunto affixed.

Dated _____

_____, *President*

_____, *Secretary*

Stub (left portion, rotated)

Certificate Number _____

For one membership

Issued To: _____

MEMBERSHIPS IN THIS
NONPROFIT CORPORATION
ARE NONTRANSFERABLE

Date _____ , _____

Received Certificate Number _____

For one membership

This _____ day of _____ , _____ ,

SIGNATURE OF MEMBER _____

Certificate

A CALIFORNIA NONPROFIT CORPORATION

MEMBERSHIP CERTIFICATE

Certificate Number _____

THIS IS TO CERTIFY THAT _____
is a member of the above Corporation incorporated under the laws of this state and is entitled to the full rights and privileges of such membership, subject to the duties and restrictions, as more fully set forth in the Corporation's Articles of Incorporation and Bylaws.

IN WITNESS WHEREOF, the Corporation has caused this Certificate to be executed by its duly authorized officers, and its corporate seal to be hereunto affixed.

Dated _____

_____ , *President*

_____ , *Secretary*

**MEMBERSHIPS IN THIS
NONPROFIT CORPORATION
ARE NONTRANSFERABLE**

A CALIFORNIA NONPROFIT CORPORATION

MEMBERSHIP CERTIFICATE

Certificate Number _____

THIS IS TO CERTIFY THAT _____

_is a member of the above Corporation incorporated under the laws of this state and is
entitled to the full rights and privileges of such membership, subject to the duties and
restrictions, as more fully set forth in the Corporation's Articles of Incorporation and Bylaws._

_IN WITNESS WHEREOF, the Corporation has caused this Certificate to be executed by its
duly authorized officers, and its corporate seal to be hereunto affixed._

Dated _____

_____ , President

_____ , Secretary

Received Certificate Number _____

For one membership

This _____ day of _____, _____,

SIGNATURE OF MEMBER

MEMBERSHIPS IN THIS
NONPROFIT CORPORATION
ARE NONTRANSFERABLE

Certificate Number _____

A CALIFORNIA NONPROFIT CORPORATION

MEMBERSHIP CERTIFICATE

THIS IS TO CERTIFY THAT _____

is a member of the above Corporation incorporated under the laws of this state and is entitled to the full rights and privileges of such membership, subject to the duties and restrictions, as more fully set forth in the Corporation's Articles of Incorporation and Bylaws.

IN WITNESS WHEREOF, the Corporation has caused this Certificate to be executed by its duly authorized officers, and its corporate seal to be hereunto affixed.

Dated _____

_____, President

_____, Secretary

Certificate Number _____

For one membership

Issued To: _____

Date _____, _____

Received Certificate Number _____

For one membership

This _____ day of _____, _____

SIGNATURE OF MEMBER

MEMBERSHIPS IN THIS
NONPROFIT CORPORATION
ARE NONTRANSFERABLE

A CALIFORNIA NONPROFIT CORPORATION

MEMBERSHIP CERTIFICATE

Certificate Number _____

THIS IS TO CERTIFY THAT _____
is a member of the above Corporation incorporated under the laws of this state and is
entitled to the full rights and privileges of such membership, subject to the duties and
restrictions, as more fully set forth in the Corporation's Articles of Incorporation and Bylaws.

IN WITNESS WHEREOF, the Corporation has caused this Certificate to be executed by its
duly authorized officers, and its corporate seal to be hereunto affixed.

Dated _____

_____ , President

_____ , Secretary

Certificate Number _____

For one membership

Issued To: _____

Date _____ , _____

Certificate Number _____

For one membership

**MEMBERSHIPS IN THIS
NONPROFIT CORPORATION
ARE NONTRANSFERABLE**

Received Certificate Number _____

For one membership

This _____ day of _____ , _____

SIGNATURE OF MEMBER

A CALIFORNIA NONPROFIT CORPORATION

MEMBERSHIP CERTIFICATE

Certificate Number _____

THIS IS TO CERTIFY THAT _____

is a member of the above Corporation incorporated under the laws of this state and is entitled to the full rights and privileges of such membership, subject to the duties and restrictions, as more fully set forth in the Corporation's Articles of Incorporation and Bylaws.

IN WITNESS WHEREOF, the Corporation has caused this Certificate to be executed by its duly authorized officers, and its corporate seal to be hereunto affixed.

Dated _____

_____ , *President*

_____ , *Secretary*

Certificate Number _____

For one membership

Issued To: _____

MEMBERSHIPS IN THIS
NONPROFIT CORPORATION
ARE NONTRANSFERABLE

Date _____ , ___

Received Certificate Number _____

For one membership

This _____ day of _____ , ___

SIGNATURE OF MEMBER

A CALIFORNIA NONPROFIT CORPORATION

MEMBERSHIP CERTIFICATE

Certificate Number _____

THIS IS TO CERTIFY THAT
is a member of the above Corporation incorporated under the laws of this state and is
entitled to the full rights and privileges of such membership, subject to the duties and
restrictions, as more fully set forth in the Corporation's Articles of Incorporation and Bylaws.

IN WITNESS WHEREOF, the Corporation has caused this Certificate to be executed by its
duly authorized officers, and its corporate seal to be hereunto affixed.

Dated _____

_____ , *President*

_____ , *Secretary*

Index

A

Form 990-T (unrelated business income), 249,
282–283
Form 1024, 9, 244
Form 2848, 200, 246
Form 5768, 60, 217–218, 246
Form 8734, 249
Form 8821, 246
Form SS-4, 193–194, 199–200
Form W-2, 287, 289
Form W-3, 287
Form W-4, 286–287
Schedule A (Form 1040), 87
See also Federal nonprofit tax exemption application
(Form 1023)
IRS intermediate sanctions. *See* Excess benefit rules
IRS publications, 62, 194, 283
appreciated property donations, 86
caution about, 20
for churches/religious organizations, 52, 194
consent to extend tax assessment limits, 234
contribution deductibility limits, 82
contribution deduction reporting, 87
employment taxes, 283, 287
excess benefit rules, 58
excise taxes, 249
exemption application help, 194
gaming activities, 218
gift valuation, 87
independent contractors, 286
for non-501(c)(3) nonprofits, 9
Package 1024, 9
political expenditures, 60
private school requirements, 56
special 501(c)(3) types, 49
IRS rulings, researching, 63, 222
IRS website
disqualified persons information, 237
exemption application form, 194
subscribing to EO Updates, 282
tips for using, 62–63
user fee amount, 238

J

Job descriptions, for directors, 27
Joint ventures, 220

L

Labor union dues, 87
Larger nonprofit rules (nonprofits with revenues of $2
million or more), 147
Law libraries, 297
Lawsuits, 10
attorney fees reimbursement, 38–39
by attorney general, 92
name/trademark disputes, 115, 116
over self-dealing transactions, 35, 39
state immunity statutes, 36–39, 41
where filed, 138, 156
Lawyers, 13, 36, 59, 296
for help with federal exemption application, 200, 202
Leases
assignment of, 187, 188, 245–246, 271–272
federal exemption application questions, 213–215,
220, 245–246
signed before incorporation, 24, 25
on state exemption application, 186–187, 188
state exemption application questions, 186–187, 188
welfare exemption and, 92, 98–99, 273
Legal research, 297–298
IRS rulings, 63, 222
Nonprofit Integrity Act, 101, 147
Legal service corporations, 7
Legislative activities, 59–61, 189, 217–218. *See also*
Political activities
Letters
cover letter for articles of incorporation filing, 131–132
federal exemption determination letter, 190, 196,
244, 248–249, 252, 281
name availability inquiries, 110
state exemption determination letter, 190, 266
Liabilities, of preexisting organizations, 253, 254, 268,
269. *See also* Asset transfers
Liability insurance, 37, 291–292
directors' and officers' liability, 23, 37–38, 39, 292
Licenses and permits, 290–291
seller's permit, 289–290
Life insurance, 11, 36
Limited liability, 10–11
promoters, 24–25
protecting, 280–281
Limited liability companies. *See* LLCs
Literary purposes, 5, 6–7, 54

Get the Latest in the Law

① **Nolo's Legal Updater**
We'll send you an email whenever a new edition of your book is published!
Sign up at **www.nolo.com/legalupdater**.

② **Updates at Nolo.com**
Check **www.nolo.com/update** to find recent changes in the law that
affect the current edition of your book.

③ **Nolo Customer Service**
To make sure that this edition of the book is the most recent one, call us at
800-728-3555 and ask one of our friendly customer service representatives
(7:00 am to 6:00 pm PST, weekdays only). Or find out at **www.nolo.com**.

④ **Complete the Registration & Comment Card ...**
... and we'll do the work for you! Just indicate your preferences below:

- -

Registration & Comment Card

NAME _____ DATE _____

ADDRESS _____

CITY _____ STATE _____ ZIP _____

PHONE _____ EMAIL _____

COMMENTS _____

WAS THIS BOOK EASY TO USE?   (VERY EASY)   5   4   3   2   1   (VERY DIFFICULT)

☐ Yes, you can quote me in future Nolo promotional materials. *Please include phone number above.*

☐ Yes, send me **Nolo's Legal Updater** via email when a new edition of this book is available.

Yes, I want to sign up for the following email newsletters:

   ☐ **NoloBriefs** (monthly)
   ☐ **Nolo's Special Offer** (monthly)
   ☐ **Nolo's BizBriefs** (monthly)
   ☐ **Every Landlord's Quarterly** (four times a year)

☐ Yes, you can give my contact info to carefully selected
partners whose products may be of interest to me.

NOLO

NON 12.0